NICHE WARS
AUSTRALIA IN AFGHANISTAN AND IRAQ, 2001–2014

NICHE WARS
AUSTRALIA IN AFGHANISTAN AND IRAQ, 2001–2014

EDITED BY JOHN BLAXLAND,
MARCUS FIELDING AND THEA GELLERFY

PRESS

Published by ANU Press
The Australian National University
Acton ACT 2601, Australia
Email: anupress@anu.edu.au

Available to download for free at press.anu.edu.au

ISBN (print): 9781760464028
ISBN (online): 9781760464035

WorldCat (print): 1224563694
WorldCat (online): 1224563779

DOI: 10.22459/NW.2020

This title is published under a Creative Commons Attribution-NonCommercial-NoDerivatives 4.0 International (CC BY-NC-ND 4.0).

The full licence terms are available at
creativecommons.org/licenses/by-nc-nd/4.0/legalcode

Cover design and layout by ANU Press. Cover photograph: Special Operations Task Group – Operation SLIPPER by Department of Defence.

This edition © 2020 ANU Press

Contents

Foreword vii
Maps, figures and images. ix
Acknowledgements xiii
Maps xv
Contributors. xxi
Glossary. xxix
Introduction 1
John Blaxland

Part 1: Policy and strategy

1. A minister's perspective 21
   Robert Hill
2. A departmental Secretary's perspective 31
   Ric Smith
3. A Chief of Defence Force's perspective. 47
   Chris Barrie

Part 2: On operations in Afghanistan and Iraq

4. Australia's intervention in Afghanistan, 2001–02 65
   Dan McDaniel
5. Air Operations Control and Reporting Centre 81
   Chris Westwood
6. Conventional stability operations at the battle group
   level in Iraq. 91
   Anthony Rawlins
7. Maritime operations 127
   Peter Jones
8. Embeds 149
   Jim Molan

Part 3: Joint forces, enablers and partners

9. Command and control 155
   Michael Crane
10. Intelligence in Afghanistan 173
    Mick Lehmann
11. Civil and humanitarian assistance 187
    Alan Ryan
12. The military and the media 201
    Karen Middleton
13. The Australian Federal Police in Afghanistan, 2007–14 ... 213
    Col Speedie and Steve Mullins
14. AusAID stabilisation 229
    David Savage
15. The gender dimension 249
    Elizabeth Boulton

Part 4: Lessons and legacies

16. Lessons and legacies of the war in Afghanistan 271
    William Maley
17. American and British experience in Iraq and Afghanistan,
    2001–04 285
    Dan Marston
18. Lessons and legacies of the use of force 295
    Peter Leahy
19. The Official History of Australian Operations in Iraq and
    Afghanistan, and Australian Peacekeeping Operations
    in East Timor 313
    Craig Stockings
20. Final reflections 325
    John Blaxland

Appendix 1: Australian units and formations deployed
to Afghanistan and the Middle East, 2001–14 335

Appendix 2: Chronology: Australia's military involvement
in Afghanistan, 2001–present 337

Appendix 3: Chronology: Australia's military involvement
in Iraq, 2003–09 357

Bibliography 365

Foreword

Several years ago, a group named Military History and Heritage Victoria formed to bring together those who were passionate about military history. After several years of examining military history up to the 1990s, we decided to look at more contemporary events; namely, the 1999 Australian-led International Force East Timor (INTERFET). In 2014, we brought together a tremendous collection of speakers to examine this key period in Australia's military history. The Strategic & Defence Studies Centre at The Australian National University partnered with us to make the event possible and, more importantly, to publish the proceedings with Melbourne University Press.[1] We would like to think that this INTERFET conference and the publishing of the proceedings contributed to the decision to commence the next tranche of Australian official histories.

Flushed with success, we then embarked on a conference regarding Australia's involvement in the wars in Afghanistan and Iraq. The Australian military has had a long involvement in the Middle East region, and Australian and coalition military involvement continues to this day in both countries. But we felt enough time had passed for us again to make a contribution by examining the period 2001–14.

We called the conference 'War in the Sandpit: Reflections on Australia's War in Afghanistan and Iraq 2001–2014'. The conference gathered a well-qualified panel of speakers, many of whom were involved firsthand in the decisions and events described. Once again, the Strategic & Defence Studies Centre at The Australian National University partnered with us to make the event possible. The proceedings are published here to add to the historical record.

---

1   J. Blaxland (ed.), *East Timor Intervention: A retrospective on INTERFET*, Melbourne University Press, Melbourne, 2015.

We know that the official history, in production at the time of writing, will produce a more informed and perhaps different record and perspective on events, but, as ever, history is not a static phenomenon. Our objective remains to examine history and seek to learn from it, drawing from the experiences and perspectives of people involved ranging from Cabinet members down to the practitioners on the ground, in the air and at sea. We hope this volume achieves that.

I would like to thank my friend John Blaxland for his support and patience in bringing these projects to fruition. We have known each other since we both first marched into Duntroon in January 1983 and served together on operations in East Timor. His contribution to the understanding of military history and more contemporary security matters has been exemplary, and we at Military History and Heritage Victoria are pleased to see this important work available for general readers to access.

Marcus Fielding
20 October 2020

Maps, figures and images

Maps

Map 1: Middle East xv
Map 2: Iraq xvi
Map 3: Areas of Australian operations in Iraq and the Persian Gulf. . . xvii
Map 4: Provinces in Afghanistan xviii
Map 5: Main areas of Australian operations in Afghanistan xix
Map 6: Afghanistan xx

Figures

Figure 1: Afghanistan airspace 85
Figure 2: Control and Reporting Centre command and
 control arrangements 86
Figure 3: Middle Eastern Area of Operations command
 and control arrangements. 160
Figure 4: Australian intelligence collection and analysis
 arrangements in Afghanistan 175

Images

Prime Minister John Howard meets soldiers of the Australian
 Special Forces Task Group deployed on Operation SLIPPER
 in Afghanistan, 2005 56

Australian personnel on guard in an Australian light armoured
  vehicle as a US Army Blackhawk helicopter takes off in
  Baghdad, 2006. 72
RAAF Control and Reporting Centre, Kandahar, 2007–09 83
Australian soldeirs check vehicles on a main supply route
  in Southern Iraq, 2008. 83
Royal Australian Air Force F/A-18A Hornets prepare to depart
  on a mission to strike a Deash headquarters compound
  in Mosul, Iraq, from Australia's main air operating base in
  the Middle East region, 2016. 93
A trooper from the 2nd Cavalry Regiment provides security
  to Japanese Iraq Reconstruction Group convoy vehicles
  in As Samawah, 2005. 97
An F/A-18 waits its turn to refuel over Iraq during Operation
  Falconer, 2003 103
HMAS *Adelaide* patrols the waters around the oil terminals in the
  North Arabian Gulf during Operation Catalyst, 2004 131
Members of the Afghan National Army, 3RAR Battle Group
  and Mentoring Task Force 4 step off on their first handover/
  takeover patrol from Forward Operating Base Mirwais in
  Chora, Afghanistan, 2012 132
A member of Mobility Support fires a 84mm Carl Gustaf
  Rocket Launcher at the heavy weapons range in Tarin Kowt,
  Afghanistan, 2012 165
Major General Michael Crane, Commander Joint Task Force 633,
  with Afghan National Army artillerymen, Camp Alamo,
  Kabul, 2013. 171
Afghan artillery soldiers fire their D-30 Howitzer as the Australian
  mentors watch on at the heavy weapons range in Tarin Kowt,
  Afghanistan, 2010 218
Lieutenant Christian Johnston, Afghan mentor team leader for
  Combat Team B, 5th Battalion, the Royal Australian Regiment,
  looks on as his Afghan National Army counterpart speaks with
  an Afghan community member near Patrol Base Mohammed,
  Uruzgan province, Afghanistan, 2010 239

An RAAF C-17 Globemaster prepares to land at Tarin Kowt, 2012 . 254

Major General Abdul Hamid, Commander 205th Hero Corps, Afghan National Army, addresses tribal elders at a Shura held at an Afghan National Army base in Chah Chineh, Afghanistan, 2013 273

Major Cootes, Chief of Engineers on Multi-National Corps — Iraq, in 2005 surveying a bridge that was partially destroyed by a VBIED attack in 2004 289

Acknowledgements

This book would not have been possible without the collective efforts of the many contributors. It is a project bigger than one person, with the diverse voices that compile this book painting a truly unique and comprehensive portrait of Australia's wars in Afghanistan and Iraq.

A key strength of the manuscript is the experiences of the authors, who were invited to participate in this project because of their close association with the topics discussed. It is a privilege and rare opportunity to be able to publish a book that includes the firsthand voices and assessments of historical participants, who include a former Minister for Defence, Chief of the Defence Force, Secretary of the Defence Department, Chief of Army, other senior Australian military and police personnel, a currently serving senator, journalists, academics and diplomats.

With such a diverse range of contributors, the manuscript covers a breadth of topics, ranging from the strategic and tactical elements of the military operations in question, and includes themes such as command, the media, and gender aspects. Its presentation of material in short chapters works well, and, given that some of the chapters rely more on the authors' recollections, is appropriate. This mixture of experiences and expertise was a real strength of the 2017 conference 'War in the Sandpit' and remains perhaps the defining feature of the book.

The absence of references in some chapters might be particularly noticeable in a university publication such as this. We would stress, however, that this is characteristic of the lack of records in the public domain and is not an indication of a lack of academic rigour.

We, the editors, have sought to increase the book's strength and appeal by inviting other experts to write chapters on topics that were not part of the conference. We are indebted to the contributors for their frankness, and for their perseverance in turning their speeches from the conference into polished chapters for this book. Regrettably, Dr Garth Pratten's paper could not be included in this volume, but his talk, along with the other speakers' talks, can be watched and heard at the Australian Army website, 'The Cove'.[1]

The conference would not have been possible without the support of the team from Military History and Heritage Victoria. Thanks must be given to Jason McGregor, Brent Taylor, Peter Fielding, Jim Barry, Peter Edwards and Michael Buckridge for their efforts in the organisation and delivery of the conference. We are also grateful to the Australian Army for the use of Enoggera Barracks in Brisbane for the conference, and the Strategic & Defence Studies Centre at ANU for its support of the conference and this publication.

We wish to express our gratitude to ANU Press for publishing this book and for supporting publications of this nature. Particular thanks go to the peer reviewers and the ANU Press Asia-Pacific Security Studies series editor, Dr Greg Raymond.

We note this work was essentially complete and ready for publication prior to the revelations made public in the Brereton Report released in November 2020.[2] The work here provides important context to much of what Brereton discussed.

Most importantly, thank you to all the men and women who served and sacrificed on behalf of Australia. To those who died serving their nation, and those who have returned bearing what John Cantwell called the 'exit wounds' that last well beyond the time on deployment, we hope this book helps to explain and do justice to your experience.

---

1 See 'War in the Sand Pit Conference—Doctor Garth Pratten', 19 July 2017, cove.army.gov.au/search/node/war%20in%20the%20sand%20pit (retrieved 27 April 2020).
2 Inspector-General of the Australian Defence Force, *Afghanistan Inquiry Report* ('the Brereton Report'), afghanistaninquiry.defence.gov.au/sites/default/files/2020-11/IGADF-Afghanistan-Inquiry-Public-Release-Version.pdf (retrieved 24 November 2020).

Maps

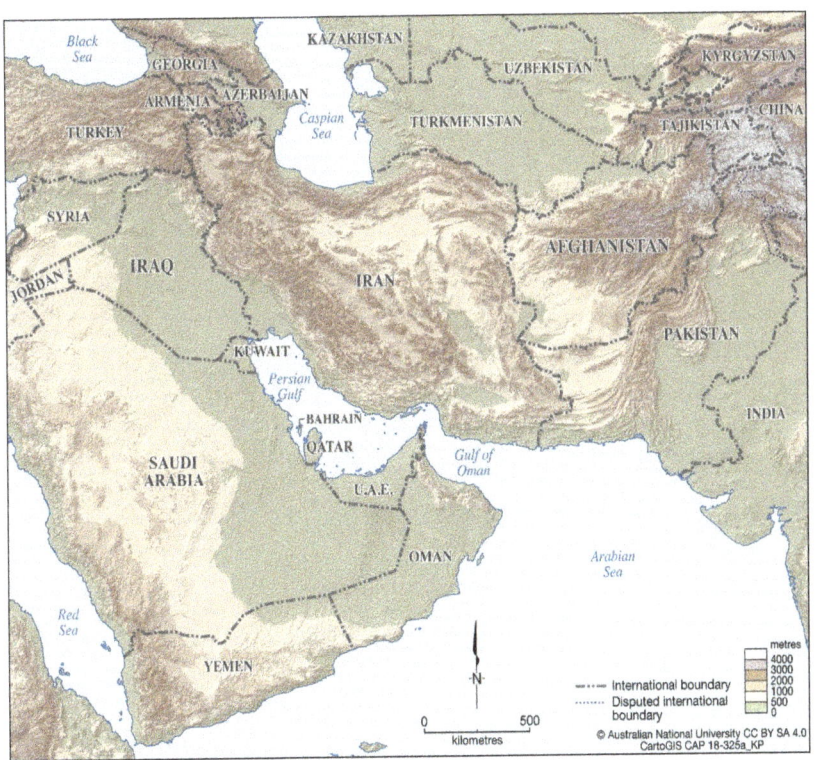

Map 1: Middle East.

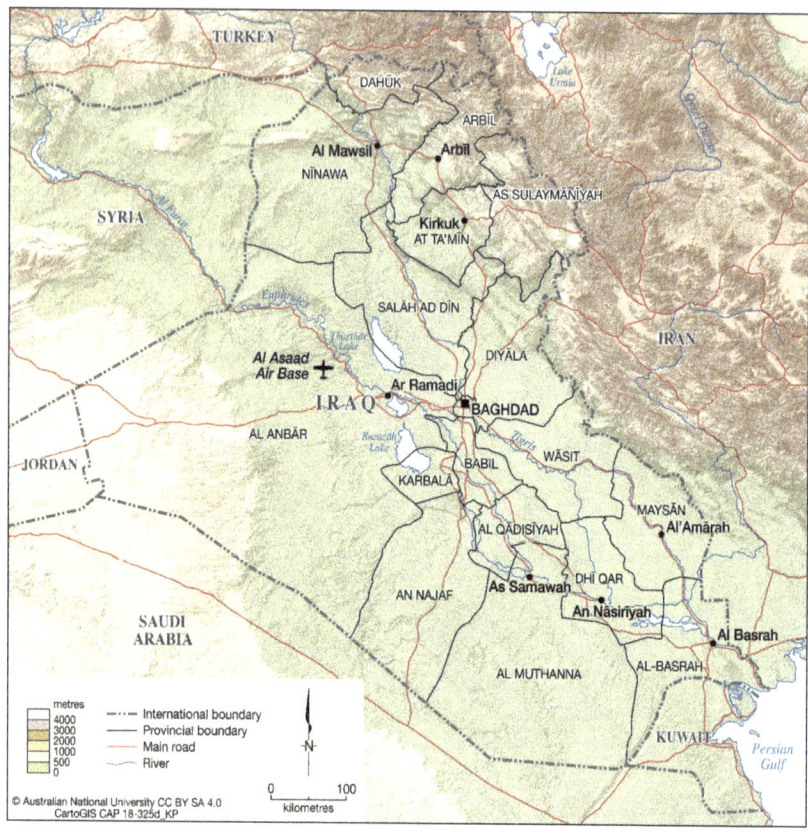

Map 2: Iraq.

Map 3: Areas of Australian operations in Iraq and the Persian Gulf.

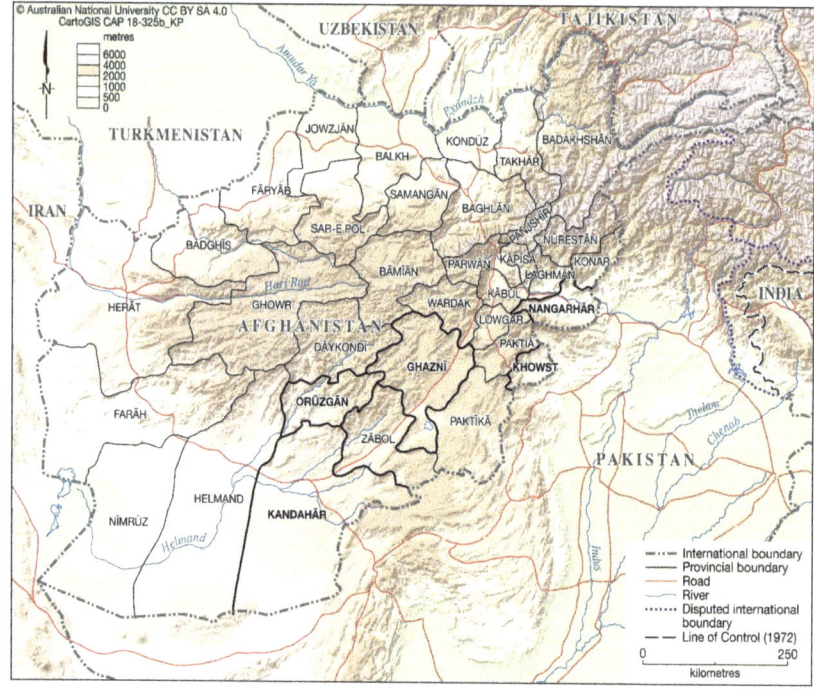

Map 4: Provinces in Afghanistan.

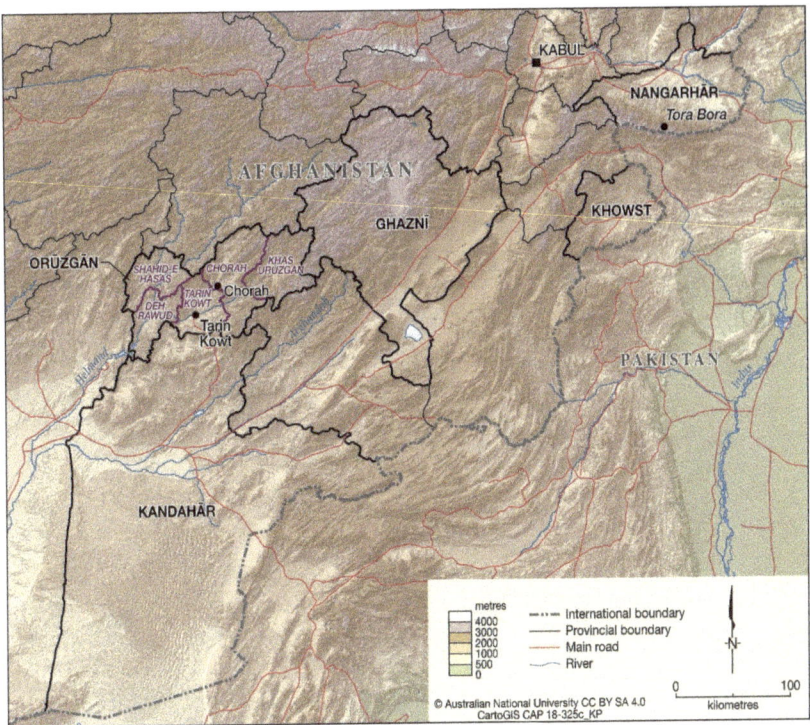

Map 5: Main areas of Australian operations in Afghanistan.

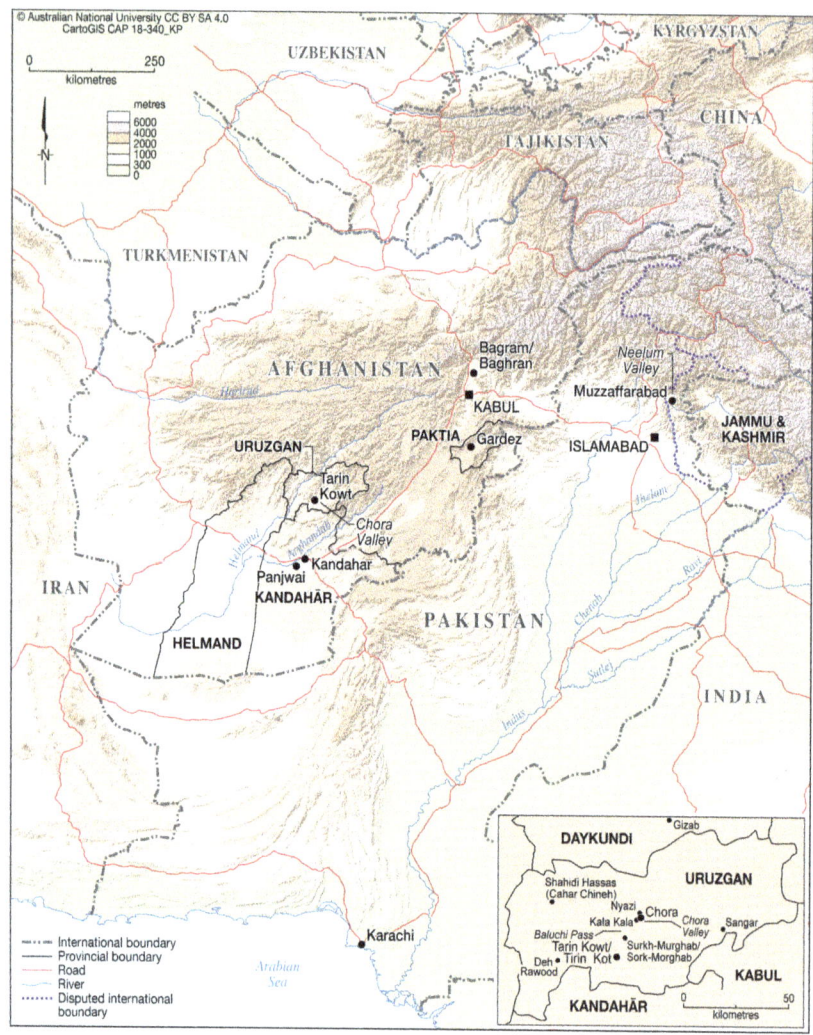

Map 6: Afghanistan.

Contributors

Admiral **Chris Barrie**, AC, was Chief of the Defence Force from 1998 to 2002. Admiral Barrie joined the RAN in 1961, and commanded HMAS *Buccaneer* from 1969 to 1970, HMAS *Stuart* from 1983 to 1984, and HMAS *Watson* from 1991 to 1992. In 1995 Admiral Barrie was appointed Deputy Chief of Navy, a role he held until he was appointed Vice Chief of the Defence Force in 1997. Following his retirement, Admiral Barrie has worked as a consultant, teacher and mentor at Oxford University, the National Defense University in Washington, DC, and at The Australian National University. Admiral Barrie chairs PTSD Australia New Zealand and is a member of the Global Military Advisory Council on Climate Change.

John Blaxland is Professor of International Security and Intelligence Studies at The Australian National University. A retired Army officer, he is also former head of the Strategic & Defence Studies Centre and a Senior Fellow of the Higher Education Academy. In 2019, the Australian Signals Directorate commissioned him to write a multi-volume history of their organisation. His publications so far include *In from the Cold: Reflections on Australia's Korean War* (2020); 'A Geostrategic SWOT Analysis for Australia' (2019); 'Tipping the Balance in Southeast Asia?' (2017); *The Secret Cold War* (2016); *East Timor Intervention* (2015); *The Protest Years* (2015); *The Australian Army From Whitlam to Howard* (2014); *Strategic Cousins* (2006); 'Revisiting Counterinsurgency' (2006); 'Information Era Manoeuvre' (2003); *Signals: Swift and Sure* (1998); and *Organising an Army: The Australian Experience, 1957–1965* (1989).

Elizabeth Boulton is a former Army officer who joined the Army in 1990 as a lieutenant in the Royal Australian Corps of Transport. She deployed to East Timor in 1999 and Iraq in 2004, and has also worked in Ghana,

Nigeria, Sudan and the Pacific Islands. Her last posting was as a research officer at Army Knowledge Centre, and she has been studying towards completion of a PhD at The Australian National University part-time.

Major General **Michael Crane**, DSC and Bar, AM, was commissioned into the Royal Australian Artillery in 1980, serving in East Timor and as Commander of the Army Recruit Training Centre. He was Chief of Staff in Headquarters Joint Operations Command from 2005 to 2006 before Commanding Joint Task Force 633 in the Middle East from 2006 to 2007. In 2008 he was appointed Head of Military Strategic Commitments, and in 2009 Deputy Director of Operations at United States Central Command. He completed a second tour as Commander of JTF 633 from 2012 to 2013 before retiring from full-time service in 2014.

Colonel **Marcus Fielding** joined the Australian Army in 1983 and graduated from the Royal Military College, Duntroon, in December 1986. He was commissioned into the Royal Australian Engineers, has held a variety of command, staff and instructional appointments, and has served on operations in Pakistan, Afghanistan, Haiti, East Timor and Iraq. Colonel Fielding transferred from full-time to part-time service with the Australian Army in 2011. He is the President of Military History and Heritage Victoria and a non-executive director of the National Vietnam Veterans Museum Ltd. He is the author of *Red Zone Baghdad: My War in Iraq* (2011) and *Dealing with a Deadly Legacy: Aussie Soldiers Clearing Land Mines in Afghanistan* (2019).

Thea Gellerfy is an early career researcher with a background in defence industry, working in support of several global military operations. She is pursuing an academic career in strategic studies, focusing on developing more robust methodologies for defence acquisitions. Her thesis with The Australian National University considers the role of emerging technologies in the maritime domain, specifically the influence of unmanned technologies in anti-submarine warfare scenarios.

Professor **Robert Hill**, AC, was a member of the Australian Senate from 1981 to 2006, representing South Australia. Hill was elected Leader of the Liberal Party and Leader of the Opposition in the Senate from 1990 to 1996 when, on the election of the Howard Government, he became Leader of the Government in the Senate from March 1996 until his resignation in January 2006. He was Minister for the Environment (1996–98), Minister for the Environment and Heritage (1998–2002) and

Minister for Defence (2001–06). Since leaving politics, Hill has served as ambassador to the United Nations and has chaired the Australian Carbon Trust (later Low Carbon Australia Ltd). He is an Adjunct Professor in Sustainability at the US Studies Centre at the University of Sydney and chairs the Control and Reporting Centre for Low Carbon Living at the University of New South Wales. He was appointed Chancellor of the University of Adelaide in 2010, a role he held until 2014.

Vice Admiral **Peter Jones**, AO, DSC, joined the RAN in 1974 and is a surface warfare specialist. His sea-going postings have included command of HMAS *Melbourne* and Commander Australian Surface Task Group. From 2002 to 2003, Jones commanded the RAN Task Group in the Persian Gulf and the multinational Maritime Interception Force. Subsequently, he has had appointments including Commander Australian Navy Systems Command, Head of ICT Operations/Strategic J6 and Head Capability Systems within Capability Development Group. In 2011 he was appointed Chief of Capability Development Group, serving in this capacity until his retirement in 2014.

Lieutenant General **Peter Leahy**, AC, served as Chief of Army from 2002 to 2008. He first joined the Army in 1971 as an infantryman, and held multiple instructional roles both domestically and abroad, including with Gurkha soldiers and at the US Army Command and General Staff College. He commanded the 8th/9th Battalion from 1990 to 1992 and the 3rd Brigade from 1997 to 1998 before assuming duties as Deputy Chief of Army in 2000. Since his retirement in 2008, Leahy has been a professor at the University of Canberra and chaired the boards of Soldier On and the Australian International Military Games.

Colonel **Mick Lehmann**, CSC, graduated from the Royal Military College, Duntroon, in 1986 and entered the Australian Intelligence Corps. He commanded the Defence Intelligence Training Centre from 2006 to 2007, and has served as senior intelligence officer at brigade and division levels. He deployed to Afghanistan in 2007, 2011 and 2015 before retiring from the Army in 2016.

Major General **Dan McDaniel** is a senior Army officer who has served in command positions several times on combat operations in the Middle East. He has led at all levels of special operations, from patrol to command. He commanded the Special Air Service Regiment from 2007 to 2008 and the Special Operations Command from 2013 to 2014. He began his Army career in 1988, and joined the Royal Australian Infantry Corps in 1989.

Professor **William Maley** is Emeritus Professor of Diplomacy at the Coral Bell School of Asia Pacific Affairs at The Australian National University. He served as the College's Foundation Director of the Asia-Pacific College of Diplomacy from 2003 to 2014. He has taught at the Australian Defence Force Academy and has served as a Visiting Professor at the Russian Diplomatic Academy, a Visiting Fellow at the Centre for the Study of Public Policy at the University of Strathclyde, and a Visiting Research Fellow in the Refugee Studies Programme at Oxford University. He is a barrister of the High Court of Australia, vice-president of the Refugee Council of Australia, and a member of the Australian Committee of the Council for Security Cooperation in the Asia Pacific.

Dan Marston is Director of the Secretary of Defense Strategic Thinkers Program (STP) and Professor of Practice at the Paul H. Nitze School of Advanced International Studies. He is a visiting professor at the US Marine Corps' School of Advanced Warfighting and an Honorary Professor at ANU. Between 2012 and 2018, he held a professorship in Military Studies at ANU and was also Principal of the Military and Defence Studies Program at the Australian Command and Staff College in Canberra. He previously held the Ike Skelton Distinguished Chair in the Art of War at the US Army Command and General Staff College. He has been a Visiting Fellow, on several occasions, with the Leverhulme Changing Character of War Programme at the University of Oxford. He was previously a senior lecturer in War Studies at the Royal Military Academy, Sandhurst. He has been a special adviser, since 2006, in Iraq and Afghanistan with the US Army, US Marine Corps and British Army.

Karen Middleton is a political journalist and Chief Political Correspondent for *The Saturday Paper*. In 2011 she published her first book, *An Unwinnable War: Australia in Afghanistan*, which told the political backstory of Australia's involvement in Afghanistan. She has worked in the federal parliamentary Press Gallery since 1989 and was the president of the Press Gallery for four years.

Major General **Jim Molan**, AO, DSC, is a Senator for New South Wales representing the Liberal Party. He joined the Army in 1968, serving as an infantryman and helicopter pilot, and in 2000 was Commander of the evacuation force from Solomon Islands. In 2004 Molan deployed to Iraq as the coalition's Chief of Operations, and upon his return to Australia commenced posts as Defence Materiel Advocate and then as adviser to the Vice Chief of the Defence Force on Joint Warfighting Lessons and Concepts. Following his retirement from the Army in 2008, Molan published books and articles on his experience in Iraq, and became a regular media commentator on defence and security issues.

Superintendent **Steve Mullins** has held a variety of roles in the Australian Federal Police, including as Senior Liaison Officer and Coordinator of Economic and Special Operations. He is now retired from the AFP.

Major General **Anthony Rawlins**, DSC, is Deputy Chief of the Australian Army. Formerly, he was Director General Military Strategic Commitments Branch, and previously he was Commander of the 7th Brigade based at Enoggera in Brisbane. He has completed operational service deployments with the United Nations Truce Supervision Organisation in Israel and Lebanon and with the Headquarters International Security Assistance Force. As Commanding Officer of 2nd Cavalry Regiment in southern Iraq, he commanded Overwatch Battle Group West (Two). Since 2017 he has been on the board of Mates4Mates.

Dr **Alan Ryan** has been Executive Director of the Australian Civil-Military Centre since 2012. He was previously Principal of the Centre for Defence and Strategic Studies at the Australian Defence College from 2006 to 2012, and Senior Adviser to the Minister for Defence, Senator Robert Hill, from 2003 to 2006. From 1999 to 2003 he was Senior Research Fellow in the Army's principal conceptual research institution, the Land Warfare Studies Centre. He has held several consulting and teaching positions, including as an assistant dean at the University of Notre Dame Australia. He served with the Australian Army Reserve between 1981 and 1994 and on attachment with the British Territorial Army from 1987 to 1991.

David Savage, AM, has been a deputy director of the Department of Foreign Affairs and Trade since 2010. He began his career in the Australian Federal Police from 1982 to 2001, contributing to peacekeeping operations in East Timor, Mozambique and Bougainville. From 2001 to 2005 he was Chief of Investigations for the United Nations Serious Crimes Unit East Timor, then worked on various overseas policing projects targeting human trafficking. In 2002, he published *Dancing with the Devil: A Personal*

Account of Policing the East Timor Vote for Independence. In 2009 he joined the International Crisis Group as a consultant researching war crimes and human rights abuses. In 2011 Savage deployed to Afghanistan as a stabilisation adviser for AusAID, returning in 2012. In 2013 he began volunteering for Soldier On Australia as a Wounded Ambassador. Savage was a Visiting Fellow with the Asia-Pacific College of Diplomacy at ANU.

Ric Smith, AO, PSM, was Secretary of the Department of Defence from 2002 to 2006. He began his career in the Department of External Affairs in 1969, serving in New Delhi, Tel Aviv and Manila. From 1987 to 1989 he was Consul-General in Honolulu, then Head of the Pacific, Africa and Middle East Division of DFAT up to 1992. In 1992 he was appointed a deputy secretary of DFAT, and in 1996 was named Australian ambassador to the People's Republic of China. From January 2001 to 31 October 2002, Smith served as Australian ambassador to the Republic of Indonesia, and in 2008 he led a review for the Rudd Government of Australia's homeland and border security. In April 2009, Smith was appointed as Australia's Special Envoy for Afghanistan and Pakistan.

Superintendent **Col Speedie** was commander of the second Australian Federal Police mission to Afghanistan from 2008 to 2009. He served in senior police executive roles in Solomon Islands and Jordan and as head of the United Nations Police in Cyprus. Following his retirement from the AFP in 2014, Speedie has been a law enforcement and security adviser and also engaged in lecturing on expeditionary policing strategy and operations, domestically and internationally.

Professor **Craig Stockings** is the Official Historian of Australian Operations in Iraq, Afghanistan and East Timor. He is a graduate of both the Australian Defence Force Academy and the Royal Military College, Duntroon, and served as an infantry officer with the 3rd Battalion, Royal Australian Regiment. From 1999 to 2000 he deployed to East Timor, then was appointed aide-de-camp to the Governor-General of Australia. He has been a lecturer and associate professor at the University of New South Wales, Canberra, since 2006. In 2016 Stockings was appointed the Official Historian for the Official History of Australian Operations in Iraq and Afghanistan, and Australian Peacekeeping Operations in East Timor.

Air Commodore **Chris Westwood** joined the RAAF in 1982 and held several executive posts, including Commanding Officer of 1 Radar Surveillance Unit in 1994, Commanding Officer 3 Control and Reporting Unit from 2002 to 2003, and Officer Commanding 41 Wing from 2004 to 2008. Westwood has been responsible for domestic defence operations, including security for the Melbourne Commonwealth Games of 2006, and deployed with the Control and Reporting Centre Afghanistan for three short visits. In 2010 he became Director General Joint Capability Coordination, a role he held until 2013 when he was appointed Deputy Air Commander Australia. Subsequently he served as Commander Surveillance and Response Group from late 2013 until his retirement in 2015.

Glossary

ACAUST	Air Commander Australia
ACMC	Australian Civil-Military Centre
ADF	Australian Defence Force
AFP	Australian Federal Police
AMCTF	Afghan Major Crimes Task Force
AMTG	Al Muthanna Task Group
ANP	Afghan National Police
ANSF	Afghan National Security Forces
ANZUS	Australia, New Zealand, United States
AO	area of operation
AusAID	Australian Agency for International Development
AUSMIN	Australia–United States Ministerial Consultation
AWACS	Airborne Warning and Control System
C2	command and control
CA	Chief of Army
CAOC	Combined Air Operations Centre
CDF	Chief of the Defence Force
CENTAF	United States Central Command Air Forces
CENTCOM	United States Central Command
CFACC	Combined Forces Air Component Command
CJIATF	Combined Joint Interagency Task Force
CJOPS	Chief of Joint Operations
CNPA	Afghan Counter Narcotics Police
COMAST	Commander Australian Theatre

CRC	Control and Reporting Centre
CSO	civil society organisation
CSTC-A	Combined Security Transition Command – Afghanistan
CTF	Combined Task Force
DFAT	Department of Foreign Affairs and Trade
EUPOL	European Union Police Mission in Afghanistan
FET	female engagement team
GA	gender adviser
GIRoA	Government of the Islamic Republic of Afghanistan
GROM	Grupa Reagowania Operacyjno-Manewrowego (Polish Special Forces)
HQJOC	Headquarters Joint Operations Command
ICRC	International Committee of the Red Cross
IED	improvised explosive device
INTERFET	International Force East Timor
IOCC	Interagency Operations Coordination Centre (US–UK)
ISAF	International Security Assistance Force
J2	Chief Staff Officer Intelligence
J4	Chief Staff Officer for Joint Logistics
JNAC	Joint Narcotics Analysis Centre
JTF	Joint Task Force
KLE	Key Leadership Engagement
LGBTI	lesbian, gay, bisexual, transgender and intersex
M2T	Mentor, Monitor and Train
MEAO	Middle East Area of Operations
MIF	Maritime Interception Force
MND-SE	Multi-National Division – South East
MNF-I	Multi-National Force – Iraq
MRE	Mission Rehearsal Exercise
MRTF	Mentoring and Reconstruction Task Force
MSC	Military Strategic Commitments
MV	Motor Vessel

GLOSSARY

NAP	National Action Plan
NATO	North Atlantic Treaty Organization
NGO	non-government organisation
NSC	National Security Committee of Cabinet
OBG(W)	Overwatch Battle Group (West)
OGA	other government agency
OMLT	Operational Mentoring and Liaison Team
OPCON	Operational Control
PM&C	Department of the Prime Minister and Cabinet
PRT	Provincial Reconstruction Team
PTSD	post-traumatic stress disorder
RAAF	Royal Australian Air Force
RAF	Royal Air Force
RAMSI	Regional Assistance Mission to Solomon Islands
RAN	Royal Australian Navy
RFA	Royal Fleet Auxiliary
RHIB	Rigid Hulled Inflatable Boat
RSM	regimental sergeant major
RTF	Reconstruction Task Force
S2	Intelligence Staff Officer
SAS	Special Air Service
SEAL	United States Navy Sea, Air and Land Team
SOTG	Special Operations Task Group
SPA	Senior Police Adviser
STABAD	stabilisation adviser
TACON	Tactical Control
TECHCON	Technical Control
UAE	United Arab Emirates
UAV	Unmanned Aerial Vehicle
UKATG	United Kingdom Amphibious Task Group
UN	United Nations
UNAMA	United Nations Assistance Mission in Afghanistan

UNFICYP	United Nations Peacekeeping Force in Cyprus
UNSCR	United Nations Security Council Resolution
UNTAET	United Nations Transitional Administration in East Timor
USAF	United States Air Force
USCG	United States Coast Guard
USCGC	United States Coast Guard Cutter
USMC	United States Marine Corps
USN	United States Navy
VBIED	vehicle-borne improvised explosive device
VCDF	Vice Chief of the Defence Force
WMD	weapons of mass destruction
WPS	Women, Peace and Security

Introduction

John Blaxland

On 11 September 2001, I was working as an integrated exchange officer of the US Defense Intelligence Agency in Washington, DC. The day before, wearing my slouch hat, I had attended a ceremony held on the sunny lawns of the Washington Navy Yard. There, President George W. Bush presented to Australia's visiting Prime Minister John Howard the bell of the warship USS *Canberra*—itself a decommissioned US Navy warship. USS *Canberra* had been given the rare honour of being named after a foreign nation's capital to commemorate the close bonds built in the Pacific War between the two nations' navies and to honour in particular HMAS *Canberra*, which was sunk while fighting alongside US warships in the Battle of Savo Island in August 1942. The gift marked the 50th anniversary of the signing of the ANZUS Treaty between the United States, New Zealand and Australia.

As it turns out, the events that followed that fateful time would not demand of Australia the kind of commitment that Australians made during the two world wars. No conscription was necessary, and no mass recruitment drive was involved. Australians instead committed carefully selected force elements from their small and boutique all-volunteer defence force. With ongoing concerns closer to home, and mindful of the considerable contributions of other partners, the Australian Government chose to make a series of carefully calibrated niche contributions, alongside allies and coalition partners, on operations in Afghanistan and Iraq. Looking back, nearly 20 years on from that moment, this book sets out to capture some of the details of what happened, examining how Australia chose to act this way, how it contributed forces and why it did so in the way that it did.

Niche Wars provides a range of rigorous academic perspectives combined with a variety of views of prominent practitioners. Of note, this book cannot hope to cover all the activities that transpired between 2001 and 2014. That is the work best left to the official historians, whose work is in progress. This book, instead, provides a snapshot of some of the problems, addressed largely thematically, without being comprehensive. To begin with, what follows is a synopsis of the contributions made by the elements of the Australian Defence Force (ADF) along the way. This is a scene-setter for the reader, providing context for the chapters that follow. The introduction then concludes with a brief overview of the structure and content of the book.

Context

Since 1885, when the colonies sent a contingent to support British objectives in the Sudan, Australians have engaged in distant military operations in the Middle East and neighbouring areas. Thereafter, Australians deployed on combat operations in the Middle East during both world wars and maintained a peacekeeping presence there for most of the years since. This reflected the consistent imperative to remain engaged with affairs in the region, particularly given the ongoing reliance of Australia on Middle Eastern oil and trade routes. Indeed, Britain remained Australia's principal trade partner for decades after the Second World War, and the main trade route was via the Suez Canal. This was vital ground for Australia.

The Suez Crisis in 1956 was an inflection point. Egyptian President Abdul Nasser nationalised the Suez Canal. Britain, France and Israel responded with force and, without knowing the details, Australia offered diplomatic support for Britain's action. US President Dwight Eisenhower, blindsided by these surprise actions, threatened economic sanctions, which forced Britain to withdraw. This also led to the creation of the first large-scale peacekeeping mission to be sanctioned by the United Nations, which was an initiative spearheaded by the Canadian External Affairs Minister Lester B. Pearson.[1] This ignominious moment saw Britain subsequently prepare to withdraw from east of Suez and Australia pivot towards working more closely on security issues in South-East Asia, but Australia's interests in

---

1   See J. Blaxland, *Strategic Cousins: Australian and Canadian Expeditionary Forces and the British and American Empires*, McGill-Queens University Press, Montreal, 2006.

the Middle East never went away. Trade, as well as the flow of oil and the call for support from allies, would continue to echo in Australia's strategic consciousness for the rest of the 20th century and beyond.

In defence policy terms, for much of the latter years of the Cold War and the early post–Cold War years, defence of Australia was the top priority, but the Middle East had still featured occasionally, and Australia made niche contributions when required. The Australian Army, for instance, sent a select group of army officers on annual rotations to the United Nations Truce Supervision Organization (UNTSO) covering Israel and Palestine. In addition, a small contingent of Royal Australian Air Force (RAAF) and Army personnel had served on rotations with the Multinational Force and Observers (MFO) in the Sinai on and off from the mid-1970s onwards. As the end of the Cold War approached, and as the Iran–Iraq War of 1980–88 came to a close, Australia contributed peacekeepers to the United Nations Iran–Iraq Military Observer Group (UNIIMOG). Australia withdrew its contribution following Iraq's invasion of Kuwait in August 1990.

Following the invasion of Kuwait by Saddam Hussein's forces, Australia was quick to join a UN-mandated coalition to liberate Kuwait. Australia supported this initiative but kept its military contribution modest, contributing some intelligence analysts, air transport and a rotation of Royal Australian Navy (RAN) warships. In that instance, three Australian warships participated in blockade operations in the Persian Gulf as part of a multinational naval interception force, to enforce the UN sanctions. Australia also provided a supply vessel, four medical teams and a mine-clearance diving team that joined a protective screen, under US operational control, around aircraft-carrier battle groups in the Gulf.

In addition to naval units, Australian personnel took part on attachment to various British and US ground formations. A small group of RAAF photo-interpreters was based in Saudi Arabia, together with a detachment from the Defence Intelligence Organisation. Four medical teams were also despatched at the request of the United States. Although the ships and their crews were in danger from mines and possible air attack, Australia's war was relatively uneventful, and there were no casualties.[2]

---

2   For an authoritative account of Australia's involvement in the Gulf War, see D. Horner, *The Official History of Australian Peacekeeping, Humanitarian and Post-Cold War Operations*, vol. 2: *Australia and the 'New World Order'*, Cambridge University Press, Melbourne, 2011.

At war's end, 75 Australians deployed to northern Iraq to assist in the provision of humanitarian aid to Kurds living in a UN-declared exclusion zone. The RAN continued its contribution to the interception operations, and several Australian naval officers commanded the multinational interception force. Australia later provided weapons inspectors in Iraq to monitor the discovery and disposal of prohibited nuclear, chemical and biological weapons of mass destruction. From then on, Australia also maintained naval ships on station in the Persian Gulf on an almost continuous basis.

A decade later, and after having had apparently quick successes in Afghanistan, the ADF was better placed and more prepared to make a more robust contribution to offensive, and inherently dangerous, military operations in Iraq. The Special Air Service Regiment contributed to a combat search and rescue force in Kuwait in 1998 in support of US-backed UN initiatives to enforce sanctions. That experience demonstrated the ease of deployment and the evident utility of special forces for contentious deployments far from Australia's shores. Howard wanted 'quick and clean' force contributions that could be 'in at the pointy end and then out fast'.[3]

Events after 11 September 2001, or 9/11 as it came to be known, would see the Middle East return to centre stage. Government policy shifted in part in recognition of the need to protect and advance Australia's national interests further from Australian shores than was envisaged in the preceding two decades.

These commitments, and the ones that would follow on a greater scale from 2001 onwards, exposed a historically deep-seated impulse to remain active far beyond Australia's shores. By 2001, however, the dynamics had shifted, with Australia still seeing the Middle East as important while looking to its near north as a priority, particularly in view of burgeoning trade connections.

President Bush called it the 'Global War on Terror'—perhaps in itself leading to a distracting focus on fighting a nebulous concept rather than a specific enemy. Sensing its awkwardness, Australia avoided endorsing the term. For Prime Minister Howard, however, 9/11 was a moment

---

3   See J. Blaxland, *The Australian Army from Whitlam to Howard*, Cambridge University Press, Melbourne, 2014, pp. 218–19.

worthy of invoking the 50-year-old ANZUS Treaty. Howard committed Australian forces, from all three services, to operations alongside US and coalition forces in the Middle East, a commitment that ended up being for a longer period than either of the two world wars. (See Appendix 1 for a table of Australian units and formations deployed to Afghanistan and the Middle East, 2001–14.) But this time they did so while avoiding the politically contentious issues of conscription and heavy own-force casualties by making niche and calibrated force contributions and by utilising only a professional, all-volunteer force.

The United States identified Afghanistan as the primary target, being the state ruled by the Taliban, which was closely associated with the terrorist group al-Qaeda, led by Osama bin Laden. The Taliban's refusal to expel al-Qaeda triggered the allied attacks aimed at their overthrow. The attacks began on 7 October, and within five weeks the capital, Kabul, had fallen to the US-led coalition's principal Afghan partners, the Northern Alliance.

A chronology of Australia's military involvement in Afghanistan commencing in 2001 is located at Appendix 2.

Few Australians realised the fight would continue for years thereafter. In reality, it would mean multiple deployments of ground, maritime and air contingents to the Middle East for the better part of the following two decades. Australians would soon be found in Iraq, Kuwait, Afghanistan, the Persian Gulf, Qatar, Dubai and beyond, as well as in transit across the Indian Ocean and on deployments alongside US and other coalition counterparts in headquarters across the Middle East and in HQ Central Command in Florida.

In contrast to the commitments in the major wars in the Middle East in the early to mid-twentieth century, Australia did not rely on mass mobilisation of troops. Instead, as the chapters in this book illustrate, the Australian Government chose to make small contributions to generate carefully constrained strategic effects—notably in support of Australia's major alliance partner, the United States. There were compelling reasons beyond the alliance relationship for Australia to engage with these security issues, as did many other powers. But with an eye to the political fallout from the Vietnam War commitment decades earlier, the government sought to minimise domestic political risk from an open-ended commitment. Each decision to commit forces therefore was evaluated for the tactical, operational and strategic consequences, as well as the political consequences likely to be generated back home. Notwithstanding these overarching constraints, operations in the Middle East would provide a wide range of unique additional challenges and opportunities for elements of the ADF to learn and adapt.

The deployments to Afghanistan and Iraq came in several iterations over the early years of the conflicts. At the outset, Prime Minister Howard wished to make a carefully calibrated, niche contribution to a US-led coalition, to ensure that Australia was not engaged in a protracted war and that it remained able to respond to any crises in our region should they arise. Hence the initial contingent deployed were special forces, with the first SAS Squadron being committed to operations in November 2001 as part of a US Marine Expeditionary Unit. Campaigning in Afghanistan ended inconclusively in mid-2002, and the special forces soldiers were withdrawn promptly.

The early success of the special forces in Afghanistan led to a similar political calculus for the deployment to Iraq in 2003. Operations BASTILLE and FALCONER were the names given successively to the preparatory operation and then the actual conduct of ADF operations as part of the war in Iraq. (See Appendix 3 for a chronology of Australia's involvement in Iraq, 2003–09.)

The controversy arising from the US Government's approach to preparations for war in Iraq generated protests around the world, notably in the capital cities of the principal participants, especially the United States, United Kingdom and Australia. That controversy would reverberate for years afterwards as the principal declared rationale for removal of the Saddam Hussein regime was the claim that he was hiding weapons of mass destruction (WMD). UN-sanctioned weapons inspectors had encountered increased wariness in Iraq, which appeared to point to Iraqi authorities having something to hide. Intelligence analysts working for countries for and against the projected war in Iraq agreed that Iraq must have a WMD program, but little thought was given to the internal logic of the Saddam regime's fear of disclosure. In hindsight, it appears obvious. Saddam did not wish to declare that he no longer had a WMD capability as it would have emboldened neighbouring Iran. Then, as war looked increasingly inevitable, he was too proud to concede and too confident that, like in 1991, the United States would not succeed in removing him from power.

The Australian Government, sensing the mood in Washington, DC, eager to support its key ally and believing the reports of an enduring WMD capability, supported military planning as part of BASTILLE and in anticipation of the switch to offensive military operations as part of Operation FALCONER. Hence, when it came finally to supporting US offensive action, the preceding preparations made the transition to FALCONER a relatively seamless one.

For FALCONER, Australia planned to make useful but niche contributions. This included an SAS squadron group, which deployed to the Iraqi western desert, supported by a squadron of RAAF FA-18 Hornet fighter aircraft and RAN fleet elements working closely with their US and UK counterparts. This was a considerably more substantial contribution than the ADF had made for the Gulf War in 1991.

The Australian special forces, as well as the RAAF contributions, were warmly received by their US coalition counterparts, who were keen to have international partners. Their presence, however, was tightly constrained to the initial phases of the war, on the understanding that after the fall of the Saddam Hussein regime they would be released for return to Australia. The realities of war in the Iraqi desert involved long distances to be covered travelling off-road, with the risk of encountering armoured opponents. Arguably, this task was better suited to Australian cavalry forces, but Prime Minister Howard was confident that the special forces could do the job and with the least risk of Australian casualties. Nevertheless the Darwin-based 2nd Cavalry Regiment, together with a company of mounted infantry, did deploy to Iraq where they were retained to form an Australian Embassy Security Detachment in Baghdad.

Over the next two years, Australia maintained a low profile in Afghanistan and Iraq. In time, however, with the war proving not nearly as conclusive as President Bush had anticipated, the security situation in both Afghanistan and Iraq deteriorated, and the United States applied considerable pressure for Australian forces to return to assist. In February 2005, therefore, Prime Minister Howard committed an additional force to southern Iraq, deployed to Al Muthanna working closely with coalition partners, including Dutch, Japanese and British troops.

Similarly, in Afghanistan, having moved on from that theatre of operations to focus on Iraq, the US departure had allowed a resurgence of Taliban forces. By 2005, the calls for coalition partners to bolster the US position there were becoming stronger. As a result, Australia weighed its options. Eager to avoid a commitment that would expose Australia to a major force commitment, significant additional expense and a heightened risk of casualties, the Howard Government decided to recommit a Special Operations Task Group (SOTG) that year under the banner of Operation SLIPPER, this time to Uruzgan Province in central Afghanistan. Special forces had proven to be reliable as being readily deployable, highly professional and less likely to face significant numbers of casualties. Following three SOTG rotations, the 1st Reconstruction Task Force (RTF1) formed and deployed to Tarin Kowt, the central town in Uruzgan. There it worked to build up Afghan society as well as defeat the Taliban. In April 2007, a SOTG returned to operate alongside the RTF to provide a kinetic war-fighting capability.

As time passed, the focus for the RTFs turned from reconstruction to mentored reconstruction. Eventually, the focus shifted mostly to mentoring the Afghan National Security Force, with the aim of developing indigenous capacity-building. As part of this approach, efforts were made to ensure that initiatives funded by the Department of Foreign Affairs and Trade and its Australian Aid projects were coordinated and that those undertaken by the Australian Federal Police were synchronised with the ADF initiatives as well. As some chapters of this book attest, this sounded good in principle but proved difficult in practice.

From one perspective, this carefully calibrated contribution made sense. The Australian commitment to operations in Uruzghan Province involved a defined physical area with agreed, limited force contributions and partnered with a prominent NATO member state, the Netherlands. Initially the Dutch would be in charge, not the Australians. This seemed to be a convenient way to ensure that the Dutch made a significant contribution to the international stabilisation operations in Afghanistan while keeping Australia's contribution in check. It also meant that Australia did not have to contribute all the force elements for an effective and holistic counter-insurgency campaign with long-term objectives in mind.

INTRODUCTION

Successive Australian governments renewed the commitment to the war in Afghanistan despite mounting losses. Over time, the ADF deployment in Uruzgan generated a growing number of casualties: 11 Australians died on operations in Afghanistan from 2002 to the end of 2009, 10 died in 2010 and 11 in 2011.

A disproportionate portion of the load fell on the shoulders of Australia's special forces soldiers who deployed in successive SOTG rotations. By 2014, many had been on several such deployments. Eventually, this would lead to over-exposure of these elite troops to the brutality and apparent unending nature of a campaign that lacked clarity of purpose. Consequently, their actions led to some highly questionable outcomes and accusations of war crimes that would prove corrosive to Australia's special forces and the broader ADF.[4] In hindsight, this probably should have been seen as the inevitable outcome of a flawed strategy. Without a holistic counter-insurgency campaign for Afghanistan, let alone Uruzgan, much of the direction of tactical actions fell on the shoulders of soldiers and commanders. In the absence of a compelling overarching strategy, the main campaign plans left Australian and coalition forces with an inadequate *raison d'être* for the brutal fight they were tasked to undertake.

Beyond the SOTG rotations and the reconstruction and mentoring task forces, Australians were seconded to (i.e. embedded in) coalition units and headquarters in Tarin Kowt, Kabul, Kandahar, Bagram and in other locations across Afghanistan. In Tarin Kowt, under the Dutch-led Task Force Uruzgan Headquarters, Australian embeds assisted in coordinating missions, campaign planning and mission deconfliction among other duties, and used this experience in joint headquarters to inform Australian planning. This embedded experience allowed Australians not only to practice the art of military operations but also to utilise the information and experience they gained to inform planning and refine processes for future Australian deployments.

Meanwhile, the RAN and RAAF continued to gain excellent operational experience from their carefully calibrated force contributions, and their experience helped to generate momentum for development, introduction into service and refinement of significant capabilities. For the Air Force,

---

4   See Australian Broadcasting Corporation, 'Killing Field', *Four Corners*, 16 March 2020, www.abc.net.au/4corners/killing-field/12060538 (retrieved 19 March 2020).

this included advances in niche capabilities including airborne refuelling, airborne early warning and control, airborne surveillance, communications and identification systems capabilities as well as ground-based air traffic control through the RAAF's deployable Control and Reporting Centre. Almost the entire RAN fleet undertook one or more deployment to participate in intervention and monitoring operations in and around the Persian Gulf for the entire period covered in this book and beyond. This experience helped to justify and refine technological advances, including weapons systems upgrades and enhancements to missile systems and phased array radars.

By 2014, about 1,550 Australian military personnel were stationed in Afghanistan as part of Australia's military contribution to the international campaign against terrorism, maritime security in the Middle East Area of Operations (MEAO) and countering piracy in the Gulf of Aden, all under the banner of Operation SLIPPER. All of this was commanded by a Joint Task Force headquarters sited in the Persian Gulf and answerable to Headquarters Joint Operations Command (HQJOC) back in Australia. An additional 830 ADF personnel were deployed across the broader MEAO, often alongside coalition partners, making discrete but important contributions. Australia also maintained a continuous maritime contribution to Operation SLIPPER, which included RAN frigates on rotation.[5]

The SOTG and the mentoring and reconstruction forces returned to Australia from Uruzghan in 2014. Australian forces had withdrawn from Iraq after Kevin Rudd's election victory in 2007, but they stayed on in Afghanistan until 2014 when a major US force drawdown took place. Yet the decisions made in 2014 did not see the end of the matter in either Afghanistan or Iraq. Iraq saw the rise of the so-called Islamic State in 2014 and a demand for a return to assist the government of Iraq alongside US and other coalition partners. How the situation arose, what transpired and how Australia responded is a separate story not recounted in these pages. Similarly, the post-2014 ADF mission in Afghanistan continued, but not in Uruzghan Province. That story, like the one for Iraq, is beyond the scope of this book.

---

5 See Australian War Memorial, 'Afghanistan, 2001 to present', www.awm.gov.au/articles/event/afghanistan (retrieved 30 March 2020).

Existing literature

Despite the publication of a number of works in recent times on operations in Iraq and Afghanistan, which focus on US, UK and Canadian experiences, only a few works capture the Australian experience.[6] This is in part due to the nature of the ongoing conflict and a general reluctance to analyse what is not yet complete; it is also due to the comparatively small role played by Australians compared to the larger coalition partners.

Chris Masters, a leading voice on Australian Middle East operations, has written such works as *No Front Line: Australian Special Forces at War in Afghanistan*, which highlights special forces operations in Afghanistan, featuring experiences and testimonies gained during his 10-year investigation.[7] Masters' work also raised difficult questions that pointed to the controversial clouds hanging over operations undertaken by the Special Forces in Afghanistan—controversies that would be considered in searing detail in the Brereton Report of 2020.[8] Karen Middleton's *An Unwinnable War* provides insight into the political motivations for involvement in the Middle East and the critical decisions that led to Australian deployment and continued presence in Iraq and Afghanistan.[9]

---

[6] There are too many to list, but some examples from the United States, the United Kingdom and Canada are highlighted here. On the United States, see J.T. Hoffman (ed.), *Tip of the Spear: US Army Small-Unit Actions in Iraq, 2004–2007*, Center of Military History, Washington, DC, 2010; S.A. Carney, *Allied Participation in Operation Iraqi Freedom*, Center of Military History, Washington, DC, 2011; N.J. Schlosser, *The Surge, 2007–2008: US Army Campaigns in Iraq*, Center of Military History, Washington, DC, 2017; B. Neumann, L. Mundey and J. Mikolashek, *Operations Enduring Freedom, March 2002–April 2005*, Center of Military History, Washington, DC, 2013; G.C. Schroen, *First In: An Insiders Account of How the CIA Spearheaded the War on Terror in Afghanistan*, Presidio Press, New York, 2005; D.P. Bolger, *Why We Lost: A General's Inside Account of the Iraq and Afghanistan Wars*, Houghton Mifflin Harcourt, New York, 2014; and T.E. Ricks, *Fiasco: The American Military Adventure in Iraq*, Penguin, New York, 2006. On the United Kingdom, see T. Farrell, *Unwinnable: Britain's War in Afghanistan, 2001–2014*, Vintage, London, 2018; C.L. Elliott, *High Command: British Military leadership in the Iraq and Afghanistan Wars*, Hurst, London, 2015; and F. Ledwidge, *Losing Small Wars: British Military Failure in the 9/11 Wars*, Yale University Press, New Haven, 2017. On Canada, see J.G. Steyn and E. Lang, *The Unexpected War: Canada in Kandahar*, Penguin, Toronto, 2008; B. Horn and E. Spencer, *Canadian Forces in Afghanistan*, Dundurn Press, Toronto, 2016; B. Horn, *No Lack of Courage: Operation Medusa, Afghanistan*, Dundurn Press, Toronto, 2010; S. Maloney, *Enduring the Freedom: A Rogue Historian in Afghanistan*, Potomac Books, Washington, DC, 2005.
[7] C. Masters, *No Front Line: Australia's Special Forces at War in Afghanistan*, Allen & Unwin, Sydney, 2017.
[8] Inspector-General of the Australian Defence Force, *Afghanistan Inquiry Report* ('the Brereton Report'), afghanistaninquiry.defence.gov.au/sites/default/files/2020-11/IGADF-Afghanistan-Inquiry-Public-Release-Version.pdf (retrieved 24 November 2020).
[9] K. Middleton, *An Unwinnable War: Australia in Afghanistan*, Melbourne University Press, Melbourne, 2011.

Al Palazzo's manuscript on the Iraq War and his more recent edited work with Tom Frame, *On Ops: Lessons and Challenges for the Australian Army Since East Timor*, consider a range of practical tactical and operational factors, including command and control arrangements and logistics difficulties, encountered during Australian Middle Eastern deployments.[10] At the 'War in the Sandpit' conference, Garth Pratten delivered an excellent account of the Australian contribution to the coalition campaign (unfortunately not included here) in which he contextualised Australian operations in southern Afghanistan.[11] In addition, my own work, *The Australian Army from Whitlam to Howard*, published in 2014, critically examines the development of the Australian Army since the Vietnam War and the influence of these developments on operations in the Middle East.

In addition to these secondary works, a range of autobiographical accounts have provided on-the-ground insight into Australia's role in Iraq and Afghanistan, notably accounts from Majors General Jim Molan and John Cantwell,[12] as well as Colonel Marcus Fielding.[13] They all describe their experiences in frank detail, greatly adding to our understanding of the wars. In 2013, Victoria Cross recipient Corporal Mark Donaldson published his own autobiographical account entitled *The Crossroad*, in which he recalled the events that led to his receipt of the highest bravery honour.[14] Publishing via the Land Warfare Studies Centre in 2011, Colonel Peter Connolly painted a critical picture of his combat experience in Uruzgan and his concern over the lack of strategy from Canberra.[15] Biographical accounts are not just written by our soldiers, with photographer Gary Ramage and defence writer Ian McPhedran's *Afghanistan: Australia's War* providing a photographic depiction of Australia's efforts in the Middle East.[16] McPhedran's commentary on Ramage's images is evocative and thought-provoking, providing details of an often unseen visual dimension to the wars.

---

10 A. Palazzo, *The Australian Army and the War in Iraq: 2002–2010*, Directorate of Army Research and Analysis, Canberra, 2011; T. Frame and A. Palazzo (eds), *On Ops: Lessons and Challenges for the Australian Army Since East Timor*, UNSW Press, Sydney, 2016.
11 G. Pratten, speech, 'War in the Sandpit' conference, cove.army.gov.au/article/war-the-sand-pit-conference-doctor-garth-pratten (retrieved 30 March 2020).
12 J. Molan, *Running the War in Iraq*, HarperCollins, Sydney, 2008; J. Cantwell with G. Bearup, *Exit Wounds: One Australian's War on Terror*, Melbourne University Press, Melbourne, 2012.
13 M. Fielding, *Red Zone Baghdad: My War in Iraq*, Echo Books, Canberra, 2016.
14 M. Donaldson, *The Crossroad*, Macmillan Australia, Sydney, 2013.
15 P. Connolly, *Counterinsurgency in Uruzgan, 2009*, Land Warfare Studies Centre, Canberra, 2011.
16 G. Ramage and I. McPhedran, *Afghanistan: Australia's War*, HarperCollins, Sydney, 2014.

The Official History of Australian Operations in the Middle East and East Timor is due to be published in 2022. In the interim, works such as this provide a new and expansive account of Australia's experience in deploying forces and conducting operations in Afghanistan or Iraq.

Outline and contributors

This collection of papers covers a range of experiences of Australia's involvement in Iraq and Afghanistan, from maritime operations in the Gulf in the 1990s to the withdrawal of combat troops from Afghanistan in 2013. The authors come from a variety of backgrounds, and each contributes their unique perspectives and voices to further the efforts to achieve a more complete view of Australia's operations in the 'niche wars' described here. The book is divided into four parts: policy and strategy; Afghanistan and Iraq; joint forces, enablers and partners; and lessons and legacies.

These chapters were all chosen for a specific purpose. Most of the authors were presenters at the 'War in the Sandpit' conference in May 2017, lending their expertise to debate and discussion there as they have to articulating their thoughts for this volume. Most importantly, they illuminate a human perspective on these operations not often otherwise considered.

The first chapter in Part 1 is the keynote and opening chapter by Professor Robert Hill, Minister for Defence from 2001 to 2006, who relates his impressions of the political lessons from Australia's military involvement in Iraq and Afghanistan. Hill summarises his involvement in key moments of the campaigns, including the decision to withdraw special forces, and debates on how many troops to commit. He concludes with poignant lessons for future campaigns for politicians, emphasising that committing the ADF is not always the most appropriate solution for a problem.

The chapter by former Secretary of the Department of Defence Ric Smith on perspectives and lessons on Iraq and Afghanistan highlights the conflict between strategic objectives and circumstances on the ground, and the ways in which successive governments have sought to maintain the overarching strategic objective of Australia's alliance with the United States despite changing circumstances in the conflicts. Writing also of his personal experience as Special Envoy for Afghanistan and Pakistan, he provides immense insight into top-level decision-making from 2001 to the withdrawal of combat forces in 2013.

Admiral Chris Barrie, Chief of the Defence Force (CDF) from 1998 to 2002, writes of his perspective on Australian military strategy following the 9/11 attacks. He relates his recollections of initial challenges relating to interoperability, and the general sentiment felt towards operations by politicians and members of the ADF. He concludes with a reflection that he believes the Australian experience of the wars in Afghanistan and Iraq have fundamentally changed the Australian approach to war.

Part 2 opens with a reflection on the early days, and, as with any reflective analysis, it is important to distil experiences from specific operational units. Brigadier Dan McDaniel, former Commanding Officer of the Special Air Service Regiment, articulates the political imperatives and pressures that led to the initial deployment of special forces troops to Afghanistan in 2001. He explains that the commitment of special forces troops was not just made in an effort to maintain the US alliance but as part of a broader effort to demonstrate the Australian commitment to the global rules-based order, and as a way to demonstrate autonomous ADF military power under worldwide scrutiny. McDaniel outlines some key lessons from the deployment. He notes what he sees as the miscalculation of the operational and practical strength of the ADF relationship with its counterpart US forces, and the need for certainty in command and control arrangements.

Air Commodore Chris Westwood, writing about his experience in the RAAF Control and Reporting Centre (CRC) from 2007 to 2009 in Afghanistan, provides a unique RAAF perspective on the conflict. He identifies key lessons from the deployment, dividing them into the broad themes of strategic, operational and tactical lessons. Westwood concludes that a successful and niche deployment should not be left unscrutinised, and that the experiences of the CRC can be extrapolated to future deployments of cyber and electronic warfare elements, among others.

In discussing his experience in Iraq, Major General Anthony Rawlins, former task group commander, reflects on Operation CATALYST and his personal experience with what he saw as strategic-tactical dissonance. He writes of the polarised perception of the effectiveness of stability operations as practised by the Australians in Iraq. He claims that the Australians played a marginal role in southern Iraq from 2005 onwards, having only a limited—even at times negative—impact in Al Muthanna and Dhi Qar Provinces. He concludes that the command and control arrangements in Iraq were not the optimal way to proceed and set a disconcerting precedent for possible involvement in future conflicts. As a result, he urges a reappraisal of the form and substance of national command and control architecture to be applied in such circumstances.

Vice Admiral Peter Jones has played several and prominent roles leading Australia's naval endeavours in the Middle East over a prolonged period, including as commander of Australian naval forces and the coalition's Maritime Interception Operations Screen Commander in the lead-up to and during the invasion of Iraq in 2003. He relates the maritime perspective of Australia's involvement in the Middle East, broadening his focus to include the ways in which the RAN combatted piracy and smugglers as part of the Maritime Interception Force (MIF). He outlines in great depth the nature and composition of naval missions from 1990 to 2003, highlighting some necessary adaptations that were made, and issues of interoperability and coalition command structures. He concludes that operations in the Gulf were largely a success in the Iraq War owing to the MIF's existing knowledge of Gulf waters and to efforts to liaise effectively with ground forces.

One of Australia's most famous integrated exchange officers, or 'embeds', Major General Jim Molan, provides a blunt but honest account of his experience as an embed in Iraq and the lessons Australian command and politicians can learn from his time. He emphasises the need for the ADF to understand the type of war they are fighting and what they are willing to sacrifice in the name of the US alliance in future conflicts, as this was a key point of contention in Iraq. He concludes with 11 generalised lessons from his time as an embed, which, he posits, can be applied in future conflicts.

Part 3, covering joint forces, enablers and partners, starts with a chapter on command and control. Major General Michael Crane has compiled his assessment of Australian command and control arrangements in the Middle East, leveraging his extensive experience as Commander of JTF 633 on two occasions, and at HQJOC and CENTCOM between 2006 and 2012. He reflects on such issues as the establishment of discrete national commanders, and his interpretation of the successes and limitations of these divergences in command structures from the arrangements employed by Australia's coalition partners. He concludes by pointing to the wide array of issues that Australia has yet to resolve in establishing an approach to command and control of operations. He notes the difficulty of objective analysis of Australia's involvement in the Middle East, given that individual perspectives are driven by the context of the observer's unique experience.

Colonel Mick Lehmann's chapter on the role of army intelligence in Afghanistan is understandably constrained by operational secrecy provisions; however, he manages nonetheless to provide a remarkable insight into the practical workings of intelligence in this campaign. He touches on the importance of actionable intelligence and the essential nature of the 'Five Eyes' relationship in Afghanistan.[17] He also outlines some of the reasons for significant failings experienced by Australian intelligence operations. Ultimately Lehmann concludes that, despite solid tactical and operational successes, the overall impact of intelligence on the strategic outcome remains uncertain and hard to measure effectively.

Dr Alan Ryan, Director of the Australian Civil-Military Centre, has compiled a chapter that provides a unique and important assessment of civil–military relations in Iraq and Afghanistan. He relates the experiences of several civilian actors in these conflicts and the challenges faced in attempting to deliver humanitarian assistance. He concludes with seven recommendations that, despite being ambitious, outline a clear path towards greater coordination and effectiveness of civilian efforts in conflict.

The role of the media in Australia's Middle East operations is of particular importance to debate. Karen Middleton, a political journalist, prominent war correspondent and author of *An Unwinnable War*, writes about her experiences as an embedded journalist on three separate occasions and how the ADF and Australian Government interaction with the media was starkly different from that of the United States. Karen emphasises the necessity of accurate and influential reporting from conflict zones and the responsibility of both journalists and the ADF not to obfuscate on operations.

---

17 'Five Eyes' refers to the intelligence-sharing arrangements between the five English-speaking nations: the United States, United Kingdom, Canada, Australia and New Zealand, which is abbreviated to reflect the caveat used on shared classified documents thus: 'AUS/CAN/UK/US/NZ Eyes Only'.

Superintendents Col Speedie and Steve Mullins offer a comprehensive account of the Australian Federal Police (AFP) deployment to Afghanistan and the various opportunities and challenges that accompanied it. In particular, they note the ways in which police, who are not trained for warlike operational environments as their ADF counterparts are, managed to adapt to the environment effectively. Accordingly, they were able to negotiate bilateral intelligence-sharing agreements, create training doctrine and become an integral part of a coalition policing effort in Afghanistan.

David Savage reflects on the AusAID experience in Afghanistan and the problems that arose from attempting to deliver effective aid and reconstruction in a highly dynamic conflict zone. He relates the difficulties present in creating ongoing relationships with stakeholders and communities, building trust and delivering aid to the areas that need it most. Ultimately, David concludes that, for all their hard work, the lack of continuity in Afghan leadership and absence of central government support for reconstruction and aid-driven projects meant that AusAID's efforts had little or no overall long-term positive impact.

Australian Army Major Elizabeth Boulton provides a comprehensive account of gender issues and debates that have arisen from the war in Afghanistan and Iraq. She highlights a positive story that these wars saw the first mass employment of women in warlike operations, in combat-related roles, in Australian history. However, Boulton also highlights that there was a strategic 'gender' blind spot, with the significance of women's contribution of operational outcomes belatedly appreciated. Ultimately, Boulton argues, deployments can be greatly enhanced by a thorough understanding of the composition of the troops and of the human terrain, both of which have gendered dimensions. She makes clear that this should be focused on more intently in strategic planning.

Part 4 of the book covers lessons and legacies from the niche wars. William Maley, an ANU professor and respected scholar of the war in Afghanistan, approaches the question of the legacy of the war in Afghanistan from the perspective not only of lessons for the ADF but also the legacy for Afghanistan. He examines the psychological and societal impacts of the coalition forces' intervention in Afghanistan on the Afghan people, and notes that the entirety of the legacy of the Afghan war cannot yet be realised. He divides lessons for military deployments into seven points, covering the necessity for deployments to be linked to political strategy, the difficulties of unintentionally fostering violence when attempting to create stability, and the impact of the miscalculation of the nature of insurgency in Afghanistan.

In the next chapter on the US and British experience in Iraq and Afghanistan, Professor Dan Marston articulates the importance of identifying military operational lessons and then analysing and debating these lessons. He criticises contemporary military leaders for rushing to declare 'lessons learned' when they have not rigorously analysed these issues in a way that is necessary if we are to avoid repeated failures in future conflicts. Marston identifies five themes that are common among the US and British experiences, and offers a starting point for further debates on these themes.

Lieutenant General (Retired) Peter Leahy was Australia's Chief of Army from 2002 to 2008, when he became Professor of National Security Studies at the University of Canberra. Leahy divides his assessment of the lessons and legacies for the Australian Army from Iraq and Afghanistan into nine strategic and operational lessons and three broad legacies. He extracts key similarities in lessons for Australia from the UK Iraq Inquiry released in 2016, and the pitfalls of maintaining an army unprepared for 21st-century conflicts. He concludes that the absence of a cohesive and enduring strategic objective was the main contributor to failings in the Middle East and that such an objective is a necessary criterion to fulfil for future conflicts. Finally, he recommends a thorough re-evaluation of the procedures that lead to Australia committing troops to overseas conflicts, and a stronger effort to care for returned troops in Australia.

As the Official Historian of Australian Operations in Iraq, Afghanistan and East Timor, Craig Stockings concludes Part 4 by imparting his initial impressions of the Official History project. He outlines the unorthodox process that led to his remit and how he has planned to approach the task of documenting Australia's involvement in these conflicts in six volumes.

We now turn to Part 1 and the opening chapter by the Honourable Senator Robert Hill.

PART 1: POLICY AND STRATEGY

1

A minister's perspective

Robert Hill

My experiences of Australia's wars in Afghanistan and Iraq are from a political perspective. My thoughts and recollections are not scholarly, and they might or might not be shared by others who were also part of the government at that time, but nonetheless allow me to relate some lessons learned.

These wars have been huge endeavours for Australia. They have touched so many Australians in different ways. And even though they continue today, it is worthwhile to pause and reflect on the experiences and lessons learned. Even to try to understand why we are still engaged, after the longest period of continuous deployment in our history, is important.

It was a privilege to be Australia's Defence Minister, and I will forever be grateful to the men and women of the services who carried out the missions set by government with professionalism and determination. I equally appreciated the service of officials of the department who were critical enablers in all missions. I was lucky to have military and departmental leadership of the highest calibre. We shared some difficult moments, and they excelled themselves.

The operations in Afghanistan and Iraq were a result of, and continue to be a result of, political decisions. I was one of the politicians making decisions at critical times, and appreciate that it is just as important for politicians to learn from past experiences as it is for the military.

I came to Defence from the Environment portfolio. I was given the Environment ministry because it had always been a conflict zone for my side of politics. I won a few of the environment battles and settled a few more by peaceful means. Nevertheless, it might still seem for military people to have been an unusual path to Defence.

There is no minimum qualification to be Defence Minister, or even to be a politician. There is no one course of study. You have to go back a long way to find a Defence Minister with military service. Occasionally there is someone in the Cabinet with military experience, but again, it is rare. It is even unusual to find someone with a background in strategic policy. It is therefore not surprising that the defence leadership sometimes finds the political world a bit bewildering, or at least untidy.

So how does a group of apparently unqualified individuals make a decision to take the country to war? Or, more particularly in the context of this conference, to deploy Australian forces to Afghanistan in 2001 and Iraq in 2003? The latter decision is still the subject of critical debate in some circles. It is easy to say that politicians make a determination of what is in the national interest. But how do they determine what is in the national interest?

Each politician is influenced by individual values and experiences. In my case, I was trained in the law. I believed in a rules-based order, both domestically and internationally. In the early 1990s I was working to build democracies in the post–Cold War era because I believed in the basic freedoms that underpin democracy. Before that I focused on getting political prisoners out of jails in Cuba and elsewhere. I believed in universal human rights. I am also a globalist. I believe in the interdependency of nation-states. I also believe in alliances based on shared values. And I have always feared the indiscriminate and destructive power of weapons of mass destruction (WMD).[1] I started working towards non-proliferation of WMD more than 40 years ago. From that background I assessed my attitude to our military participation in the wars in question.

---

1   That is, nuclear, radiological, chemical or biological weapons that can cause mass killings or great damage.

In relation to Afghanistan, the cruelty and barbarism and the inter-territorial nature of the 9/11 attacks on the United States had an enormous effect on me. Even today, I cannot stand on the World Trade Center site in New York without shaking my head in disbelief. How could this happen? What is the world coming to?

The attacks on the United Sates led our Prime Minister, John Howard, immediately to invoke the ANZUS Treaty, although in technical terms that was a decision for Cabinet, which we made a few days later on his return from the United States. We all saw this as not only an attack on our ally the United States but also, and fundamentally, an attack on our shared values.

I remember the meeting by telephone of the leadership group within Cabinet, held the morning after 9/11 when we took advice from our intelligence agencies and took decisions to ensure Australia's immediate security. We saw the attack on the United States as equally directed at us, and sadly we were proven right sometime later, when those who shared the al-Qaeda ideology deliberately targeted Australians in Bali and Jakarta in 2002 and 2005, in neighbouring Indonesia, as well as in Afghanistan.

ANZUS might be primarily a commitment to consult, but in the circumstances I have just sketched it is not surprising that a short time later we took the decision to commit forces to Afghanistan and against the Taliban regime. In Afghanistan, al-Qaeda was permitted bases and given support. To remove the threat also required the defeat of the Taliban. The Afghanistan response had United Nations Security Council support and was not particularly controversial. Removing the Taliban did run the risk of creating a vacuum in governance, but this was a responsibility the United Nations was willing to assume.

It is interesting to reflect on the fact that if the Taliban had not provided comfort and support to al-Qaeda, it might have been permitted by the international community to continue to abuse its own Afghan people for some time. In Australia this was regarded as an internal affair, even if we did not approve of it.

Afghanistan

Australian troops were deployed after I became Defence Minister but pursuant to a decision made before my appointment. I remember visiting Kabul after the deployment and meeting the UN Secretary General's Special Representative, Lakhdar Brahimi. It was in part to brief him on the Australian mission objectives and in part to explore how Australia might assist the post-war reconstruction and transition in governance. It was all reasonably orthodox in an environment where the operations seemed to be going well.

I guess the first mildly controversial decision I was involved in was the government's decision to withdraw special forces from Afghanistan. It was said by some that this was in preparation for pending operations in Iraq. In truth, both the government and I were concerned with avoiding mission creep. The advice of the Defence leadership was that the task for which our special forces were sent had been achieved.

The next big government decision in relation to Afghanistan was to return to the theatre with both special forces and a Provincial Reconstruction Team (PRT). I had been a strong advocate of the need for the international community to support the development of sustainable institutions and basic necessities such as health, education and infrastructure. It is not only a good thing to do in development terms but also guards against the return of another extremist regime. However, the overlap between the role of the military in providing security and civilians in providing humanitarian and development aid is complicated, even in seemingly straightforward circumstances. In this scenario, it was made more difficult by the fact that Afghanistan was never really post-conflict. Nevertheless, to me, development was essential if Afghanistan was to ever stand a chance of normalcy.

I took to the National Security Committee of Cabinet a bid for a PRT and came out with not only a PRT but also a government decision to return the special forces to Afghanistan. This was an acknowledgement of the need to transition to development and a recognition that the security situation was not as far advanced as we had earlier believed.

The role of the military in nation-building is not straightforward. With its 'can do' attitude, the military sometimes overestimates what it is able to achieve. It is for the politicians to set the mission parameters, and they should be realistic in assessing what is for the military and what requires other elements. The challenge is to get the right mix. I do not think the international community invested enough in nation-building in Afghanistan. But if they had, it still might not have worked. Unfortunately, Afghanistan will be a work in progress for a long time.

Iraq

Despite what some might say, the intervention in Iraq did not commence as an operation against terrorism. Certainly, for our part, it was not an operation to secure oil, but was a response to the perceived threat posed by Saddam Hussein's WMD program.

Saddam Hussein had had WMDs, and even used them against his own people, at little international cost. What had changed was the risk threshold the United States was prepared to accept. As with Afghanistan, this related to 9/11. President Clinton knew al-Qaeda in Afghanistan posed a threat, but his limited response had not removed that threat. No subsequent president could take the same risk after 9/11.

President Bush saw Saddam Hussein in the same light. He was a threat. He had previously invaded his neighbours and drawn the United States, Australia and others into that conflict. The inability of the UN processes to satisfy the US administration that Saddam had both forgone his mass destruction weaponry and complied with UN Security Council resolutions that he disarms and verify left a risk too great to accept.

History showed that conflict in the region flowing from Saddam Hussein's unquenched expansionist goals would in all likelihood again draw us in. But this time it might subject Australian forces to chemical and biological weapons. This was a risk we felt was too great for us to bear. The national interest was therefore to support our ally in the heavy lifting and to protect against what might become a direct threat to Australians and their interests.

At the time of the Iraq invasion, did Saddam Hussein still possess weapons of mass destruction? I had watched the UN processes intently. There was always an ambiguity in Saddam Hussein's response. He always seemed to be hedging. There were a lot of wise heads after the event, but my intelligence briefings at the time were that he did maintain those capabilities, biological and chemical, but not nuclear. In fact, I was briefed on what was believed to be his command and control regime, including who would give the command for the use of those weapons. I will never forget the briefings. Defence insisted that I be inoculated against anthrax before travelling to Iraq.

Nevertheless, I wanted to hear different perspectives. I travelled to the United States and listened to their intelligence services. Their brief was similar, although in some aspects they were even more confident. I followed this with further briefings in the United Kingdom. Again I was presented with similar views, and their assessment was shared by intelligence services in France, Israel and Russia. So this was hardly an invention of politicians.

It is easy to be wise after the event, but decision-makers do not have the benefit of hindsight. It would seem that intelligence services around the world got it wrong. I accepted intelligence assessments that turned out to be wrong in their conclusions. That is no one's fault. Intelligence assessment is not a precise science. Rather, it is a judgement based on the best available information at the time.

I certainly accept that Australia's intelligence agencies were acting professionally and in good faith. But they were clearly influenced by Saddam Hussein's past record, as were we. The complication here was that Saddam Hussein ruled through fear, and WMD and his willingness to use those weapons helped to safeguard his survival. It would seem that he had complied with the Security Council resolutions, but to ensure his authority internally and in the region, he chose to maintain an ambiguity.

Saddam Hussein apparently believed that leaving an element of doubt on the question of whether he had disposed of his WMD would not lead to a military intervention by the United States. This was a bluff he lost, because he failed to appreciate how the risk appetite in the United States had changed after 9/11. The Taliban had made a similar mistake in Afghanistan.

I also want to address the allegation made by some that we had committed to war in Iraq before the Cabinet decision that immediately preceded the public announcement. There is a distinction between preparing for the decisions Cabinet might make and the making of such a decision. No decision was made until it was made by Cabinet.

I had been party to decisions over some time to support the ADF being prepared in the event that Cabinet made a decision to commit Australian forces to combat. It always struck me as a sensible thing to do, and I said so on a number of occasions. Even without my endorsement, I would expect the ADF to be planning for various scenarios. It is what good militaries do. But some preparations, such as entering the US planning process, did require my political imprimatur.

I concede that this is a difficult area. If it came to pass that we chose to be part of a US-led military operation, the more we understood about the objectives and plans the better off we would be, not only in maximising the effectiveness of our contribution but also in minimising casualties. The worry is that by undertaking such preparations, our ally assumes a commitment that had not been made. It is even trickier if we are in fact contributing to the development of the plans. Therefore, the decision to enter preparations at this level had to have political endorsement.

The legal basis for the war was another area in which we were criticised by some. An Australian Government will not commit to military operations without being satisfied that the decision is sound in law. We believe in a rules-based international order. In this instance, the legal premise was Iraq's failure to comply with the UN Security Council resolutions designed to remove the threat associated with Saddam Hussein's WMD through a direction to disarm and verify. We decided that the UN processes designed to lead to a peaceful solution had been exhausted and that we should join a so-called coalition of the willing. This was a political judgement for which we must accept responsibility.

On a personal basis, I would argue that a contemporary interpretation of the doctrine of self-defence might also have provided a legal justification. It seemed to me that the construct of self-defence in relation to WMD is very different from a construct of what amounts to self-defence in relation to traditional threats.

One political lesson learned from this conflict was the need for a well-developed plan to address the 'day after' issues. What was to happen the day after the removal of Saddam Hussein and his regime? There was not going to be a UN Security Council administration. This was a coalition of the willing, and the partners had to have a plan for governance as well as security. It was on my mind, because it might be said that the ADF was part of an occupying force and therefore had legal responsibilities. In the end, we sidestepped this responsibility, arguing that we were not an occupying party.

In this instance the plan was not as well developed as it should have been. I do not think the development of the plan should have been left to the United States. To accept responsibilities in a coalition of the willing should also include accepting a share of responsibility in what was to follow. To be fair, I do not think we were even consulted on what turned out to be two of the most unwise decisions following the conflict: to disband the Iraq army and the Ba'ath Party. On the other hand, I think we preferred to pass these responsibilities to others. Before the war, when talking about building democracies, I used to stress the importance of growing institutions. New institutions cannot simply be imposed if the goal is a democratic and stable state.

Another area that turned out to be quite challenging and in which there was overlap between the ADF and political decision-makers related to the rules of engagement. We of course made the decision that we would be part of a US-led force, but with Australian forces under Australian command and operating to Australian rules of engagement. The rules under which we operated would be different from some others who were not parties to the same humanitarian conventions.

By and large, from my perspective, the United States was respectful and accommodated the differences, particularly in the early years. Problems tended to develop more in the frustrations of the occupying power, as the war became an insurgency operation, particularly in relation to Australians embedded in US force structures. The Australian chain of command became more of a formality than a practice. Australia's responsibilities in relation to prisoners was contentious and would have benefited from more forethought.

Lessons

There are a few lessons that I think should be learned by the political class. Both conflicts have demonstrated the effectiveness and limitations of military force. Routing al-Qaeda and removing the Taliban from government on the one hand, and defeating the orthodox military of Saddam Hussein and removing him from office on the other, were relatively straightforward and successful operations. Western military forces are good at such work.

Combatting the insurgencies that subsequently evolved, in part in response to the ongoing presence of foreign forces and the application of asymmetric warfare,[2] proved much more difficult and should have received more thought. This reconstruction of the battlespace should have been anticipated. We were naïve to believe the Iraqi people would simply rise up and fill a vacuum, particularly after we disbanded their institutions.

Continuing military operations have been largely couched as counter-terrorism when the real challenge has been nation-building, for which militaries are not well suited. Sometimes politicians over-rely on defence forces to solve problems for which force is not the best solution. A military presence might be necessary because of an ongoing security threat, but it must be a supportive element.

Both conflicts illustrated how little we in the West knew or understood about both societies, including the tribal divides in Afghanistan and the sectarian divides in Iraq. We do not fight wars in a vacuum, and politicians need to better appreciate the social and cultural environments to which we send our forces

---

2   Asymmetric warfare concerns warfare between forces with greatly differing power whereby one side seeks to gain advantage through the use of unconventional weapons and tactics.

2

A departmental Secretary's perspective

Ric Smith

I should begin with two caveats. First, when I left Defence after four and a bit years as Secretary, I did not take with me a diary or any papers of consequence, and nor did I keep any from my time as Special Envoy for Afghanistan and Pakistan. So what follows is a hybrid of personal memory, with all its faults, and from reading some of the writings, a few conversations with others who were engaged and, in the case of Afghanistan, at least some work I did for Defence—and ultimately for the National Security Committee of Cabinet—on the lessons to be learned from our 'whole-of-government' mission in Afghanistan.

Second, and more important, while I appreciate the reasons we are addressing the Iraq and Afghan conflicts together, we should not forget how different they were. The justifications for each, the international structures around them, the nature of their endorsement by the United Nations and their standing in international law, the way they were fought, the issues we were dealing with on the ground, and domestic or popular perceptions are unique. In short, one was a conflict fought in the context of what was then being described as the 'Global War on Terror', and the other was a war against a state; that is, the state of Iraq. And one—Iraq—was arguably more a war of choice than the other.

There is a risk in works of this kind that we will find ourselves over-analysing, and thereby complicating unduly, our accounts of significant events. In fact, government decision-making in most fields is usually best understood in its simplest forms. For good or ill, what you see from government in these areas these days is mostly what you get, and that was so in the case of the original decisions about Afghanistan and Iraq.

Afghanistan I

Taking these in sequence, the first was of course the decision announced on 17 October 2001 to deploy a force to Afghanistan. For me, two points stand out about that decision and the way it was announced. The first is that it was placed squarely in the context of what the government saw as Australia's commitment to the United States under the ANZUS Treaty, which of course had been invoked in the wake of 9/11. The decision was straightforward, and enjoyed wide public support.

The second point is this: in announcing the decision, the Prime Minister emphasised its limited nature, and referred to Afghanistan only once in a one-and-a-half-page statement—to say that the F/A-18 Hornet fighter aircraft being deployed would not operate in Afghanistan.[1] In other words, the US alliance apart, the mission was primarily about terrorism, not Afghanistan.

In subsequent media comments, the Prime Minister and ministers emphasised that our commitment would remain limited in scope and time. For instance, Foreign Minister Downer said:

> We don't want to get ... bogged down in Afghanistan. We don't want Australian troops to be part of managing and running Afghanistan for the next five or six years ... We don't really have a great desire to get into the long-term management of Afghanistan.[2]

In part, statements of this kind reflected an abiding, in-principle reluctance to be drawn into long-term or open-ended roles in this distant theatre and, in this sense, foreshadowed the initial positions we were to take a year later about post-conflict roles in Iraq. The government's preferred approach in both cases was captured in John Howard's later

---

1   Prime Minister the Hon. J. Howard MP, 'Australian troops to be deployed to Afghanistan', statement, 17 October 2001.
2   P. Bongiorno, interview with Foreign Minister the Hon. A. Downer MP, 'Meet the Press', Network 10, 18 November 2001.

statement that 'the right combination was to provide sharp-edged forces for a limited period of time during the hot part but not get bogged down in long drawn-out peace-keeping operations'.[3]

But in my view, Downer's remarks were also early signs of an underlying and persistent wariness about the Afghanistan project, reflecting a keen sense of the risks that Afghanistan posed. I will return to this point, but suffice for now to note that, in this event, these concerns not to be dragged into Afghanistan beyond the initial assault on terrorist positions were overridden as the conflict unfolded, as they were in Iraq.

After a year in Afghanistan as part of Operation ENDURING FREEDOM, the government was satisfied with what we had done and, consistent with its preferred approach, withdrew the deployment. In announcing this on 20 November 2002, Defence Minister Hill noted that 'the focus of the operations has moved towards supporting the reconstruction of Afghanistan';[4] *ipso facto*, we were no longer involved. And so from April 2003 to August 2005, we had only two ADF officers in country: one in a liaison position with United Nations Assistance Mission in Afghanistan, the other in the Mine Action Coordination Centre.

Iraq

By the time we withdrew from this first mission from Afghanistan, planning for a possible deployment to Iraq was well in hand. I did not take up duty as Secretary until 18 November 2002, but when I did, the first two orders of business were a briefing on the status of our contingency planning for Iraq and the announcement (two days later) of our withdrawal from Afghanistan.

The government had not by then made a decision to go to war in Iraq. It can be argued that this was only a technical matter and that the decision had effectively been made. But in fact many in government still hoped that Saddam Hussein would submit on the issue of WMD and that war would

---

3   Quoted in Middleton, *An Unwinnable War*, p. 38.
4   Senator the Hon. R. Hill, Minister for Defence, 'Australian special forces to return from Afghanistan', media release, MIN 664/02, 20 November 2002.

be avoided at the last moment. There was still a view, shared with the UK Government, and indeed with US Secretary of State Colin Powell, that we should have tried to put another UN Security Council resolution in place.

In the event that that was not achieved, the ADF leadership was concerned with being well positioned so that if the government made a decision to commit to conflict, we would not be caught with our forces unprepared or in a long transit. The government accepted this view.

In a frantic period, two things stood out for me. The first was the great care that the CDF and the service chiefs were giving to the selection of the capabilities we would offer and to the personnel who would lead in the field. The capabilities would be niche, but they had to be in areas where their presence would matter and be noticed. The second was the intense effort, led by Defence but with the close involvement of the Department of Foreign Affairs and Trade (DFAT), to ensure access to basing and support facilities in the Gulf—a very successful effort, of course.

As to why we became involved in the war, what you saw was what you got. In a taxonomy that I heard for the first time only recently from a very senior figure in the government at the time, there was a justification for the war and a reason for our involvement in it. The justification was Iraq's possession of WMD and the risks following from that, including the risk of terrorist groups gaining access to them, and Iraq's refusal to comply with UN Security Council resolutions in respect of the WMDs. And the reason for our commitment was the policy imperative that the government saw to support our US ally.

The justification of course was to prove flawed, and the process around it exposed serious failings both in the US-led intelligence community and at the higher policy level in Washington, which led for instance to Colin Powell's UN speech of 5 February 2003 in which he confidently stated that Hussein possessed WMDs. This was disillusioning for many of those involved, not least for Powell himself, and in the longer term embarrassing for others, in particular British Prime Minister Tony Blair and, arguably, to a lesser extent for our own government.

But for the Bush administration as a whole it might not have mattered so much at the time because other considerations were in play. As our ambassador in Washington, Michael Thawley, had told John Howard at the time, the 9/11 attack had ensured that 'Iraq would be back on the agenda for the Americans'.⁵ And in addition to retribution, US policy came to embrace regime change and democratisation as well as the WMD issue.

In my view, this was not the case for Australia. As I recall, neither formally nor in any informal discussions did the Howard Government's deliberations embrace regime change as an objective in itself, evil as Saddam was seen to be. 'Democratisation' for its own sake was certainly not on our agenda, and any references to terrorism related not to 9/11 but rather to the fear that WMDs might find their way from Iraq into the hands of terrorist organisations.

As Allan Gyngell puts it in his recently published, and excellent, history of Australian foreign policy, Howard's speeches were 'absent the moral universalism which informed Bush's language when he spoke to the American people'.⁶ In my recollection, this was true of discourse among ministers, which was typically functional and prosaic.

Nor incidentally did I see or hear any reference to oil as a reason for us to be in the Middle East—at least not until the then Defence Minister Brendan Nelson made a comment in 2006 suggesting an oil motive, on which he was quickly corrected. The fact is that, as students of the Middle East will know, the United States' obsession with the region goes back way beyond oil—and incidentally way before Israel. Anyway, oil supplies were not at risk under Saddam Hussein.

In short, there was no conspiracy in Australian policy. Some critics have difficulty accepting this, but the fact is that, right or wrong, for the Australian Government the WMD issue was the sole justification for the war, and at the time a sufficient one. Although the Defence Intelligence Organisation had noted some doubts about the claims made by Secretary Powell in his UN speech, it took time for the government to be convinced that there were no WMDs. As late as mid-April 2003, when the Defence Minister, CDF and I were preparing to go to Iraq, we were vaccinated against anthrax, as our troops had been, and we had professional teams in the field continuing the search long after hostilities concluded.

---

5   J. Howard, *Lazarus Rising: A Personal and Political Autobiography*, HarperCollins, Sydney, 2010, p. 425.
6   A. Gyngell, *Fear of Abandonment: Australia and the World Since 1942*, La Trobe University Press, Melbourne, 2017, p. 259.

Mistaken as that justification turned out to be, it does not follow that the reason for our involvement was invalid. We did provide support for our alliance partner. If there is argument on this matter, it relates more to what we actually did in Iraq. There is a view, fashionable among some in the ADF, that we did not do enough to win much kudos from the US armed forces, and indeed one very senior officer has claimed to me that our efforts actually attracted derision from his American counterparts. The credibility of our forces is always important, but it would surprise me if anyone was suggesting that the seriousness of our commitment should be measured in casualties.

Yes, our force for what was called Operation FALCONER was structured carefully for impact. It might well be that concerns were expressed in some quarters about the adequacy of our post-war roles. It would be wrong, however, to underestimate the value of what the SAS units did in western Iraq, especially in ensuring that no missiles could be launched at Israel, and the RAN's work in the Al-Faw Peninsula, in the initial stages of the war.

More importantly, the government's purpose was not to impress the American military commanders in the field—rather, it was to signal policy and political support for the Bush administration in a world in which it had few friends. And sustaining that support in the face of widespread international criticism at home and abroad added to the value of that support in Washington. In this regard, the Howard Government could argue that its objectives were met, whatever the view of American military commanders in the field, and I would expect that this remains John Howard's view.

Through all of this there is one other consistent policy factor that proved a mitigating factor against a larger Australian contribution to the coalition in Iraq. While the Australian Government was always conscious that these Middle East operations were important to Australia's policy interests, there were potential challenges closer to home that could at any time demand a response from the ADF and for which significant force elements needed to be kept available.

This was not mere rhetoric. During Australia's time in Afghanistan and Iraq, additional deployments had to be made to East Timor and to Solomon Islands. This was not a matter of 'defence of Australia'; rather, it was well-founded prudence and, as Howard used to say, the most important contribution Australia could make to the Alliance would be to do what was needed in Australia's own region.

It was not only in relation to the WMD intelligence issue that the US system was found wanting. The absence of a credible post-victory plan—a plan for 'phase 4', as the Americans called it—was hardly less a contribution to the huge problem that Iraq became, not least by leaving the way open to some poor—and poorly made—decisions about 'de-Ba'athification' and the disbandment of the Iraqi army.

While Australian planners did not foresee the intelligence failure, there were concerns from the outset about the absence of a serious plan for 'phase 4'. Australian officers persisted in expressing these concerns up to the commencement of the war. I recall an especially frustrating meeting in Washington in late January 2003, to which we sent Canberra-based officers and officials from DFAT, AusAID and Defence. The United Kingdom, which of course had a considerably greater stake in the conflict than we had, pushed even harder but with no more success, and the State Department shared these concerns. In short, in Washington, the Pentagon—and Secretary Donald Rumsfeld in particular—had run away with the game.

That said, it is worth recalling that while we were making known our concerns about the post-conflict situation, the Prime Minister and ministers were also making clear that Australia did not wish to be involved in any post-war occupation of Iraq beyond humanitarian aid, and possibly some military specialists. While our policy position in this regard might have been different had there been a well-developed post-war plan, in the absence of one it was thus consistent with the approach we had taken to Afghanistan—and proved no more enduring.

And so it was that we withdrew most of the force committed to Operation FALCONER from Iraq when the major hostilities ended in 2003. Unlike the United States, the United Kingdom and Poland, we did not commit forces to post-war reconstruction until early 2005. In 2005, the government announced the deployment to Al Muthanna Province in what was called an 'Overwatch' role, which came to include training Iraqi forces as well. My own recollection of this is that while the United States wanted us more engaged, it was in the end the British who leaned hardest, Al Muthanna being in the area of Iraq in which they were leading in the name of the Multi-National Division (South East) based in Basra.

Most of our remaining forces were withdrawn by June 2008 following the election of the Rudd Government in December 2007. By that time, I was no longer in government, but my sense was that while the Labor Party policy on withdrawal was unequivocal, Rudd tried to cushion the impact in Washington by taking some time over the decision, leaving at least some elements behind—and moving on to do more in Afghanistan.

Afghanistan II

In the meantime, a decision had been taken in mid-2005 to return to Afghanistan. This decision was taken not long after the government decided to take on the new role in Al Muthanna, but it was clearly a much bigger decision than the Al Muthanna decision, and it had very much greater implications.

There were two elements to the decision the Prime Minister announced on 13 July 2005. The first was about the deployment of a Special Forces Task Group to undertake a 'security task very similar to the task that was undertaken by an SAS taskforce that went in 2001'. The second was confirmation that the government was considering 'the possibility of sending a Provincial Reconstruction Team [PRT] to Afghanistan'.[7]

I think it is on the public record that the Defence Minister's initial proposal was for a contribution to a PRT. The decision that the Prime Minister announced was again more cautious, focusing on a renewed special forces deployment and only foreshadowing a possible PRT contribution.

There has been speculation about whether we had come under 'pressure' from Washington to recommit to Afghanistan. This is not my recollection, at least as far as the policy and political levels of government were concerned.

It is worth reflecting in this regard on another aspect of the Prime Minister's announcement of 13 July 2005. He said that Australia had:

---

7   Prime Minister the Hon. John Howard MP, 'Troop deployment to Afghanistan', press conference transcript, 13 July 2005.

received requests, at the military level, from both the United States and others and also the Government of Afghanistan and we have therefore decided in order to support the efforts of others to support in turn the Government of Afghanistan to despatch … some 150 personnel …⁸

The emphasis on the requests having been made at the 'military level' is consistent with my recollection about the absence of pressure at the political level. The reference to our 'supporting the efforts of others' reflects the importance attached to our being part of the coalition—by then a proxy term for the alliance—and at the same time suggests again a degree of wariness about the whole project.

We had of course been watching the changing picture in Afghanistan since 2002 closely, and were very much aware that the role of the coalition there—by 2005 called the International Security Assistance Force (ISAF)—had changed significantly and was taking on more 'pacification' or 'stabilisation' functions. Above all, the coalition had come under NATO leadership (formally at least) and grown very considerably to include roles for Canada and New Zealand, among many others.

There was therefore a sense among senior ministers that there was a legitimate and important international effort underway, backed unequivocally by UN Security Council resolutions, and that our non-involvement sat oddly with the interests we shared with most coalition members and with our traditional view of Australia's place in the world. As well at that time, there was, as a matter of policy, great interest at the political level and among the ADF leadership in getting closer to NATO.⁹ Indeed, the NATO Secretary General, Jaap de Hoop Scheffer, was welcomed in Canberra in the first part of 2005. As consideration of a PRT deployment continued through the latter half of 2005, Afghan's President, Hamid Karzai, weighed in during a media conference with Prime Minister Howard, on a visit to Kabul, to encourage the idea.

As the PRT proposal firmed up in the course of these deliberations, the international politics became intense while we sorted out with NATO and individual members just who it was we would partner with. In the end, the Dutch won the prize, an outcome encouraged by NATO and especially, as I recall, by the United Kingdom.

---

8   Ibid.
9   An interest incidentally that I did not fully share at that time, and still do not.

Thus, on 21 February 2006, the Prime Minister announced the deployment of an ADF Reconstruction Task Force incorporated in a Netherlands-led PRT in Uruzgan Province as part of ISAF's Stage III expansion. A visit to Canberra by the Dutch Prime Minister followed in March 2006. From this beginning our contribution grew incrementally over the following seven or so years to encompass various reconstruction, mentoring and force protection roles, then a PRT leadership role, and eventually leadership of the Combined Team – Uruzgan as well as 'embeds' and others in Kabul and Kandahar.

2005–08

From a national policy point of view, what is especially interesting is how a limited and cautious decision in 2005 for the ADF to 'help others help Afghanistan' followed by another to deploy an 'ADF Reconstruction Team' evolved into a genuine whole-of-government effort, and why. This evolution took place in two stages. The first was from 2005 to 2008. By committing in early 2006 to join a PRT, and to partner with the Dutch in Uruzgan, we implicitly accepted the case for a broader civil–military approach. We wanted to do, and be seen to be doing, more or less what the others were doing, and once there, of course, we wanted to do it well.

This meant engaging agencies beyond the ADF. Institutionally, AusAID, DFAT and the AFP were not reluctant to take on roles, and indeed they had plenty of volunteers once their roles were established. But the government was always cautious, and very conscious of the costs and the risks. While the ADF was funded by the usual 'no-win, no-loss' financing provisions, funding to support non-Defence deployments remained parsimonious ('out of hide') through to about 2008.

Nevertheless, the aid program that had delivered some $94 million to Afghanistan between 2001 and 2005 was stepped up. In the period 2005–08, some $236 million was disbursed through AusAID, most of it through multilateral agencies and the Afghan Reconstruction Trust Fund in largely hands-off ways. However, some aid went directly into Uruzgan, and the ADF delivered aid worth about $117 million on the ground in the province, in large part with the aim of ensuring community support for our military presence. As the focus moved more to direct aid, the first AusAID civilian was posted to Uruzgan in 2008. In the same period, to 2008, the ADF presence grew first to about 900, then to 1,100 through numerous evolutions of role and title: Reconstruction Task Force, then Mentoring Reconstruction Task Force and so on.

The AFP mission also grew, and from 2007 shifted to Regional Command South in Kandahar, where it played a useful role in counter-narcotics support for the Afghan National Police. Whereas before 2005 Australia's ambassador to Afghanistan had been accredited to Kabul from Islamabad, in 2006 the government opened a small embassy in Kabul, first in the Serena Hotel until it was attacked, then located temporarily in ADF House. It subsequently relocated to a donga in the US Embassy compound, where it clung on until 2009 in circumstances that have to be described frankly as demeaning.

2009–13

Thus government concerns were eased, the idea of a PRT was acculturated at ministerial level, and the mission grew, leading to the second stage and to what became a whole-of-government endeavour, which lasted until 2013.

The biggest steps in this journey were announced by Prime Minister Rudd on 29 April 2009 in a major statement on Afghanistan in which he linked military and civil endeavours more explicitly than hitherto.[10] The ADF role was further enhanced, and a significant increase in Australia's aid commitment announced, with much more to be spent on the ground. This was together with an increased mentoring role for the AFP in Tarin Kowt, although at cost to the work they had been doing in regard to counter-narcotics work in Kandahar.

DFAT staff were to be posted to Tarin Kowt, more AusAID staff added and the embassy upgraded and relocated into its own premises. With increased force protection requirements, the ADF presence reached—and was capped at, officially at least—1,550, making the Australian force the 10th largest in a coalition, which was growing towards 50 members.

---

10 Prime Minister the Hon. K. Rudd MP, press conference, Parliament House, Canberra, 29 April 2009.

Rudd also announced the appointment of a 'Special Envoy for Afghanistan and Pakistan', and that is where I came in. I was living in Washington, doing my own thing at the Woodrow Wilson Center, when the Prime Minister asked me to take on this 'special envoy' task. For the first two months I worked from there, visiting the State Department frequently, the Pentagon and other agencies as I could, and working especially with Richard Holbrooke, the US Special Representative.

Holbrooke's appointment was significant. He had expected to be Secretary of State in a Hillary Clinton administration. His new position was created, I believe, because the Obama administration accepted that the war could not be concluded by military means alone, and that the State Department and its counterparts in coalition countries should be written into the script to help develop a different approach. This would be immensely time-consuming, and the Secretary herself would not be able to devote that time to the issue, so Holbrooke's very senior position was created.

Australia, by now one of the larger contributors to the coalition, was asked explicitly to nominate a person to work with Holbrooke and an initially small group of 'special representatives' or envoys. Their role at the outset was one of statecraft, although over time—and especially after the United States began its drawdown—it evolved more in the direction of stagecraft.

Holbrooke's formative years, incidentally, had been as a civilian adviser in Vietnam. He believed strongly in the need for a civilian role in delivering aid, fostering governance and working the political leadership, although he was realistic about the challenges in this area. He also thought there was an important role for regional countries, not least in trying to influence Pakistan and in reaching out to the Taliban. He believed personally that a political settlement would be necessary sooner or later, and, although I suspect Obama as well as Clinton agreed with this, the Pentagon effectively vetoed it as a policy. It was not until after Holbrooke died—tragically, from an aneurism suffered in Hillary's office in December 2010—that she first spoke of a 'negotiation', by which she meant a negotiation to separate the Taliban from al-Qaeda. By then it was 2011, and the United States had reversed its 2009 surge. The United States was clearly preparing its way out, so the Taliban had no reason to talk seriously.

As to Australia's mission, it quickly became evident to me as Special Envoy that while we had an 'all-of-government' presence, it was not functioning optimally on the ground, and was not coming together quite as well as it should in Canberra. There were the usual hardworking inter-agency task forces, but by then our commitment in people, treasure and policy capital demanded more than that.

So when I returned to Canberra in August, I helped put together an inter-agency group that operated at the CDF/Secretary/agency-head level, chaired by the National Security Adviser in the Department of Prime Minister and Cabinet, which met at least fortnightly. In time, that led to what I think was a pretty optimal all-of-government functioning in Canberra, better advice to the National Security Committee and a better connected performance on the ground in Afghanistan.

By the time the government decided to withdraw from Tarin Kowt in 2013, ADF, DFAT, AusAID and AFP leaders on the ground were agreed that, after some pain along the way, the whole-of-government effort there was as good as we had ever had, including joint civilian–ADF leadership in Tarin Kowt and close working relationships in Kabul.

In the meantime, the government had taken three significant policy decisions about our presence. The first was to take over leadership of the PRT from the Dutch when they left in 2010, but to decline leadership of the Combined Team – Uruzgan, leaving that to the United States. The second was to reverse that decision in 2012 and agree to take over from the United States.

Why the reversal? It was never made explicit to us as officials, but my hunch, not entirely uninformed, is that the government feared that if we had taken over in 2010, the United States would have withdrawn its enablers from Uruzgan, leaving us to hold a much larger baby than we wanted or could afford. But by 2012 that concern had been mitigated, and it was clear we were on the way out anyway.

And the third great decision in this period was of course the ultimate one: to withdraw from Uruzgan at the end of 2013 after progressively handing over to the Afghan security forces throughout 2012 and 2013. Incidentally, once the decision was made to be out by the end of 2013, there was some surprise in government about the pace at which the ADF moved—the military planners in effect set policy over the closing months.

Why were we leaving? Because the cost had been great, and the coalition partners, especially the United States, were tiring and leaving. We—that is, the coalition—had in the meantime given ourselves an 'out'.

With the Afghan security forces much improved through the training and mentoring of coalition partners, and now larger and more generously resourced than ever before, Afghanistan's future could surely be placed in their hands.

All of the change that our presence in Afghanistan underwent in the period 2005 to 2013, and especially after 2008, has led to debate about whether Australia's national strategic objectives changed in Afghanistan during the decade we were there. Having thought a lot about this, my answer is that they did not, and that what changed was the means by which the government, and the 50-member international coalition, sought to achieve those objectives. The two key themes had been reiterated consistently by government leaders from 2001 to 2013.

At the outset, Prime Minister Howard and his ministers had emphasised that the mission was aimed at ensuring that Afghanistan could not remain or become again a safe haven for international terrorists, and was undertaken in support of our alliance interests. These aims were restated when our enhanced deployment in 2005 was announced, although with additional (but passing) emphasis on the importance of safeguarding the elections about to be held in Afghanistan because, 'if democracy takes root [in Afghanistan] … then a massive blow is struck in the war against terrorism'.[11]

In his major speech of April 2009, Prime Minister Rudd made the same points in his own language. He spoke about 'the need to deny sanctuary to terrorists who have threatened and killed Australian citizens', and about 'our enduring commitment to the United States and the ANZUS Treaty'. He contended that what we were seeking was the 'stabilisation of the Afghan state through a combination of military, police and civilian effort to the extent necessary to consolidate [the] primary mission of strategic denial'.[12]

In 2010, Prime Minister Gillard said explicitly that 'Our mission in Afghanistan is not nation-building', and in 2011 reaffirmed the government's objectives: 'there must be no safe haven for terrorists in

---

11   Prime Minister the Hon. J. Howard MP, 'Address to the Australian troops', Campbell Barracks, Perth, 24 August 2005.
12   Rudd, press conference, 29 April 2009.

Afghanistan. We must stand firmly by our ally, the United States.'[13] And in his speech in Tarin Kowt marking the closure of our base there in October 2013, Prime Minister Abbott again reflected the two key objectives of our mission when he said: 'The threat of global terrorism is reduced. Our reliability as an ally is confirmed.'[14] In short, while the rhetoric wandered about at times, and the nature of what we did on the ground went through many changes, the strategic policy objectives remained the two we had started with.

Let me conclude with three points. The first reflects the 'lessons learned' work I did with the Australian Civil-Military Centre, at Defence's request, about government decision-making and whole-of-government processes in relation to Afghanistan.[15] There were many lessons: about aid programs, communications, resourcing of agencies, working with allies, detainee management (a matter of particular sensitivity, incidentally)—all the things you would expect.

But one that I think matters particularly is this: we must accept that when we commit the ADF to operations abroad, significant whole-of-government and foreign policy implications are bound to be generated. Rather than trying to retrofit additional machinery to an ADF operation, DFAT and other agencies as necessary should be fully properly engaged from the outset on the ground as well as in Canberra, and resourced through Defence-like 'no-win, no-loss' provisions.

Second, I referred earlier to my sense that there was always a degree of caution about Afghanistan at the highest levels in Australia. Governments of both kinds were highly sensitive to the risks implicit in the Afghan project, risks that were of three types: to personnel, later to the budget, and to policy interests—what could be achieved, and how distracting would it be? This is reflected not only in the statements made by prime ministers and ministers, but also in some of the lively exchanges I can recall with and among ministers about what Australia was doing and could achieve in Afghanistan.

---

13   Prime Minister the Hon. J. Gillard MP, Speech to the House of Representatives, Ministerial Statements, Commonwealth Parliamentary Debates, 19 October 2010, pp. 692–4.
14   Prime Minister the Hon. T. Abbott MP, Address at Recognition Ceremony, Tarin Kowt, Afghanistan, 28 October 2013.
15   A public version of the report on this study has been released: Australian Civil-Military Centre, *Afghanistan: Lessons from Australia's Whole of Government Mission*, ACMC, Queanbeyan, 2016.

Finally, a word about a subject that comes up so often in discussion about conflicts of this kind: exit strategies. We have seen how the approaches of successive governments to the implementation of their policy objectives evolved in Afghanistan and Iraq during our missions there. At the outset in both cases, government asserted its determination not to be there for the long haul and not to become involved in occupation or reconstruction roles. But in time, in both cases, the elected government of the day decided, for what it considered good and sufficient policy reasons related as much to the company we were in as to circumstances on the ground, to do those things, and more. Government would have so decided even if it had had the most rigidly defined exit strategy or end state from day one.

Circumstances changed, and national policy implementation changed with it, even if the strategic objectives did not. As ever, when we become involved in conflicts in which the national interest is defined more in terms of policy benefits than national survival, and in which we are a member of a wider coalition, we will—as the Chinese would say—be 'crossing the river by feeling the stones'.

3
A Chief of Defence Force's perspective

Chris Barrie

Prelude

In my four-year term of office as the Chief of the Defence Force (CDF), there are three major operational commitments that stand out.

The first, and perhaps most important, commitment from a strategic and national point of view was the UN-mandated operation to provide security in East Timor carried out from 20 September 1999 until 28 February 2000. The International Force East Timor (INTERFET) mission stands as a watershed moment in Australian military history and for our nation; it was for the first time that Australia had to put together and lead an internationally sanctioned coalition operation in our neighbourhood using military forces from many nations. As a result, Australian military doctrine had to be changed rapidly for our leadership role and the resulting requirements for interoperability—that is, to be able to work effectively with counterpart forces from coalition partners.

The second major operational commitment was the provision of security for the Sydney Olympic Games in 2000. This operation involved a substantial force of about 4,500 full-time and part-time ADF members who had to learn to work effectively with a variety of domestic law enforcement agencies and Olympic organisers before and throughout the Games. The ADF also had significant training responsibilities for the provision of specialist security forces, including forces able to respond to a terrorist incident.

The third major operational commitment had its genesis in the 9/11 attacks in the United States.

At the time of the 9/11 attacks, the ADF was already engaged in two significant operational commitments. The first commitment was a follow-up to the security operation in East Timor: Operation TANAGER, involving about 1,600 personnel supporting the United Nations Transitional Administration in East Timor (UNTAET). The second commitment was mounting Operation RELEX from 3 September 2001 until 1 July 2002 to deter people-smugglers selling one-way overland bus trips and boat passages intended to bring people into Australia without proper authority.

With this as background, I will examine the main events in the post-9/11 military world until I retired from command of the Defence Force. I will add some observations about unfolding operations in Afghanistan and Iraq after July 2002. I will then finish this chapter with my assessment of the implications of these events for the ADF and the nation.

The attacks of 9/11 in context

On 26 February 1993, terrorists detonated a truck bomb in the basement of the World Trade Center. It killed six people and injured more than 1,000 people. The intention of these terrorists was to send the North Tower crashing into the South Tower, thus bringing both towers down and killing tens of thousands of people.

Investigations now show that Ramzi Yousef, the mastermind of this operation, had spent time in al-Qaeda training camps in Afghanistan before 1991 when he began the planning of a bombing attack inside the United States. He later said that the 1993 attack was in vengeance for US support for Israel. Letters sent to media outlets in the United States just before the attack demanded that America end all aid to Israel, terminate diplomatic relations with Israel and end interference in Middle East countries' interior affairs. If these demands were not met, the letters threatened, further attacks would take place.

Yousef's uncle, Khalid Sheikh Mohammed, later considered to be the principal architect of the 9/11 attacks,[1] gave tips and advice to Yousef on the telephone. He also supported financially a co-conspirator, Mohammed Salameh, with a small wire transfer to him of US$660.[2] The records now show that Khalid Sheikh Mohammed was a skilful terrorist committed to the cause of attacking the West.

In 1996, Tom Clancy's new bestselling Jack Ryan book, *Executive Orders*, was released in the United States.[3] The back cover of the book had the following synopsis:

> A runaway Jumbo Jet has crashed into the Capitol Building in Washington, leaving the President dead, along with most of the Cabinet and Congress. Dazed and confused, the man who only minutes beforehand was confirmed as the new caretaker Vice-President is told that he is now President of the United States.

The full story is in the opening pages of the book. Therefore it is possible that the breathtaking conception of using US technology to attack the symbols of US global leadership, such as the Pentagon and the World Trade Center, might have had its genesis in Clancy's work of fiction. Indeed, in 1996 Khalid Sheikh Mohammed presented Osama bin Laden with an outline of an idea along these lines.[4]

It was on my watch that the tragic 9/11 attacks occurred. I was dining with a friend in Perth when ADF Operations alerted me to an unfolding event in New York City. I turned on the television in time to see live coverage of the second aircraft fly into the South Tower. However, what became quite clear within hours of the collapse of both towers from the television coverage, supplemented by upgraded intelligence reporting, was the imperative for the United States to take immediate action in response in Afghanistan. Additional measures to safeguard communities who were in fear of what might happen next would also be necessary.

By midnight Perth time, I had decided I needed to return to Canberra as quickly as I could as I knew the Prime Minister, accompanied by a strong team from Australia, was in Washington, DC, for an official visit. We took the first available flight to return to Russell Offices and my headquarters.

1 Included in the 9/11 Commission Report.
2 Khalid Sheikh Mohammed, globalsecurity.org, from an original on 21 October 2008.
3 T. Clancy, *Executive Orders*, G.P. Putnam's Sons, New York, 1996.
4 BBC News, 'Suspect reveals 9/11 planning', 22 September 2003.

In the immediate aftermath of the attacks, there was a lot of uncertainty, including when our national leadership team would return from the United States. We tried to obtain more detail about exactly what had happened, as well as engaging with US military authorities on likely response options.

The timing, coordination, imagination and audacity of these attacks took the world by surprise. This was in spite of knowledge that al-Qaeda was a force to be reckoned. It had mounted successful attacks on USS *Cole* on 12 October 2000 and other attacks on US interests, such as the attacks on US embassies in Kenya and Tanzania on 7 August 1998. The intelligence agencies had been doing their best to anticipate al-Qaeda's next moves, but this was one they missed.

After the tragedy that befell New York, the Pentagon and the passengers and crew members of all four large-body aircraft used in the attacks, the world watched and waited for the next big event. For some time after 9/11, it was thought that other 'spectacular' events had been planned. People watched and waited, while we were doing our best to try to outsmart al-Qaeda.

The British historian Niall Ferguson has summed up the position well, as follows:

> The defining event of this century's first years was an attack on the financial and transport networks of the United States by an Islamist gang that is best understood as an anti-social network. Although acting in the name of al-Qaeda, the 9/11 plotters were only weakly connected to the wider network of political Islam, which helps explain why they were able to escape detection.
>
> There was an evil genius to what the attacks of 11 September 2001 did. In essence, they targeted the main hubs of America's increasingly networked society, exploiting security vulnerabilities that allowed them to smuggle primitive weapons (box cutters) onto four passenger planes bound for New York and Washington, respectively the central nodes of the US financial and political systems … the al-Qaeda operatives achieved the greatest coup in the history of terrorism. Not only did they generate an atmosphere of fear in the United States that persisted for many months; more importantly, they precipitated an asymmetrical response by the

administration of President George W. Bush that almost certainly did more over the succeeding years to strengthen than to weaken the cause of Salafist Islam.[5]

Post 9/11

The Bush administration, with the support of Congress, responded quickly to these attacks with a statement of intent. During a televised address to the nation from the White House in the evening of 9/11, President Bush said, '[W]e will make no distinction between the terrorists who committed these acts and those who harbor them.'

From an Australian perspective, my recollection is that an urgent meeting of the National Security Committee of Cabinet (NSC) took place in Parliament House on Wednesday afternoon following my return from Perth. This meeting was chaired by the Deputy Prime Minister, John Anderson MP, and it included a hook-up with Prime Minister Howard in Washington, DC. The meeting canvassed a range of possibilities that might affect Australian security interests in the forthcoming weeks and the implications of a commitment to invoke the ANZUS Treaty as a framework within which to conduct consultations with the United States. The matter of the return to Australia of the Prime Minister's party was also discussed.

The government announced the activation of the ANZUS Treaty on 14 September after Howard's return to Australia. This was followed in Parliament on 17 September by a resolution that 'fully endorses the commitment of the Australian Government to support within Australia's capabilities United States-led action against those responsible for these tragic attacks'.[6] Clearly, the government had set a high priority on the ADF doing as much as was prudent to assist the United States in its efforts to combat terrorism.

Within the Australian Defence Organisation, the Secretary, Dr Alan Hawke AO, and I discussed implications for our own security. We were anxious about further attacks on targets of opportunity, certainly within the United States, and possibly with close allies like Australia. As a matter

---

5   N. Ferguson, *The Square and the Tower: Networks, Hierarchies and the Struggle for Global Power*, Allen Lane, London, 2017, pp. 333–4.
6   House of Representatives, Debates, 17 September 2001, p. 30739.

of urgency, we lifted the security watch at all ADF bases in Australia. I was also concerned that small groups of 'sleeper' terrorists in our community might decide to attack ADF members, and possibly their families, as a means of demonstrating al-Qaeda's reach and the seriousness of its agenda. Consequently, I decided to write a personally signed letter to families of ADF members in Australia emphasising the need to consider personal security measures, including the use of different travel routes to and from work, and schools where appropriate, as well as being watchful about their homes and within their communities.

Given the nature of our close relationship with the United States, it did not take long before the phones and the emails were running hot between US Pacific Command in Hawaii and, less frequently, the chairman of the US Joint Chiefs of Staff in Washington, DC. Our Defence staff in Washington, DC, and our consul-general in Hawaii were also busy discussing options for the conduct of immediate response operations in defence of our interests and to support the United States in the prosecution of al-Qaeda terrorist training camps, certainly in Afghanistan, and possibly in other places of interest.

Another proposal being pursued vigorously by the United States was the patrolling by naval ships of the Malacca Strait and the management of appropriate interception operations there. Early on it was evident that finding sufficient naval ships from reliable allies and partners of the United States would be troublesome. Australia was unable to participate in this activity owing to other operational priorities.

I was also conscious, particularly in the context of Malacca Strait operations, that there might be sensitivities in Jakarta to any US requests for support. Accordingly, I visited Jakarta to explain to colleagues there that any US requests for help should be taken seriously. I also pointed out that US officials might become tense if they encountered inexplicable obstacles. I had the impression at the time that my trip was worth the effort.

Providing air defence assets to protect the US naval support facility, US Marine Corps pre-positioned ships and US Air Force (USAF) bases in the British Indian Ocean Territory of Diego Garcia was another US priority. From an Australian perspective, the request to mount this operation with RAAF resources could be undertaken quite easily within the constraints of ADF priorities. The government readily accepted arguments for participation in these operations by RAAF Hornet aircraft from the Air Combat Group. This deployment began on 9 November 2001 and lasted until 7 May 2002. The air defence of Diego Garcia was the first time since the Korean War the RAAF had been tasked to conduct potentially hostile air operations using our fighter aircraft.

Concurrent tasks, as pointed out already, severely limited Australia's ability to carry out substantial additional operations to support the US military effort. The ADF was still involved in Timor Leste as a priority, providing training to the new country and managing security operations under the leadership of UNTAET. For the Navy, and with some army support, Operation RELEX began on 3 September following the MV *Tampa* incident. Several fleet units were deployed in northern Australian waters to carry out patrols and conduct interception operations to frustrate the activities of people-smugglers.

Operation ENDURING FREEDOM, the US-led international effort to oust the Taliban regime in Afghanistan and destroy Osama bin Laden's terrorist network based in Afghanistan, began on 7 October 2001. For the ADF, major operations in support of ENDURING FREEDOM demanded the highest attention during October and November 2001. Australia's parallel Operation SLIPPER, beginning on 22 October 2001, was marked by the political leadership farewelling in Perth our first contingent of special forces troops bound for Afghanistan.

The land operation was to deploy a highly mobile special operations force into Afghanistan to neutralise and, if necessary, destroy the al-Qaeda terrorists sheltered by the Taliban government. The naval operation in the Indian Ocean operation and sea areas adjacent to Middle East coastlines was to support our deployed ground forces and, if necessary, interdict unwelcome forces elsewhere. Both these operations formed the mainstay of the Australian Government's commitment to the United States under the ANZUS Treaty. The focus of these operations was a significant move away from our traditional area of operations in the Pacific and our relationship with Pacific Command. Quickly we had to build up a new relationship with US Central Command (CENTCOM) that would soon take priority over the long-standing relationship we enjoyed with Pacific Command.

How did we select these forces and not others? I was particularly concerned that we should include an amphibious ship (Landing Platforms Amphibious or LPA) in the force to ensure the presence of an Australian medical capability nearby if needed by our special forces in Afghanistan. The inclusion of Australian special forces in a US operation would involve acquiring some new skill sets and equipment, but we were confident that operations on the ground would be relatively easy to conduct.

What was not going to be so easy was how we might provide support to other deployed forces, especially if things started to go wrong. We also needed to consider the resources for the rotation of deployed forces if these operations were needed for an extended period. For example, in the context of support to other deployed forces, we needed special diplomatic arrangements to operate RAAF Boeing 707 air-to-air refuelling aircraft from airfields close to Afghanistan, yet far enough away to offer a measure of security. Accordingly, we dispatched our Chief of Air Force, Air Marshal Angus Houston AO, to the region with a brief to find us an airfield and a government that would be useful for our needs. He was able to arrange for Manas airfield in Kyrgyzstan to be used.

I had visited Washington on 30 September for the change of command ceremony when General Myers became chairman of the US Joint Chiefs of Staff on 1 October 2001. While in Washington, I also had the privilege of a brief in the National Military Command and Control Center in which thinking about the range of operations being considered by the US military was outlined. I can say, from my perspective, that there were no surprises in anything I heard. At the end of the brief, I spoke about our base defence security enhancements and the letter I had written to ADF families about the need to look to their personal security.

The day following the change of command ceremony, exactly three weeks after the 9/11 attacks, my team and I flew on American Airlines flight 77 (the Pentagon crash flight) from Washington to Los Angeles. At Dulles Airport, near Washington, most of the terminal was deserted.

To complicate matters further, the writs for a federal election in Australia were issued on Monday 8 October for an election to be held on Saturday 10 November 2001. This meant that most of our response operations would commence during the caretaker period. Consequently, with the approval of the government, a considerable effort was made to keep the federal Opposition, and particularly the Leader, Kim Beazley MP, fully apprised of the government's intentions and the implications for our

3. A CHIEF OF DEFENCE FORCE'S PERSPECTIVE

alliance relationship. I spent several hours with Beazley and his leadership team going over the key issues for our deployments. He seemed interested to ensure the best possible support for our deployed special forces group.

Once operations began in Afghanistan in October 2001, our ADF planners became closely involved with US Central Command, something quite new and different from working with our customary friends at US Pacific Command. In a sense, the dice were being loaded towards Australian involvement in all further operations that could be connected to the outcomes of 9/11.

Interoperability issues: Prisoner handling

In January 2002 during a trip to the region with our Defence Minister, Senator Robert Hill, I visited various ADF units deployed on Operation SLIPPER. Everywhere, I found that our forces had integrated well with US counterparts at sea and in Afghanistan. All operational issues were being carried out in the professional manner we have come to expect from the ADF. Of particular note was our visit to Bagram air base in Afghanistan where our special forces people were working closely with their US counterparts in headquarters and in the field. But, while our interoperability was as good as we might expect and the practice consistent with doctrine of its day, there was an important gap in interoperability that had to be sorted out: prisoner handling.

For my own part, this oversight was a surprise. I recall that during the Australia–United States Ministerial Consultations (AUSMIN) talks on 3 November 1999 in Washington, DC, I had introduced a discussion item into the agenda on interoperability. The intention was to show that interoperability was based on more than shared equipment and communications, extending to shared values and doctrine. This point was picked up in paragraph 13 of the AUSMIN communiqué, which stated:

> Australia and the United States noted that interoperability remains a priority goal of the alliance. Rapid technological changes require both governments to maintain an open dialogue and continue to explore exchanges focused on interoperability.[7]

---

[7] Archived in Australia–United States Ministerial Consultations, 1999 Joint Communiqué, 3 November 1999, para 13, dfat.gov.au/geo/united-states-of-america/ausmin/Pages/australia-united-states-ministerial-consultations-1999-joint-communiqu.aspx (retrieved 31 March 2020).

Prime Minister John Howard meets soldiers of the Australian Special Forces Task Group deployed on Operation SLIPPER in Afghanistan, 2005.
Source: Courtesy of the Department of Defence.

In field operations by our special forces in Afghanistan it did not take long to appreciate that on some occasions al-Qaeda and Taliban fighters would offer their surrender rather than becoming casualties of combat action. For Australia, as a signatory state of all the Geneva Conventions and Protocols, this presented a serious problem if the number of deployed personnel was to be kept low.

Unlike Australia, the United States is not a signatory of all the Geneva Conventions and Protocols, and for prisoner-handling this presented a problem as we could not simply hand our prisoners over to US forces without breaking the Conventions. The Geneva Conventions require that the state accepts responsibility for the treatment of any prisoners that surrender to its forces, including under Article 3 in circumstances where the conflict does not involve one state fighting another.[8]

For the initial deployment to Afghanistan, the effect of the Conventions would have meant the deployment to Afghanistan of a considerable number of additional personnel to set up and manage a 'prison' in which

---

8   The Third Geneva Convention is about the treatment of the prisoners of war. Article 3 of this convention applies in non-international conflicts; that is, when the combatant parties are not states.

Australia would bear full responsibility for the treatment of its prisoners. But, in the context of the early commitment to Afghanistan, it was highly desirable to find a solution for this problem. After briefing ministers about the problem and a possible solution, I wrote a letter to my opposite number in Washington suggesting that the creation of an Australian prison in Afghanistan would not be sensible if another solution could be found.

The letter resulted in a written assurance from the Chairman, US Joint Chiefs of Staff that all prisoners taken by US military forces in Afghanistan would be treated in accordance with the provisions of the Geneva Conventions and Protocols. This letter was taken as the basis for the Australian Government to agree that it would not be necessary for the deployment of a 'prison' to Afghanistan if arrangements could be made in the field for a US military officer to accept the surrender of any captives taken during Australian operations. This turned out to be a neat solution to an important interoperability issue.

Iraq

In the lead-up to the Iraq invasion I was retired, working in Oxford, watching carefully how things were unfolding from a UK perspective (now the subject of the Chilcott Report), and paying little attention to Australian events. I did, however, check the ABC News website to gauge community responses to the government's decision to commit Australian military forces to the invasion force, under US leadership, on 18 March 2003.[9] I was surprised, and a little pleased, to see on that website ADF personnel responding to some people in the community who wanted to label ADF members as 'war-mongers' by reminding them that the ADF was a 'force for good'!

I spent some time trying to work out what knowledge might have brought Bush, Blair and Howard together on such a joint venture. At that time my presumption was that highly classified intelligence assessments about Iraqi WMD capabilities were such that the three leaders became united in their intent, despite their differences in politics. No other scenario is credible.

---

9   See 'Howard commits troops to war', 1 March 2003, www.smh.com.au/articles/2003/03/18/1047749732511.html (retrieved 31 March 2020).

The invasion of Iraq took place nearly nine months after I handed command of the ADF over to General Peter Cosgrove. I cannot know what took place in classified conversations from the time of my retirement until the invasion of Iraq. But, at the time of my departure in early July 2002, it was my opinion that no special evidence existed to make an invasion of Iraq essential, which became one topic of conversation during my final call with the Prime Minister.

Australian information available to me at the time seemed to focus on the simple decision by Prime Minister John Howard that Australia should join its alliance partners to invade Iraq, even though the contrast between Australia and the United Kingdom, in terms of community responses, could not have been more different. I remember well the UK campaign 'Not in Our Name', which sought to undermine Prime Minister Tony Blair's willingness to go along with President Bush's plans for toppling Saddam Hussein. I did not find much reporting of similar community opposition to the invasion of Iraq in Australia. But, in my view, the wisdom of crowds as witnessed by the opposition campaign in the United Kingdom has now been sustained through the exposure of systemic failings outlined in the Chilcott Report, which shows how misguided the invasion turned out to be.

In Australia, it seemed, the executive power of the government was sufficient to begin what we would now describe as the 'long campaign of war', which grew to include Afghanistan as well as Iraq. This revealed once again, as in Vietnam, fundamental weaknesses in conceptions of the usefulness of strategic military power in circumstances short of total war. Reporting from the press after the government's announcement of our contribution to the invasion of Iraq showed that voters were strongly against a war in Iraq without UN support, even though 61 per cent of the same voters would have supported the invasion if it had been backed by the United Nations.

The unconscionable cost for our all-volunteer forces—some members of which have now served in conflict overseas for longer than anyone did in either of the two world wars—is incalculable. Many of the consequences, in terms of casualties, destroyed family relationships, mental illnesses and disabled veterans, will be a burden on our society for decades to come. Yet the only people who really noticed were surviving members themselves and the families of those who are suffering, wounded or have been killed.

Once committed, of course, successive Australian governments of both political persuasions have not been able to do much other than follow the US grand strategy. Hence, it is possible to argue that the only superpower that existed in 1945, having triumphed in the European and Pacific theatres of war, has learned that short of total war, a determined and intractable enemy can succeed despite all the trappings of power—in Vietnam, in Iraq and in Afghanistan. What is even more curious is that we have failed to learn from the lessons to be drawn from these expeditionary fights.

Afghanistan after the invasion of Iraq

At the turn of the century, well before I handed command of the ADF over to General Cosgrove, two books were published under my signature by the Australian Defence Organisation. The first of these books is titled *The Australian Approach to Warfare*, and the second is titled *Force 2020*. I commend them both not because of the wisdom in them but because they are a useful summary of our thinking in the early part of the 21st century. I note that, on page 33 of *The Australian Approach to Warfare*, we show a war on terrorism from 2001 to the present being listed as 'Participation in US-led campaign against international terrorism'.[10] None of us at that time—even though there was strong recognition that the post–Vietnam War era had passed—could have predicted that more than 15 years later Australia would still be involved in the Middle East and Afghanistan combating terrorism.

Final thoughts

It involves a great deal of complexity to assess fully the outcomes of our involvement in the 'long war' (as operations in Afghanistan have become known). More likely, it is far too early to make such a call. In making an interim assessment, however, we must take into account the important assumption that Australia would not have been involved in military operations in Iraq or Afghanistan—or indeed anywhere else in the Middle East—in the absence of significant pressure from the United States to

---

10   Department of Defence, *The Australian Approach to Warfare*, Department of Defence, Canberra, 2002.

support its agenda in the region. It also follows that Australian forces will not be operating anywhere in the Middle East after a withdrawal by the United States.

To place the 'long war' in context, there are two points that I think would be important to assessments of success or failure.

The first perspective relates to the 13 years of campaigning involving the ADF as an all-volunteer force. In effect, ADF personnel at the centrepiece of our consideration have undertaken combat operations in the full knowledge that people in Australia, apart from their own families, would barely notice. I am aware that some ADF personnel have participated in more than 10 deployments to Iraq and/or Afghanistan. This raises a question about the serious limitations of undertaking extended duration and extensive operations without the benefit of national service.

The second perspective relates to Australia's ability to conduct its own campaigning. As a relatively small contributing nation, Australia was involved in two significant coalition operations (Afghanistan and Iraq) in which the United States asserted its primacy as the lead nation. This has meant a return to the pre–East Timor doctrine in which Australia would always be operating as a small component of a much larger multinational coalition. Presumably, although we continued the practice of deploying an Australian national command headquarters into the combat zone, there have been implications for our ability to be fully in charge of our own operational imperative in both conflicts.

On reflection, I think the 9/11 attacks fundamentally changed the dynamics of the Australian approach to war. Just as Operation RELEX was launched to counter people-smuggling, the responses to these attacks were not deliberate. We learned as we went. In the three months after 9/11, these responses were cobbled together as the world held its collective breath awaiting news of the next attacks. We simply had no idea of the possible nature and scale of what might follow. But what we did know was that the basis of our security was under serious threat from experts in asymmetric warfare; this has been a common characteristic of all groups intent on using terror to achieve their objectives.

As with INTERFET, the initial insertion of our special forces into Afghanistan was accompanied by a clear exit strategy. Success was defined as the destruction of al-Qaeda terrorist training camps in Afghanistan and

3. A CHIEF OF DEFENCE FORCE'S PERSPECTIVE

significantly reducing its presence in country. This success we achieved quite quickly, but then the priorities and complications presented by the invasion of Iraq meant that we took our eyes off this ball too early.

Now, it seems evident that the search for WMD was an artifice to cover the real intent of the invasion of Iraq, which was to topple Saddam Hussein. In May 2002, at a meeting with senior administration officials in the US Department of Defense, we were told that planning for a campaign in Iraq was for contingency purposes only. It is now rather revealing from the books written by Bob Woodward that US intentions over Iraq had firmed in December 2001, beginning with a high-level meeting of the administration at President Bush's Crawford ranch just before Christmas.

In my tour as CDF, we transitioned from a focus on our region and relative peace into the post-9/11 age when, having been caught short over Osama bin Laden and al-Qaeda, we suddenly woke up to the fact that the world had been undergoing changes that entailed significant new challenges to the established order. Whereas in the previous four years we had been the lead nation in the UN-mandated coalition operation to restore security to East Timor involving 26 other countries, we now returned to an operational environment in which the United States called the shots.

Notably, at the time of mounting INTERFET in East Timor, I do not think that Australia would ever have contemplated invading Indonesia to set East Timor free. If we had invaded Indonesia to set East Timor free, the dynamics of our region would have been reshaped quickly in ways that would not have been good for Australia as it is hard to believe that war with Indonesia would not have resulted. By 2003, it seemed we were more circumspect in 1999. In today's world it seems it is much easier to invade a country that is not your neighbour.

Finally, I cannot help but observe that while Parliament has held a full inquiry into the circumstances of 'Children Overboard' and other matters resultant from certain events of political interest during Operation RELEX in October 2001, it has not yet held an inquiry into the circumstances leading up to and during the 'long war' from 2001 until the present.[11] Given the cost of the long war to the nation, this failure to examine

---

11 Parliament, Senate, *Select Committee on a Certain Maritime Incident* (report), The Committee, Canberra, 2002.

fully all these issues beggars belief about our priorities and the impact of political expediency. This failure also lends support to those who call for a change to the processes we use in Australia to decide on war.

If national service of some kind had been required in the United States and in Australia before embarking on the invasion of Iraq in 2003, the decisions for war would have been a lot more difficult to make.

PART 2:
ON OPERATIONS IN AFGHANISTAN AND IRAQ

4

Australia's intervention in Afghanistan, 2001–02

Dan McDaniel

I met the former US Senator Charlie Wilson at midnight in Kandahar when it was 30 degrees Celsius. Standing outside in the dark with three US officers, Charlie said to us, '[Y]ou boys are finishing off what we started, but you're doing it a whole lot better than we ever did.' Privately, I disagreed. It was now 2009, I was on my third tour and the coalition did not seem to be winning a counter-insurgency that was quite different from the counter-terrorism mission I was sent to fight in 2001–02.

Back in Charlie Wilson's day, in response to the Soviet Union invasion of Afghanistan in 1981, the United States supported the Afghan mujahideen to fight the Soviet forces efficiently and effectively, famously providing them with a Stinger missile to shoot down Soviet helicopters. US support for the mujahideen largely ceased once the Soviet Union withdrew from Afghanistan and the United States judged that it had achieved what was in its primary national interest.

Twenty years later, the 2001 US-led invasion of Afghanistan and the operations immediately following were similarly well focused and fairly well executed under the circumstances. Al-Qaeda was the enemy, the Taliban its support. While some contributing nations had broader national agenda, the primary objective of removing the terrorist group al-Qaeda and denying it Afghanistan as a safe haven was clear in the minds of the US-led coalition forces.

Then a major, I led the first SAS Squadron, under an Australian Special Operations Task Force Headquarters.[1] We entered Afghanistan in early December 2001, through Forward Operating Base Rhino, a former drug-smuggling hub located in the desert south of Kandahar. Following the fall of Kandahar in late December, during which Australian forces supported the combined US special operations forces and Northern Alliance efforts, the Task Force's base of operations moved to Kandahar airfield. Although the base was home, much of the squadron's time was spent outside it on long-range and long-duration patrols and shorter direct-action tasks. In March 2002, the Task Force temporarily relocated to Bagram Airfield to support Operation ANACONDA in attacking Taliban and al-Qaeda forces in eastern Afghanistan. My squadron was rotated out and replaced by a second squadron in March–April 2002, at which time Bagram Airfield became the permanent base for the Task Force headquarters. The final squadron rotation occurred in September 2002, and Australian special forces were withdrawn from Afghanistan in December 2002.

This chapter reflects on the first year of the commitment of Australian special forces to combat operations in Afghanistan, from the invasion in 2001 through to withdrawal at the end of 2002. It is intentionally focused at a level higher than specific tactical actions, most of which remain classified. Instead, its focus is on Australia's national strategy, the missions and the broad lessons. It will also briefly reflect on Australia's exit strategy.

These reflections are deliberately limited to those of the tactical troops and commanders of 2001–02; it captures the rough, blunt perspectives of then junior troops rather than the analytical and polished evaluations of now senior soldiers and officers. This account and any inaccuracies are my own; however, in preparation I interviewed many of the SAS commanders of the 2001–02 deployments and others who were senior officers at the strategic level in Australia at the time.

---

1   This chapter numbers the SAS squadrons by the order in which they were deployed to Afghanistan, not by their formal subunit titles; i.e. 'the first squadron deployed' rather than '1 SAS Squadron'.

National strategy—ANZUS, entry and the Australian reputation

At the time of the September 11 attacks, I and elements of the squadron were on a separate deployment and did not learn of the attacks until some days afterwards. We were swiftly recalled to Australia and, in November 2001, the squadron was sent to the Middle East.

Prime Minister John Howard's swift decision to stand alongside the United States and commit troops to combat operations in Afghanistan demonstrated the level of Australian national intent. Although the Special Forces Task Force was issued a mission to defeat al-Qaeda and deny Afghanistan as a terrorist safe haven, we had no real relationship with Middle Eastern nations. Furthermore, each of our traditional coalition partners was focused on their own national agenda, and the United States was focused on its own plan rather than on forming and supporting a broader coalition. This left us with the problem of securing a base in the Middle East, entry to Afghanistan, US command and control 'sponsorship' (i.e. the US host formation to which Australians could attach) and logistics support necessary to achieve the national will. There were no favours—nothing was offered and nothing was simple.

The Task Force faced some active resistance from other coalition partners who were positioning themselves within their own national agenda, and there were some follow-up discussions between the Australian Prime Minister and US President to finally secure support. The Task Force Commanding Officer, supported by the deployed national commander, Brigadier Ken Gillespie, had to work hard to secure a base in the Middle East. He had to work hard for US command and control sponsorship. This eventually came in the form of a US Marine commander by the name of Brigadier General James Mattis, who would go on to become the US Secretary of Defense under President Trump, and then Gillespie had to work harder to actually get the force into Afghanistan. There was a lot of work to be done before the real work began.

Once the Task Force was deployed to Afghanistan, all ranks of the squadron felt keenly a responsibility to reinforce Australia's military reputation on this world stage. The soldiers understood that the Task Force was representing not only the Australian military but also the Australian nation, including its commitment to the global rules-based order and the

US alliance. At the tactical level, the soldiers knew that actions in this war zone would shape the coalition's judgement of the professionalism of Australian soldiers.

Early on, my boss, the SAS Commanding Officer, made a tactical decision that had strategic impact: the decision to deploy with our own ground transport in the form of the SAS's modified Land Rover Perenties. Australia's was one of the few coalition special forces that brought its own vehicles. This provided autonomy and flexibility, and the ability to conduct a wider range of missions, thereby allowing a modest-sized squadron to make a disproportionately large contribution to the US-led effort. For a period in the midst of winter of 2001–02, Australia was one of the few nations conducting long-duration special reconnaissance patrols, reporting on the presence of al-Qaeda and the broader mood and perceptions of the Afghan people across the east and south of the country. Each individual Australian patrol was tracked at the US Central Command (CENTCOM) Headquarters in the mainland United States, and its reporting was being briefed at the highest levels of the US military and administration. The information provided was highly regarded, and the Australian patrol flags on the map at CENTCOM Headquarters were a powerful demonstration of Australian commitment. However, it was Operation ANACONDA that showcased Australian professionalism and influenced the course of the commitment of Australian special forces for the remainder of 2002.

Operation ANACONDA's objective was to destroy a large al-Qaeda–Taliban force located in the Shahi Kot valley, in Ghazni Province in central eastern Afghanistan. Unlike earlier Afghan-led operations in the Tora Bora region of Nangarhar Province, north of Khost, Operation ANACONDA was to be a coalition-led combat operation that would commit more than 6,000 conventional and special operations forces. During the course of this operation, Australian patrols directed air power on to al-Qaeda targets all day and night for more than a week, killing significant numbers of enemy fighters, destroying enemy equipment and on more than one occasion protecting the lives of coalition soldiers fighting in the valley. The action resulted in the awarding of a Distinguished Service Cross to an SAS sergeant patrol commander and a US Silver Star, the US military's third-highest personal decoration for valour in combat, to a United States Air Force member attached to one of the SAS patrols.

About the time of Operation ANACONDA, the Australian Government was considering that there would only be a single squadron commitment with no rotations. The Task Force performance on Operation ANACONDA persuaded senior US commanders that the Australian force was one worth lobbying for. The Australian Government agreed to remain committed and deployed a second squadron to Afghanistan to take over from the first.

Not surprisingly, the squadron rotations were the subject of deliberate government consideration and decision. No rotation was assured and, in both cases, the decision to continue the deployment was not made until four to six weeks before departure. This process was apparent to the deployed force, with the tempo of operations reducing around the times of Australian Government consideration.

As the deployment progressed into mid-2002, it became clear that most al-Qaeda forces had departed Afghanistan. At this point, the national intent seemed less clear. There was still work to be done to ensure that pockets of al-Qaeda were dealt with, but the focus of the deployed forces shifted a little, which is probably best understood through the missions assigned to each SAS squadron.

Missions

The first SAS Squadron's mission was clear and without restriction—it was essentially to deny Afghanistan as a firm base for al-Qaeda's global terrorism campaign in order to reinforce Australian national interests. The ruling Taliban regime was of interest and clearly important in terms of Afghanistan as a safe haven for al-Qaeda; however, the focus was very much on hunting al-Qaeda forces. The mission was simple, clear, executable and aligned from the tactical to the national level.

There might have been some surprise at the wide range of the mission at the time of Australia's deployment. The US and UK special forces had made early gains before we departed Australia, and indeed the tactical situation did evolve from September to early December 2001. The Australian Government probably could have reduced the breadth of the Task Force mission but chose not to, which sent a strong message of Australian national commitment.

While throughout 2002 the mission remained focused on al-Qaeda and denying Afghanistan as their base, by the second squadron rotation the Taliban started to feature more prominently in tasking. Following Operation ANACONDA, it was increasingly clear that the bulk of the remaining al-Qaeda forces had departed Afghanistan and moved largely into Pakistan. As a result, the second and third SAS Squadrons' tasking shifted from directly targeting al-Qaeda forces to a more traditional reconnaissance role, focusing on remaining pockets of al-Qaeda forces, their support networks and their movement routes along the various 'rat lines' between Pakistan and Afghanistan. Australian forces were now also tasked with stemming the flow of Taliban figures along the same movement routes. A particular focus became protecting Kabul from attack to facilitate the conduct of the strategically important national Loya Jirga to select a future President and Government of the Islamic Republic of Afghanistan.[2]

The mission assigned to the first Task Group deployed to Afghanistan provided the freedom to exploit fleeting opportunities. The Task Group commander had the flexibility to move his forces wherever necessary within Afghanistan to achieve the national intent and the tactical direction of his coalition commander, Brigadier General Mattis. As I said earlier, the first assigned mission was simple, clear, executable and aligned from the tactical to the national level. It remains the finest example of mission command I have experienced,[3] and was one of the many useful tactical lessons of this deployment.

Lessons

From its first rotation, the first squadron documented more than 200 lessons and recommendations. They ranged from a lack of modern anti-tank capability to 5.56mm weapons being outranged, a lack of a mature joint tactical air control capability, the advantage of a varied fleet of helicopters and of course experiences in cold weather warfare. The following strategic, operational and tactical lessons are worthy of note.

---

2 Pashto for 'grand council', a Loya Jirga is a mass national gathering that brings together representatives from the various ethnic, religious and tribal communities in Afghanistan. See www.rferl.org/a/afghanistan-loya-jirga-explainer/25174483.html (retrieved 31 March 2020).
3 Mission command involves the trusted delegation of authority to undertake a mission within the parameters of a commander's guidance.

Strategic lessons

The first lesson concerns the issue of the reasons for intervention in a nation's external affairs versus its internal affairs and the associated national strategic decisions, preparation and level of national commitment in time, resources and casualties.

The 2001 invasion was about intervention in Afghanistan's external affairs; that is, al-Qaeda and the safe haven it had in Afghanistan from which it was planning and carrying out global terrorist operations. While Taliban regime change was a predictable (and potentially US-planned) consequence, it was not the primary aim, certainly not of Australian forces, and might not have happened had the Taliban eventually given up al-Qaeda forces early during the invasion, as the United States had requested. To succeed in this mission, the Task Force needed only a fairly basic understanding of Afghanistan: its strategic relationships and influencers, its history, its people, its first and second level of tribal affiliations and its geographic environment.

Contrast this with intervention in Afghanistan's internal affairs, which might include installing and maintaining a pro-Western government, imposing Western-style values, systems and processes, nation-building, protecting human rights and reversing the oppression of women and minority groups in a complex tribal environment where subtribes and their associated dynamics extend eight, nine, even 10 levels. This involves a far deeper and greater level of planning, cultural understanding and immersion, risk, inter-agency commitment in time and resources, and a deeper assessment of Australia's national interest. I do not believe that any one nation demonstrated an appreciation of this until much later in the occupation and, as a result, I do not believe that any contributing nation, including Australia, prepared well with a strategy for the level of commitment necessary for intervention in Afghanistan's internal affairs.

Australian personnel on guard in an Australian light armoured vehicle as a US Army Blackhawk helicopter takes off in Baghdad, 2006.
Source: Courtesy of the Department of Defence.

Second, and a lesson that is topical given current geostrategic circumstances, the Australian military needs to work at understanding the alliance with the United States and not take it for granted. Despite the many activities and interactions with the United States at many levels, the initial problems we had with securing basing, sponsorship and entry to Afghanistan taught us that we were not as 'tight' with the Americans as we thought. Despite shared history over many of the world's major conflicts in the last century, it was apparent at the tactical level that at that time the United States really did not know us, understand us or necessarily trust us.

The fact that this relationship was not automatic was a surprise but clear to those deployed. It did not seem as clear to the Defence organisation in Australia, which appeared critical of the Task Force's early inability to gain the tactical traction necessary to meet the national intent. There seemed to be in Australia an assumption that trust automatically came with Australia's decision to commit ground forces, which was not the experience of those deployed. The military outcomes of Australia's alliance with the United States require constant work at many levels and ongoing and realistic assessment.

Operational lessons

Beyond the strategic-level lessons observed during this phase, three lessons stand out at the operational level. First, the Australian military overseas exchange program reaps dividends and must be continued. In 1998, I spent a year posted to the United States serving with different units of the US special operations fraternity. Fast forward to Afghanistan in 2001. Following our occupation of Kandahar airfield, we had identified some areas of interest in the Helmand region but were being denied the safe passage through Kandahar city necessary to travel to the Helmand area. The US Special Forces unit that, with Hamid Karzai and his Northern Alliance soldiers, had secured Kandahar city had either not received our formal requests or ignored them. My commanding officer and I travelled into Kandahar city to try to negotiate passage with the US Special Forces commander. Upon arriving at the makeshift US Special Forces Headquarters, I met a senior US warrant officer with whom I had worked closely while on exchange in the United States and who was now a senior member of this US Special Forces group. After recounting old times, he organised an immediate meeting with the US Special Forces commanding officer who, as it happens, I had met at a social function while on the same US exchange. The US commander promptly offered us passage through Kandahar city whenever we required it.

Admiral Bill McRaven, a former commander of US Special Operations Command, was fond of what he termed the Special Operations Force truth that 'you can't surge trust'. Notwithstanding my earlier comments regarding our broader military relationship and alliance with the United States, the one-on-one trust that is built through the exchange program has paid off at the tactical level time and again. It is important to note that the Australian Special Operations Commander in 2001, Major General Duncan Lewis, had attended the US Army War College. Additionally, one of the Australian deployed commanding officers in 2002 had attended the US Marine Corps Command and Staff College.

The second lesson concerns Australian national command. It would not be an Afghanistan discussion without mentioning command and control and, most particularly, what the term 'national command' actually means and how Australia applies it. Australia established a national commander and headquarters from 2001; the first national command headquarters was lean and comprised a commander, a handful of staff officers, some logistics personnel and a signals detachment.

Before deploying the first squadron, the then Chief of Defence Force, Admiral Chris Barrie, made it clear to my commanding officer that the 'national command' function had two purposes: first, a backstop and support should he face tasking that was outside the national interest, and second for Australia to exert influence at senior levels in the coalition. The national command function was not designed to command or control the commanding officer; rather its mandate was to allow him the freedom to make rapid decisions within Australia's strategic intent and, in so doing, exploit fleeting opportunities without reference to higher mission command.

Throughout 2002, and probably specifically after Operation ANACONDA, there was anxiety at senior levels within Defence that the Special Operations Task Force would draw itself further into whatever fight presented, regardless of national intent, and wedge the Australian Government into remaining committed to Afghanistan. This suspicion led to pressure on the national commander and his staff to be more involved in managing priorities and directing the Task Force and its actions.

Over the years, Australia's national command headquarters grew and on occasions seemed to assume a greater level of almost operational command of Australian task groups, parallel to and sometimes in competition with the coalition operational command and control arrangements. The Australian national command headquarters often provided outstanding support for deployed task groups; however, its status and responsibilities were inconsistent and seemed to depend on the intent of the appointed national commander rather than on the need or indeed direction from Canberra. The national command function started with a clear role and mandate that grew hazier. Certainly, each time I deployed I felt the need to test what it thought it was doing against what I had been briefed before departing Australia.[4]

The point is that the ADF needs to better define and implement the mandate, tasks and responsibilities of a national commander. Further, it needs to be clear on its national command and operational command and control models to ensure the most efficient employment of finite staff resources. One alternative model used by other nations was to add national command responsibilities as a function of its most senior deployed headquarters or staff, which in our case would have rested with the Task Force commander.

The third lesson concerns Army and ADF policy on a war footing. Despite the then ongoing operations in Timor Leste, Australia had not been engaged in many of the policy challenges that we faced since the Vietnam War. Rules of engagement for war, a lack of detention policy and a lack of detainee interrogation policy were a few of the operational issues that I had to work through. However, the most troubling issue was that of managing wounded soldiers back in Australia with what seemed primarily peacetime personnel policies. Quite different from today's practice, back in 2002 wounded soldiers had to comply with medical and fitness policies that did not seem to appreciate the impact of their war service.

In one case a soldier had lost a portion of his foot and significant leg function to an anti-personnel mine but was penalised for not being able to complete portions of the Army basic fitness assessment. While he ultimately and probably correctly discharged on medical grounds, upon return from that first tour it felt as if ADF policies were too slow to adapt

---

4   I served under its national command three times in eight years.

to the commitment of its people to war. Defence needs to ensure that its policies remain combat focused and do not lazily drift into those policy settings best for managing an ADF at peace.

Tactical lessons

Beyond the operational level, there are three tactical lessons that stand out from that first year of service in Afghanistan.

First, this was the first real dawning of the necessity of a new suite of enablers to which we were exposed, such as long endurance, armed Unmanned Aerial Vehicles. There was a growing awareness that Australian special forces needed to lift its modernisation game but without becoming over-reliant on technology. We had observed this over-reliance in the lead-up to Operation ANACONDA. Our Special Forces Task Force had independently discovered the significant al-Qaeda presence within the Shahi Kot valley a few months before Operation ANACONDA and was reporting from manned observation posts. The US command, however, ordered the Australian patrols to leave the area for fear of compromise, and instead manned and unmanned reconnaissance flights were flown to establish enemy dispositions. These flights failed to identify all of the enemy strong points that did much of the damage to coalition forces during the first hours and days of Operation ANACONDA. It was our view that the coalition was too reliant on technology for its reconnaissance and that reporting from manned SAS observation posts, combined with the overhead imagery, would have provided planners with a more complete picture of enemy dispositions. We believed that Australia needed to embrace new technology and ways of operating but that the soldier remained the critical piece. The answer was better enabled soldiers, not soldiers enabling technology.

Second, our tactical self-sufficiency was a key factor in our early success and overall reputation. While other coalition Special Operations Forces elements were competing for limited US vehicles and helicopters, the squadron's fleet of Long Range Patrol Vehicles, communications suite and fairly rough but workable logistics chain provided an agility that was attractive to the Americans, who needed to service the demands of a growing number of less robust coalition partners. The Australian force was light, agile, self-sufficient and therefore attractive to our US allies.

Third, the deployment validated the SAS maintaining a broad suite of equipment and capabilities. There had been much discussion in the 1990s about the SAS's focus, and at one stage the organisation debated disbanding the vehicle-mounted capability and disposing of the fleet of Long Range Patrol Vehicles. The first rotation validated the breadth of unit capabilities. The SAS squadron's ability to conduct a wide array of missions, from pinpoint direct-action attacks to reconnaissance across thousands of kilometres; the diverse skill sets, ability to plan and execute missions rapidly and such tactical skills as sniping and cold weather warfare were but some examples. The Special Forces Task Force delivered a high level of versatility, agility and adaptability that was attractive to the coalition command.

Exit strategy—mission accomplished or Iraq looming?

Beyond these strategic, operational and tactical lessons, I cannot comment on whether there was a formal exit strategy as its existence was never clear to me at the tactical level. Only those in the senior political and military machine at the time would be able to verify the existence of a formal exit strategy and whether such a strategy was used to guide key decisions throughout 2002. What I do know is that while the national intent and mission was clear, the strategy for exit was less so.

Some thought that there might be only one deployment of troops and that withdrawal would follow. Indeed, when the first commanding officer was rotated, it was widely communicated that his replacement was there to pack up and return the Task Force to Australia at the conclusion of Operation ANACONDA.

Around each rotation decision there were high-level teleconferences between Australia and the United States during which the United States pressured Australia to remain. Following Operation ANACONDA, Australia decided that it was so engaged in the fight and relied upon by the coalition that its forces should remain. So, in my view, the Australian Government decided to continue to commit ground forces not just for the sake of the US alliance but also because militarily Australia was delivering tactical effects upon which the coalition relied.

At the tactical level, the fairly blunt and unsophisticated view was that a one-year commitment would suitably demonstrate national will. A year also suited the SAS as it could be broken up into three four-month rotations, which would effectively manage the high intensity of the deployment and expose most soldiers to this combat environment. I doubt that anyone assessed at that point that the Australian special forces community would have more than enough exposure over the next 15 years.

Iraq was looming towards the end of 2002, and many at the tactical level felt that the evident geographic shift of US assets and the shift of US staff focus started to distract from the job in Afghanistan. The mission that underpinned the invasion of Afghanistan was, in my view, achieved by the end of 2002, so the force withdrawal in December of that year was prudent from an Australian national perspective. While I say this, one wonders what would have happened had it not been for the planning for the invasion of Iraq. I suspect that it was potential future operations that ultimately determined the timing of the withdrawal of Australian special forces from Afghanistan.

In terms of the decision to commence another operation in Iraq, my personal view in 2002–03 was that quite aside from the justification for invading Iraq, opening a second front in the Middle East at that time seemed militarily unwise. I viewed such a rapid pivot to Iraq as a military and strategic mistake, simply because it would stretch resources too thin, and that if the job in Afghanistan was to shift from countering terrorism to nation-building, then it was nowhere near done to the extent necessary for assets and staff to be reassigned to another invasion and major conflict.

Even in April 2002, my view was that the Taliban would return and behave in much the same way as the mujahideen of the 1980s. I did not share the view that even a massive military coalition had the resources to win, then hold Afghanistan and concurrently win in Iraq. My expectation was that in 2003, significant counter-attacks would be launched from countries bordering Afghanistan. In the end I was wrong, and the coalition faced only a limited insurgency in 2003. The Taliban could have made it more difficult in that first year of operations in Iraq; however, that was to come.

Conclusion

This first year and, indeed, the first rotation were wild times when boundaries were set only by where the enemy were. I had the view that rather than making history, our squadron was dropped in the middle of it. One day while on patrol I met a former Afghan mujahideen fighter from the Soviet era who handed me a photo of Ronald Reagan. On the back was written the name 'Mike' and a phone number. The Afghan told me that he had been 'working with Mike some time ago' but that his radio batteries had gone dead and he needed new batteries so they could get back in contact. 'Mike' was clearly of the US Central Intelligence Agency and had likely dumped this Afghan contact back in the 1980s when the Soviets withdrew from Afghanistan. I suspect that 'Mike's' CIA colleagues were probably as keen to speak to the Afghan contact now as he was to take their money. It struck me then that the game was back on and that, in an Afghan sense of time, the break between the Soviets and our invading force was merely a half time.

The missions and freedoms assigned to us in that 2001–02 period were an example of what right looks like, and Australia managed it well. Our task of removing a terrorist force and the conditions that allowed it to grow was clear, was aligned from the national through to tactical levels, and represented the essence of mission command. Its ultimate test was that it allowed deployed forces the necessary freedoms to best achieve Australia's national objectives, which the Task Force did. Although we did not find Bin Laden, the invasion was a success, the strategy and mission were clear and our exit roughly aligned with achieving that mission; denying al-Qaeda safe haven in Afghanistan.

5

Air Operations Control and Reporting Centre

Chris Westwood

Much had happened in Afghanistan following the withdrawal of the Special Forces Task Group in 2002. Australian land forces returned in 2005. Thereafter calls were being made for additional niche contributions, including critical capabilities in relatively short supply. This included calls for capabilities to manage the increasingly busy airspace over Afghanistan, such as the RAAF's Control and Reporting Centre (CRC), a field deployable unit designed to manage the use of airspace in a war zone.

The 2007–09 deployment of the RAAF's CRC was drawn from No. 41 Wing, Surveillance and Response Group (SRG). The CRC was responsible for deconflicting civilian and military air traffic over Afghanistan as well as ensuring that all military aircraft, both manned and remotely piloted, were properly marshalled within the area of operations. The CRC deployment represented only one small but important part of a significant RAAF contribution to operations during this period. This contribution included the following elements:

- Air Mobility—86 Wing (C-130 Hercules air transport and air-to-air refuelling aircraft)
- Heron unattended aerial vehicles—5 Flight (used for reconnaissance and surveillance)
- APC3 Orion surveillance aircraft—92 Wing (used for maritime as well as land surveillance over Iraq from 2005 onwards)

- Air Traffic Control—44 Wing (personnel deployed at various airfields alongside US and coalition counterparts)
- An Air Task Group, consisting of the following two components:
  1. Air Combat—81 Wing (F/A-18 Hornet fighter aircraft deployed particularly for Operation FALCONER in 2003 over Iraq)
  2. Air-to-Air Refuelling—33 Squadron (operating Boeing 707 and later KC-30 refuelling aircraft throughout the Persian Gulf region)
- Intelligence—87 Squadron (collection, analysis and reporting for deployed force elements)
- Medical—Aeromedical Evacuation, Role 2 (deployed with the land forces in Tarin Kowt, Uruzgan)
- Joint Terminal Attack Controller—4 Squadron (providing precision targeting assistance to deployed forces)
- Combined Air Operations Centre (CAOC; RAAF contribution comprising personnel assigned to various command, operations, intelligence and logistics appointments alongside US Air Force and other coalition personnel managing coalition air operations across the Middle East)
- Various units delivering communications, combat support and supplementing joint staff appointments
- Control and Reporting Centre (CRC)—41 Wing.

In short, for the period 2001–14, lots of great Air Force people were doing great things. The forthcoming official histories will provide coverage of the breadth and depth of the RAAF's operations in the Middle East.[1] So I will simply acknowledge the great achievements of the RAAF in general, and individual members in particular, and move on to the CRC.

A niche deployment such as the CRC is generally overshadowed in discussions regarding air power by fast jets and bombs. Perhaps not surprisingly given my background, I believe there is much to be learned from examination of these smaller capabilities such as the CRC. And lessons drawn from such examination are relevant not just to CRC or even broader command, control, communications, computer, intelligence, surveillance and reconnaissance (C4ISR) operations, but also for all small, high-end niche capabilities.

---

1   See Australian War Memorial, 'Historians: Official History of Australian operations in Iraq, Afghanistan and East Timor' at www.awm.gov.au/learn/understanding-military-history/official-histories/iraq-afghanistan-timor/oh (retrieved 21 October 2020).

5. AIR OPERATIONS CONTROL AND REPORTING CENTRE

RAAF Control and Reporting Centre, Kandahar, 2007–09.
Source: Courtesy of Air Commodore Chris Westwood.

Australian soldeirs check vehicles on a main supply route in Southern Iraq, 2008.
Source: Courtesy of the Department of Defence.

The CRC by definition includes sensors—in this case our own Lockheed Martin TPS-77 radar, plus access to all other deployed radars; an operations facility—contained within a series of ISO containers inside a large tent; and some link (military tactical data exchange networked communications) capabilities and facilities both at the CRC site and scattered around the theatre. The CRC compiled an air picture characterising the Afghanistan airspace from this facility and provided that to various agencies, primarily the CAOC. The CRC also used their air picture to provide 24/7 air battle management throughout the Afghanistan airspace.

The role of the CRC is simple: to ensure we have the right aircraft with the right weapons and fuel load in the right place at the right time to support the joint (interservice) fight—our priority was to support the troops in contact with adversaries.

This was the first RAAF CRC offshore operational deployment in 50 years. It was fair to say that at the time, while we were good at moving capabilities around Australia, we had little offshore deployment experience or culture, and operating inside a deployed Joint Task Force (JTF) was reasonably foreign. So we had a steep learning curve. However, there was no better operational or technical CRC capability of its type at the time on the planet—including the operators and technicians (and support staff) who were, and still are, highly trained.

In terms of operational statistics, there were 196,000 sorties that came through the CRC in the 23-month deployment, more than any operator would see in a full career. The CRC supported 7,000 troops in contact during that time—something we are particularly proud of. This was a busy operational deployment in the busiest airspace in the world at the time.

In addition to these key operational achievements, there were some impressive technical statistics as well. In the 23 months of operations, the capability operated 24/7, achieving close to 100 per cent availability. This was a big ask for this type of sensitive electronic equipment, which included many single points of failure, operating in such a harsh climatic zone and under considerable operational pressure. Credit needs to go to our outstanding technical teams who took these challenges in their stride.

Figure 1 shows the airspace divisions in Afghanistan at the time of the RAAF CRC deployment. There were three Air Battle Management agencies controlling three Afghanistan Battle Management Areas (BMAs): an RAF CRC ('Crowbar'), a US AWACS ('Wizard') and our RAAF CRC ('Taipan'). The RAAF CRC was the primary agency and had Operational Control (OPCON) of the RAF CRC and US AWACS. Effectively, the RAAF CRC 'controlled' the Afghanistan skies for 23 months. In the context of the ADF, this represents a historically significant achievement.

5. AIR OPERATIONS CONTROL AND REPORTING CENTRE

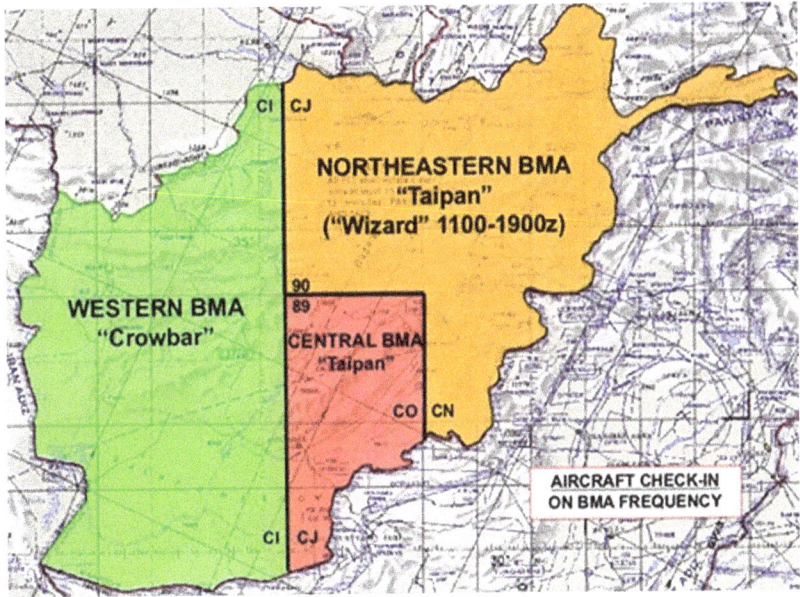

Figure 1: Afghanistan airspace.
Source: Courtesy of Air Commodore Chris Westwood.

Lessons

There were myriad lessons at all levels and from many perspectives concerning this deployment. In compiling these lessons, I spent a bit of time with many of the key players involved in the deployment. In particular, I would like to acknowledge Group Captain Richard Pizzuto. Richard was one of the deployment commanders and maintains a keen interest in capturing the history of the CRC deployment. I have collated these lessons into strategic, operational and tactical categories and listed the top ones of each.

Figure 2 shows a simplified command and control (C2) diagram. Operationally, the CRC worked for the CAOC. Everything was real time, which challenged those well-intentioned staff officers who were used to making decisions in days with well-crafted decision briefs.

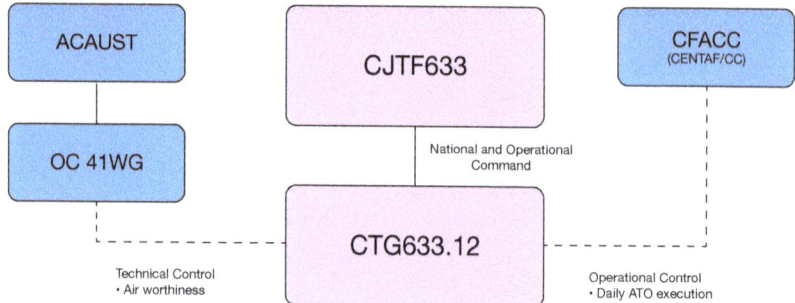

Figure 2: Control and Reporting Centre command and control arrangements.
Source: Courtesy of Air Commodore Chris Westwood.

Strategic lessons

The value of high-end niche capabilities such as this to Australia's alliance relationship with the United States cannot be overstated. US CRC capabilities were very tired, technically and personally. US Marines and USAF personnel had many rotations since 2001. Even in major forces, the pool of personnel and equipment available to service deployments of this type is limited and can be overused. Frankly, the US people and equipment were looking for an opportunity to reconstitute the force. Deploying the RAAF CRC into Kandahar for two years was a great way to give our US counterparts a well-earned and much-needed break—and they were extremely grateful.

Being offered a significant C2 role in a combined force, such as the Air Battle Management OPCON role of the CRC, with so much direct operational interaction with allied forces, demonstrated the trust the United States had in our CRC. Our operators and commanders had to be known and trusted by our allies, with compatible if not common doctrine and procedures. Things such as Air Battle Management, tanking (refuelling) procedures, 'Link 16' data communications doctrine and protocols and so on cannot be learnt on the fly. This underscores the importance of investment in high-end exercises to continually prepare and develop forces, and expose personnel to partners. Exercises such as Red Flag, where high-end capabilities can be tested and integrated with allies and put on show, are critical. Australian exercises need to be complex and attractive to the full range of partners, and need to include genuine, demanding, warlike scenarios. Trust is critical.

There is also a need to invest in education. Broad education among the key stakeholders can make or break a deployment. Very few people in the ADF, at all levels, understood the nuances of the CRC capability—which is perfectly understandable. The same, no doubt, is true for many current high-end niche capabilities such as electronic warfare, cyber and information operations for instance. More time spent demonstrating the CRC capability, and explaining where the 'one sizes fits all' mentality might not work, would have been useful. Niche technical capabilities of this type tend to be locked up and somewhat hidden behind secure doors. This is not always helpful. Everyone we depend on to make operational deployments successful needs to understand what these niche capabilities do and what their unique requirements might be.

Most important of all is relationships, of course. Knowing and trusting each other at all levels fixes most problems. Having RAAF officers as Deputy Combined Forces Air Component Command (CFACC) and CAOC directors, as well as valuing long-standing relationships between senior officers throughout the RAAF, the Australian Army and Navy, US forces and RAF, was a great aid in working through local issues—including getting the local C2 squared away. Likewise, relationships in Headquarters Joint Operations Command (HQJOC) at all levels helped work through many teething issues. Relationships always have been and always will be the key to success. Knowing each other through courses, exchanges and exercises can create the rapport and trust necessary to overcome problems at all levels.

Operational lessons

As I have mentioned, Afghanistan was the first deployment of the RAAF for 50 years. We, of course, had moved the CRC capability around Australia on many occasions, which did develop some reasonable technical deployment skills, but it was clear that some of the more JTF-level skills needed to be developed. The CRC team learnt quickly, but there were tears along the way.

For example, the CRC did not engage the JTF staff effectively in the pre-deployment phase. Hence JTF personnel did not understand the CRC's deployment needs, and CRC personnel did not understand their processes. The result was that pre-deployment reconnaissance was somewhat underdone. What should have been a dedicated activity was instead tagged on to a special forces reconnaissance, which clearly had different priorities. The CRC Recon Team was subsequently slashed—even losing the logistics officer. Deployment planning therefore became that much harder, and the advance party ultimately had a more difficult task as a result.

The CRC also had an unusual in-theatre training and assessment requirement for operators, which the JTF personnel staff never did quite get to grips with. This was the busiest operational airspace in the world. There was no way to simulate the intensity. None of the team had experienced the sheer volume of aircraft and the absolute urgency of operations. The Mission Rehearsal Exercise (MRE) that was developed by 41 Wing was as good as it could be, based on in-theatre Air Task Orders and Airspace Control Orders, and using a representative simulation capability. It was good enough for the USAF to adopt, but it still could not replicate the intensity or tempo of real operations. As such, operators were put through a 2–3-week training program on arrival in theatre before facing an assessment that, if passed, certified them for live operations. Unfortunately, a handful of operators (about eight over the 23 months of the deployment) could not make the jump from MRE to live operations, and they were tagged for compulsory return to Australia. This invariably invoked lengthy engagements with the JTF personnel and legal staff, who did not appreciate the due process and rigour that had already been applied; sometimes they insisted on adding their own review. Such reviews might take a week, during which time the CRC would be short an operator.

Being something of an unknown capability to many in the JTF and HQJOC, the CRC always forced an uphill battle to justify its existence or, more precisely, its workforce. This was a particular issue in Afghanistan, where the government imposed a hard limit on the number of 'boots on the ground'. The CRC had a 75-person footprint that replaced a US footprint approximately twice the size. That is not unusual. The ADF has long prided itself on multiskilling and doing more with less. This reflects the demands of operating a mid-size force with best of breed equipment. It seems fine on paper until illness strikes or when someone does not come up to speed and needs to be replaced. There were unique challenges in this regard, yet the operational personnel allocation table was considered sacrosanct. The concept of 'one size fits all' is outdated and largely irrelevant in a modern force.

Finally, at the operational level, I must mention the redeployment. 41 Wing (under the TECHCON umbrella) had planned the extrication of the CRC in detail to ensure the protection of millions of dollars' worth of equipment from packing and handling mistakes. The wing's concerns were not shared by the JTF staff, however, who insisted yet again on applying the standard model, a model that did not include the deployment of a specialist pack-up team as planned by the wing. The resulting damage to the $20 million radar when it struck the boom gate as it was driven off the site by a contractor easily accounted for any savings garnered by the decision not to deploy the specialist 41 Wing team.

Tactical lessons

One lesson at the tactical level concerned workforce sustainment. The CRC initially deployed for two rotations and one 12-month deployment. Once the deployment of the wing was extended (no real surprise), there were numerous workforce sustainment and concurrency issues, many unique to small, highly specialised capabilities of this type. My message is twofold: first, there is a clear need to be flexible and innovative as a whole force with workforce sustainment (medical, rotation durations and so on), and second, there is a need to listen to those who understand the specific workforce pressures of these capabilities. One size does not always fit all.

Summary

Overwhelmingly, this was a great deployment that achieved great results, and one of which those involved can be proud. That is important. The commitment and professionalism shown by the 400 or so ADF members who deployed with the CRC was yet another example of the remarkable people who serve in the ADF. And finally, there is plenty to learn about deploying niche capabilities. These will become more and more crucial to the joint and integrated force as fifth-generation technology takes hold. The lessons drawn from the CRC deployment are relevant for future high-end niche capabilities, be they cyber, electronic warfare or whatever comes next. So we should not be shy about discussing them now.

6

Conventional stability operations at the battle group level in Iraq

Anthony Rawlins

While Australia's military presence in Afghanistan ebbed and flowed, pressure was also on Australia to deploy land combat forces to support the coalition facing massive challenges in Iraq. On 16 July 2003, Operation FALCONER ceased and Operation CATALYST commenced, heralding a transition from a focus on combat operations towards the rehabilitation and reconstruction of Iraq.

In 2005 Australia committed the first of six conventional battle groups to security and stability operations in Iraq. This deployment was in direct response to broader US requests for increased coalition contributions to counter-insurgency operations. Australia's response focused on training indigenous Iraqi Security Forces to assume the lead for security under a new and democratically elected national government.

The decision to continue military operations remained a sensitive political issue. From the outset the decision to commit to the war in Iraq had never won bipartisan political or mainstream electoral support.[1] The government's decision to remain committed was carefully considered,

---

1 The Opposition Leader at the time, Simon Crean, stated: 'Labor opposes your commitment to war. We will argue against it and we will call for the troops to be returned.' House of Representatives debates, 18 March 2003, p. 12512, www.aph.gov.au/About_Parliament/Parliamentary_Departments/Parliamentary_Library/pubs/BN/0910/ParliamentaryInvolvement (retrieved 31 March 2020).

finely calibrated and specifically messaged: this was to be a transition from combat-focused operations reflecting ongoing coalition progress in Iraq.² Previously the government had sought to justify military commitments on the basis of Iraq's breaches of UN resolutions, catalogued in United Nations Resolution 1441. As counter-insurgency operations deepened, coalition casualties mounted, and the likelihood of discovering a WMD 'smoking gun' diminished, debate about the value and legitimacy of continued military participation escalated.

With the announcement of an imminent withdrawal of Dutch forces from Iraq's southern provinces, the government now contemplated a US request for an Australian force element to replace them. On 22 February 2005, Prime Minister John Howard announced the deployment of a conventional battalion-sized group to Al Muthanna Province, designated the Al Muthanna Task Group (AMTG). Its mission was to provide a stable and secure environment for the Japanese Reconstruction and Support Group undertaking humanitarian, engineering and reconstruction tasks in the area, and to assist in the training of Iraqi army units in the province.³ Working in support of the Interim Iraqi Government, AMTG-1 would provide a visible and tangible Australian contribution to multinational efforts to develop a more secure and stable Iraqi nation-state.

Over five subsequent evolutions, this task group, later redesignated the Overwatch Battle Group (West) (OBG(W)), undertook a variety of activities to expedite the capacity of Iraqi Security Forces and local government to buttress local security, support civic control and deliver good government. Australian forces oversaw the inaugural and largely successful transition of Al Muthanna and Dhi Qar provinces from coalition to Provincial Iraqi Control, the first two provinces in Iraq to achieve this milestone. Australian forces then transitioned into a loosely defined but ostensibly supportive 'operational overwatch' configuration until the last Australian battle group withdrew in 2008. Despite numerous engagements with adversary groups—particularly the Jaysh al-Mahdi militia (a group that emerged in 2003 led by firebrand Shia cleric Muqtada al-Sadr)—no Australian soldier from any contingent was killed in action. This combination of progressive Iraqi success, zero fatalities and American political praise for Australia's contribution has since facilitated generally positive mainstream analyses of Australian efforts on Operation CATALYST.⁴

---

2   Blaxland, *The Australian Army from Whitlam to Howard*, p. 218.
3   Department of Defence, *Annual Report 2004–05*, Department of Defence, Canberra, 2005, p. 161, www.defence.gov.au/annualreports/04-05/downloads/0405_dar_10_full.pdf (retrieved 31 March 2020).
4   See for instance Blaxland, *The Australian Army from Whitlam to Howard*, p. 244.

6. CONVENTIONAL STABILITY OPERATIONS AT THE BATTLE GROUP LEVEL IN IRAQ

Royal Australian Air Force F/A-18A Hornets prepare to depart on a mission to strike a Deash headquarters compound in Mosul, Iraq, from Australia's main air operating base in the Middle East region, 2016.
Source: Courtesy of the Department of Defence.

In contrast, the academic commentary has been more probing and the praise less effusive.[5] Analysis and critique has focused more on the motives and means by which this carefully nuanced military contribution achieved its professed political and strategic objectives. Although the general consensus suggests that Australia adroitly managed its participation and achieved its desired strategic outcomes at very little cost, some have contended that at the tactical level, Australia's reputation as a 'heavy lifter' in the coalition community actually suffered. Within the Australian Army itself, a parallel and equally critical dialogue appraising the means by which senior leadership chose to manage the political–strategic military requirement for government has also been evident.

This academic dialogue formed the touchstone for my presentation to the 'War in the Sandpit' seminar at Gallipoli Barracks, Enoggera, on 12 May 2017. Invited to speak as a former Commanding Officer of Overwatch Battle Group (West)-2 (OBG(W)-2), I chose to recount my experience of the deleterious impact of strategic–tactical dissonance during this deployment; that is, the subtle but visceral impact on the practice of mission command emanating from uncertainty as to the strategic objective of the mission. I settled on this approach following near-unanimous concurrence among six the AMTG and OBG(W)

---

5 Ibid., pp. 244–5.

commanders that higher-order strategic imperatives—specifically, a clear national intent—had not been adequately or accurately communicated to the tactical level of command. The consequences, certainly in my own personal experience, manifested in some strategically counter-intuitive and tactically debilitating outcomes unlikely to have been evident at the highest levels of command, but which I now recognise as needing to be highlighted as containing important lessons for the future.

My observations, assessments and deductions on this issue, presented to many academic, military and political leaders at the seminar, proved polarising. Not surprisingly, in the post-seminar wash-up, my observations seemed to resonate favourably with those who operated at the tactical level but attracted scepticism amounting to outright rejection the more senior the stakeholder involved was in the chain of command, particularly so the more personal their involvement in the planning or execution of Operation CATALYST. Some media personalities saw my assessments as a potential smoking gun, seemingly confirming their long-held suspicions of duplicity between the government's declared and unstated motives for engagement in Iraq and its commitment to coalition efforts. Despite what some might have thought, my motives were neither to denigrate my military superiors, criticise government capacity or commitment to furthering Australia's national interests, nor the means chosen to achieve them. Nor was it to suggest that Australia should have committed more heavily to combat operations during Operation CATALYST.

Rather, my intent—which can be more fully outlined in this chapter—was to examine in greater detail the means by which our military elected to exercise command and control, and apply the concept of mission command in the conduct of security and stability operations in Iraq. Not surprisingly, in light of my own and most of my counterpart commanding officer experiences, this examination has precipitated a reasonably critical view of our command and control architecture, emanating from what I do believe to have been the highly politically charged and nationally sensitive nature of this operation.

In attempting to understand why a restrictive and directive means of national command and control was employed, undermining the practice of mission command at the tactical level, I have relied upon third-party assessments. I must emphasise that I was not privy to the discussions and debate at the strategic and operational levels that would no doubt have informed the development of this command and control system.

Very few at the most senior levels of command would have been party to these discussions. Nevertheless, in my own mind, the search for reasons is important, given that the tenets of mission command were both doctrinally prescribed and professionally accepted in the Australian Army at that time, yet were seemingly either consciously or subconsciously discarded during many of the task or battle group deployments.

In the final analysis, much (I now suspect) revolves around the question of whether there was an express or implied direction for Australian battle groups to limit operational activity to avoid casualties. To this day I can neither unequivocally confirm nor deny whether this was the case; although it was certainly a topic of hot discussion within most contingents, no such direction (to my knowledge) has been confirmed as either an express or implied requirement. At best my personal experience and discussion with other tactical commanders confirms that remained a metaphoric 'elephant in the room' for most contingents deployed on Operation CATALYST.

This chapter therefore allows me to amplify the position put forward in my verbal presentation to the 'War in the Sandpit' seminar. It outlines my personal understanding of the background, objectives and nature of tactical operations in Iraq during Operation CATALYST. It leverages third-party accounts of the strategic and operational decision-making processes to discover what the national strategic intent might have been, which would have informed force design and development of a command and control architecture to give best effect to the political objective. It is my personal view, and that of most of my counterpart commanders on Operation CATALYST, that the command and control architecture chosen and employed was non-doctrinal and suboptimal for prosecuting contemporary operations. Our recounted experiences suggest the exercise of mission command at the strategic through to tactical levels was frequently undermined by an unfamiliar national command framework. This chapter seeks to discover the reason for this and in so doing highlights a potential lesson for Army: the importance of communicating strategic intent down to the tactical level as an essential prerequisite for the practice of mission command on complex operations.

The strategic context

Essential reading for anyone interested in Australia's military activities in Iraq is the abridged history and analytical study of the war in Iraq by Albert Palazzo, *The Australian Army and the War in Iraq: 2002–2010*. The Australian Army directed Professor Palazzo to undertake this study in order to critically review Australia's involvement in this contemporary campaign for future learning. His work, heavily redacted for release at the unclassified level, still provides a comprehensive history and—for many—a broad-ranging insight into the operational and strategic considerations at play at the time.

His study highlights that the commitment of Australian forces to Iraq, from the commencement of combat operations through to stability and security operations, remained a politically sensitive issue for government. The conduct of this seminar confirms that many in the policy and academic community are comfortable with recognising that a principal determinant in Australia's decision to commit to the war in Iraq was a calculated intent to enhance the strategic relationship between Australia and the United States. The seminar served to further confirm the strategic intent and outcome suggested by Palazzo in the Lowy Institute's blog, *Interpreter*:

> Australia joined the war to advance its own policy objective: to improve its relationship with its great power protector. It achieved this goal with great skill and at very little cost, and showed that it is possible for a junior partner to advance its strategic interests within a coalition dominated by a great power. For Australia, what mattered most was not what was happening in Baghdad but in Washington.[6]

---

6   A. Palazzo, 'The making of strategy and the junior coalition partner: Australia and the 2003 Iraq War', *Infinity Journal*, art. 6, vol. 2, no. 4, 2012, pp. 27–30, quoted in Palazzo, 'We went to Iraq for ANZUS', *Interpreter*, 25 March 2013, www.lowyinstitute.org/the-interpreter/we-went-iraq-anzus (retrieved 31 March 2020).

A trooper from the 2nd Cavalry Regiment provides security to Japanese Iraq Reconstruction Group convoy vehicles in As Samawah, 2005.
Source: Courtesy of the Department of Defence.

This policy objective, coupled with the political landscape, would have heavily influenced military planning, force design and the selection of operational areas for Australian forces. It would also have informed mission specification, pre-deployment training and the overarching national command and control architecture. In contrast to the more combat-oriented counter-insurgency operations being undertaken by US and British forces, the Australian mission set was carefully calibrated to enliven the strategic focus on provincial reconstruction and rehabilitation. Nevertheless, given the potential sensitivity of the electorate to Australian casualties, design and provisioning of the force ensured that it would be capable of defending itself in combat operations against any conceivable adversary in its area of operations.

The prescribed area of operations and mission set for the inaugural AMTG deployment clearly reflected these strategic considerations. In the largely peaceful province of Al Muthanna, AMTG-1 was to provide a stable and secure environment for the Japanese Reconstruction and Support Group undertaking humanitarian, engineering and reconstruction tasks in southern Iraq, and to assist in the training of Iraqi army units. The force, a 'square' battle group comprising a light armoured (cavalry) squadron and a protected motorised infantry company, along with combat support and combat service support company-sized subunits, was deemed more than capable of overmatching expected levels of opposition in the area.

However, during the third AMTG rotation, the Japanese force withdrew from theatre as Al Muthanna transitioned to Provincial Iraqi Control. This transition in July 2006 marked the formal handover of primary security duties for the province from coalition forces to the Iraqi Government and its indigenous security forces. With this change, the ostensible and predominant function of Australian military forces in Al Muthanna had been removed. AMTG-3 therefore relocated to Ali Air Base, Tallil, in the neighbouring province of Dhi Qar. By way of new function, the task group was now assigned the rather ill-defined task of operational overwatch of Al Muthanna Province, which still entailed continued training and development of Iraqi Security Forces under the capstone program known as Mentor, Monitor and Train (M2T).

Dhi Qar was the next province to transition to Provincial Iraqi Control on 21 September 2006, as the Italian contribution previously overseeing provincial security withdrew in the following month. In response to coalition (predominantly US) representations to replace them, Australia agreed additionally to assume operational overwatch of Dhi Qar Province, and with this expansion and consolidation of duties the AMTG was then retitled the Overwatch Battle Group West (OBG(W)), with AMTG-3 becoming the inaugural OBG(W)-1.

This change in title reflected a fundamental change in the mission and objectives of the Australian force, with the battle group being more heavily focused on training and developing the capacity of the Iraqi Security Forces while maintaining a preparedness posture to provide support if the security situation degenerated beyond their capacity. However, the simple reality is that this 'intervention' posture was more illusory than real, crafted more to bolster the confidence of the local Iraqi Security Forces than to backstop them militarily. Operational overwatch was also cleverly conceived to present a positive strategic picture of Australia as a coalition partner engaged in 'heavy lifting', particularly as the insurgency in Iraq grew increasingly virulent, although the scale and intensity of counter-insurgent activities in Al Muthanna and Dhi Qar provinces remained well below the national average.

I describe the mission set of 'overwatch' as something of a facade on the basis that the provision of combat support to the Iraqi Security Forces was really nothing more than a fictional construct, and the provision of combat support resided well outside the decision authority of the local battle group commander. Activation required a complex, lengthy and largely ill-defined series of approvals from local to national Iraqi, coalition and then Australian governmental approval chains. It was made clear to successive tactical commanders that Australia would approve such a request only on formal application from the government of Iraq to the Australian Government, requiring that government prove that the situation outstripped the capacity and capability of national security resources. Iraqi Government inability or unwillingness to commit national resources would not constitute sufficient reason for the battle group to engage in supportive combat operations. In a hypothetical crisis, this high threshold for action meant that any Australian intervention would have come late, following the commitment and overmatch of all national and other regional coalition forces in order to stabilise the situation before it spiralled out of control and generated a public affairs disaster for the coalition.

This arrangement meant that there was never any conceivable likelihood of the battle group being able to support local Iraqi forces constructively and decisively in combat operations to maintain stability in the province, at least not before it had escalated out of control, requiring a larger and more immediate coalition intervention to stabilise the situation.

This significant practical impediment was certainly not reflected in the Multi-National Division – South East (MND-SE) mission orders for the Australian force. In order to manage British (and potentially also US) expectations, it meant that the bulk of OBG(W) activity focused on supporting activities to maintain stability in the provinces, rather than actively pursuing destabilising elements. This translated into daily activity sets including Key Leadership Engagement (KLE) with local leaders, collective and individual training of provincial leaders and Iraqi army elements, force protection of coalition forces and installations, and intermittent support to various local Provincial Reconstruction Teams (PRTs). These efforts have been accurately characterised as 'preventing the insurgent's cause from gaining purchase in the prevailing society' rather than on combat operations against the enemy.[7] It proved—in large measure—to be a successful approach, although it was periodically upset by events occurring in other parts of Iraq, which served also to destabilise the local security situation.

---

7   Blaxland, *The Australian Army from Whitlam to Howard*, p. 242.

It is a matter for historical record that, over time, the insurgency in Iraq grew ever more emboldened, increasingly contesting the authority and control of national and provincial governments and the capabilities of the Iraqi Security Forces. This national trend periodically affected southern Iraq, most notably during coalition counter-insurgent surge periods in central and northern Iraq. It translated into more dangerous operating conditions for several OBG(W) rotations, particularly in the conduct of movement, patrols and KLE in Dhi Qar Province. It was frequently asserted that the former Italian contingent had negotiated an agreement or 'detente' of sorts with the Jaysh al-Mahdi militia in Dhi Qar Province. In exchange for some measure of financial assistance, the Italian contingent could operate without the militia contesting their presence. This arrangement was never confirmed, but it goes without saying that a 'contract' of this nature would never have been contemplated by—let alone authorised for—Australian forces operating in Iraq. In accordance with the operational mission specified in orders from Headquarters MND-SE, OBG(W)-2 thus began to expand its capstone overwatch and training activities into Dhi Qar Province, bringing it into closer contact with insurgent forces frequently using Dhi Qar as a 'rest and recreation' locale from insurgency activity in other parts of Iraq.

This seems to have been the catalyst for increased scrutiny and directive control from the national command chain, as OBG(W)-2 began to orient towards the operational overwatch and friendly force protection components of the mission in response to local assessments of security conditions. This reorientation inevitably brought the battle groups into closer contact with the Jaysh al-Mahdi militia, the stakeholder most likely to contest their presence. Attacks on coalition logistic convoys and indirect fire attacks against the Tallil Air Base also began to increase at this time. This deterioration in provincial security conditions and the greater level of insurgent activity in Dhi Qar Province might have tripped risk sensitivities in the Australian national chain of command. This in turn gave rise to a perception of increased scrutiny and intervention in tactical decision-making by the Australian headquarters of Joint Task Force 633 (JTF 633), ostensibly to assess and regulate tactical activities in Dhi Qar in accordance with Australian national intent.

Certainly, during the OBG(W)-2 deployment, the Australian national commander in JTF 633 now specified a requirement for advance notification of all tactical activities through provision of plans and orders to the national headquarters in Baghdad. This gave rise to frequent episodes of Commander JTF 633 reserving (and frequently exercising) the right to veto tactical activities, including patrols aimed to counter improvised explosive devices (IEDs), interdicting the main coalition supply route from Kuwait to Baghdad, and clearing patrols to known rocket launch sites. This veto frequently took the form of directing the commanding officer to canvas other coalition forces on Tallil Air Base to execute these activities, all well understood to be within the Australian mission remit according to operational orders from Headquarters MND-SE. This approach generated significant tension between myself and the commander of JTF 633, as I continually asserted that these tasks were well within our mission set. It also generated tension between the OBG(W) and local coalition force elements, given their loss of confidence in Australian capability and resolve, which also gravely wounded morale within the Australian contingent. The question of just why we were frequently precluded from executing approved mission sets for which we had been trained and assessed as mission capable during our final Mission Rehearsal Exercise was the source of great confusion among the contingent.

This dissonance between implied strategic intent and tactical freedom of action during my deployment suggested a critical omission in the national command architecture—a failure effectively to communicate national intent or strategic objectives from which we could purposefully orient our tactical actions. We understood our tactical mission and tasks articulated in the operations order from Headquarters MND-SE, which was provided in the traditional, well-understood coalition mission orders format. These orders expressly contemplated combat action against the insurgency in support of provincial stability and security, support to friendly forces in contact, and integral force protection activity. To my recollection, each and every task and battle group before ours had extensively trained to this mission set during its Mission Specific Training and Mission Rehearsal Exercise before deployment. These were enduring tasks, and while they were articulated in the UK-led Headquarters MND-SE operations order, they had been ratified by previous Australian national command chains so as to inform Mission Specific Training and Mission Rehearsal Exercise training and certification.

The Australian national command also intervened in the tactical activities of other task and battle group contingents. This was presumably to ensure that tasks allocated in mission orders from Headquarters MND-SE did not breach or contravene Australian national interests. This in theory should not have presented a problem, as this is the express role and function for a national command entity in Australian operational doctrine. The problem was manifest in its execution rather than the theory.

Herein lay the essential problem for myself and many other tactical commanders attempting to execute operational orders from Headquarters MND-SE: what were Australia's national interests in southern Iraq? Without this clear articulation at the tactical level of command, the only means by which Australian national interests could be properly interpreted, preserved and/or protected was through incessant intervention by the national command chain to authorise, modify or veto tactical activities based upon an isolated and segregated assessment of strategic intent. This translated into a highly variable level and poor understanding of the risk management frameworks of each national commander.

The criticality of communicating national intent

Australian military doctrine itself highlights that without clear articulation of intent, the foundational basis for the application of mission command will be absent. ADF doctrine directs commanders to make sure that subordinate commanders *understand* the higher commander's intent, their own missions and the operational context before planning tactical activity. Articulation of intent forms the conceptual basis for mission command, as subordinates can then be told what effect they are to achieve and the reason it is necessary. Their superior commander will tell them what to achieve, but should not tell them how to achieve it—the 'how' is the preserve of the tactical commander, who is acknowledged as being in the best position to read and understand local conditions and situational variables.[8]

---

8   Land Warfare Doctrine 0-0, 'Command, Leadership and Management', chapter 2, section 2-2, 10 June 2008, para 12.

6. CONVENTIONAL STABILITY OPERATIONS AT THE BATTLE GROUP LEVEL IN IRAQ

An F/A-18 waits its turn to refuel over Iraq during Operation Falconer, 2003.
Source: Courtesy of the Department of Defence.

The experiences of Australia's tactical commanders on Operation CATALYST suggest that this most basic of doctrinal stipulations was at best only partially enacted, often in an ad hoc and informal manner. The commanding officer of the first Al Muthanna Task Group (AMTG-1), then Lieutenant Colonel Roger Noble, recalls that the strategic intent for the mission was verbally communicated to him by both the Chief of Defence Force (CDF) and Chief of Army (CA) before his deployment. However, written versions of Australian strategic and operational orders were neither drafted nor made available until well into the AMTG-1 deployment. Given that he recalls writing his own mission orders in the absence of anything other than verbal context, it is likely that national orders were retrospectively drafted to conform to the tactical orders he had written. By way of comparison, Noble recalls the operational orders provided by the higher coalition headquarters (MND-SE) to be both precise and well articulated, with clear intent provided in both written and verbal media. Somewhat incongruously, he recalls a lack of interaction with the Australian theatre commander, Chief of Joint Operations (CJOPS), until such time as his first visit during the deployment. This suggests either an implicit acceptance that coalition orders were compatible with Australia's strategic intent or, alternatively, that either the tactical commander or Australian national commander would be required to manage and ameliorate any inconsistency on the ground.

AMTG-1 was the inaugural deployment and at short notice, and therefore an element of 'catch-up' could be countenanced. Subsequent commanders did not receive a similar level of pre-deployment interaction with either CDF, CA or CJOPS, thereby precluding this personal conveyance of strategic intent. In the absence of this personal interaction and clear written articulation of national intent, most tactical commanders have expressed different levels of confidence that the strategic intent was sufficiently discoverable or could be properly implied. Of those most confident that the strategic context and command intent was implicitly discernible, the commanding officer of AMTG-3/OBG(W)-1 recalls:

> [R]eviewing the intent that I drafted as part of our in-theatre review (completed at the end of the first month in theatre) it was pretty clear that I understood the strategic aim ... In terms of Australian interests it was clear to me that we had an 'enabling role' and that the confluence between tactical mission and Australian interests lay in us providing an 'overt demonstration of relevance and the continual delivery of positive outcomes or effects'. The Task Group had 'to provide a balanced, agile and highly relevant military response'. The mission was on the nose politically and the US was in the midst of the 'cut and run' debate so it was clear that at the political–strategic level our masters were searching for answers and leaning very heavily on the military to come up with a solution. This was clear across the board within the coalition chain of command. I knew I wasn't going to get any coherent guidance and decided to embark on our own approach[,] building on the conceptual work done by AMTG-2.[9]

Other commanders, however, cite lower levels of confidence in attempting to discern the strategic intent in light of the evolving political context. This was my own personal experience. Despite the extensive mission specific training and Mission Rehearsal Exercise regime, I remained unsure as to what express or implied strategic caveats or limitations would circumscribe my tactical freedom of action. I therefore undertook a self-funded trip to Canberra during my pre-deployment leave in order to gain a better understanding of the strategic context and any national caveats from our strategic headquarters in Canberra. I particularly wanted to confirm the veracity of rumours circulating in our mounting base that we were to avoid casualties at all costs.

---

9   Discussions with author.

I therefore organised an impromptu visit to Military Strategic Commitments at Russell Offices in Canberra. None of the senior appointments were available for me at the time I visited. In speaking to the relevant desk officer for Operation CATALYST, asking for advice as to what I needed to do to meet the strategic intent and what I needed to avoid, the response was disappointingly blithe and vague. The advice was simply 'Just don't f*#k it up' [sic]. When I asked what this actually meant, I was told that I would very quickly discover what I was doing wrong if I 'skied off-piste'. At his level of authority and understanding, the desk officer simply could not cogently articulate what sort of things were 'on' and what was 'off-piste'. It was not very reassuring, but by the same token I was relatively comfortable that the pre-deployment training had provided me with an operative understanding of what we were there to do, and what tools and tactics were available to me as a commander in seeking to execute this amorphous 'national intent' in the absence of specific national orders.

Other tactical commanders recount a similar personal requirement to determine implied strategic intent through their mission analysis process. The provision of coalition operational orders during pre-deployment training provided a solid understanding of coalition operational intent. However, Australia's military orders tended to focus almost exclusively on the administrative or procedural aspects of constituting, concentrating and deploying the force into theatre. Reassurance was derived from the assertion that operational orders from Headquarters MND-SE had been vetted at the Australian theatre command level, and it was assumed that instructions to overcome any incongruence would be articulated in individual directives, national orders from Headquarters JTF 633 or in the CJOPS campaign plans. As a matter of doctrine, they would also be addressed 'on occurrence' by the national command chain in theatre—the *raison d'être* for a national commander in theatre. But the lack of a clear, cogent statement of national intent through the doctrinally accepted orders process clearly complicated the pre-deployment preparation of respective force elements. A heavy focus on the administrative and governance aspects of deployment served more to distract rather than assist tactical commanders in this respect. The commanding officer of AMTG-3/OBG(W)-1 recalled:

> The hierarchy of military orders didn't flow naturally within the coalition but, as mentioned before, I was conscious of the dissonance within the coalition and also of the governance focused (and therefore limited utility) of national directives. By way of example, the mounting order out of Headquarters 1st Division came too late to make any difference and the deployment order arrived a day after our advance party had left.[10]

This diffuse process also resulted in a lack of discernible communication as to any national caveats or 'red cards' to the tactical commanders through Australia's operational chain of command, at least not before interaction with the national commander in theatre.

However, if the national intent or caveats took time to discern for Australia's tactical commanders, there was little doubt that—over time—they came to be well understood by the higher coalition headquarters. In the short period in the transition between the first and second AMTGs, it appears that Headquarters MND-SE had already determined that national strategic intent was curtailing the Australian tactical commander's freedom of action. This interpretation was not complimentary, but it was generally understanding of the circumstances in which the Australian force element had to operate. The Commanding Officer AMTG-2 lamented:

> I never received orders. I just took Roger's orders and typed a '2' over the '1' and no-one noticed. By the time I arrived in theatre, the Brits had given up on us as far as contributing to their plan. The British Brigade Commander in Basra gave me his Brigade operational orders and asked me to fill in the blanks for AMTG-2—this is true! As there was no formal direction from Australia, I therefore made it up. No one ever took me aside and told me what the actual (not for public consumption) reason for us was for us being in Iraq. It certainly wasn't to defeat anti-Iraqi Government forces and it was also evident that the Japanese weren't totally incapable of looking after themselves. I had a conversation with Chief of Army just before we left and confirmed the real reason, but it wasn't until day 3 on the ground in theatre when I think when I realised that all we could do was stuff things up ... As-Samawah was as good as it was ever going to get![11]

---

10 Discussions with author.
11 Discussions with author.

As foreshadowed earlier, this absence or informality in the articulation of strategic intent was accompanied by a bureaucratic and forensic involvement in the administrative aspects of the deployment by various headquarters in the national command chain. According to the commanding officer of AMTG-3/OBG(W)-1:

> the operational concepts were developed by us and briefed to all of the supporting commanders and also those in our tactical chain, and they were agreed without too much fuss. Fortunately, no one else was doing it at the time and, although some train-spotting [i.e. higher-level engagement with the details of our planning] occurred, it was inconsequential. Orders were largely written by us for insertion into the relevant orders (mainly divisional orders). HQ JTF 633 orders were largely administrative.[12]

The commanding officer of AMTG-2 similarly recalls an absence of articulation of national strategic intent, coupled with an overbearing and unhelpful focus on administrative control driven by internal military politicking:

> In the early days, AMTG was to be a 12-month commitment with two six-month tours, the 2nd Cavalry Regiment being first. I was involved in much of the early discussions and planning as it was obvious to us in 1 Brigade that the follow-on force would have to be 5/7 RAR. What I didn't factor on was a senior officer in Headquarters 1 Division wanting a 3 Brigade unit to go next. It meant that for the next four months, I had no authority to spend money or do anything really to prepare the force (training, equipment and even my reconnaissance) and everything I did was through begging, borrowing, stealing and bluffing. I had to fight constant little 'pissant' battles to get simple requests filled like automatic sniper rifles, and if it wasn't for Chief of Army showing such an interest in us and thus being available for me to speak directly to when he visited, I wouldn't have got the very little I asked for. In the end, I was described by a colonel in Army Headquarters as a 'typical whinging CO'. I also had to deal with personnel and families who wanted to know what was going on, plans, career courses, postings, and the like. I rolled the dice and bluffed through it, telling everyone it was up to us to do.[13]

---

12 Discussions with author.
13 Discussions with author.

These experiences suggest that there were significant deficiencies in the articulation of intent at the operational level in Australia's chain of command, potentially owing to a more incumbent focus on the administrative aspects of preparing and deploying operational contingents. Nonetheless, it seems clear from a subsequent reading of Palazzo's study that Australia's strategic leaders had actually developed and were maintaining a high level of strategic unity. This seemed to have been well in place during the inaugural Australian deployment, with the commanding officer of the first AMTG recalling:

> [The Chief of the Defence Force] articulating his intent and then reinforcing this during his visits meant that it worked—without that we would have deployed with no orders. Actually, both the Prime Minister and Minister for Defence were also very clear on their intent when they visited us.[14]

Although in Palazzo's estimation politico-military unity might have endured throughout Operation CATALYST, the articulation of national intent and military strategic objectives down through the operational to tactical levels clearly seems to have fallen away in subsequent rotations. This might have been because the political and military strategic leadership remained confident that the initial parameters had been set by the first AMTG deployment; therefore only minimal ongoing dialogue was required to maintain a steady state. Alternatively, it might have been that as the tactical situation on the ground became more dangerous, particularly with the assumption of responsibilities in Dhi Qar Province, the risk of Australian casualties demanded closer scrutiny and control of tactical activities by the Australian national command. Irrespective of either possible motivation, what resonates most strongly is a definitive procedural failure to convey the strategic intent—the fundamental strategic context—down to the tactical level as the tenets of mission command suggest is essential for unity of effort.

---

14 Discussions with author.

Intent and the practice of mission command

Articulation of command intent, from strategic down to tactical levels, forms a bedrock principle of the philosophy of mission command. Without this clear articulation, unity and synchronisation of effort suffer:

> Mission command and control relies on the use of mission tactics in which seniors assign missions and explain the underlying intent but leave subordinates as free as possible to choose the manner of accomplishment. Commanders seek to exercise a sort of command by influence, issuing broad guidance rather than detailed directions or directives. The higher the level of command, the more general should be the supervision and the less the burden of detail. Commanders reserve the use of close personal supervision to intervene in subordinates' actions only in exceptional cases. Thus, all commanders in their own spheres are accustomed to the full exercise of authority and the free application of judgment and imagination. Mission command and control thus seeks to maximize low-level initiative while achieving a high level of cooperation in order to obtain better battlefield results.[15]

Australian Defence Doctrinal Publication 0.01 (ADDP 0.01) and Land Warfare Doctrine 0-0 (LWD 0-0) are typical of the genre in that they restate most of the universally accepted prerequisites for the successful application of mission command. These include the concepts and precepts of doctrine, reliability, trust, understanding and risk.[16] Western military doctrine specifies that for mission command to be effective, each tenet must be well understood and accepted at all levels of command, and then vigorously enacted in practice.

However, during Operation CATALYST, the philosophy of mission command was not formally entrenched as the joint command philosophy for the conduct of operations by deployed forces. The ADF's capstone command and control publication in effect at the time was *Australian*

---

15   United States Marine Corps, *Command and Control*, Doctrine Publication 6, Department of the Navy, Washington, DC, 1996, pp. 109–10, www.marines.mil/Portals/1/Publications/MCDP%206.pdf?ver=2019-07-18-093633-990 (retrieved 31 March 2020).
16   Land Warfare Doctrine 0-0, 'Command, Leadership and Management', chapter 2, section 2-2, 10 June 2008, para 13.

Defence Force Joint Operational Command and Control,[17] issued on 14 December 2001, operative as interim command and control doctrine until formally superseded by Australian Defence Doctrine Publication 00.1 (ADDP 00.1), *Command and Control*, on 27 May 2009.[18]

Nevertheless, at this time subscription to the philosophy of mission command as an operational command and control construct was well established within the Australian Army. At the time Land Warfare Doctrine 0.0 (LWD 0.0) *Command, Leadership and Management* prescribed mission command as the Army's extant philosophy of command and control system for the conduct of operations. In advocating the well-established tenets of mission command, it specified that subordinates were to be given a clear indication of their commander's intent—the result required, the task, resources and any applicable constraints—but the subordinate commander was to be afforded freedom to decide how to achieve the required result.[19]

Equivalent doctrine and practice was also operative among the various nations commanding and controlling operations in Iraq, most notably the US and British contingents. The Australian concept of mission command had been closely modelled on equivalent US and UK doctrine, and was therefore consistent with Multi-National Force – Iraq (MNF-I) and Multi-National Division – South East command and control systems. MNF-I and MND-SE mission orders were developed and executed on the basis of the tenets of mission command familiar to Australian military forces. All the Australian commanders throughout this period readily acknowledge that the philosophy of mission command was applied as the capstone command philosophy in the development of their operational and tactical mission orders.

---

17 *Australian Defence Force Joint Operational Command and Control*, Provisional Edition, Commonwealth of Australia, 14 December 2001.
18 Australian Defence Doctrine Publication 00.1 (ADDP 00.1), *Command and Control*, formally introduced mission command as applicable to the ADF, stating: '[T]he ADF has adopted a command philosophy known as "mission command" that promotes flexibility by rewarding initiative, ingenuity, innovation, resourcefulness, and devolution of authority in achieving the commander's intent. Understanding the strategic and operational context within the joint operational framework allows tactical commanders to react quickly and appropriately to demanding situations.' ADDP 0.01, *Command and Control*, para 2.18, p. 2-8.
19 Land Warfare Doctrine 0.0, 'Command, Leadership and Management', Department of Defence (Australian Army), Canberra, 17 November 2003.

Similarly, Australian commanders unanimously confirm that during the conduct of pre-deployment training, mission command was empowered and employed, including the development and execution of operational orders. Following the original AMTG-1 deployment, extant operational orders from higher coalition headquarters in Iraq were always made available, allowing the deploying force to develop its derivative operational orders. These coalition mission orders had all been 'vetted' and approved by Australian national commanders at the theatre command level. While some specific caveats on such issues as national rules of engagement and compliance with specific international and domestic legal considerations were widely acknowledged and accepted by coalition commanders, no task or battle group commander could recall any specific operational caveats placed upon any missions or tactical objectives assigned to them by Headquarters MND-SE.

These factors suggest that all the essential precursors for the effective application of mission command were functionally in place for Australian forces, particularly given that the campaign in Iraq was predominantly a land component operation with army commanders in command at coalition and Australian strategic, operational and tactical levels of command. Accordingly, it is clear that the underpinning philosophy for command and control in Iraq was in fact *mission command*; that is, the superior commander would direct *what* was to be achieved while leaving the subordinate commander free to decide *how* to achieve the assigned tasks.[20]

The experiences of many task and battle group commanders was that this was variably practised, with different levels of application depending upon the command style and approach of respective national commanders. Given Palazzo's assertion of strong politico-military unity, leading to potentially invasive strategic control at the tactical level, I therefore sought the views and experiences of Australia's task and battle group commanders in terms of understanding how three essential elements of mission command were applied in practice during their deployments. My enquiry centred on three broad questions: first, whether the national strategic intent was clearly conveyed to them; second, whether this allowed them to reconcile potentially divergent Australian and coalition tactical requirements; and

---

20   ADDP 0.01, *Command and Control*, para 2.19, p. 2-8.

third, whether the exercise of Australian national command affected their ability to apply mission command in seeking to achieve both coalition and national objectives.

What follows are select snapshots of the experiences of several of Australia's tactical commanders in an attempt to reconcile Palazzo's assertion of strategic success with the suboptimal conditions experienced in the application of mission command on the ground. I have sought to understand whether the Australian philosophy of mission command was actually applied, and, if it were effectively applied under these conditions, whether it might have contributed to the successful strategic outcome described in Palazzo's study.

In correlating their experiences, it appears that the unreliable transmission of national or strategic intent through the layers of command might also have affected the ability of the Australian national commander in theatre to exercise cogent national command. This observation is based mostly on my personal observations, where wide variations in the interpretation of national intent between commanders at strategic, operational and tactical levels were frequently encountered. By way of example, in one illuminating personal exchange between myself, commander JTF 633 and CJOPS during the latter's visit to OBG(W)-2 in theatre, glaring differences in the interpretation of my authority to intervene to support coalition forces in contact illuminated an embarrassing level of confusion as to my command authority.

COMD JTF 633 had previously instructed me that I was not authorised to intervene on behalf of coalition forces in contact without his express authorisation. It remained a point of contention between us throughout my deployment, as I constantly contested his interpretation of my authorities based upon my pre-deployment training and understanding of previous task and battle group standard operating procedures. Given this dispute, I took the opportunity to confirm this with Australia's theatre commander during his visit. In confirming that this was—in fact—within my authority (the fact that I had even asked greatly aggravated COMD JTF 633), CJOPS stated that my authority to intervene in support of coalition forces in contact extended to combat operations in support of British elements in the adjoining and highly dangerous MND-SE provinces of Basra and Maysaan. This revelation stunned COMD JTF 633 and myself, as this was never considered within the authority of either of us, and seemed contrary to the implied national intent to focus on reconstruction and training tasks and avoid combat. Our interpretation had been that a request of this nature (crossing provincial boundaries) would require express governmental authorisation.[21] Irrespective of the correct interpretation, to my mind the dissonance between we three commanders at respective levels of command (strategic, operational and tactical) was a seminal example of prevalent deficiencies in the articulation of command intent through the Australian chain of command during Operation CATALYST.

This, and the previously recounted experiences of other tactical commanders, suggest that the articulation of intent—the doctrinally essential precursor for the effective application of mission command—was frequently absent or at best episodic. In seeking to understand the reasons for this during our discussions, given the relatively mature understanding and subscription to the tenets of mission command within the Army at the time, most tactical commanders put forward a variety of speculative explanations. These included either operational immaturity in the Australian operational command chain, individual failings by particular national commanders, or a relatively laissez-faire sense that articulation of Australian intent could be achieved through vetting of coalition operational orders.

The most concerning explanation put forward by several commanders and some of their battle staff was a sense that Australia's most senior strategic and operational commanders simply did not want to articulate Australia's calculated strategic intent formally, as described by Palazzo, because of its political sensitivity:

> [Of] second importance to Howard was the opinion of the Australian domestic audience and he recognised the necessity of minimising casualties. In this the Prime Minister successfully managed a potentially divisive issue. Events in Iraq, by comparison, were considerably less important to the achievement of Australia's policy goal.[22]

---

21 The rationale for this was that an arrangement existed between Australian and British forces whereby mutual support would be provided between provinces where the respective nation's forces were in danger of defeat. In order for the task group or battle group to be able to rely upon support from the British, it would need to be responsive to requests from British forces in Basra and Maysaan provinces. This determination that a decision to deploy to another province to support British forces in heavy contact was within the battle group commander's authority was dubious, given the implied caveats on battle group operations in so many other respects.
22 A. Palazzo, 'Assessing the war in Iraq', Address to the Royal United Services Institute of New South Wales, 31 July 2012, p. 15, www.rusinsw.org.au/Papers/20120731.pdf (retrieved 31 March 2020).

To have overtly communicated this type of political consideration to the tactical level would risk its public disclosure, resulting in political embarrassment and undermining efforts to buttress the alliance. While limited combat exposure by Australian forces might have been widely suspected within the coalition, in the absence of formal orders to this effect, it remained plausibly deniable. Confirmation of any belief that Australian military forces were only there to 'put a flag in the sand', and nothing more, in order to shore up the alliance would likely prove an embarrassing revelation for the government and Australia's military leadership and soldiers. Formal correspondence illuminating the calculated nature of Australia's military involvement could also wound the strategic enterprise. Some commanders and staff suggest that given the experience and professionalism of Australia's senior leaders, it might also have been that they were embarrassed in being privy to a mission in which Australian troops were committed to a dangerous and complex operation where their freedom of action to achieve the coalition intent was so heavily and deliberately constrained.

If this more calculated approach to preserving the sanctity and secrecy of the national strategic intent is taken to be credible, or even possible, then it would strike at the heart of one of the most essential tenets of mission command: the clear articulation and understanding of higher intent at the tactical level. If it was not possible to bring tactical commanders 'into the tent' in terms of the true strategic intent and sensitivity to casualties, it would therefore be necessary to constrain tactical activity in order to ensure that pursuit of coalition tactical outcomes would not threaten the sanctity and integrity of the national political intent to demonstrate commitment without suffering casualties.

The impact of constraining tactical freedom of action

Australian Army doctrine operative at the time highlights two essential components of the operative philosophy of mission command: (1) commanders using a minimum of control so as not to limit the subordinates' freedom of action unnecessarily; and (2) subordinates deciding for themselves how best to achieve their missions.[23] Given the

---

23   Land Warfare Doctrine 0-0, 'Command, Leadership and Management', chapter 2, section 2-2, 10 June 2008, para 15.

limited and episodic articulation of strategic intent previously outlined, and the lack of any real and express limitations on a tactical commander's freedom of action through formal national orders, what remains untested are assertions that tactical freedom of action was deliberately constrained through the national command chain, in particular by the Australian national commander located at HQ JTF 633 in theatre.

In seeking to determine whether the Australian national command element in theatre enabled or undermined mission command, the task and battle group commanders cited a variety of different experiences. The commanding officer of AMTG-1 recalls that the Australian embedded staff officer at Headquarters MND-SE was excellent for advice, and that the commander of JTF 633 was also generally very helpful. His experience with other Australian headquarters at the operational level outside theatre was generally less positive. In stark contrast, the commanding officer of the second AMTG was scathing of the interference of the Commander JTF 633 in unnecessarily constraining his tactical freedom of action to achieve designated and endorsed mission outcomes:

> When we did receive [national command] guidance it was ad hoc and always centred on stopping us from doing something. First example—the Brits had responsibility for providing security assistance to the Iraqis for the December 2006 elections. It was in all our interests to coordinate and assist in this regard. We were told via [national command] we had no role and were to stay out of it. I attended the British lead planning meetings and contributed what we could by just advising how we would conduct our normal security roles, which would assist 'naturally', but it was a professionally humiliating time for us. Another example—we received what was assessed by the intelligence agencies to be credible intelligence that we would be hit by an improvised explosive device on one of the routes within the tactical area we were responsible for. We planned an operation to interdict it. The Land Commander found out and denied us this action and insisted the British execute it, despite the threat fitting within our remit and emanating from our area. I was mortified … it was so embarrassing in that it was professionally humiliating and a part of my respect for our organisation died that day.[24]

---

24   Discussions with author.

I recall numerous and similarly invasive interventions by the Australian JTF 633 commander during the deployment of the OBG(W)-2. After a period, these interventions caused me to question not only the basis of the authority of the national commander to intervene in my tactical decision-making, but also his tactical competence in seeking alternatives to the courses of action being proposed.

By way of example, within a week of the OBG(W)-2 arriving in the province, Jaysh al-Mahdi launched a coordinated and heavy attack on the Police Headquarters in As-Samawah when the police refused to accede to demands for prisoner release. Surprisingly, and reassuringly, for the first time the local Iraqi police and army elements combined and cooperated to defeat this attack. The militia returned in numbers, bolstered by insurgent fighters from other provinces, and laid siege to the provincial headquarters. The situation in the city became dire; the Iraqi Security Forces were both outgunned and outnumbered, so the local commanders called us for combat support and an urgent resupply of ammunition. I was fully aware of our restrictions on intervention—at best we could arrange for an aerial resupply of ammunition. But I resolved to move the battle group tactically to a secure location in the desert just outside the capital. This was not to intervene in the fight but to create a ruse to deceive the insurgents that we were in fact about to commit in support of the Iraqi Security Forces, to unsettle the militia and bolster the confidence of the local Iraqi commander. Whether the ruse was successful or not remains unknown. Either way, the Iraqi Security Forces remained steadfast and the militia eventually withdrew without achieving their objective.

When I informed the JTF commander later that night that I had done this, he was apoplectic, insisting that I had intervened in express contravention of both national and coalition orders. His assertion was—and I recall this precisely—that I did not have the authority to 'step up' the battle group, which required his express permission as national commander. This flabbergasted me. If I could not even manouevre my force without his permission, what tactical authority did I possess as battle group commander? In seeking to clarify command options available to me in future, I recounted an exhaustive list of actions we had been instructed on and trained for on the Mission Rehearsal Exercise, including actions that previous task and battle groups had frequently undertaken in theatre. Each was serially rejected as being outside my remit, including even the option of aerial overpasses by coalition aircraft or authority to observe engagements via our unmanned aerial vehicle. With command caveats of this nature, mission command had clearly given way to directive control of tactical activity.

The commanding officer of the second AMTG recalls similar invasive episodes with HQ JTF 633 during his deployment, leading him to conclude:

> [HQ] JTF 633 was just a conduit for getting reports out and acting as the scout for Big Brother. I realised very early to play it 'grey' and stay under their radar or invite the 10,000-kilometre screwdriver. I was lucky to have great individuals as respective national commanders during my time as they understood and applied mission command and gave me freedom of action. They were cut from the same cloth, and I was fortunate in this respect. Both applied mission command and both were very supportive. So, I was free to plan and conduct tactical level operations so long as I kept things low profile. To this day, I can only shudder at the thought of the meddling and obstacles I would have experienced if the operation had been more kinetic.[25]

This inconsistency in variable involvement of the national commander in tactical decision-making proved puzzling to many commanders, as did the roles and remit of other embedded national officers in coalition headquarters. The commanding officer of AMTG-2 recalls:

> We also had a colonel senior national representative (SNR) embedded with the British Division based at Basra. I had no formal instructions as to how this individual featured within our command and control chain. On national command issues I worked directly to [Commander] JTF 633. I was more of the understanding the embedded SNR was [Commander] JTF 633's representative in Basra with no direct authority in my chain of command. I had little contact with the SNR because I didn't feel a need to engage them and to their credit, they didn't try and impose themselves upon them. But in knowing them personally, I also knew they were available to me if I wanted to engage them informally.[26]

---

25 Discussions with author.
26 Discussions with author.

Given the variable nature of experiences with the Australian national commander in theatre, it would seem that much came down to the personality of the individual and their corresponding interpretation of the role of the national commander and their role in preserving Australia's strategic intent. While many acted in what was described as an impediment to mission command, through an expressed requirement to 'approve' task and battle group operational orders and activities, others maintained more of a mentoring and enabling role for the tactical commander. Different tactical commanders also recount varied tolerances for risk with their respective national commanders, giving rise to markedly different stipulations on reporting tactical plans on an ongoing basis.

These variable experiences recounted by tactical commanders in terms of the freedom of action granted does not necessarily support the assertion of *strategic* micromanagement of tactical activities as suggested by Palazzo. Most tellingly, no task or battle group commanders recall any explicit intervention by the Chief of Defence Force acting as personally as a 'strategic corporal' in their tactical decision-making. The most deleterious interventions in tactical decision-making recalled by all tactical commanders were always exercised at the operational level through the national command element, usually by the Commander JTF 633 himself.

However, the varied experiences certainly tend to suggest either a lack of clear articulation or strategic intent and/or national caveats down through the national command chain, or alternatively a willingness by some national commanders to loosen the reins and allow tactical commanders freedom to manoeuvre. Clearly, one of the key bases driving the approach of the national commander towards allowing or constraining the freedom of action of the task or battle group commander was the relationship of trust between them.

Trust

Australian and Western military doctrine also posits that for the tactical commander to be able to exercise judgement and freedom of action in achieving this higher intent, an essential enabler is trust. That is, once the senior commander has articulated the results to be achieved and assigned the appropriate resources, he/she must have trust in both the professional understanding and ability of the subordinate commander to be able to achieve the outcome desired. Again, in light of Palazzo's assertions of close strategic supervision bordering on tactical micromanagement, I also sought to determine whether the prerequisite level of trust was afforded to task and battle group commanders to properly enable mission command at the tactical level.

It is important to note that trust between military commanders engaged in operational activity is always a two-way relationship. Western military doctrine insists that mission command requires a high level of mutual trust at all levels of command. Subordinates are trusted in the allocation of sufficient resources to carry out their missions, and commanders are trusted to keep control to a minimum so as not to constrain their subordinates' freedom of action to achieve their intent. The inverse is that commanders will rely upon subordinates to provide accurate and timely information to achieve operational success. Hence, doctrine highlights that high demands are made on the leadership qualities of subordinates, on their initiative and on their sense of responsibility to carry out assigned tasks.[27]

Once again, great variability in the experiences of respective task and battle group commanders is registered in relation to the sense of trust afforded them and their trust in their senior command chain. The commanding officer of AMTG-3/OBG(W)-1 recalls:

> Both Commander 1 Division and Commander 3 Brigade were clear in their discussion with me prior to deploying about the political sensitivities but neither were prescriptive in their guidance, showing great faith and trust. The Brigade Commander completed a reconnaissance concurrent to mine (covering off on the strategic and theatre issues) and we debriefed him on our appreciation while heading home out of Kuwait. He gave guidance but knew from his previous experience at US Central Command Forward and also with INTERFET that guidance would remain fluid and that if we didn't stay a bound ahead in our thinking then we would be caught flat-footed.[28]

---

27   ADDP 0.01 stipulates that 'The ADF's mission command philosophy is realised in the commander's confidence in delegating responsibility to subordinates, and the professional discharge of those responsibilities of command by subordinates. This is of particular importance in response to fleeting windows of opportunity during the conduct of operations, and contingencies where no specific direction has been given to the subordinate.' ADDP 0.01, *Command and Control*, para 2.31, p. 2-12.
28   Discussions with author.

Conversely, the relationship between myself and the Commander JTF 633 in theatre was marked by an absence of mutual trust. Given the earlier exchanges on differences in perceived authorities, based upon the expressed stipulation that all battle group operational orders were to be vetted by the national commander, by late in the deployment we were selectively providing redacted operational concepts of operations and operational orders to HQ JTF 633. From discussions with his staff, it was also evident that his relationship with his own staff was similarly affected by a lack of trust and regard. I had determined some protocols with the Chief Operations Staff Officer (J3) at HQ JTF 633 by which sufficient information could be provided to inform the national commander of our tactical activities without invoking his suspicion or tripping his risk sensitivities. I had lost confidence in his tactical acumen, and was failing on most occasions to articulate tactical ideas, concepts or options without attracting his ire. Instead I chose to seek counsel, advice and mentoring on the merits and appropriateness of proposed tactical operations with my parent brigade commander back in Australia. I felt very strongly that our relationship and the constraints being imposed on my tactical authority were jeopardising the lives of OBG(W) soldiers. This was confirmed in my own mind during one particular incident late in the deployment.

During an indirect fire (rocket) attack on the base, the insurgents fired a second salvo from the exact same point of origin at the 30-minute mark, which was instructive that (1) they knew our protocols (i.e. all clear after 30 minutes), and (2) they were confident that there was going to be no response from us to clear or contest the firing site or point of origin after the first salvo. I believed the latter had come to pass because we had had several previous exchanges with the Commander JTF 633, who insisted that our job was not to seek engagement with the enemy nor was it to protect the base. If a response to indirect fire attacks was required, his view was that the Americans or another contingent should do it—even though one of our approved mission tasks was to patrol suspected indirect fire sites within our designated security area outside the base.

This incident emphasised that his risk aversion was proving highly detrimental to our own force protection, and having to vet immediate tactical action through the national chain of command was untenable. In this case I was unable to convince Commander JTF 633 that aggressive patrolling and/or clearance of launch sites was actually a self-defensive measure, an action to protect ourselves, and I was not—as he suggested— 'under the spell of the Americans'. I clearly remember at this point convening a 'war counsel' with my senior staff officers and combat team commanders on this issue, at which point we resolved deliberately to withhold future patrolling plans from him on the basis that to do otherwise might cost Australian lives and continue to adversely affect Australian morale and reputation on the base. This exchange conclusively demonstrated that there was simply no vestige of mutual trust and that I had lost all respect for his tactical judgement of our situation from afar. I required another mentor, with whom I had professional trust and respect, to discuss tactical options and to ensure that I was acting in accordance with what I perceived to be the 'national interest' and derivative mission orders.

The commanding officer of AMTG-3/OBG(W)-1 had what could only be described as a diametrically opposite experience, with both national command chains forward and rear:

> [National Command] worked as well as it could, and worked because they supported us and didn't interfere. The national commander was an excellent mentor and supporter. As I have said before, I put this down to his operational command experience.[29]

Every tactical commander remains adamant that the doctrinal philosophy of mission command was entirely appropriate for the complex operating environment in which we operated, including the complexities concomitant to coalition operations. None recall any suggestion or discussion within the Australian chain of command that the philosophy of mission command would be relevant only to a high-end war-fighting environment and inappropriate for security and stability operations. In fact, its pointed relevance to the current operation inspired the commander of the first AMTG to publish an article on the application of mission command on his return to Australia, in which he emphasised the centrality and applicability of mission command to Operation CATALYST. A central observation was that the effective application of mission command demanded more than rhetorical subscription to the doctrine:

> The key to effective, focused action is mission command. The philosophy of mission command must be believed and nurtured. To be effective, it must be built on the intellectual components of clear intent, trust and accountability. The central moral

---

29   Discussions with author.

component is trust. A physical framework must also be established to support decision-makers at every level, especially those in the midst of chaos and in close contact with the adversary.[30]

Yet despite this seemingly universal subscription to the relevance and utility of mission command, dissonance appears evident in its application within the Australian national command in Iraq. The personal experiences of respective Australian tactical commanders reveal common dynamics at play in seeking to apply mission command in operational practice. Their recollections and observations give rise to familiar revelations about the relevance, effective application and ultimate utility of mission command in modern, complex operations. Most peculiarly, the Australian experience on Operation CATALYST highlights contemporary challenges in fully enabling mission command as a theatre framework providing connectivity and between the strategic, operational and tactical levels of war. This experience is reflective of the issues faced by Western military forces on modern operations, which might be highly politicised and conducted by individual nations within a complex coalition architecture.

Counter-intuitive outcomes

In another article, 'The making of strategy and the junior coalition partner: Australia and the 2003 Iraq War', Palazzo argues that the Iraq campaign was a masterstroke of Australian policy-making.[31] His previous assertion that it had little to do with events in Iraq is an intriguing observation for those who deployed, seemingly inimical to the traditional military view that in war, strategic success emanates from successful actions or military 'victories' at the tactical and operational levels of war.

Palazzo's hypothesis is antithetical in contending that achievement of coalition military objectives was neither the principal aim nor ultimate determinant of Australian strategic success:

> Unusually, strategic calculation was at the forefront of the Australian Government's senior political leaders and their military advisers. The Australian Government of Prime Minister John Howard saw

---
30   R. Noble, 'The essential thing: Mission command and its practical application', *Australian Army Journal*, vol. 3, no. 3, 2006, p. 124, researchcentre.army.gov.au/sites/default/files/aaj_2006_3.pdf (retrieved 31 March 2020).
31   Palazzo, 'The making of strategy and the junior coalition partner', pp. 27–30.

the War in Iraq as an opportunity to advance a long-held security objective, one that had little to do with events in the Middle East. For Australia, the policy goal for its participation in the Iraq War was the opportunity to enhance its relationship with the United States. In achieving this objective Australia identified factors by which a junior coalition partner can set and attain its own policy goals, and, importantly, avoid creating a conflict with the objectives of the coalition-leader.[32]

Palazzo suggests that tactical 'victories' were neither necessary nor encouraged by Australia's strategic leaders. The mere presence of Australian forces would be sufficient to achieve the desired strategic objectives, provided that tactical involvement was carefully orchestrated and controlled to prevent any semblance of tactical 'defeat'. Task and battle group actions would need to be carefully controlled to ensure strategic visibility while minimising the force protection risk. This complex formula necessitated clear unity of purpose between government and the military in order to achieve the desired strategic outcome:

> Australian political–military divisiveness was not evident in the Iraq War. Howard and his senior general, the Chief of Defence Force General Peter Cosgrove (and later Air Chief Marshal Angus Houston), acted as one in regard to Iraq. Cosgrove understood the government's purpose and worked towards that goal. To keep the ADF on target the CDF tightly controlled the mission and kept the Prime Minister informed of its progress. Contemporary military theory contains numerous references to the effect of the 'strategic corporal'. In Iraq the influence of the junior ranks was minimal as Cosgrove aspired to be the 'tactical general'. Throughout the Iraq War no issue was too unimportant for the CDF's strategic-level oversight. The commander of Australia's headquarters in the Middle East also served as Cosgrove's strategic-level theatre representative. He had direct access to the CDF—outside the formal chain of command—and kept Cosgrove alert to all activities across the Coalition that might have an effect upon Australia's ability to secure its goals.[33]

This strategic scrutiny and control of tactical freedom of action often had debilitating effects on morale at the task and battle group level. The policy of constraining tactical activity at the strategic and operational levels

---

32 Palazzo, 'Assessing the war in Iraq', p. 13.
33 Ibid., p. 14.

without national context confused Australian soldiers as well as their higher coalition headquarters in theatre. Without a cogent explanation for curtailment of tactical activity, coalition forces frequently interpreted these inexplicable constraints as a lack of courage and resolve. Irrespective of strategic interpretation, this also generated a highly counter-intuitive but easily foreseeable result: the Australian Army's professional credibility and standing as a trusted, capable and committed alliance partner often suffered at the tactical level. Perceptions of risk aversion to casualties had a gravely deleterious impact on the reputation of Australian forces on the ground.

This trend was visible even before assumption of operational overwatch activities in the more dangerous province of Dhi Qar. During the AMTG period, Professor John Blaxland registered and reported a growing sense of disquiet developing among Australian soldiers and coalition partners in Al Muthanna Province, most particularly within the British contingent. This disquiet morphed into open hostility in later evolutions where tactical freedom of action to intervene in support of coalition forces in contact was constrained, becoming the root cause of verbal disdain for Australian forces:

> As one Australian officer observed, British senior officers 'understood' the constraints of the Australian rules of engagement. But the British soldiers, 'the squaddies, called the diggers cowards to their faces. At least some of the diggers agreed.' The net effect of this government-driven tactical approach was the absolute minimisation of Australian casualties. But this approach came at a price in terms of credibility with Australia's allies and coalition partners and soldier's morale.[34]

Final thoughts

Ironically, Operation CATALYST has proven true to its operational nomenclature (title), although it is far more likely in buttressing the Australian–US alliance at minimal political and human cost (battlefield casualties) rather than a catalysing impact on the Iraqi nation-state and regional geopolitical landscape. Whether it had this latter effect is a separate question not addressed by this chapter. Of greater importance,

---

34 Blaxland, *The Australian Army from Whitlam to Howard*, p. 242.

as evidenced by discussion and debate during the 'War in the Sandpit' seminar, is that it seems to have polarised opinion among political, academic and military commentators as to the most appropriate measure of appraising success.

There is, however, an alternative perspective: at the tactical level, many officers and soldiers viewed this operation as a confusing, disappointing, deeply embarrassing and professionally disheartening experience. For many, our ability to put our hands on our hearts and declare unequivocal mission success remains an elusive and deeply soul-searching endeavour. To the casual observer, this might sound odd, given that many contemporary measures of operational success were present, no soldier was killed in action, and our casualties were often minor despite some intense engagements with opposition forces. Surely this would tend to connote that strategic success was built upon highly professional efforts and outcomes at the tactical level.

The observations outlined in this chapter suggest the means by which Australia's strategic leaders chose to achieve the desired strategic outcomes actually mortgaged professional pride and military reputation at the tactical level. Australia's national command and control architecture contributed to debilitating strategic–tactical dissonance, through either a conscious or an unconscious failure cogently and reliably to communicate strategic (national) intent down to the tactical level of command in a complex coalition operating environment. This did our soldiers a massive disservice in that it returned counter-intuitive results in giving justifiable cause to a cadre of coalition officers and soldiers, and likely also Iraqis, to appraise Australian contingents as 'talking the talk but failing to walk the walk'. I have no doubt that we could have done better in this regard while still achieving the strategic objectives desired by government. We simply needed to be true to our capstone operational doctrine of mission command.

In suggesting this, I remain aware of the dangers of binary thinking. That is, with the benefit of hindsight it is easy to identify the disadvantages of a particular approach, leading to the trite assertion that a different approach would generate a better outcome. My peculiar advantage in this respect is being able to look back with the benefit of the great contextual analytical work by Professor Palazzo and others. Having now also occupied a number of different positions at tactical, operational and strategic levels of command, I have a more informed perspective of the difficult and competing interests and issues at play and therefore the strategic context within which the various task and battle groups operated.

Even so, I would still strongly contend that this manifestation of national command control cannot be considered an optimal means by which to wage war, enforce the peace or deliver humanitarian assistance or disaster relief. To prevent strategic–tactical dissonance, and the accompanying deleterious impact upon the morale and well-being of a deployed force, our strategic leaders must strive to get the national command and control architecture right, both in form and in substance. This demands an honest, considered and principled approach to the application of mission command to ensure that those at the most risk on the battlefield understand precisely what it is that they are being asked to do and what they are risking their lives to achieve. This starts with a clear and honest articulation of national intent being cogently communicated down to, and understood by, tactical commanders.

My personal belief is that the means by which we as a military chose to deliver the political outcomes demanded by government on Operation CATALYST did not keep faith with our history, traditions, doctrine or national character. The arguably duplicitous approach we took as a nation to committing our troops to stability operations in Iraq, ostensibly to put an Australian flag in the sand in support of our major ally, generated mixed and equivocal results—some very good (mostly at the strategic level) but many very bad (at the tactical level). This chapter should not be interpreted as suggesting that we should be a reflexive slave to any particular operating methodology, but my view is that we should always understand the reason for taking a different line or treading a different path. We should also understand the potential second- and third-order consequences inherent in any departure from proven doctrinal approaches. To my mind, this is what the 'War in the Sandpit' seminar has allowed me to do: articulate some hitherto unseen or vaguely perceived negative consequences of suboptimal national command and control on a contemporary coalition security and stability operation.

If we do in fact wish to achieve articulated strategic intent, as in this case to buttress and enhance our strategic alliances, and be seen to deliver on our commitment to a rules-based global order, we must ensure that our actions truly reinforce that intent at every level. As a professional military we owe that to ourselves, to our government and—most importantly—to our soldiers and their families.

7

Maritime operations

Peter Jones

Australia's maritime military operations are unique among those of the broader Australian Defence Force (ADF) because the Royal Australian Navy (RAN) has had ships more or less continually deployed to the Persian Gulf or the Red Sea since Saddam Hussein's invasion of Kuwait in 1990.[1]

During both the 1990 Gulf War and the 2003 invasion of Iraq, the RAN's contribution was a three-ship task group and a clearance diving team, with an embarked task group staff and logistic support element (LSE) ashore. However, for most of those long years the contribution was a single frigate integrated into the multinational Maritime Interception Force (MIF). In the period between the 9/11 attacks and the immediate aftermath of the 2003 hostilities, the Navy bolstered its contribution to two or three ships with a task group commander and staff.

During the 1990 Gulf War, while the RAN provided three ships to the large multinational armada and a mine-clearance diving team, its task group commander did not have a command role in the multinational organisation.

---

1 For further information and sources consulted, please see P. Jones, 'The maritime campaign in Iraq', in *Naval Power and Expeditionary Wars: Peripheral Campaigns and New Theatres of Naval Warfare*, ed. B.A. Elleman and S.C.M. Paine, Routledge, New York, 2011, pp. 167–81.

A generation of officers and sailors had therefore become increasingly familiar with the Persian Gulf, the inshore waters of Iraq, their allies, the at times aggressive neutrals in the case of the Iranians, the myriad of shipping and not least their prospective enemy, the Iraqis.

The other benefit of this exposure was the growing confidence of the US Navy in Australia's ships and, from 2001, in its task group commanders. This meant that often the Australian naval task group commander was dual-hatted and had, in addition to command of the RAN task group, alternating command of the MIF with a US Navy captain.[2] This was very much a conscious decision on the part of the US Navy. For example, in the lead-up to the 2003 Iraq War, my superior, Rear Admiral Barry Costello, USN, told me that because of my time in theatre, I, supported by my staff, would fill the role of Maritime Interception Operations Screen Commander, and not a US Navy captain, as originally conceived.

Overview of operations, 1990–2003

The enduring thread from 1990 to 2003 was therefore maritime interception operations with their asset-intensive surveillance and boarding operations. This was first to enforce sanctions imposed under United Nations Security Council Resolution (UNSCR) 661 and then, after the Iraq War, under UNSCR 687, to maintain security, prevent smuggling by non-state actors or promote freedom of navigation.[3]

Such surveillance and boarding operations date back to the age of sail. They can be conducted for many years and require endurance, patience and a sea-going temperament. They also needed a sophisticated naval organisation to meet the unremitting tempo. History records that such operations, if well conceived, are effective. The blockade of Napoleonic France in the first decade of the 19th century and the Kaiser's Germany in the second decade of the 20th are two such examples, and, I would contend, that of Iraq up to 2003 was also effective.

---

2   The US Navy captain was the Commander Destroyer Squadron 50, normally based at Fifth Fleet Headquarters at Bahrain.
3   UNSCR 661 was adopted in August 1990 to sanction Iraq following its invasion of Kuwait. UNSCR 687 of 1991 outlines the terms imposed on Iraq after the expulsion of Iraqi forces from Kuwait. See en.wikisource.org/wiki/Portal:United_Nations_Security_Council_Resolutions (retrieved 31 March 2020).

7. MARITIME OPERATIONS

The nature of such operations is not something all governments and policy-makers understand. In respect of the sanction enforcement on Iraq, while the first Bush and then the Clinton administration largely understood the purpose of these operations, the second Bush administration did not.

The command arrangements for operations in the Gulf were complex. The Commander US Fifth Fleet was the operational-level commander based ashore in Bahrain. He was also the Maritime Component Commander to Commander United States Central Command (CENTCOM) based in Tampa, Florida. The commander of the on-station carrier battle group provided the operational-level command of naval forces. The command of the MIF was typically exercised from a US Navy cruiser or destroyer.

During the period from 1990 to 2001, there had been occasions when land- and sea-based air strikes and Tomahawk land attack missile launchings had been conducted against Iraq. These were generally in support of the efforts to disarm Iraq of weapons of mass destruction (WMDs) or in response to breaches of the Iraqi no-fly zone. Targets struck included military command and control and civil telecommunications facilities. The cumulative degradation of command and control capacity had an important impact on the ability of the Iraqis to respond to the 2003 invasion.

During that same period, however, the effectiveness of the MIF was less than optimum. Smugglers of oil and other goods seeking to circumvent the embargo would often use the presence of Iraqi shore-based missile batteries on the Al-Faw Peninsula and a passage through Iranian territorial waters to avoid interception. On occasion, the MIF would conduct night surge operations near the mouth of the Khawr Abd Allah and Shatt al-Arab waterways to increase their chances of intercepting smugglers, clearing the coast before sunrise. These operations had little strategic effect on sanction enforcement. The strategically vital offshore oil terminals near the mouth of the Khawr Abd Allah and Shatt Al-Arab would remain of enduring significance and a high priority to be secured in the event of the outbreak of conflict and before oil could be released into the Gulf.

Post-9/11 operations

The most significant development in this protracted sanction enforcement campaign was the attacks of 11 September 2001. In their wake, not only were the naval forces infused with a significant increase in ships from the long-standing contributors but also other navies contributed forces to assist in the Global War on Terror. This blurring of mission between UNSCR enforcement against Iraq and the anti–al-Qaeda Global War on Terror differed between nations. Some nations would deploy forces only in and around the north Persian Sea and Gulf of Oman as well as the Gulf of Aden to cut al-Qaeda lines of communication, while other nations such as Australia grouped the two missions together.

Like the conduct of many naval operations of the past, the post-9/11 phase of operations shifted in response to a confluence of strategic-, operational- and tactical-level developments. The increase in naval forces in the Persian Sea and Persian Gulf enabled the Commander Fifth Fleet to deploy separate coalition task groups in the north Persian Sea/Gulf of Oman and the Gulf of Aden. These forces not only provided a capability for the Global War on Terror but also, as events unfolded, would by their presence provide enhanced security for the 2002–03 force build-up before commencement of the US Operation Iraqi Freedom.

The MIF was also to enjoy a substantial increase in force levels. But before additional forces arrived, a significant tactical shift took place. The immediate response to the 9/11 attacks made it necessary temporarily to detach US Navy Tomahawk fitted ships from the MIF. This left the depleted MIF under the command of Captain Nigel Coates in HMAS *Anzac*. Coates, in response to the drastic reduction in force numbers, used his ship's shallow draft and national rules of engagement to move into Iraqi territorial waters at the mouth of the Khawr Abd Allah waterway. This shift to a close blockade had an immediate effect on smugglers.

HMAS *Adelaide* patrols the waters around the oil terminals in the North Arabian Gulf during Operation Catalyst, 2004.
Source: Courtesy of the Department of Defence.

The initial success was limited by few warships having sufficiently shallow draughts to allow them to operate close inshore. For the close blockade to be effective, continuous inshore frigate presence was required. This capability was provided by an increased number of British Royal Navy and RAN warships. From 2001 to 2003, the crews of these ships built up considerable knowledge of the shallow waters, thus allowing incrementally greater freedom of manoeuvre. This would prove invaluable during OIF.

For their part, the smugglers responded to the new challenge posed by the MIF. A move and counter-move ensued until 2003 with smugglers welding doors and hatches, electrifying guardrails and attempting mass breakouts to swamp the MIF. The MIF replied with acetylene cutters, greater coordination and training. By mid-2002 the larger merchant ships were effectively submitting to being searched and trying to hide modest quantities of oil in hidden tanks. In the last six months of the sanction enforcement, only two merchant ships escaped the interception force's net, and even then the MIF successfully encouraged the Islamic Republic of Iran Navy to apprehend them in their territorial waters.

Members of the Afghan National Army, 3RAR Battle Group and Mentoring Task Force 4 step off on their first handover/takeover patrol from Forward Operating Base Mirwais in Chora, Afghanistan, 2012.
Source: Courtesy of the Department of Defence.

The main focus became smuggling in much smaller dhows. Night mass breakout attempts of 40–60 dhows were not uncommon. The MIF responded with improved tactical cohesion between the boarding parties of the RAN, US Coast Guard, Royal Marines and US Navy. These conventional forces were augmented at night on a regular basis by Polish special forces (Grupa Reagowania Operacyjno-Manewrowego or GROM)[4] and US Navy Seals, who were based in Kuwait. In addition to the boarding parties, helicopters were used to vector boarding parties to breakouts.

Over the years the boarding parties benefited from design improvements in the Rigid Hull Inflatable Boats (RHIBs), which resulted in boats of greater endurance, reliability and comfort. Having said that, in the early months of the year boarding parties could risk hypothermia if not well equipped and their on-water time closely managed.

---

4   In English, Group [for] Operational Manoeuvring Response.

In the air, US Navy Seahawk helicopters fitted with the Hawklink tactical data link allowed video streaming of the dhow breakouts to the MIF commander's command ship. This visual perspective was invaluable in coordinating modest MIF resources.

The two other actors in this complex and shifting maritime scene were the naval forces of Iran and Iraq. Iran had units of both the Iranian navy and the Iranian Republican Guard Corps Navy. The latter was the most active in the northern Persian Gulf and at times unpredictable. Its small craft irregularly swept through waters at the mouth of the Khawr Abd Allah and boarded vessels and harassed crews. In contrast, the Iranian naval presence was weighted more in the central and southern Gulf. The Iranian navy proved helpful when cued through interlocutors to intercept smugglers transiting through Iranian territorial waters or responding to search and rescue incidents.

The Iraqi Navy largely confined itself to its two bases of Umm Qasr and Basra. However, in mid-2002 their PB-90-class patrol boats initiated solitary daytime patrols in the Khawr Abd Allah approaches. There was concern in US Navy Fifth Fleet headquarters that the close proximity of the Iraqi PB-90 to MIF warships might allow the patrol boats to inflict damage to the larger ships in a surprise attack. To ward against that possibility, the MIF invariably had a missile-armed helicopter airborne and would warn the Iraqi PB-90 not to interfere with interception force operations. Once again, the Hawklink-transmitted video stream allowed the MIF commander to monitor deck movements on the PB-90 in this situation, although the PB-90 was significantly less capable than the units of the MIF. The naval forces were in a unique position whereby they saw their prospective foes on a regular basis and had an opportunity where possible to intimidate them.

Preparations for Plan 1003V: The invasion of Iraq

The operational plan to invade Iraq and disarm the regime of WMD was developed by CENTCOM under the command of General Tommy R. Franks. It was designated Plan 1003V. Work commenced in 2002 and was refined in numerous iterations. The maritime elements of this plan were developed by the Commander of the US Fifth Fleet, Vice Admiral Timothy Keating, and his staff both in Tampa and in Bahrain.

The central characteristic of the maritime campaign was the diverse nature of the tasks assigned to the navies and marines. These tasks included:

- Protecting of focal points from the Suez Canal to Kuwait to ensure the massive logistical build-up of supplies for land, air and sea forces. As with Operation DESERT STORM, the overwhelming bulk of material was shipped by sea.
- Facilitating the entry into Iraq of special forces and other covert elements before hostilities.
- Providing a sizeable proportion of the air power for the operation. This requirement was significantly increased when sorties could not be flown from air bases in Turkey, nor over-fly rights obtained from that country. A significant element of this air power would be sea-based Tomahawk strike missiles in the initial 'shock and awe' wave of attacks on Iraqi infrastructure and leadership.
- US Marines and the Royal Marines providing a significant element of the land force. The marines would be involved in securing southern Iraq, including the ports. Some elements would move north to Baghdad.
- Securing the Mīnā' al-Bakr and Khor al-Amaya offshore oil terminals to prevent a catastrophic oil spill into the Gulf and ensure their preservation for the benefit of post-war Iraq.
- Countering Iraqi naval operations, including any mining.
- Ensuring the merchant ships and dhows (potentially more than 400 vessels) holed up in the Khawr Abd Allah (estuary) and the Shatt Al-Arab (river) did not interfere with coalition operations along the length of the Gulf.
- Forcing entry to the Khawr Abd Allah and facilitating the port of Umm Qasr into a hub for humanitarian aid. This would inevitably involve a significant mine counter-measures effort.
- Deterring any attempt by the Iranian naval forces or al-Qaeda seaborne elements from interfering with coalition operations.

The campaign had to factor in the possibility of Iraqi use of biological and chemical agents. This threat, despite subsequent absence of WMD, was deemed to be a major risk to coalition forces.

The missions and tasks required a significant force build from about 50 warships to 150. This build-up began in November 2002. The coalition force was centred on the newly arrived USS *Constellation* carrier battle group (Rear Admiral Barry M. Costello) and the USS *Abraham Lincoln* battle group (Rear Admiral John M. Kelly), which returned following a short break in Australia. In assigning responsibilities, Vice Admiral Keating gave Rear Admiral Kelly the role of commanding the strike elements and Rear Admiral Costello the multifaceted sea control missions. There were other subordinate command arrangements, which reflected the shift of Fifth Fleet missions from one of UNSCR enforcement and sea control to combat operations in the littoral. Like many operations, the command arrangements were a compromise between clear lines of accountability, national sensitivities and assessments of likely rates of effort of US and supporting coalition naval vessels.

A central feature of Plan 1003V was the significant application of naval air power. This was achieved with the deployment of four carrier battle groups to augment those two already in theatre. USS *Kitty Hawk* and later USS *Nimitz* joined the two carriers in the Gulf while the USS *Theodore Roosevelt* and USS *Harry S. Truman* carrier battle groups would operate from the eastern Mediterranean Sea. To facilitate the integration of naval and air force assets, Rear Admiral David C. Nicholls became the Deputy Joint Force Air Component Commander at the Prince Sultan Air Base in Saudi Arabia. US Navy personnel also integrated into the air planning staff.

The United States also deployed the specialist forces that Plan 1003V needed for success. These included:

- mine counter-measures vessels US Ships *Ardent, Cardinal, Dextrous* and *Raven*
- mine-clearance diving teams employing remotely operated underwater vehicles as well as dolphins to detect bottom mines
- MH-53E Sea Dragon minesweeping helicopters
- the heavily armed patrol boats USS *Firebolt* and USS *Chinook* as well as the US Coast Guard cutter *Boutwell* and the US Coast Guard patrol craft *Adak, Aquidneck, Baranof* and *Wrangle* for the envisaged inshore operations
- the high-speed catamaran USS *Joint Venture* deployed to support special forces
- additional replenishment ships and the hospital ship USNS *Comfort* pre-positioned in the Gulf.

Britain's Royal Navy deployed the UK Amphibious Task Group (UKATG), centred on aircraft carrier HMS *Ark Royal*, into the Gulf. This was under the command of Commodore A.J.G. Miller. The *Ark Royal* was configured as a helicopter carrier and had not embarked Harrier strike aircraft. The other major UKATG ships were the helicopter carrier HMS *Ocean*, the aviation support ship RFA *Argus* (fitted as a hospital ship) and the landing ships RFA *Sir Tristram*, RFA *Sir Galahad* and RFA *Sir Percivale*. These ships were escorted by the destroyers HM Ships *Liverpool*, *Edinburgh* and *York*, frigates *Marlborough*, *Chatham* and *Richmond*, minehunters *Grimsby* and *Ledbury*. They were supported by the tankers RFA *Fort Rosalie* and RFA *Orangeleaf*. In addition, the survey ship HMS *Roebuck* would undertake surveys of the north Persian Gulf. The Tomahawk-fitted submarines *Splendid* and *Turbulent* would be multitasked in the operation.

The RAN deployed the amphibious ship HMAS *Kanimbla* to bring to the Gulf stores for the Australian joint force. While originally intended to join the logistic forces in the Gulf, as Australian Naval Task Group Commander, I had her reassigned to the MIF where her amphibious, command and communications capabilities proved invaluable. Indeed, once *Kanimbla* offloaded her stores, my staff and I shifted the MIF command function from the Arleigh Burke destroyer USS *Milius* to *Kanimbla*. Her planning spaces were extremely useful in the lead-up to the conflict. To compensate for this reassignment, *Kanimbla*'s Sea King helicopter joined the US 'Desert Duck' logistic helicopter effort one day a week. *Kanimbla* joined the frigates HMAS *Anzac* and HMAS *Darwin*, which had their time in theatre extended. The Navy also deployed Clearance Diver Team 3 to work with other coalition diving teams under the command of US Navy Commodore Michael P. Tillotson.

The Polish Government deployed GROM, and a fresh crew was flown into theatre for its support ship ORP *Kontra Admiral Xavier Czernicki*, which was assigned to the MIF. Her ability to embark additional boarding teams and boats would prove very useful.

Contribution of the Marines

The US Marines and the Royal Marines made a substantial contribution in size and combat power. The campaign represented the largest marine deployment since the Gulf War of 1990. The US contribution included elements of the 1st Marine Expeditionary Force, commanded by

Lieutenant General James T. Conway. The force would number 65,000 personnel supported by 142 MIAI tanks, 606 amphibious assault vehicles, 279 light amphibious vehicles, 105 howitzers, 7,000 trucks and 454 Marine Air Wing aircraft. The vast majority of these forces would be pre-positioned in Kuwait.

The British provided the 3rd Commando Brigade, Royal Marines, under the command of Brigadier James Dutton. The force would also pre-position ashore in Kuwait from the UKATG. The initial requirement was to secure the ports of Umm Qasr and Az Zubayr from land. This was undertaken by the 15th Marine Expeditionary Unit (15th MEU) while the Royal Marines combined with the British Army's 1st Armoured Division to secure Basra following an air assault on the Al-Faw Peninsula.

Information and communications technology

For the first time in a major naval conflict, satellite communications would play a pivotal role not only in long-haul strategic communications but also between ships and formations. Commercial software tools such as email, chat and web surfing became critical command and control aids and proved vital to the success of the mission. The allocation of satellite bandwidth became a matter of close attention for commanders.

Chat was of particular significance in passing orders and disseminating information. It allowed ships to join in a 'meeting room' with their task group commanders where reports would be made and orders given. Chat proved excellent for providing shared situational awareness and fostering task group cohesion. For example, one-on-one 'whisper boxes' between task group commanders and individual ships allowed details to be sorted out before posting orders in open meeting rooms. Innumerable task-specific chat rooms proliferated throughout the theatre for such functions as logistics, air warfare or shore bombardment. There were, however, challenges with this novel tool. Information overload was a risk, as was providing too much transparency to higher commands who became tempted to micromanage issues. In addition, chat could distract the eyes of operations crews from radar screens and charts.

Lead-up to the Iraq War

Critical to the operation's success was the massive build-up of materiel for the land, air and sea forces. As in 1990, the vast bulk of equipment and stores came by sea. From January until the end of April, the US Military Sealift Command moved about 21 million square feet of materiel and more than 261 million gallons of fuel. The commander of the Military Sealift Command, Vice Admiral David L. Brewer III, attributed this achievement to the adoption of lessons from the Gulf War. The large, medium-speed, roll-on/roll-off ships were such an example and became the prime movers with a carrying capacity of 300,000 square feet per ship. The surge of the Military Sealift Command was assisted by Ready Reserve Force roll-on/roll-off ships from the US Maritime Administration and commercial charter. The protection of these ships from interference from al-Qaeda, Iran or Iraq was of critical importance. Ships were provided not only naval escorts (often by the MIF) as required but also on-board US Navy and US Marine Corps security teams.

From January 2003, ships stationed in the Gulf began to receive additional training and had defects repaired. An example of this training was naval gunfire support drills for the Australian and British frigates designated for this mission. In preparing for the likely conflict, the MIF identified four worst-case scenarios: Iraqi mining, short-range Iraqi missile strikes from the Al-Faw, a blue-on-blue incident, and a collision involving helicopters unfamiliar with the confines of the north Persian Gulf. The MIF developed enhanced procedures to mitigate these risks. They included improved reporting and tracking procedures for merchant ships, aircraft and boats, and a range of visual and procedural tools to confirm identity. The MIF Commander became the North Arabian Gulf Local Surface Warfare Commander and Local Air Warfare Commander. These small but important steps were to ensure not only that the MIF could operate in a broader warfare context but also that when the inevitable force build-up occurred, the much-enlarged coalition force could operate safely in this relatively confined area.

A key to the cohesion between not only the on-station ships but also newly joined forces was the long-standing ties between most of the naval forces. In particular, American, British and Australian sailors had long association and familiarity. Extensive use of embedded liaison officers in the different levels of command helped to resolve issues and promote cohesion.

The new joiners also had the benefit of chat rooms to immerse themselves as they steamed in theatre. The Royal Navy frigates were visitors to MIF chat rooms from the point when they commenced steaming down the English Channel. This accelerated their eventual integration into the MIF.

While the coalition forces prepared for war, the Iraqis began to rebase their warships from Umm Qasr to Basra. This unprecedented redeployment of all major ships included Saddam Hussein's presidential yacht, *Al-Mansur*. It was assessed that Iraqis thought Basra offered more protection for these ships, as well as allowing a short passage across the Shatt Al-Arab to Iran if considered expedient to do so and should Iran prove to be accommodating.

As part of revised command and control arrangements, Commodore John W. Peterson in the cruiser USS *Valley Forge* was made the North Arabian Gulf Commander. He had extensive north Persian Gulf experience and had been heavily involved in developing the maritime plan. His new purview was operations off both the Khawr Abd Allah and Shatt Al-Arab, and supporting special forces operations. He also had to align the activities of the coalition with the Kuwaiti–Bahraini–Emirati Defence of Kuwait Task Group now at sea. Major General Ahmed Yousef al-Mulla, Commander of the Kuwait Naval Force, in the United Arab Emirates frigate *Al Emirat* commanded this task group as it operated in the western sector of the north Persian Gulf.

From mid-February to early March, the planning tempo increased significantly. An important issue was aligning the different components of the plan to reduce the possibility of fratricide.

On 1 March 2003, we scrutinised the plans for the clearance of merchant and dhow traffic from the Khawr Abd Allah. We desired clearance of the channel to ensure that delivery of humanitarian relief to Umm Qasr could occur within 72 hours of the adjacent land sector being secured. The plan involved *Kanimbla* being used as a command platform with the MIF to oversee a force of 38 RHIBs inspecting, clearing and directing dhows and merchant vessels to designated holding areas. All vessels would be searched for explosives, mines, weapons and contraband material before being allowed down a defined route into the central Persian Gulf. US Navy and US Coast Guard patrol boats, as well as Kuwaiti patrol vessels and maritime interception operations helicopters, would support operations. In addition to the organic RHIBs, *Kanimbla* and *Czernicki* would host additional boats and associated personnel from other non-MIF warships operating further down the Gulf. Later, part of the MIF would deploy forward to protect the mine counter-measures effort and patrol the river once cleared.

The proposed use of naval gunfire support in the assault on the Al-Faw Peninsula became a contentious issue. Four frigates in two fire support areas planned to provide fire across the whole of the Royal Marines' 40 Commando area of operations and on to 42 Commando's insertion point. Despite US concern about deconfliction with air assets and an initial lack of Royal Marine support, it was agreed that naval gunfire support would become a feature of the plan. The planning work and assiduous advocacy by the commanding officer of HMS *Marlborough*, Captain Mark Anderson, was instrumental in this outcome. As events were to unfold, naval gunfire support was to prove invaluable to the assault.

On 11 March 2003, Rear Admiral Costello convened a final planning conference on board USS *Constellation* in which all plans were outlined. Elaborate anti-fratricide measures for the small boats were also briefed. Such was the concern about fratricide that Costello directed that a weapons safe posture was to be adopted, with engagement of the enemy to be directed by him unless in self-defence. This approach reflected the preponderance of coalition military power and the confined nature of the battle space. More challenging was the deconfliction between maritime and land operations in the littoral. Despite the sharing of plans, albeit often later than desirable, and the exchange of liaison officers, there remained doubt as to whether all risks had been retired.

Rear Admiral Kelly's remit was complex and required the integration of the naval air and strike assets into the coalition air and targeting plans. In addition to striking Iraqi targets, the naval forces had to complement operations to ensure air superiority over both Iraq and Kuwait. A particular challenge was to protect Kuwait city from a possible short-range missile attack from Iraq. The US Army deployed Patriot anti-air missile batteries around the city, and the destroyer USS *Higgins* was fitted with additional equipment to provide early warning and tracking for these forces.

The Iraqis had developed defensive plans that were being incrementally implemented. In the first instance, the Iraqi navy moved the last of its larger ships from Umm Qasr to Basra. Some tugs, small patrol craft and a barge were fitted with disguised mining rails to enable them to lay defensive minefields at the mouth of and along the Khawr Abd Allah. Plans were also put in place to destroy navigational markers along the waterways. Small inflatable boats were also rigged as suicide boats from components of Iraqi-built LUGM-145 naval moored contact mines. These boats were to be deployed from the Al-Faw, enabling coalition warships to be attacked from the Khawr Abd Allah and Shatt Al-Arab waterways.

The MIF, through its contact with merchant ship and dhow crews, had learnt of some of these plans, including the threat to navigation marks and the Mīnā' al-Bakr and Khor al-Amaya offshore oil terminals. As a result, all Iraqi government vessels were trailed by MIF RHIBs while at the entrance to the Khawr Abd Allah to monitor their actions.

During the evenings, there had been a noticeable increase in smuggler movement with increased desperation to exit the Khawr Abd Allah. On the evening of 15 March 2003, a Kuwaiti patrol boat fired warning shots at an exiting dhow that had not responded to its order to stop. The ill-directed fire hit an Indian crew member. A medical team from HMAS *Anzac* was unable to save his life, and the dhow was directed back up the Khawr Abd Allah. Perhaps, as a result of this event, there was a marked reduction in dhow activity.

On the arrival of the UKATG in the north Persian Gulf, pre-positioning of the Royal Marine force in Kuwait commenced with US and Australian assistance. Reconnaissance of the peninsula, commenced by Royal Navy airborne Sea King Mk 7 helicopters fitted with early warning radar, provided synthetic aperture radar images of the terrain and installations. HMAS *Kanimbla* was used as a forward operating base for crew swaps and refuelling. Tragically, on 22 March 2003, two of these helicopters collided with the loss of seven lives.

On the afternoon of 17 March, 38 dhows attempted an unusual daytime escape of the Khawr Abd Allah. Their crews had heard erroneous news reports of the impending start of the war. In their desperation they started to jettison cargo. Vice Admiral Keating approved the recommendation of the MIF to clear the Khawr Abd Allah rather than turn the dhows around in accordance with the UN sanctions. It was a historic moment because it was the effective end of the 12-year embargo. The well-developed plan of the MIF was activated. All dhows were anchored and searched for arms, explosives, mines and deserting Iraqi leadership before being physically marked, cleared and directed south along the designated track called Red Route 1. Coalition aircraft and warships monitored their passage down the Gulf.

For their part, once the dhows' crews understood what was happening, they were compliant. For some boarding teams and dhow crews, it was a poignant moment. After months, if not years, of being boarded and being turned back, this was to be their last meeting. Among those vessels cleared was the Indian dhow that lost her crew member two nights earlier.

As expected, the word of the clearance quickly spread up the Khawr Abd Allah, and the following day the merchant ships made their outbound passage. Fifty-six dhows and 47 merchant ships were inspected and cleared in about three days. This early clearance emptied the waterway in preparation for combat operations.

In the early morning of 19 March, UN officials on the Mīnā' al-Bakr and Khor al-Amaya oil terminals were detained and taken to Basra in an Iraqi government tug. There were fears that they would find themselves used as 'human shields' just as such people had been used during the earlier Gulf War. To prevent this, CH-47 Chinook helicopters intercepted the tug, removed the UN workers, and allowed the vessel to proceed on its way. The UN workers reported that Iraqi military were present on the two offshore oil terminals with some suspicious equipment. This corroborated earlier reports from merchantmen that Iraq might detonate explosives on the terminals.

Hostilities

On the evening of 19 March 2003, US Navy Seals and Polish GROM, under the overall command of US Navy Commodore Robert S. Harward, conducted a sea and airborne assault on Mīnā' al-Bakr and Khor al-Amaya oil terminals. HMAS *Anzac* stood by to extract these forces if the assault was repulsed. However, the attack proceeded to plan, and both platforms were quickly secured. Iraqi explosives were present on the platforms but had not been fitted. At the same time as the oil terminal operation, US Navy Seals secured the two related oil manifolds on the Al-Faw Peninsula.

This operation was soon followed by the first wave of Tomahawk land attack cruise missile launches from US Navy cruisers, destroyers and submarines as well as British submarines. In all more than 800 Tomahawks were fired from 35 coalition ships from the Mediterranean, the Red Sea, the Persian Sea and the Persian Gulf, with almost half of those being fired in the first 24 hours. A third of the missiles were launched from submarines, including from the British submarines.

7. MARITIME OPERATIONS

The Al-Faw coalition aircraft commenced strikes on Iraqi army positions, augmented by 148 Battery Royal Artillery firing from Bubyan Island, the largest island in the Kuwaiti coastal island chain in the north-western corner of the Persian Gulf. On completion of this bombardment, Royal Marines conducted an airborne insertion on the Al-Faw Peninsula.

Soon after the commencement of hostilities, an Iraqi navy PB-90 patrol boat proceeded down the Khawr Abd Allah to attack coalition warships. En route it was detected by a AP-3C Orion from Patrol Squadron 46, which relayed its location to an AC-130 gunship then supporting the Al-Faw operation. In a brief exchange of fire, the PB-90 blew up under the hail of fire from the aircraft's 76mm gun. Three survivors, suffering from hypothermia, were picked up at daylight by Adak. They were expeditiously recovered to HMAS *Kanimbla* where they told their tale of survival.

At around 0200 on 20 March 2003, HMS *Marlborough*, HMAS *Anzac*, HMS *Chatham* and HMS *Richmond* were detached for shore bombardment duties. The passage to assigned fire support areas was challenging with a strong tidal stream, poor visibility and shallow waters. The Royal Marines encountered stubborn resistance from Iraqi forces and called for naval gunfire support at 0604. The ships engaged command posts, bunkers and artillery positions. In one action, HMAS *Anzac* destroyed a T59 artillery piece in a fire mission of three rounds. Such was the unprecedented accuracy of the frigates that spotters used single rounds to direct Iraqi troops up the peninsula. Very accurate fire was provided by frigates at near maximum ranges with Royal Marines in close proximity waiting to exploit the effects. Naval gunfire was used to encourage capitulation by Iraqi forces with success on a number of occasions. The battery commander reported: 'Success on the Al-Faw was due to the aggressive use of indirect fire support, especially the swift response from naval gunfire support ships which had a huge impact on the ground and shattered the enemy's will to fight.' A total of 17 fire missions were executed with just 155 rounds of 5-inch and 4.5-inch ammunition expended.

During the night another aspect of the operation was executed. This was the protection of an amphibious transit lane for the fast landing craft air cushion (LCAC) hovercraft to take equipment from Bubyan Island across the Khawr Abd Allah to the Al-Faw Peninsula. USS *Chinook*, USS *Firebolt*, USCGC *Adak* and USCGC *Aquidneck* reported three Iraqi tugs and a barge coming down the Khawr Abd Allah. It was discovered that the tug *Jumariya* had a barge with 20 Manta and 48 LUGM contact mines concealed in its hull, while the tug *Al Raya* contained 18 LUGM mines. The mines on the upper deck of the *Al Raya* were concealed by hollowed-out 50-gallon barrels. The barrels were lined in rows, simulating a cargo barge and tug. An Australian Army LCM-8 landing craft ferried the 38 Iraqi crewmen to a US Navy designated prisoner-holding amphibious ship. SEALs from USS *Joint Venture*, which had come up the channel west of Bubiyan Island, then confirmed that there were no additional Iraqi mine barges further up the Khawr Abd Allah.

Later in the day, four small Iraqi suicide boats proceeded down the Shatt Al-Arab. They were pursued by Iranian naval forces and beached themselves. In response to this threat, I detached HMS *Chatham* and HMAS *Darwin* as a Surface Action Group to the mouth of the Shatt Al-Arab. The ships possessed a good combination of weapon systems to deal with small inshore contacts. The ships remained off the mouth of the Shatt Al-Arab until the danger of these boats had passed.

The anticipated short-range Iraqi missile attacks from the Al-Faw did materialise on 20 March, but the target was Kuwait city, not coalition warships. At least six SCUD missiles were fired with limited damage sustained. The Patriot missile defence batteries, with cueing from USS *Higgins*, intercepted at least two SCUDS, destroying them in mid-flight.

While this activity was occurring at the mouth of the Khawr Abd Allah, the US, British and Australian clearance diving teams had driven across the desert from Kuwait behind the leading 15th Marine Expeditionary Unit elements into Umm Qasr. Once the port had been secured, they commenced mine clearance of the port precinct. Australian, British and US Navy diving teams were complemented by dolphins trained by the US Navy to locate bottomed mines. The mine clearance forces were supported from the amphibious ship USS *Gunston Hall*.

On 20 March, US Marine Corps Task Force Grizzly advanced to South Rumaylah to prevent Iraqi efforts to destroy the oilfields. However, the main effort of the US Marines was to push into Iraq and approach Baghdad from the south-east, securing vital points en route. Meanwhile, the Royal Marines and British Army units focused on securing the south and took Basra on 6 April. By 10 April 2003, the US Marines had established themselves in Baghdad. The focus then shifted to stabilisation and security operations.

Meanwhile, the aircraft carriers maintained continuous air missions to support the air campaign, while the Tomahawk armed cruisers, destroyers and submarines also contributed to operations. More than 400 navy aircraft from six fighter wings flew more than 7,000 sorties in support of Operation IRAQI FREEDOM between 20 March and 14 April. Among the many Iraqi targets struck were the remnants of the Iraqi navy tied up alongside in Basra, including *Al-Mansur*.

The US Marine Air Wing flew some 9,800 sorties and expended nearly 6.25 million pounds of ordnance during the operation. Owing to the shortage of airfields and other considerations, their AV-8B Harriers operated from their amphibious ships. This demonstrated the US Marines' 'Operational Manoeuvre from the Sea' concept, which is premised on a largely self-contained force being able to project force and sustain operations from its offshore support ships, integrating all joint, combined and organic assets.

During the next couple of days events moved quickly. Once the Al-Faw was secured, the coalition mine counter-measures vessels HM Ships *Bangor*, *Blyth*, *Brocklesby* and *Sandown*, as well as US Ships *Dextrous*, *Cardinal* and *Ardent*, complemented by the two Sea Dragon helicopters with towed sidescan sonars, commenced counter-mine operations. MIF patrol boats and RHIBs protected these forces through ever-lengthening riverine patrols. On one such patrol, USS *Chinook* observed suspicious activity on the Al-Faw shoreline. On landing a team ashore, they chased away Iraqis who left a semi-inflated boat and a cache of rockets and other weapons. The MIF continued riverine patrols until the Al-Faw was secured.

The campaign plan called for clearing of mines in the Khawr Abd Allah up to Umm Qasr within 72 hours. But this goal proved unrealistic owing to the large number of mine-like objects littering the riverbed. This was hardly surprising as the Khawr Abd Allah has been a battle zone on several occasions in the 20th century. To speed up the clearance, the normal mine counter-measures process of detect, identify and destroy was modified to detect and destroy mine-like objects. In the end, the coalition mine counter-measures forces cleared the equivalent of 913 nautical miles of water in the Khawr Abd Allah and Umm Qasr port area. Eventually, 21 berths for ships were opened in Umm Qasr, and this cleared the way to allow the first coalition humanitarian aid shipments into Iraq on board RFA *Sir Galahad* on 28 March.

The maritime component of operations to dislodge the Saddam Hussein regime was long in the build-up but short in duration. On 12 April 2003, Baghdad fell to coalition forces. Even before that day, once the land forces had secured Umm Qasr and Basra, the primary role of maritime forces fell to contributing to the air campaign.

At this phase of the campaign there was a strong desire to rapidly draw down on forces. This was not only because of their attendant logistic and fiscal burden but also because they could become a target for local insurgents, al-Qaeda or misadventure. In consultation with the overall campaign commander, General Franks, the naval footprint was therefore rapidly decreased.

In coming months, however, there was much work to be done by coalition naval forces in stabilising the post-Saddam Iraq. This included opening up ports and waterways and, most importantly, protecting the vital offshore oil terminals through which more than 90 per cent of Iraq's foreign earnings flow.

Summation

The maritime campaign to oust the Saddam Hussein regime was noteworthy for the diverse range of missions undertaken by an integrated multinational force. The Deputy Maritime Component Commander, Rear Admiral Snelson, on reflection stated: 'Overall, the campaign was a classic use of maritime power in support of initial diplomatic and coercive objectives and then in support of a joint war-fighting campaign.'[5]

The success of the maritime element was based on a number of factors. Key among them was 12 years of experience operating and sustaining naval forces in the narrow confines of the northern Gulf. Related to this experience was the high level of interoperability among participants. This was a testament not only to the experience of working together but also to the widespread use of liaison officers and the development of mission-specific procedures and doctrine for the operation. An example was the elaborate identification procedures to prevent friendly fire on RHIBs. Rear Admiral Snelson stated:

---

5   D. Snelson, 'Liberating Iraq—The UK's maritime contribution', *Naval Review*, vol. 91, no. 4, 2003, p. 328.

> This very close integration of forces practised by the Australian Navy as well as the US [Navy] and [Royal Navy], resulted in unparalleled unity of effort that paid dividends in preventing friction, blue-on-blue engagements and forcing the sharing of intelligence and C2 connectivity.[6]

This integration extended to the higher levels of command and planning. Vice Admiral Keating remarked:

> This was a different war, perhaps obviously, but for not-so-apparent reasons. It was joint war-fighting at the highest form of the art I've ever seen. The component commanders (air, land, sea) working for General Tommy Franks had spent about a year formulating this plan.[7]

Despite the complexity of the operation, the relatively sophisticated command and control tools allowed large amounts of information to be disseminated. This allowed units to be multitasked or retasked. Vice Admiral Keating remarked, 'We were able to keep up with the rapidly dynamic and changing war in ways that were, in my experience, unprecedented.'[8]

The most decisive strategic effect created by the maritime component was the generation of air power from six carrier air groups in an operation where constraints were placed on land-based air power. The second crucial effect was sea control that enabled the build-up and sustainment of all land, air and sea forces. This sea control also enabled the strategically vital offshore oil terminals to be secured before oil could be released into the Gulf by Saddam Hussein's regime. The consequences of such a release could have been catastrophic. The coalition's sea control also prevented sea mining of the Gulf, which could have had serious implications on the coalition's conduct of operations. Finally, deployment of significant marine forces made a notable contribution to the success of the land campaign.

---

6   Ibid., p. 326.
7   T.J. Keating, 'This was a different war: Interview with Vice Admiral Timothy J. Keating', *US Naval Institute Proceedings*, vol. 129, no. 6, 2003, p. 30.
8   Ibid., p. 30.

Post–Iraq War operations

Following the Iraq War, the thread of maritime interception operations and the provision of good order at sea was once again picked up. Initially, the environment was benign, but then Iraqi insurgents and later al-Qaeda and Islamic State terrorists posed a threat in the northern and southern Gulf. Seaborne forces had the opportunity to disrupt the drug trade between the subcontinent and Africa. These and the earlier operations showed the utility of naval forces that are capable of both sustained maritime interception operations and, if needed, littoral warfare.

8
Embeds

Jim Molan

I saw three Iraq wars: the first Iraq War in 1991, otherwise known as the Gulf War; the second Iraq War from 2003 to 2011, being the invasion and stabilisation of Iraq by counter-terrorism and counter-insurgency; and the third Iraq War, being 2014 to perhaps 2017–18, against ISIS. There is a popular view that there was just one war and that it was all the fault of the United States, President Bush, or the invasion of Iraq in 2003. But in fact—and I acknowledge that this is a contentious view—the only thing common across the three wars was the geography of Iraq.

From 2004 to 2005, I was an embedded member, an 'embed', of the Headquarters Multi-National Force – Iraq (MNF-I), and probably the most senior Australian soldier deployed. During that time, I was chief of operations in Iraq. My experience was an American experience of what our US comrades considered to be a war of necessity. For the US Army at least, this was a war of necessity, and the achievement of the mission was more important than the lives of soldiers, so greater risks and more casualties were accepted by the United States. For the allies, this was a war of choice, and most allies chose to prioritise the lives of their soldiers over the achievement of almost any mission.

I discussed the various views of my task as chief of operations in my book, *Running the War in Iraq*. I made the point that my experience was an American experience as I worked as a lone Australian (except for my brilliant executive officers and my extraordinary bodyguard) in the headquarters and throughout Iraq with almost no contact with other

Australians. I was told by the Australian Chief of Defence Force to ensure that the commanding general was aware that I was working for him alone. Suffice to say that since 2004, as the ADF and the government's exposure to war increased, Australia has become much more competent in giving direction to its deployed soldiers through military directives.

The war in which I was involved as an embed was big. Most Australians are unaware how big it was or how vicious the fighting was. When I was there, there were 150,000 to 175,000 coalition troops, and we built the Iraqi army up to 125,000 troops and police over a year. The United States had 20 combat brigades deployed but, strangely, only had 413 hospital beds over the entire theatre because of the capability to evacuate casualties. Out of the 10 combat divisions that the full-time US Army possessed, the equivalent of three and a half were deployed at any one time in Iraq. Given the US world responsibility, this illustrates how desperately short the United States is in terms of land combat forces and how much the United States needs its allies. But in Iraq, the allies were not there.

To illustrate the level of combat in this counter-insurgency fight, I spoke briefly about the second battle of Fallujah, in November 2004. This was a conventional 'divisional' attack on a city that had 3,000 to 6,000 dug-in insurgents defending it. That this should occur within a counter-insurgency, which most Australians seem to associate with jungles and communist terrorists, was somewhat counter-intuitive. To show how one type of traditional but complex conflict has merged into other types of complex conflict, I described Fallujah as 'a conventional operation as part of a stabilization campaign to achieve an integrated political effect against an insurgent and terrorist force that stayed and fought'.

I commend to you Dr Albert Palazzo's 572-page report on Australia's participation in the Iraq War,[1] which has recently been made available through a Freedom of Information request by the *Sydney Morning Herald*— but with 500 redactions by Defence.[2] The *SMH* quoted Defence as referring to the report as an 'unofficial history that reflect the author's own views', the author being referred to as an 'Army official'. In that report, I was referred to as 'the ADF member most directly involved in fighting the insurgents', and I consider this report to be a good summary of our participation in the Iraqi war up to 2010. The author of the report considered that Australia's

---

1 Palazzo, *The Australian Army and the War in Iraq: 2002–2010*.
2 See www.smh.com.au/interactive/2017/pdfview/ViewerJS/#../The_Australian_Army_in_Iraq.pdf (retrieved 3 April 2020).

participation in the war was 'inconsequential and confused, timid even', and observed: 'It would be interesting to know the reaction of US personnel who served in Iraq to Australia's timidity.' Well, as someone who lived within the beast for a long time, and became familiar with the US personnel at the top, let me tell you that whenever they thought of it, which was not often because they were running serious operations and battles, they were not impressed, and we were just another ally.

This issue goes to the importance of military credibility in an alliance. Because the centre point of our defence policy is an expectation that the United States will come to our aid in an extreme military situation, it is important that the United States feels that Australia will share the burden not just of military expenditure but also of combat. This was not a view that seemed to be accepted by Australian defence civilians in the room, the flippant comment being made that 'we do not go to war to impress the US military'. My view is that Australia's credibility as an ally is crucial to our defence policy if we base that policy on US assistance in an emergency. This does not mean that we accept US policy always or that we follow the United States like a deputy sheriff.

If we consider that a war should be fought, and we are prepared to put troops into that war, then we should realise that it is against our interests for us to be popularly considered the 'new French', as the British called us in Al Muthanna Province because we would not fight. The alternative is to not rely on the United States and to put our minds to defending ourselves, which we are unlikely to do. Regardless of what the United States says to us or to our allies, the United States understands which nations are truly prepared to carry the burden of world security with them. Many defence civilians seem to think that 'showing the flag' is clever when we send troops to Iraq at a time when the United States is desperate for assistance, and we decide that we will support the war rhetorically, so that we will send our troops there but not fight. Then of course many of the same people point out how we are 'punching above our weight' in an appalling show of insensitivity.

Ignorant people think that the United States does not need its allies and that it has infinite military strength. It did not then, and after 16 years of one or two wars, eight years of President Obama and congressional sequestration, the United States needs its allies like it has never needed them before. And Australia needs to have a clear-eyed view of what it contributes to the alliance.

My favourite lesson from Iraq was about allies, and it was that it took the coalition eight years to win a war that in my judgement (and in retrospect) we should have won in two years. Why? Because the allies, like Australia, refused to help effectively. Twenty-eight countries were present in Iraq when I was there, yet one, or maybe two at times, were doing all the fighting.

By way of conclusion, I came up with a number of generalised lessons put as simply as possible, as follows:

- Counterinsurgencies are not quick, cheap or easy. But they are winnable.
- Get serious or get out.
- Security forces are not the only answer, but they are normally the first answer.
- The amount of strategic benefit derived from a 'niche' or 'token' deployment is in direct proportion to its value to an ally.
- You will never 'do strategy' if you cannot balance the objective with the costs (mainly time and casualties).
- Close combat is so ugly that everyone is looking for alternatives—except the modern insurgent.
- A comprehensive inter-agency approach is not just a set of words; it is real resources (time, money, lives, reputation).
- 'End-states' (i.e. the conditions to be achieved at conclusion of the operation) specified before the start of a war are an interesting academic exercise.
- It is much harder to get out of a war than to decide to get into a war in the first place.
- Avoid simple solutions—they are likely to be wrong.
- Avoid the four standard errors:
  1. allocating insufficient troops initially
  2. insisting that reconstruction start before there is security
  3. failing to provide even the non-military resources necessary
  4. stretching the involvement beyond the limits of your home nation's resolve.

These are the lessons about winning wars that embeds can provide.

PART 3: JOINT FORCES, ENABLERS AND PARTNERS

9

Command and control

Michael Crane

Command and control, or C2, is an issue of keen interest to both students and practitioners of the military art because the C2 arrangements go a long way to establishing the tenor of any operation. As General David Petraeus used to say when I worked for him at US Central Command (CENTCOM), if you get the C2 right the rest will follow. At the other end of the spectrum, poor command and control arrangements create ambiguities and frictions that distract the attention and energy of commanders. After all, C2 structures are about power relationships: who gets to give orders and who has to take them. An examination of command and control arrangements is therefore very important to understanding Australia's recent operations in the Middle East.

I present here a personal perspective, and my observations should be seen in that light. I served twice as Commander Joint Task Force 633, so my assessments are developed primarily through the lens of national command. But in the period under consideration I also served as Chief of Staff at Headquarters Joint Operations Command (HQJOC), Head Military Strategic Commitments (HMSC) and Deputy Director Operations at CENTCOM, so what follows also reflects some flavour of those appointments.

I do not propose to dwell at any length on why national command is so sensitive to Australians; our experience in two world wars is widely known and understood. Neither will I trace the detailed development of higher ADF command structures from Federation; such an exposition is not necessary for this discussion, and in any case others have done that very elegantly elsewhere.[1]

Instead, I want to focus on the Australian command and control arrangements that I experienced in the Middle East Area of Operations (MEAO) in 2006 and 2012. I begin by describing the original structures and how they evolved over time to the points at which I found them. I then canvass some of the critiques of the model and offer my perspectives. Finally, I turn briefly to select other issues that I grappled with on a day-to-day basis during my tenure in command.

Australian Middle East Area of Operations command and control, 2001–14, in outline

As we have seen in earlier chapters, Australia's most substantial recent involvement in the Middle East had its origins in the terrorist attacks in the United States in September 2001. In response to those attacks, the ADF deployed ships to support the Maritime Interception Force (MIF) in the Persian Gulf, a special operations task group to Afghanistan, and aircraft to different locations in the region. Operation SLIPPER, as it was known, was commanded by Commander Australian Theatre (COMAST), Rear Admiral Chris Ritchie. 'Australian Theatre', or AST, is the precursor title of HQJOC. Ritchie's concept for the operation was endorsed by the Chief of Defence Force and the Strategic Command Group, and he was then left to run it.

We did not deploy a Joint Task Force (JTF) headquarters for Operation SLIPPER in 2001, but we did deploy an Australian national commander, Brigadier Ken Gillespie. He was based in Kuwait, where he was co-located with the US Land Component Commander and handy to the other US component commanders. Gillespie reported to COMAST, but did not himself exercise much control over the deployed Australian forces. Instead, on national matters, the commanders of the tactical elements reported directly to their respective Australian Theatre component

---

1   See in particular D. Horner, 'The higher command structure for joint ADF operations', in *History as Policy: Framing the Debate on the Future of Australia's Defence Policy*, ed. R. Huisken and M. Thatcher, ANU E Press, Canberra, 2007, pp. 143–61. Much of my description of the early years in the Middle East Area of Operations is drawn from this rich source.

commanders—that is, to the maritime, special forces and air component commanders. Gillespie was kept informed so that he could veto Australian participation if required, but on operational matters, the tactical commanders worked under the operational control of their respective US component commanders.

The command arrangements for the 2003 Iraq War, Operation FALCONER, had some similarities. The Australian national commander, Brigadier Maurie McNarn, was co-located in Qatar with the US commander General Tommy Franks. As in Operation SLIPPER, McNarn reported to COMAST, who by then was Rear Admiral Mark Bonser. As before, the several deployed task group commanders were placed under operational control of the coalition component commanders. But this time they reported through McNarn on operational matters and to COMAST on technical and administrative matters. The big differences, though, were at the strategic level. First, for reasons of secrecy, Operation FALCONER was planned in Canberra by Strategic Operations Division in Defence Headquarters, and Bonser was brought in only later. And second, in addition to reporting to Bonser, McNarn also reported directly to the Chief of Defence Force, General Peter Cosgrove, who wanted a more direct connection with his commander in the field because of the rapid pace of operations.

After the successful invasion of Iraq, Operation FALCONER came to an end and a new operation, CATALYST, began. While several units returned to Australia, the remaining force still contained a variety of naval, land and air elements, and at this point a joint task force was established: Joint Task Force 633 (JTF 633). The first Commander JTF 633, Air Commodore Graham Bentley, was given operational control of all Australian elements, which he in turn delegated to coalition commanders. He reported to COMAST but retained a direct link to the Chief of Defence Force.

In the period following the establishment of JTF 633, there were some seismic changes in arrangements at the strategic and operational levels.

- In 2004, Headquarters AST became HQJOC; COMAST (a two-star appointment) became the Deputy Chief of Joint Operations (DCJOPS); and the three-star appointment, Vice Chief of the Defence Force (VCDF), was double-hatted as Chief of Joint Operations (CJOPS).

- At the same time, Strategic Operations Division was disestablished, and a smaller Military Strategic Commitments (MSC) Branch was established at one-star (brigadier or equivalent) level to support the Chief of Defence Force (four-star ranked appointment) and VCDF in their operational roles.
- In 2007, the roles of CJOPS and VCDF were separated, so that for the first time we had a three-star officer (lieutenant general or equivalent) focused entirely on commanding operations on behalf of the Chief of Defence Force.
- At the same time, HQJOC (the rebadged Headquarters Australian Theatre) expanded considerably as it moved from Potts Point in Sydney to Bungendore in rural New South Wales, not far from Canberra, and absorbed the component headquarters.
- Finally, the MSC Branch was expanded to a small division, headed by a two-star officer (major general or equivalent) as Head MSC (HMSC).

At the JTF 633 level, though, the basic command and control construct remained remarkably stable for more than a decade. Commander JTF 633 exercised operational control over a number of task groups dispersed across the MEAO, most of which were then delegated under the operational control of coalition commanders. Commander JTF 633 also commanded a significant national logistic element, which was designed to reduce our impost on US resources.

There were, of course, a number of changes in the JTF over time.

- In 2006, in response to our renewed and growing commitment in Afghanistan, a deputy national commander was established in Kabul, Colonel Dick Stanhope being the first incumbent.
- In 2007, the rank of the Commander of JTF 633 was upgraded from one-star to two-star level, and the rank of the deputy in Afghanistan was later upgraded from O6 (colonel or equivalent) to one star.
- Having moved to Baghdad in 2003 soon after the end of the Iraq War, in late 2008 the JTF headquarters moved to the United Arab Emirates. A move was necessary because the UN mandate in Iraq was coming to an end, but it also reflected the realisation that the weight of Australian operations was by then in Afghanistan.

9. COMMAND AND CONTROL

- At about the same time, the various air elements of the JTF were assigned to an Air Task Group under a group captain, rather than reporting directly to the commander of the JTF as they had done previously.
- And in 2011, the new CJOPS, Lieutenant General Ash Power, assigned units under operational command of Commander JTF 633 rather than operational control. By so doing, the Commander JTF 633 could exercise the further delegation of authority, rather than that function being mandated directly from HQJOC.

By the time I arrived in the United Arab Emirates to assume command in September 2012, the JTF command and control arrangements were largely well settled, although, as Figure 3 illustrates, it was somewhat complex. The blue lines show the basic national command arrangements. CJOPS exercised theatre command,[2] with national command[3] and operational command[4] being delegated to me as Commander JTF 633. In turn, I exercised national command of those units based in Afghanistan through my deputy in Kabul, Brigadier Peter Short, while those outside Afghanistan worked directly to me. Also in the national space were multiple chains of technical control, shown in Figure 3 in green, running from a range of agencies in Australia to units based in the Middle East. These chains dealt with matters ranging from airworthiness and special forces operations to finance and other administration. In fact, some detachments were not strictly even working for me at all—for example, the Diggerworks team at Tarin Kowt was an army unit focused entirely on learning lessons about our land materiel, and I had no responsibility for it other than to provide it with protection and logistic support.

---

2 Theatre Command is the authority given by CDF to CJOPS to command assigned forces to prepare for and conduct operations (campaigns, operations, combined and joint exercises) and other activities as directed.
3 National Command is a command that is organised by and functions under the authority of a specific nation.
4 Operational Command is the authority granted to a commander to specify missions or tasks to subordinate commanders, to deploy units, to reassign forces and to retain or delegate OPCON, TACOMD (Tactical Command) and/or TACON as may be deemed necessary. It does not of itself include responsibility for administration or logistics.

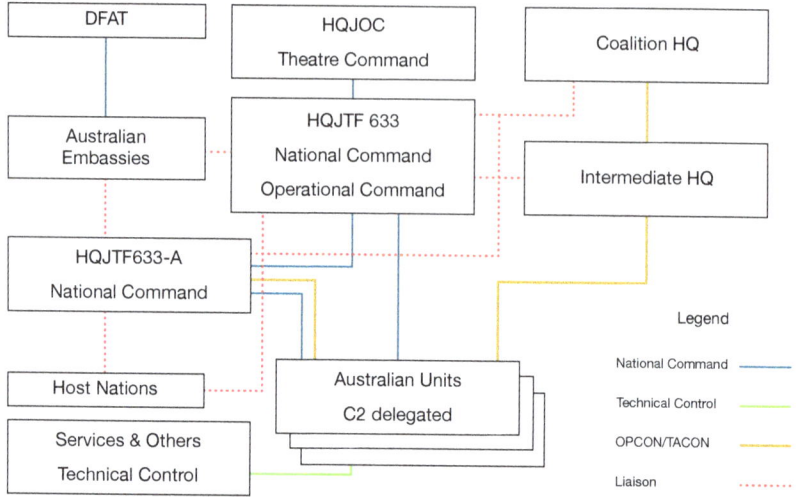

Figure 3: Middle Eastern Area of Operations command and control arrangements.
Source: Courtesy of Major General Michael Crane.

Authority to employ Australian units for the conduct of operations was delegated to coalition commanders (the linkages are illustrated in Figure 3 in brown). Australian units were generally allotted under Operational Control (OPCON)[5] or Tactical Control (TACON)[6] of the supported coalition headquarters, depending on the requirement. The picture is greatly simplified, of course, because there were multiple coalition headquarters, and some of them had multiple linkages to Australian units. For example, our ship in the MEAO worked for Combined Task Force (CTF) 150 on maritime security, CTF 151 on counter-piracy and CTF 152 on Gulf security, with the command and control arrangements switching at any given moment to suit the immediate requirement.

It is interesting to note that Peter Short exercised more than just national command on my behalf. When the Dutch left Uruzgan in 2010, Australia began holding and interrogating detainees in its own right for the first time.

---

5   Operational Control is the authority delegated to a commander to direct forces assigned so that the commander may accomplish specific missions or tasks that are usually limited by function, time or location; deploy units concerned; and retain or delegate TACON of those units. It does not include authority to allocate separate employment of components of the units concerned. Neither does it, of itself, include administrative or logistic control.
6   Tactical Control is the detailed and, usually, local direction and control of movements or manoeuvres necessary to accomplish missions or tasks assigned.

Given the obvious sensitivities, the deputy commander in Afghanistan was made responsible for oversight of detention and interrogation operations, and the respective units were allotted OPCON to him.

Finally, another critical element of the C2 architecture was the liaison network that Peter Short and I operated, shown in Figure 4 in red. Peter worked all his contacts in Afghanistan assiduously and did a great job on my behalf in keeping his finger on the pulse from day to day. That meant I did not have to visit Afghanistan as frequently as I might have done otherwise, and it freed me to focus on relationships in the Gulf.

For example, I called on the US naval, land and air component commanders several times during my tour to get their assessment of their operations, to check whether there were any issues for Australia and, of course, to touch base with the Australians working in their respective headquarters. Working also with the Australian ambassadors in the region, I routinely called on representatives of the host governments on whose support we relied so heavily.

The critiques

Despite their longevity, the command and control arrangements described above have been critiqued routinely. Most of the main concerns are summarised in a scoping study for a review of strategic C2 lessons, conducted by Noetic Solutions in July 2013.[7] The study claims that there are 'very few JTF 633 "fans" in the ADF', and found 'near-uniform questioning of [the JTF's] role, size, location and function'. JTF 633 was generally perceived, the study said, to be 'at best marginally contributory to the work people did, and was described variously as "a self-licking ice-cream", overly controlling, risk averse, disruptive and interfering'.

The study found that those consulted had several concerns. First, they felt that the appointment of a discrete national commander, rather than the role being assigned to a senior embedded officer, confused senior coalition officers and other coalition members. Second, they felt that this separation of functions rendered the Australian national commander just another

---

7   Noetic Solutions, 'Strategic Command and Control Lessons—Scoping Study', Noetic Solutions, Canberra, 2013, www.defence.gov.au/FOI/Docs/Disclosures/343_10_11_Document.pdf (retrieved 31 March 2020).

visitor to the headquarters who merely added to the staff workload. They felt that any perception of special influence or access was probably largely illusory. Finally, they felt that the connection between the various activities being conducted did not support the need for a JTF—in other words, that the various task groups were essentially conducting discrete tasks through different coalition chains of command. They argued that, with the introduction of the various environmental directors general, HQJOC had evolved beyond an integrated model. Under these changed circumstances, the task groups could have been commanded directly through these 'components', with the logistic and force support elements being made direct command units—presumably through the Chief Staff Officer for Joint Logistics (or J4) at HQJOC.

At the other end of the spectrum, another former JTF 633 commander, Major General Craig Orme, makes a quite different criticism.[8] Orme assesses that the command and control arrangements were not sufficiently strategic and that JTF 633 could have had an even wider role. He argues that we only ever had a tactical vision for each operation, and came to understand the need for an MEAO theatre architecture only after some 15 years of operations. He makes the point that, had we had such an architecture to tie the theatre together from the outset, the transition to new operations as conditions changed would have been much smoother. He also argues that such an architecture could have included the minor operations, including in South Sudan, the Sinai and Palestine.

Finally, Brigadier Anthony Rawlins in Chapter 6 of this book raises another critique based on his experience as commanding officer of Overwatch Battle Group (West)-2 (OBG(W)-2) in Iraq's Al Muthanna Province in 2006–07. If I understand it correctly, it is that the national chain of command failed to articulate a clear intent for OBG(W) operations, then leave the commanding officer to get on with implementing that intent in accordance with the principles of mission command.[9]

---

[8] Major General C.A. Orme, DSC, AM (Retd), private communication, April 2017.
[9] ADF doctrine does not define mission command, but describes its effects. Perhaps the most precise description (in a somewhat unsatisfactory section of the doctrine) is 'Under Mission Command … the superior commander directs WHAT is to be achieved but leaves the subordinate commander free to decide HOW to achieve assigned tasks'. See ADDP 0.01, *Command and Control*, pp. 2–8.

Now, the data for the Noetic study was developed via an email questionnaire sent to just 14 senior ADF and Department of Defence officers. The authors are quick to point out that their study makes no claim to being comprehensive. Accordingly, we should take care in deciding what weight to give expressions such as 'few fans in the ADF' and 'near-uniform questioning'.

That said, the people canvassed represent an impressive body of experience. The group included two former JTF 633 commanders and two others who would go on to command it. It also included former senior embedded officers, a former CJOPS and a former Commander Special Operations, as well as senior Defence headquarters and staff from HQJOC. Further, Craig Orme's and Anthony Rawlins's experiences speak for themselves.

So each of these critiques deserves to be examined in detail, and no doubt, as historians mull over the evidence in years to come, a clearer picture will emerge. Let me offer a few observations that the historians might include in their considerations.

First, I agree that the idea of a discrete national commander did bemuse some coalition officers, but I never thought they were confused, and I never found it an insurmountable issue. Actually, some senior Americans rather liked our system, because it was quite clear which officers were doing national tasking and which ones were engaged in coalition work.

For my own part, I have always thought there were good reasons not to have an embedded officer as the senior national representative. Underlining that distinction between dedication to national tasks and coalition effort is one. Another is that, presumably, an embedded officer's embed duties are sufficient to fill his or her days in their own right without loading national responsibilities on top. I certainly found that was the case when I was an embedded officer at CENTCOM. If it is not, somebody should probably be reviewing whether that embed position is really necessary. Finally, I am not sure that embedded officers can bring a sufficiently hard-headed national focus to the national command role. My experience throughout more than a decade suggests that embedded officers are quickly institutionally captured by their coalition headquarters. And that is as it should be—we want them to be the best coalition staff officer they can be because it is in Australia's interest for them to be seen to be a loyal team member. But that does make it difficult for them to judge priority between coalition and national interests.

I also agree that my visits to coalition headquarters did make some work for coalition staffs, but it was minimal. I was being reminded of the sensitivity to my visits, particularly by our embeds and national staff in Afghanistan. I do not know how my predecessors or successors did it, but I tried to time my visits appropriately, and I always made them low key. I was not interested in getting detailed briefs from the coalition staff. I was focused on engaging the commanders themselves, and those who were worth their salt were always willing to give me their time. Of course, I also wanted to hear the views of our embedded staff on how the operation was going and whether their individual roles were useful, and to talk to them about how they were going personally. If that took up some of their time, I make no apology for that.

As to whether we received any special access or influence by virtue of having a discrete national commander, I am not sure we ever made that claim. I believe that such special access and influence as we had has come from the US experience of Australia as an ally and partner: we came to the party when they asked us; we then tried not to ask too much of them in terms of support; and we always said which part of the job we would do, then did it.

A more interesting question is whether we had it right in having our national support infrastructure, including our headquarters and commander, based in the United Arab Emirates from 2008 rather than, say, in Kabul. To me, the argument for the United Arab Emirates was reasonably compelling. From a security point of view, it was far superior to anywhere in Afghanistan, and not having it in Afghanistan reduced the load on the International Security Assistance Force (ISAF). Also, having been based in Baghdad in my first tour, I found the United Arab Emirates much more convenient for visiting the dispersed elements of the JTF and our coalition and host nation partners.

Perhaps another variation would have been to appoint Peter Short as national commander in Afghanistan, working either to me as the regional national commander or directly for the CJOPS. I think Short would argue that he could have done that and that, in many ways, it was the de facto situation anyway. I will simply say that I think it is easier to make the case for that kind of arrangement than it is for double-hatting an embed, which would be my least preferred option.

9. COMMAND AND CONTROL

A member of Mobility Support fires a 84mm Carl Gustaf Rocket Launcher at the heavy weapons range in Tarin Kowt, Afghanistan, 2012.
Source: Courtesy of the Department of Defence.

The 'no need for a JTF' critique is also interesting: could we have done away with Headquarters JTF 633 altogether and run the entire operation through the HQJOC components and Joint staff? Well, of course anything is possible, and in fact we do run some minor operations that way—Operation SOLANIA in the Pacific, for example.

But I believe it would have been difficult to do it through HQJOC and the components of the headquarters in the early days in the MEAO because of the limited capacity of HQJOC before the 2007 expansion. Perhaps the components could have run the operational task groups, but the J4 at HQJOC certainly could not have run the national support side with the staffing levels it then had. And of course, the doctrine we were moving towards at the time was the creation of an integrated HQJOC with no components, so such an approach would have swum against the prevailing philosophical tide.

Beyond matters of capacity, there is also the question of whether we should have run the operations in the MEAO directly through HQJOC, even if we could have. Perhaps one could make the case that this would have eliminated overlap and shortened lines of command and control, but in my view these are marginal benefits. HQJOC is, after all, designed to run all operations worldwide at the operational level, and running task groups directly would inevitably draw it down into the tactical to the detriment of its higher command functions. So, for me, the answer to this question is no.

Craig Orme's concern that we did not take JTF 633 far enough has greater merit. I was in Baghdad in late 2008 trying to negotiate a new Status of Forces Agreement with Iraq, so I saw firsthand the disruption to Headquarters JTF 633 as it moved down the Gulf to the United Arab Emirates. I have heard service chiefs lament the way we walked away from some Gulf countries when we no longer needed them after the successful invasion of Iraq, only to have to rebuild our bridges when we needed them again. So there is definite appeal in the idea of a solid foot on the ground with an enduring remit to manage Australia's military footprint in the MEAO on behalf of HQJOC.

I believe, however, that such an idea quickly founders on the rocks of reality. Wish it otherwise as we may, all our operational commitments in the Middle East from 2001 to 2014 were developed incrementally and were therefore tactical in their focus. There was no sense of being engaged in a campaign, at least not in the early years. Winning resources was difficult, as successive governments prescribed numbers for task elements almost to the individual soldier level. In such an environment, winning support for a JTF headquarters with a more expansive mandate would simply not have been possible. That said, we should certainly note the potential of this idea for future operations, even when they start small and tactical.

As to Anthony Rawlins's concerns, let me just say that, in my view, the OBG(W) task and the constraints around it were clear. We were, at that stage, in our province, past any free-flowing manoeuvre warfare, with its inherent ambiguity, where there is a need for subordinate commanders to have freedom of action and room for them to express themselves with flair and élan. The task the Australian Government had taken on just had to be ground out, and there was not anything pretty about it. That OBG(W) soldiers did not like the task, or that there might have been more professionally interesting jobs elsewhere, is of little account.

As an aside, when Ken Gillespie was VCDF and dual-hatted as CJOPS, I accompanied him on a call on the British two-star commander of Multi-National Division – South East (MND-SE), who made a strong play for OBG(W) to be allowed to reinforce in what was by then a difficult situation in Basra. Gillespie had little patience for this request. He reminded our host that the difficult situation was of British making. He pointed out that we had a long history of being asked by the British to do things that were not in our interests, and said we would not be so easily drawn again. He noted that we had already undertaken to do the job in Al Muthanna, and declared his intention that we would see it through. Perhaps we failed to communicate this intent adequately to OBG(W), but there was certainly no doubt in our commander's mind about what he wanted to do—and what he did not.

Where I could agree with Rawlins is that perhaps Australia missed an opportunity to leave Al Muthanna when the Japanese did, which would have saved our soldiers from what was apparently an unpopular mission. Of course, that would have meant that somebody else had to do it. In any case, for its own reasons the government decided that we would not leave with the Japanese, so the job just had to be done, like it or not.

Selected other issues

I want to leave the critiques there and touch briefly on some other issues. There are many we could consider, but I will focus here on just a few.

First, let me touch on national caveats and the so-called red card. In any coalition, national caveats are a sensitive issue. They are a significant factor for the coalition commander because they constrain the employment of his force. General John Allen used to track them personally when he was Commander of ISAF in Afghanistan, and I recall that during one of my visits to Kabul he produced a matrix that showed the various caveats—and it was a very complicated chart indeed.

But from a contributing country's point of view, national caveats are critical to sustaining national will for the contribution. They are usually finely calculated, balancing the need to make the force useful with a clear assessment of national appetite for risk.

Australia's history is replete with examples in which those we have fought alongside have asked us to do things that were not necessarily in our interests, and since we first invoked the idea of a national commander, standing up for those interests has been a key part of the role.

As a general statement, our caveats in the MEAO in 2006–07 and 2012–13 were reasonably modest. The Australian forces assigned for tasking in Al Muthanna in Iraq and Uruzgan in Afghanistan were not to operate outside those areas without explicit national approval; the ship could work with some task forces but not others; and things of that ilk. Of course, Anthony Rawlins has drawn to our attention his concerns about the constraints around OBG(W) operations (see Chapter 6), but even those caveats were modest compared to those imposed by some other nations.

I only ever really came close to pulling the national 'red card' once. It was right at the beginning of my second tour, in early October 2012, and, oddly enough, it arose out of an ISAF requirement, not an Australian one. It was not long after we had suffered the tragedy of losing three soldiers to an attack by the treacherous Afghan, Sergeant Hekmatullah. That attack precipitated a significant review of ISAF force protection protocols. One of the outcomes was a requirement that 11 specified criteria had to be satisfied before a combined ISAF–Afghan National Army patrol could be sent outside the wire, although an ISAF Forward Operating Base commander could give a waiver on up to three of those criteria if he was satisfied that the risk had been adequately mitigated. At that point, the Americans were still leading in Uruzgan, and two nights in a row the evening report from our deputy, Colonel (now Brigadier) Ben James, advised that the US commander proposed to send out a combined Australian–Afghan patrol the following day, on the basis that he had waived three of the 11 criteria.

On the first night, I called James and asked which of the criteria had been waived and on what basis the Combined Team – Uruzgan commander felt that the associated risks had been adequately mitigated. An explanation followed, and I thanked James and let it go, but when the same thing happened the following night—again initially without explanation—I called James again to express my concern. I do not recall exactly what I said, but it was to the effect that as the Australian national commander, I was becoming uneasy about what appeared to be a routine acceptance of additional risk for Australian soldiers that seemed to circumvent Commander ISAF's intent.

James accepted my concerns, and from then on a thorough justification accompanied advice of planned combined patrols. As things turned out, it was not long before ISAF set aside the requirement to satisfy those criteria explicitly and the risk was managed in different ways. But from a perception point of view, the damage had been done. When I went to visit Uruzgan a few weeks later, there was still an undercurrent of concern about my 'meddling' in operational matters, and Commander Regional Command (South) made an oblique reference to the issue during a later visit by the CJOPS.

This incident serves to illustrate just how important but also how sensitive the role of a national commander can be. These were not even Australian rules—they were ISAF's—yet what I thought were quite reasonable questions provoked a minor storm. But I cannot agree with Anthony Rawlins that mission command says I should have just stepped back. We must never forget what has been done to us by others in their own interest, and national commanders must continue to advocate for Australian interests when they see them threatened.

It is worth mentioning briefly that the command and control arrangements concerning embedded officers is not straightforward. Certainly, controlling them is not easy, principally because most of them work deep within a coalition chain, there is rarely direct Australian supervision, and they are, after all, Australians—they are outcome focused and they have a 'can-do' attitude. So, for example, when the one-star Australian director of the Combined Air Operations Centre in Qatar boarded a US aircraft and went on a bombing mission over Afghanistan one day in 2007, it caused me some concerns. To this day, I do not know whether he was within his personal directive and rules of engagement to do so, but the point I made to him was that I would have minded less if he had told me about it before he went on the mission rather than after. That way I could have at least been prepared to manage the fallout if anything went wrong.

Graham Bentley first began the task of crafting directives to embeds in 2003, and they have grown like Topsy since. The early ones were a bit light, and if anything, the current versions are probably too prescriptive. But it is important that embeds do have clear guidance because laissez-faire is simply not a workable approach to managing them.

Another interesting dimension of our command and control arrangements in the MEAO was the relationship between the JTF and Australia's diplomatic missions in the region. Our ambassadors in the various countries up and down the Gulf were, of course, important in helping to assure ongoing support for our basing presence. But the two key diplomats, to my eyes at least, were the ambassadors in Baghdad and Kabul, and of those I met and worked with, two merit mention here.

I first met His Excellency Marc Innes-Brown in Baghdad in late 2006, when my predecessor, Brigadier Mick Moon, took me for an introductory call during our handover. Innes-Brown had been ambassador since August that year. I do not recall what we talked about in that introduction, but I do remember that he had red hair and a reputation of being pretty fiery to go with it.

Just a couple of weeks later, my senior operations officer walked into my office to advise that His Excellency had requested that we send over some staff to brief him on current operations. That seemed a little odd—after all, he had an attaché resident in the embassy. I asked whether we had given such briefs before and found we had not. Then I consulted our operations order and my directive from the CJOPS, and, as I recall, I found that both were silent on any formal command and control relationship between the JTF and the embassy beyond a requirement for us to provide force protection and some enabling logistic support.

Yet clearly it was imperative that there be a relationship that ran deeper than just force protection and logistics. While I was not required to consult or report through the ambassador on operational matters, the JTF was a big focus for him in its own right and, beyond that, our activities obviously had the potential to affect his broader work. Reciprocally, he had access to a range of information that lent context to what I saw happening in the coalition, and he could work to shape things in the diplomatic arena if I felt I needed such help.

In the end, I declined to provide staff to give Innes-Brown his brief—I felt that our headquarters was busy enough doing its core tasks without adding jobs that we were not resourced to do. But I did offer to go across to the embassy to give him a personal update, and he accepted with alacrity. That approach seemed to work well in terms of both meeting his information need and deepening our personal relationship. So I made the journey across to the Red Zone every fortnight or so for the remainder of my tour, combining the brief to the ambassador with visits to our embedded staff and calls on senior coalition officers.

9. COMMAND AND CONTROL

Major General Michael Crane, Commander Joint Task Force 633, with Afghan National Army artillerymen, Camp Alamo, Kabul, 2013.
Source: Department of Defence.

In 2012, my relationship with the ambassador to Afghanistan began differently. In May that year, I attended the force preparation course in Sydney, only to find that the then ambassador-designate, Jon Philp, was also enrolled. This extraordinary step on Philp's part had two important outcomes: it gave him some insight into the way the ADF perceived Afghanistan and its operations there, and, perhaps more importantly, it allowed us to begin to develop our personal relationship before becoming immersed in our respective responsibilities. Over dinner one night that week we agreed that, while we would likely have different perspectives on many issues, nothing would be important enough to allow it to disrupt our personal relationship. We settled on a protocol under which, if we could not agree, we would refer a matter to our superiors and each abide by their decision. This approach served us well, and I am delighted to say that we never needed to ask for adjudication from Canberra.

Successful as our personal relationship was, I should close by observing that the formal arrangements between the JTF and the embassy in Kabul (or lack thereof) were broadly similar to those I had experienced in Baghdad in 2007—although in Kabul there was not yet a resident attaché. We probably need to give that some more thought.

Conclusion

As I have said, there are many other issues relating to command and control I could have discussed. Should we revisit the idea of a standing deployable JTF headquarters? How did Headquarters JTF 633 perform technically, and should we rethink our individual trickle flow reinforcement system? Why did Australia come to have its own campaign plan for Afghanistan and how was that managed? How did we get to be leading in Uruzgan Province when we had fought for so long not to be in charge there? At the strategic level, how far have the services really come in ceding control of assigned forces to the CJOPS? And so on.

There is obviously still a lot of work to be done by historians in sorting through these issues. One factor that will complicate their task is that everybody's experience is different. If you are Major General Paul Symon, who commanded in the early days, your concern is whether we should have had a properly organised standing national headquarters to get us started. If you are Major General John Cantwell in 2010, you are worried about HQJOC reaching past you into Afghanistan, and the extent to which you yourself have to lean into Afghanistan to feed the Canberra beast. If you are Major General Craig Orme in 2014, you are concerned about how you ramp up again in Iraq when Australia has only just removed the last remnants of its military presence there. And, of course, Anthony Rawlins has set out his concerns earlier. So, where you stand on our command and control arrangements very much depends upon where (and when) you sit.

10

Intelligence in Afghanistan

Mick Lehmann

The role of intelligence in war tends to be unclear, at least until enough time passes to allow the declassification of records necessary for historians to ply their trade. In the Second World War, for instance, revelations of the Ultra secret almost three decades after the end of the war substantially altered judgements on what transpired.[1] However, intelligence on the wars in Iraq and Afghanistan has been subject to a significant amount of public reporting thanks to a number of unauthorised disclosures. This reporting, together with personal experience, makes it possible to sketch a picture of the role intelligence played in supporting Australian operations in Afghanistan.

The aim of this chapter is to provide a personal perspective of intelligence support to land operations in Afghanistan from 2007 to 2014. In doing so, the chapter will touch on three main areas: organisation and structure, strategic support, and intelligence effectiveness.

When reading this chapter, a number of caveats should be borne in mind. The first is that intelligence remains *sub rosa*—subject to secrecy—and this is a fundamental constraint on what can be said by the author. The second is that much of the intelligence story in Iraq and Afghanistan—particularly in the air and at sea—is not mine to tell. Finally, this chapter is based on my experience of four and a half years of direct involvement in operations in Afghanistan, more than two of which were deployed.

---

1 See for instance F.W. Winterbotham, *The Ultra Secret*, Weidenfeld & Nicolson, London, 1974.

In regard to wisdom, this chapter is dedicated to the memory of Graeme Clarke, a man who shaped the majority of today's Australian Army Intelligence Corps personnel through his experience, knowledge and peerless passion for one of the oldest of professions.

In writing this chapter, I have been mindful of the words of General Peter Cosgrove, who wrote in his biography that intelligence officers should 'bring you the facts, their careful deductions, [and] from time to time a courageous conclusion'.[2] I hope I have done justice to the General, Graeme Clarke, and the men and women I served with.

Context

There is, of course, history to this history. For army intelligence, the period leading into 2001 had not positioned it well for operations in Iraq and Afghanistan.

Following Australia's military commitment to East Timor (1999 to 2005), the Australian Army Intelligence Corps was heavily committed and understaffed. Additionally, many of the Army's core intelligence collection capabilities, such as electronic warfare and human intelligence, were the victims of benign neglect. The deployment to East Timor in 1999 had also seen an ugly public brawl erupt between Cosgrove's chief intelligence staff officer (J2), Lieutenant Colonel Lance Collins, and the Defence Intelligence Organisation (DIO). This dispute revolved around Collins's reported concerns about pro-Indonesian bias in DIO and the alleged switching off of a strategic intelligence pipeline from Canberra to the field.[3] Relationships were not what they should have been.

The organisational consequences of these issues played out during operations in Afghanistan and Iraq, forcing the Army's intelligence efforts into a decade of improvised and ad hoc arrangements, practices, technological innovations and tactical support structures.

With this context in mind, and to the extent that it is possible to describe an organisation across two theatres and over 10 years, what did intelligence in Afghanistan look like?

---

2   P. Cosgrove, *My Story*, HarperCollins, Sydney, 2007.
3   P. Flood, *Report of the Inquiry into Australian Intelligence Agencies*, Department of Prime Minister and Cabinet, Canberra, 2004, Chapter 3.

The organisation and structure of intelligence support to operations in Afghanistan

While intelligence operations in Iraq and Afghanistan changed in structure and functional capability, there were three generic constants in its framework (see Figure 4).

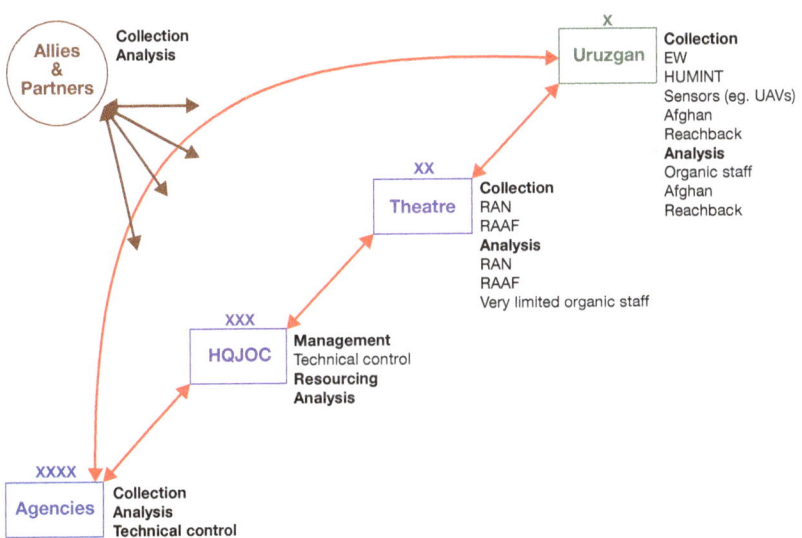

Figure 4: Australian intelligence collection and analysis arrangements in Afghanistan.

The first constant was coalition intelligence support. Australian intelligence efforts did not, of course, occur in a vacuum. Integral to intelligence, from the strategic to the tactical level, was the network of international resources from which the Army, Navy and Air Force could draw, be they Five Eyes, Nine Eyes (Five Eyes plus four close European partners),[4] Fourteen Eyes (the extended network of NATO-linked international military partners operating in Afghanistan) or wider coalition. Indigenous intelligence reporting, with its own strengths and weaknesses, was also available. Of these, in my experience, I would contend that Australia benefited

---

4 See E. MacAskill and J. Ball, 'Portrait of the NSA', *Guardian*, 3 November 2013, www.theguardian.com/world/2013/nov/02/nsa-portrait-total-surveillance (retrieved 26 April 2020).

most from the Five Eyes relationships, thanks to the level of coverage, the resources available in support, and the depth of often complementary analysis undertaken by the various components of the coalition.

The second constant was Australian-based support. Forces in the area of operations (AO) were supported by strategic and operational intelligence efforts based in Australia. These efforts served four main functions: feeding the needs of their respective Canberra audiences (including Defence and wider national security intelligence, operations and policy circles); managing the intelligence resources provided to the AO; providing direction and oversight for intelligence operations in the AO; and providing support of varying degrees of usefulness to those within the AO.

Finally, there were the deployed ADF intelligence assets. Each of the services deployed elements to meet their own intelligence needs and to contribute to the joint picture. For example, there were specialist Air Force and Navy intelligence elements protecting platforms and providing intelligence support to their respective tasks, including counter-piracy, counter-smuggling and counter-terrorism. Then there were the deployed land intelligence elements, contributing to planning, force protection and situational awareness through sensors on such platforms as the Heron Unmanned Aerial Vehicle (UAV), and through such functions as human intelligence, electronic warfare and signals intelligence, and geographic intelligence. Ultimately, this information was, through the science of analysis and the art of fusion, turned into intelligence by analytical staff. While driven by the needs of commanders, this intelligence was basically focused on fighting the insurgency and understanding the muddled tapestry of Uruzgan's population and its power structures.

At this point, it is proper to recognise the contributions made by deployed civilians. Across all three of these constraints, civilians provided specialist expertise otherwise unavailable to the Army, which was particularly valuable in allowing our forces to leverage the capabilities of national agencies. This included the deployment of Defence civilians to Afghanistan to provide trusted and close intelligence support. These deployed civilians fully deserve the Operational Service Medal, and I am proud to have served with them.

10. INTELLIGENCE IN AFGHANISTAN

Strategic support to intelligence operations in Afghanistan

In Afghanistan, the majority of my experience was with operational and strategic intelligence support, including direct support to deployed forces.

Drawing on the incomparable capabilities of allied partners, the scale of strategic intelligence support provided to deployed forces was considerable. In keeping with their acknowledged roles of supporting military operations and protecting Australian troops, Defence's three intelligence agencies: the Defence Intelligence Organisation, the Australian Signals Directorate and the Australian Geospatial-Intelligence Organisation, all had deployed staff. These deployed elements provided, at least, liaison officers who were able to task their agencies in what was known as reach-back support. Each agency provided a unique service, which grew in utility over time. This utility was a product of both the significant resources committed and a developing understanding of how to support the deployed chief intelligence officer, J2 or S2 (at the lower echelon), of the Joint Task Force (JTF) and its respective subordinate units.

However, I do recall multiple conversations when ADF colleagues would criticise strategic support to deployed forces. Barbs might include that the agencies deployed people to be seen to be relevant, that the agencies did not trust ADF personnel with their capabilities, or that agencies wanted to prevent their capabilities from diffusing down into the Army. I also remember hearing several times that agency liaison officers would run single-source reports to commanding officers, without telling the Intelligence Staff Officer (S2), in a form of intelligence one-upmanship. I personally never saw failings of this nature, and the vast majority of agency staff I encountered were professional and dedicated.

So why mention what might be nothing more than rumours? Well, what I can say with certainty is that the central role of the S2 was assisted immensely by Headquarters Joint Operations Command (HQJOC) regularly evaluating the effectiveness of the supporting intelligence efforts. This held everyone, including agencies, accountable.

In my observation, there was a mostly healthy rivalry between the agencies, although there were times, often associated with particular personalities, when this was tested. I do recall seeing a poster in Tarin Kowt on the differences between the agencies. This poster expounded the virtues of signals intelligence, and contrasted it with another intelligence function, represented by a stick figure holding what might have been a weapon, and the assessment: 'There are bad men in Afghanistan.'

To my mind, one of the most important contributions made by strategic agencies was the provision of 'actionable' intelligence for targeting purposes. This type of intelligence is precisely what it sounds like. It involves a cycle of identifying individuals as insurgents, presenting this intelligence as part of a command decision to target, or not, and then providing accurate information to allow duly authorised action to be taken.

It is a matter of public record that intercepted phone calls informed decisions on who should be targeted by special forces. Media reports claim that mobile telephones can be located when an emitter is used to mimic a mobile telephone tower, convincing a target phone to connect through it.[5] If the emitter is itself mobile, then triangulation can occur as the platform moves around and measures the target phone's signal strength. It is a covert but deadly game of 'Marco Polo'.

In 2011, an article in the *Australian Army Journal* titled 'Australian special forces in Afghanistan: Supporting Australia in the "long war"' stated that special forces, specifically Task Force 66, had the capabilities and role to 'incapacitate' the Taliban's leadership. The author went on to conclude that 'the effectiveness of these operations has ... been significant'.[6]

The ABC television program *Four Corners* later reported that Australian special forces had killed 'dozens' of Taliban commanders. It quoted an unnamed lieutenant colonel as saying that special forces missions to target insurgent leaders were provided with 'very good' intelligence, drawn from national agencies and ADF sources, on which decisions were based. It was claimed that the intelligence available to Task Force 66 often allowed it to 'find' and 'fix' a specific insurgent at a specific location, regardless of their physical appearance, clothing or efforts to avoid detection.

---

5   See for instance V.J. Appelbaum, J. Horchert and C. Stöcker, 'Catalog advertises NSA toolbox', *Der Spiegel*, 29 December 2013, www.spiegel.de/international/world/catalog-reveals-nsa-has-back-doors-for-numerous-devices-a-940994.html (retrieved 14 March 2020).
6   I. Langford, 'Australian special forces in Afghanistan: Supporting Australia in the "long war"', *Australian Army Journal*, vol. 7, no. 1, 2010, pp. 21–32.

The Taliban were reportedly aware of the coalition's ability to track their mobile phones, at least as early as 2008. This was thought to have been behind their threat to attack cellular towers that were not turned off at night—when special forces often staged their counter-leadership operations.

The experience of Major General Jim Molan in Iraq was that US Special Forces, supported by their unique intelligence feeds, played a 'key part' in targeting the insurgency. In talking about the operational and legal considerations of actioning a target, he records himself thinking: 'God, let there be special intelligence so that the decision will be straightforward.'[7]

My experience was that intelligence support to Australian special forces in Afghanistan was as important as that described by General Molan. One of my most treasured mementos is a letter I received in mid-2013 from an officer in the Special Air Service Regiment in which he talked of the 'lasting impression' left by this support, while noting that 'few appreciate [its] impact'.

Overall, I am comfortable in asserting that, in the history of Australian military operations, there has not been a better resourced or more sustained targeting of an adversary's operational and tactical leadership.

Additionally, I am strongly convinced that intelligence support to targeting in Afghanistan was tactically and, at times, operationally effective. But—in terms of influence on strategic decision-making—there is clearly room for debate. The former Director of the US signals intelligence organisation, the National Security Agency, General Michael Hayden, has acknowledged this, saying: 'If you radiated on an American battlefield, you were likely to die. Less certain, though, was our ability to inform broad questions of policy.'[8]

However, it is important to note that strategic support was about more than targeting. It played a key role in many force protection operations. One example is in the December 2011 seizure of 3.55 tonnes of ammonium nitrate in Zabul. This stockpile was enough to make more than 250 improvised explosive devices, the majority of which were probably bound for Uruzgan.

---

7   See Molan, *Running the War in Iraq*.
8   See M.V. Hayden, *Playing to the Edge: American Intelligence in the Age of Terror*, Penguin, New York, 2017.

In his fascinating but frustrating book, *Intelligence in War*, John Keegan wrote that all history of the Second World War written before 1974 was 'flawed' simply because the story of Enigma and Magic, the breaking of German and Japanese wartime codes, was unknown before then.[9] There is a lesser but still enthralling history waiting to be told about the people and impact of technical intelligence in Iraq and Afghanistan.

The dusk of a 'golden age' for intelligence?

Afghanistan might very well be a high-water mark for intelligence support to military operations. Afghanistan had a relatively unsophisticated communications network, and the distance between Uruzgan's insurgents and their leadership in Pakistan forced them to use these networks at least part of the time.

A very considerable intelligence enterprise exploited technological and practical factors, particularly as the balance between operations in Iraq and Afghanistan changed. I believe this coincidence of technology, geography and resources is unlikely to be seen again.

Second, despite the strain it caused on the limited numbers of intelligence personnel, the scale of strategic support was mirrored by deployed tactical capabilities, which at one time included intelligence specialists embedded at the company level.

It did not, however, begin this way. For example, in 2001, there were six Australian Army Intelligence Corps specialists and liaison support from two agencies supporting special forces in Afghanistan. At one stage, the S2 for our special forces was an SAS officer rather than an intelligence specialist. By 2010, in the words of an intelligence colleague, the intelligence support available to the Special Operations Task Group (SOTG) was 'a massive evolution by any measure'. Analyst numbers had greatly increased; sensitive collection capabilities had been added; there were more agencies with more staff and more embedded capabilities; and there were Australian specialists in two coalition intelligence cells in Kandahar. I am aware that these capabilities continued to grow through to 2013, creating a truly robust presence.

---

9   J. Keegan, *Intelligence in War*, Pimlico, London, 2004, p. 370.

Overall, I would liken the level of intelligence support received in Afghanistan by our brigade minus-sized forces to have been roughly equivalent to what a reinforced division might have hoped to receive in the field in other contingencies. This was a laudable focus of Defence intelligence resources on the mission, but I doubt that this level of resources could be expected in future.

My concern is that the experience in Afghanistan has created a generation of commanders, particularly special forces patrol leaders, who might regard the intelligence support they received in Afghanistan as the norm. As long as Australia has the strategic luxury of choosing the extent of our involvement in conflicts, this is likely to be the case. But if a future enemy removes this choice from us, I see a strong possibility of unmet expectations and, consequently, accusations of intelligence failure.

Iraq, weapons of mass destruction and the role of intelligence

In regard to failures in this period, the 800-pound elephant in the room would have to be the presence, or not, of weapons of mass destruction (WMDs) in Iraq leading into 2003. General Hayden recalls that there was a genuine consensus that 'there was a case' for WMD but that ultimately the intelligence community 'just got it wrong'.[10] In the Australian context, Dr Albert Palazzo's previously classified work concluded that WMD judgements were based on 'faulty' assessments and therefore that Iraq was an intelligence failure.[11] I do not propose to go into this further; however, those who want a more detailed account of Australian intelligence assessments of the WMD threat posed by Iraq might start with Phillip Flood's 2004 inquiry into the Australian intelligence community.[12]

Ultimately, this begs the broader question of the relationship between intelligence and decision-making, and the fine balance that needs to be struck so that the first informs the second without being suborned by it. In my opinion, this balance, extrapolating slightly from a recommendation of the Flood Inquiry, is best served when the leadership of intelligence

---

10 Hayden, *Playing to the Edge*, p. 50.
11 Palazzo, *The Australian Army and the War in Iraq: 2002–2010*, pp. 27–8.
12 Flood, *Report of the Inquiry into Australian Intelligence Agencies*.

assessment organisations comes from those whose professional life has been spent mastering its nuances, complexities, limitations, relationships and legalities.

Intelligence effectiveness in Afghanistan: Kicking goals in a game of cricket?

Looking at the operational and tactical levels, to what extent did they also suffer from intelligence failures? Or, as I have pondered since I left Afghanistan in late January 2016, was intelligence kicking goals but playing a game of cricket? In other words, were the achievements by one measure largely irrelevant in terms of the measure that counts the most: the final outcome?

For me, one of the most striking public critiques of the effectiveness of intelligence was in the report *Fixing Intel: A Blueprint for Making Intelligence Relevant in Afghanistan*.[13] This public report was scathing of the efforts of US intelligence in Afghanistan, describing them as 'only marginally relevant', obsessed with the insurgency, and 'unable to answer fundamental questions' that would leverage popular support and thereby delegitimise the insurgency. It is not just the content of this document that is striking; it is the fact that it was written by the senior US military intelligence officer in Afghanistan at the time, Major General Michael T. Flynn.

The solutions proposed by Flynn are grassroots, community-based intelligence collection, focusing on governance, development and stability. Of course, like all things, there is a context, and a debate had raged in 2009 over the relative merits of a counter-insurgency or counter-terrorism-based strategy in Afghanistan. It is clear whose side Flynn was on. However, even if one accepts that counter-insurgency was a valid approach in the Pashtun-dominated areas of Afghanistan, I am not aware of any evidence that this report substantially changed the way the United States approached intelligence there.

---

13   M.T. Flynn, M. Pottinger and P. Batchelor, *Fixing intel: A blueprint for making intelligence relevant in Afghanistan*, Center for a New American Security, Washington, DC, 2010.

Returning to kicking goals in a game of cricket, I have quoted General Cosgrove's view on intelligence officers. The general also said that a key attribute of intelligence officers was experience, and opined that this usually had 'scars attached'. Personally, as I look back over my time involved with operations in Afghanistan, there are 'scars' that I bear and that I will now recount. I leave it to others to judge whether these were failures, but they certainly were not successes.

The first 'scar' came from the two occasions when my team was unable to support operations. One occasion followed the conclusion of Operation ATHENA and the Canadian withdrawal from Kandahar. This left portions of Route Bear to the south of Tarin Kowt (connecting Tarin Kowt with Kandahar) potentially vulnerable and—quite rightly—generated a desire to exert influence there. The second occasion was similar. It followed the withdrawal of our Dutch partners from Uruzgan and the subsequent Australian decision to penetrate into the Tangi Valley to the west of Tarin Kowt.

In both cases, my collectors and analysts had no baseline to work from. Australian troops were to be committed into what was effectively a black hole for my teams' intelligence function. While we worked to fill that void, all we could do was inform commanders, so that this gap could be taken into account in their planning. Intelligence training stamps into you the absolute necessity to say 'I don't know' when that is the case. That does not make it any easier when lives are at stake.

The second 'scar' was also operational, and it was our lack of success in being able to provide actionable intelligence on arguably the most effective of the senior Taliban field commanders for Uruzgan—Objective Katana. Although he was the enemy, I came to regard Katana with a grudging respect. He was a competent and committed leader, who was not afraid to leave his Pakistani sanctuary and venture into Uruzgan. The fact that he was able to do so was a testimony to his operational security practices, as well as to the respect he commanded from the Taliban, who knew of his travels. Regardless, an Afghanistan with men like Katana in charge will be poorer by any Western measurement—except, possibly, stability.

Finally, there was the period between 2009 and 2012 when the number of attacks by Afghan security personnel on coalition soldiers—that is, the so-called green-on-blue attacks—skyrocketed. There were significant losses to coalition forces as the result of such attacks, including seven Australians who were killed and 12 who were wounded.

Consequently, there was an unrelenting focus on combatting green-on-blue attacks. However, technical intelligence proved to be unsuitable for the task. Essentially, unless the potential attacker associated himself with known insurgents or was brought to our attention by other reporting—counter-intelligence, human intelligence or reports of suspicious behaviour from the field—then technical means were likely to be useful only after an attack.

This turned out to be the case. Australian intelligence played the key role in bringing justice to all three rogue Afghans who fled after their attacks: Objectives Morningstar, Jungle Effect and Shady Igloo.

There is scant detail publicly available about the hunt for Lance Corporal Jones's killer, Shafidullah, although the then Defence Minister Stephen Smith acknowledged that intelligence tracked him to his home where he was shot when he pulled a pistol on special forces troops.

In August 2013, Prime Minister Rudd announced that Mohammad Rozi, an Afghan soldier who attacked and wounded Australian and fellow Afghan soldiers almost two years before, had been killed. Using 'focused intelligence' (drawing on a range of sources in a concentrated effort to weave together the strands and make sense of the situation and deliver timely and actionable intelligence), Australian forces had tracked Mohammad Rozi from Uruzgan to Pakistan and then to Takar Province in northern Afghanistan.

Later that year, the direct role of intelligence in the capture of the Patrol Base Wahab attacker, Hekmatullah, was clear in the description of the operation as a 'hi-tech spy hunt' using 'a combination of electronic eavesdropping, human intelligence and detailed satellite imagery'.[14]

---

14   C. Stewart, 'How they found the Diggers' killer Hekmatullah', *Weekend Australian*, 3 October 2013, www.theaustralian.com.au/national-affairs/defence/how-they-found-the-diggers-killer/news-story/6883aa8eee237dcac676c67f259073d2 (retrieved 14 March 2020).

Perhaps illustrating the difficulty of predicting individual behaviour, the Queensland Coroner's report on the August 2012 attack at Patrol Base Wahab concluded that there were no indications that Hekmatullah was a threat and that it was not possible to draw a conclusion on his true motivation for the attack. Almost exactly the same findings about indications and motivation were made about the earlier green-on-blue attack that killed Lance Corporal Jones in May 2011.

As I have said, the techniques that were successful in providing actionable intelligence against Taliban leaders in Uruzgan were unsuited to pre-emptively combatting green-on-blue attacks. This inability to contribute to the prevention of green-on-blue attacks weighs heavily on me. It is my greatest professional regret.

Finally, I do not think that any discussion on the 'scars' left by this war would be complete without acknowledgement of the enduring and terrible psychological legacy it has left some with. In the context of my experiences, I want to take this opportunity to touch on a facet of psychological risk that I encountered during this time: vicarious trauma. Vicarious trauma is what can happen when a person is exposed to something in which they did not personally participate. For example, it could result from seeing graphic images or listening to potentially distressing material.

The danger of this sort of exposure was first brought home to me in the aftermath of a successful strike against a target. Immediately following the strike, we were looking to assess the longer-term impact on the insurgent network. The information collected was graphic, detailing the physical effects of the strike and the emotional toll it had on certain key figures. As the direct result of exposure to this material, a young analyst working for me starting showing signs of distress. Over some days, it became clear that it was having an effect both at work and at home, including significant loss of sleep and nightmares. Ultimately, this exposure to the brutality of war meant that this analyst—who was very good at their job—had to move to another area.

As a footnote, this episode also carried a warning, although a different one, for me. When I was exposed to the same material that had caused the young analyst psychological distress, my reaction was laughter. Beyond any degree of reasonable professional satisfaction, I felt something bordering on euphoria at the results of the strike. It was only when my analyst's reaction became known that I took time to reflect on the dangers of dehumanisation.

While psychological stress affects individuals in different ways, this legacy of operations in the Middle East will be with us for decades, and the care and treatment that we offer our people who suffer must continue to be a priority for government and Defence.

Conclusion

What I have described in this chapter is my perspective on intelligence support to land operations in Afghanistan, from 2007 to 2014. This story begins poorly. Its opening features an Australian Army Intelligence Corps tired and under-resourced from its years in Timor, as well as an intelligence system whose relationships were not as harmonious as they could have been. However, over time, the story becomes one of success, although this success is far from unqualified and is not synonymous with a satisfactory ending.

Ultimately, however, this is the story of men and women, military and civilian, making a clear difference to Australian operations in Afghanistan and to the soldiers who conducted them. It is the story of men and women who did precisely what their country asked of them and who did it very well indeed. In the fullness of time it is a story that deserves to be told in its entirety.

I am very proud to have been a part of this intelligence effort, as we did our best to pierce Clausewitz's fog of war and to ensure that the Australian Army was forewarned and forearmed in Afghanistan.

11

Civil and humanitarian assistance

Alan Ryan

> If I were to fault the process ... [of planning the effort in Afghanistan] ... I would say that vastly more attention was focused on every aspect of the military effort than on the broad challenge of getting the political and civilian part of the equation right. Too little attention was paid to the shortage of civilian advisers and experts: to determining how many people with the right skills were needed, to finding such people, and to addressing the imbalance between the number of US civilians in Kabul and elsewhere in the country.
>
> – Robert Gates, US Secretary of Defense, 2014

My brief in writing this chapter is to provide an Australian Civil-Military Centre (ACMC) view on the contribution of civil society organisations (CSOs), non-government organisations (NGOs) and other government agencies (OGAs) in Iraq and Afghanistan 2001–14. I have already failed because to arrive at a holistic view that makes sense is impossible. Iraq and Afghanistan were two distinct conflicts—the cultural, political, social and economic circumstances were fundamentally different. So too were the array of different humanitarian, development, advocacy and private sector actors. Over 13 years the story changed considerably as the relationship between humanitarian actors and the military shifted. Finally, CSOs, NGOs, OGAs and, yes, humanitarian relief organisations are not the same thing at all. Even within government the tendency to sum up the full array of 'other government agencies' with an easily dispensable acronym misses the point that all government departments and agencies possess their own mission and mandate. With respect to national and international civil society aid, advocacy and development organisations, it can be deeply offensive to be lumped together as an amorphous 'other'. Nonetheless, in too many historical accounts of conflict the greater weight of attention is given to war-fighting and security operations, and the rest, the odds and sods, find themselves in a single chapter.

This is not that chapter. As it is impossible in single short essay to capture the scale of the non-military enterprise in two separate wars, I propose to make a few corrective observations.

First, as long as the history of contemporary conflict in the Middle East focuses on combat operations rather than peacebuilding, it is only a discussion about treating the symptoms, not the causes of violence. The next time members of the international community mount an intervention on the scale of Afghanistan or Iraq, greater attention must be given to the critical nature of civil–military interaction in planning and executing stabilisation and reconstruction. Because if we do not, we had better resign ourselves to winning wars quickly on our own terms and then rapidly losing the peace because we missed the point of what conflict is all about.

Second, the history of conflict is only in part the story of combat operations. I have heard too many veterans of both of these conflicts rail at the insult to their professionalism at not being able to fight the insurgent war on their terms. The next generation of war-fighters must understand that there is a never-ending supply of people to kill. As one special forces operator put it, there are tactical achievements more important than 'killing farmers and two dollars-a-day Taliban conscripts'.[1] All wars end, and the military will play a constructive role only if they have established a close and constructive relationship with the peace builders. Very few of those peace builders wear a uniform, so the effective military officer had better develop an idea of who they are and learn how to work with them.

Third, these conflicts resulted in a blurring of the lines of international humanitarian action. The emergence of something termed the 'new humanitarianism' created challenges to the way that civilian

---

1   C. Masters, *No Front Line: Australia's Special Forces in Afghanistan*, Allen & Unwin, Sydney, 2017, p. 425.

aid, development and advocacy groups operate in persistent warfare. Militaries and governments used aid and stabilisation packages to support their own national and political objectives in both Iraq and Afghanistan. While meeting short-term requirements, the lack of coordination between themselves and with host nation authorities too often meant that these efforts did more harm than good. Too often if the military was providing assistance to build hearts and minds, it meant that other, more expert and/or appropriate agencies were prevented from doing their jobs. As Nick Guttmann and Sean Lowrie, the chair and director respectively of the Start Network (the Consortium of British Humanitarian Agencies), wrote: 'Civil society delivers some 70 per cent of the last mile of international humanitarian assistance. A crisis for NGOs would mean a crisis for the entire humanitarian system.'

In this chapter, I briefly identify the types of civilian actors that were active in these conflicts, consider the challenges that these conflicts represented to the humanitarian response system, and outline some of the lessons from Afghanistan and Iraq that will continue to apply in the future.

The search for common ground in civil–military–police interaction

In an introduction to a recent book on civil–military interaction, Admiral James Stavridis, Supreme Allied Commander Europe at NATO (2009–13), wrote that we need effective civil–military interaction as there are countless operational issues 'that the military are not necessarily willing or able to address themselves':

> [T]here may be issues of neutrality, impartiality and independence that the military find difficult to meet, as in medical support, humanitarian operations and disaster relief. Without resolving this myriad of challenges, the modern multifaceted mission will not fulfil its mandate … It takes non-military partners, governmental and non-governmental, to achieve that.[2]

---

2   G. Lucius and S. Rietjens (eds), *Effective Civil–Military Interactions in Peace Operations: Theory and Practice*, Springer, Berlin, 2016, p. vi.

This issue of 'partnership' is a fraught one. The then US Secretary of State, Colin Powell, talking to a group of NGO leaders in the immediate aftermath of 9/11, famously stated:

> I have made it clear to my staff here and to all of our ambassadors around the world that I am serious about making sure we have the best relationship with the NGOs who are such a force multiplier for us, such an important part of our combat team.[3]

The speech prompted outrage from the international humanitarian community. In the years that followed, his comments might even have operated to frustrate their intended effect. Secretary Powell might have meant to suggest that the military and humanitarian organisations worked in common cause to make the world a better place. But civilian organisations operating by the principles of humanity, independence, neutrality and impartiality were never going to subscribe to their enlistment into the US military 'combat team'.

Western militaries have had to overcome the notion, often inculcated in the past at remote combat training centres, that fighting would occur in a 'people-free zone'. The experience of both Afghanistan and Iraq was not only that there were large civilian populations present, but also that a large number of other national and international professionals had a stake in achieving peace, security and economic sustainability. It is one of the major lessons of these conflicts that force preparation training in Australia now involves exposure to a range of non-military actors and scenarios.

In both Afghanistan and Iraq, coalition military forces faced considerable challenges reconciling their combat mission with the desire of the international political coalition to make meaningful change in politics, the economy, the legal system, health and dealing with the grinding effects of poverty.

There is a reason for that. As the US Joint Chiefs of Staff own counter-insurgency doctrine states:

> Long-term security cannot be imposed by military force alone; it requires an integrated, balanced application of effort by all participants with the goal of supporting the local populace and

---

3   C. Powell, 'Remarks to the National Foreign Policy Conference for Leaders of Nongovernmental Organizations', Washington, DC, 26 October 2001, avalon.law.yale.edu/sept11/powell_brief31.asp (retrieved 1 April 2020).

achieving legitimacy for the HN [host nation] government. Military forces can perform civilian tasks but often not as well as civilian agencies with people trained in those skills. Further, military forces performing civilian tasks are not performing military tasks. Diversion from those tasks should be temporary and only taken to address urgent circumstances … Military forces should be aware that putting a military face on economics, politics, rule of law etc, may do more harm than good in certain situations.[4]

For their own part, many members of the international humanitarian community now question the degree to which they can afford to be impartial and apolitical if they are to have any chance of achieving their objectives.

The complexity of the environment that emerged from Iraq, Afghanistan and subsequently Syria was captured by Claudia McGoldrick, Special Adviser to the Presidency of the International Committee of the Red Cross (ICRC). Questioning the very existence of an international humanitarian system, she wrote:

> At best there may be multiple 'systems'—working on local, national and international levels—with varying degrees of organization, different approaches and different goals. This broad humanitarian landscape and all of its features are evolving constantly, shaped by the increasing complexities of the causes and consequences of war, violence and disasters, and will inevitably assume quite a different shape in the years to come.[5]

Complexity, multinational operations and the art of the possible

You will have noticed that there is not much reference to Australian actors here. There will not be. That is not because there were not many Australians working for NGOs, UN agencies, private sector organisations, diaspora and civil society groups. There were, and there still are. However, when considering Australia's participation in the multination coalitions in Afghanistan and Iraq, we need to appreciate the subnational, multinational

---

4 Department of Defense, *US Army Counterinsurgency Handbook*, Skyhorse Publishing, New York, 2007, p. 2.42.
5 C. McGoldrick, 'The state of conflicts today: Can humanitarian action adapt?', *International Review of the Red Cross*, vol. 97, no. 900, 2015, p. 1180.

and supra-national character of the many civilian actors with which Australia interacted. The other harsh reality is to accept the fact that in the many histories of both conflicts that are emerging, Australia rarely, if ever, makes it into the index. If Australia expects to make a more significant contribution to future international interventions, it will not be because of the ADF's war-fighting prowess, no matter how good it is, or how many bitter sacrifices it accepts. It will be because Australia has figured out how to work with the non-military elements of local, regional and international elements of power. It will be because the country recognises and has adapted to the demands of complexity.

That said, operations in Afghanistan and Iraq represented a steep learning curve for all Australian government agencies that found themselves in these theatres of operations. While operations in the Middle East have realised the predictions that it would be a long war, it is easy to forget how novel these commitments were in the first years of the 21st century. Both Afghanistan and Iraq saw an initial military-only, war-fighting phase. The ADF's involvement in Afghanistan was drawn down in December 2002 to only two officers until the second phase of Operation SLIPPER commenced in August 2005. Combat forces committed to the invasion of Iraq in 2003 for Operation FALCONER were withdrawn at the end of the invasion, and it was not until April 2005 that troops redeployed for Operation CATALYST to Al Muthanna Province. In both countries, the initial focus was on participating in the Global War on Terror and ensuring the disarmament of Iraq. In November 2001, Foreign Minister Downer made it clear in a media interview that 'nation-building' was no part of Australia's mission in Afghanistan:

> We don't want to get ... bogged down in Afghanistan. We don't want Australian troops to be part of managing and running Afghanistan for the next five or six years ... we want to help with the war on terrorism, to destroy al-Qaeda and its network and so on. But we don't really have a great desire ... to get into the long-term management of Afghanistan.[6]

---

6   A. Downer, interview transcript, 'Meet the Press', 18 November 2001.

Announcing the conclusion of combat operations in Iraq in May 2003, Australia's Prime Minister John Howard stated:

> Our military deployment will be limited given current commitments in our own region. Many other nations have indicated a willingness to provide peacekeeping assistance in Iraq. The government has made clear all along that Australia would not be in a position to provide peacekeeping forces in Iraq. Our coalition partners clearly understood and accepted our position … Australia takes its rehabilitation responsibilities very seriously. Our contribution—as in the conflict phase—will focus our limited resources in niche areas where we have expertise and where a concentrated effort can make a difference. We have committed some $100 million in aid. We have provided highly skilled personnel to contribute to key humanitarian planning and reconstruction efforts.[7]

The emphasis in both cases was to make a clean break with military operations but not to become embroiled in the 'messy' business of civil–military interaction in what Australia hoped were post-conflict societies. Of course, the reality that emerged was very different, particularly when Australia re-engaged in both countries with provincial reconstruction efforts.

From 2005 onwards, it became increasingly obvious that Australian government agencies—not just the ADF but also DFAT, AusAID, the AFP and subject matter experts drawn from a variety of other agencies and departments—needed to develop expertise in dealing with the civil society sector in all areas of operations. This should not have been such a surprise. The principle was well accepted at the time in the operations that Australia led in East Timor and Solomon Islands. Even as a junior partner in a large and diverse international coalition, we needed to understand the governance and humanitarian context. This understanding cannot be achieved by departments and agencies planning in stove-pipes. Nor are inter-agency committee meetings sufficient to develop the level of environmental expertise necessary for effective integrated national policy. It is difficult to criticise voluntary civilian agencies for not getting aid and assistance right when state actors were incapable of it too.

---

7   J. Howard, Ministerial statement to Parliament on Iraq, 14 May 2003.

The ACMC report *Afghanistan: Lessons from Australia's Whole-of-Government Mission*[8] found that the evolutionary and changing nature of operations in Afghanistan meant that both the international community's and Australia's approach to aid delivery at national and provincial level was uncoordinated. The report concluded that a lesson for the future was that 'whenever a whole-of-government mission is considered, all departments and agencies involved should participate in an inter-agency planning team to plan the mission'.[9] The importance of a deliberate approach to the delivery of aid and development assistance and the coordination of national contributions with host nation and civil society efforts was underscored by twin recommendations. Where aid delivery is funded or delivered by government agencies and is a requirement of the mission,

I. Aid objectives should be defined clearly from the outset and advice provided to government on whether the aid is most appropriately delivered by DFAT or the ADF, or a combination of both, and in the case of DFAT aid, which agencies (including the AFP) would be best placed to deliver it.

II. Whichever agencies are responsible for delivering the aid program, it should be regarded as a whole-of-government program from its outset and be planned and coordinated by an inter-agency group, supported where possible by a parallel group in the field, which includes representation from the resident diplomatic mission.[10]

Providing humanitarian and development assistance in a political minefield

Drawing on the experience of operations in Iraq and Afghanistan, as well as knowledge derived from regional operations in Timor and Solomon Islands, the ACMC describes the civil society environment in these terms:

> In addition to national authorities, international military, police and the aid community are likely to encounter a range of other important and influential stakeholders in the host country. Stakeholders include local civil society and NGOs, tribal and factional leaders, religious organisations and the private sector.

---

8   Australian Civil-Military Centre, *Afghanistan: Lessons from Australia's Whole-of-Government Mission*, ACMC, Queanbeyan, 2016.
9   Ibid., p. 8.
10   Ibid., p. 10.

These entities range from credible, professional organisations with strong popular support to ineffective organisations or groups with criminal ties. It is important to remember that not only is the affected population always the first responder, but that, when possible, local capacities should be an option of first resort in facilitating a comprehensive response.[11]

Among themselves, the realities of providing humanitarian assistance in both Iraq and Afghanistan drove a deep rift through the many organisations providing assistance. Two issues predominated: (1) protection, and (2) the source and influence of donor funding for reconstruction and development projects.

As the security system in both countries deteriorated, humanitarian relief organisations were often faced with a stark choice: whether to work within the security umbrella provided by the coalition or to remain neutral and independent. Accepting a degree of coalition protection did not necessarily increase security—it risked being identified as being aligned to one or more parties in the conflict. But even that was rendered irrelevant as terrorist groups actively targeted humanitarian groups as a means of enhancing their own profile.

In particular, the politicisation of aid delivery in Afghanistan posed enormous challenges to the United Nations, to the major humanitarian relief organisations, and to international organisations such as the ICRC. NGOs were receiving large sums from state donors, but this money rarely came without strings attached. In the aftermath of the overthrow of the Taliban, Paul O'Brien, now Vice President for Policy and Advocacy at Oxfam America, wrote while still an adviser on aid coordination, development planning and policy reform to the Afghan Government:

> The global importance of what was going on in Afghanistan was hard to miss. The new rules for international engagement were being written here, and they posed interesting challenges for NGOs. In other post-conflict reconstruction contexts, NGOs had been strengthening governments for years. But this was different. An internationally orchestrated regime change had taken place, and state-building was clearly part of a larger plan to promote one type of regime over another. By accepting donor funds to

---

11 Australian Civil-Military Centre, *Same Space—Different Mandates: A Civil–Military–Police Guide to Stakeholders in International Disaster and Conflict Response*, ACMC, Queanbeyan, 2015, p. 12.

strengthen the new government, NGOs would implicitly support this strategy and would jettison their pretensions at political independence from explicit donor agendas.[12]

The tendency of more naive military and political actors from many countries to describe all non-military actors as 'NGOs' exacerbated these problems in both Afghanistan and Iraq. Across Afghanistan, at the provincial level, local military commanders and government aid officials focused on the need to complete projects that would demonstrate results during their deployment and in their area of operations. In both countries the division of security responsibility among different coalition members resulted in inconsistent approaches being applied at a national level. Provincial Reconstruction Teams (PRTs) came to be seen as the best way for states to reconcile their security and stabilisation objectives, but the composition of these teams was very much a national preference. By 2008, there were 26 PRTs in Afghanistan, led by 13 different nations.

In an excellent analysis of the use of PRTs in Afghanistan, completed for the British Humanitarian Policy Group, Ashley Jackson and Simone Haysom argued:

> Many aid actors strongly objected to the presence of PRTs on the grounds that they, and the broader stabilisation approaches of which they were a part, militarised and politicised assistance. They often lacked the skills and tools required to ensure that their work was appropriate, effective and sustainable, and that it supported (rather than undermined) Afghan institutions. There were also significant problems with coordination, both among PRTs and in their interactions with aid agencies. While ISAF (International Security Assistance Force) assumed command of all the PRTs in Afghanistan in 2006, in practice they were controlled by lead nations with seemingly little uniformity or coordination with ISAF HQ or the Afghan Government. The structure and activities of individual PRTs varied widely, as did the financial resources each PRT lead nation spent.[13]

Coalition members' desire to demonstrate progress often resulted in questionable alliances with local warlords and investment of both military and aid resources in unsustainable or unnecessary projects. Countries were

---

12   Letters to author.
13   A. Jackson and S. Haysom, *The Search for Common Ground: Civil–Military Relations in Afghanistan, 2002–13*, Humanitarian Policy Group, London, 2013, p. 3.

also often confused by the fact that different humanitarian actors behaved very differently, and this led to a perception that some, or all, civil society actors were unreliable. For example, there was a clear division between larger international humanitarian agencies who were able to sustain principled neutrality and local NGOs who were more likely to pursue pragmatic accommodation with government representatives. The Dutch scholar Georg Frerks wrote:

> This does not support the conclusion, however, that international agencies represented the moral high ground, while local NGOs are unprincipled and money-driven. Firstly, the INGO [international non-governmental organisation] position is not just a principled one, but also a material one: they can afford to keep their distance from the military and function in relative autonomy. Secondly, many local agencies are not unprincipled, but differently principled as they feel that humanitarianism is primarily about helping people as much as you can.[14]

Conclusions and recommendations

There remains a perception in some areas and some countries that the national interest of donor countries should take priority over mission results. This perspective is extremely short-sighted. States may achieve short-term operational gains in terms of government 'announceables', local security or tactical battlefield success, but if the overall strategic objective of reconstruction and stabilisation at the national level is not achieved, all the effort is for nought. The unstructured approach to the delivery of reconstruction assistance in both Iraq and Afghanistan resulted in enormous duplication of effort and the waste of scarce resources. The former Chief of Army, now Professor, Peter Leahy summed it up succinctly when he suggested that aiming for a Western-style liberal democracy was unrealistic, 'But, gee whiz, with the amount of effort going in there and the number of troops, I'd be looking for black-and-white cows and people yodelling.'[15]

---

14 G. Frerks, 'Who are they?—Encountering international and local civilians in civil–military interaction', in *Effective Civil–Military Interaction in Peace Operations*, ed. Lucius and Rietjens, p. 41.
15 Middleton, *An Unwinnable War*, p. 316.

Civilian, military and police participants on conflict, stabilisation, reconstruction and peacebuilding need to be pragmatic. Sometimes it is impossible to reconcile all their efforts or to achieve more than partial cross-sectoral understanding. Nonetheless, being aware of the limitations on civil–military engagement does not mean that we should not make best efforts to promote coordination in a complex emergency. We can draw a number of recommendations from our experience in Iraq and Afghanistan.

First, network analysis of all major humanitarian, host nation and civil society actors needs to be incorporated in a structured way from the very beginning of operational planning. It needs to be continually revisited and updated. It needs to take into account the fact that different organisations need to be dealt with differently and that at the same time the humanitarian landscape is constantly changing. To fail to invest in a rigorous assessment of who is doing what is to accept the likelihood of duplication of effort and waste.

Second, within government a strong policy basis requires structured engagement with policy experts resident outside government; in universities, civil society groups, international organisations, the private sector, diaspora movements and host nation institutions. Nothing will replace this engagement. If it is not resourced appropriately, sustained and integrated at the strategic, operational and tactical levels, then missions are operating blind.

Third, partnerships between military and civilian organisations need to be founded on formal understandings wherever possible. These understandings should spell out the terms on which they will engage, including the terms on which parties do not want to engage. In both Iraq and Afghanistan there were many examples of excellent temporary or personal understandings that did not survive posting cycles and personality changes. Leaders need greater visibility of counter-part relationships, and those organisational relationships need to be given some degree of protection from the depredations of the 'new broom'.

Fourth, we need to stop believing our own propaganda. All organisations inevitably report that their activities are successful. We all like to believe that our inter-agency and counterpart relationships are as good as can be achieved. Investment in real-time and concurrent operational evaluations generally produce more mixed messages, but equally provide civilian and military leaders and policy-makers with the information that is essential to enable them to adjust their approach.

Fifth, humanitarian assistance and reconstruction efforts should be devolved to the local level wherever possible.

Sixth, consistency matters. When an intervention is managed by a coalition, every effort needs to be made to ensure that post-conflict operations are conducted with the integration of national effects in mind. The uncoordinated delivery of support at the provincial level by multinational teams with different budgets, operating procedures and policies is a recipe for disaster. Rather than seek out operational autonomy for provincially based teams, countries contributing to a coalition should seek to be better integrated in the joint, inter-agency and multinational effort.

Finally, preparedness is essential. To achieve the necessary level of preparedness for complex operations comprising rapidly assembled civilian, police and military elements, contributing nations need to have invested in building common military doctrine and training, and established a firm appreciation of the principles of civil–military engagement between national elements, NGOs and international organisations. They need to have conducted exercises to hone all participants' awareness of the need for the application of the integrated approach.

All of these recommendations are likely to be dismissed as requiring too high an overhead in terms of more assessment, and leading to more civilians sticking their noses into the business of the military. But building peace in post-conflict societies is not blitzkrieg—it is a long, slow, careful process, and it needs to be based on evidence, not a sense that an enhanced body-count will somehow 'break' the enemy. The people who will determine the conditions of the post-conflict settlement are rarely the people we are fighting. The next time Australia considers a commitment to an offshore intervention, better that we overinvest in achieving a sustainable solution than underinvest. All wars end, and it is the investment that we make in peacebuilding that will be the most decisive in the long run.

12

The military and the media

Karen Middleton

In the first line of his autobiographical novel *Blood Makes the Grass Grow Green*, American soldier Johnny Rico makes a disclaimer of sorts: he wrote it under orders. At the funeral of one of their colleagues, he says his sergeant major told him and other members of C Company, 2nd Battalion, 5th Infantry of the 25th Infantry (Light) Division that it was their duty to tell their own stories.

'[He said] that there was a lot of negative publicity circulating out there about the Army and that each one of us has an Army story, and it was our responsibility to have it told,' Rico explains, before presenting the reader with a raw, darkly funny glimpse into his time in Afghanistan—as he terms it, 'a year in the desert with Team America'.[1]

Rico concedes that his tale might not be quite what the sergeant major had in mind but jokes that absent more specific instructions, this was what he produced. 'I write', he says, 'because I want to be a good soldier.' Fictionalised in parts—he does not say which parts—Johnny Rico's story rolls from expositions on loyalty, honour and authority into reflections on grinding disillusionment, sometimes from a vantage point that feels like the outer edges of sanity. The book is well and truly unvarnished. Even published as it was after Rico left the Army, it is hard to imagine

---

1   J. Rico, Prologue, *Blood Makes the Grass Grow Green*, Presidio Press, New York, 2007, p. xiii.

this kind of thing being written by an Australian soldier and certainly not at the urging of a superior. Here in Australia, the prevailing culture is the opposite.

The Australian Defence Force prefers a more polished presentation and, with its supporting department, has historically invested so much in varnish that it almost deserves its own budget line item. The instruction from Johnny Rico's sergeant major implies that the publicity around the US Army was negative because it was not the whole truth; not the real truth, the *soldier's* truth. In Australia, Defence's complaint historically seems to have been that any negative publicity via the nation's media stemmed from their failure to present its *official* version of the truth—the airbrushed, cheerleader version written in a world where nothing ever goes wrong and nobody should be either embarrassed or to blame. Defence would likely respond that the media only look for trouble, and when they do not find it, they make it.

Maybe in some cases that is true. But what is also true is that hostility and suspicion seek each other out, and if that is what greets journalists—if obfuscation and obstruction are the starting points for media–military relations—then it is likely to be what is returned. The relationship between Australia's defence apparatus and its media has improved considerably in recent years, thanks largely to the high tempo of operations and a commitment to embedding reporters with the ADF in the field. But there is still a way to go. Wherever the relationship falls short, some fault lies on both sides.

Chasing 'clicks' online to attract dispersed and flagging advertising revenue, media organisations are increasingly impatient with the nuances of policy and particularly of conflict. Some organisations look less for the whole story than for the most dramatic version of it to be produced in the shortest possible time. The daily newspaper deadline is giving way to minute-by-minute coverage, with stories updated and published as they develop. There is a new unofficial (and unflattering) motto in the online news world: you're never wrong for long. Each item, whether for print or broadcast, is less and less part of a curated whole news presentation than a stand-alone attracter of readers and viewers. This does not always help to build trusting relationships, including with Defence.

Another significant contributor to the mutual suspicion is the political culture that pays lip service to openness and the role of the 'Fourth Estate' in a democracy while working hard to keep as much as possible secret. As senior military officers themselves are increasingly concluding, using that method to try to win hearts and minds often has the opposite effect. Whenever Defence's objective is seen to be controlling the message and avoiding scrutiny, the media will instinctively want to sidestep the control and amp up the scrutiny. If ADF personnel and Defence officials refuse to answer questions, journalists will fall back on that old rhetorical one: what do they have to hide?

In his book *Don't Mention the War* on Australian media–military relations during the Afghan conflict, Monash University historian Kevin Foster observes, correctly, that the Australian media have depended heavily on the ADF for news from Afghanistan, mostly through journalists being embedded in their ranks. The public has relied on the media for the same. Foster describes what he asserts has been the public's 'apparent ignorance' of what was actually going on over there, calling it 'a critical failure of coverage'. 'The media have to bear their share of the responsibility for this failure,' Foster says. 'But one must also acknowledge that journalists cannot report on events that they cannot access.'[2]

This culture of secrecy comes from high up, beyond the top of Defence to the senior ranks of government—regardless of which side is in power. It is a shut-them-out culture that infects the military–media relationship and the quality of what Australians are told. Australia's political system is much less steeped in accepting the public's right to know than those of our biggest allies, especially the United States.

Australian military public affairs officer Colonel Jason Logue canvassed the process and history of embedding media with the Australian Defence Force on operations in his paper *Herding Cats*. Logue, then a lieutenant colonel, compared the Australian experience with those of counterparts from the United States and Britain, explaining how embedding had been part of the US military's media strategy in previous conflicts. But in the opening stages of the war in Afghanistan after the attacks on US soil on 11 September 2001, the US Defense Department had deemed it too risky to take journalists to the battlefield. Journalistic integration was such

---

2   K. Foster, *Don't Mention the War—The Australian Defence Force, the Media and the Afghan Conflict*, Monash University Publishing, Clayton, Vic, 2013, pp. xiv–xv.

an accepted part of US operations that a Defense official had publicly apologised to members of the Pentagon press pool for their lack of access during the conflict's first phases.[3]

In Australia, the notion that a Defence Department official—or anyone from government—would offer a public apology to the media for locking it out is so beyond comprehension as to be laughable. Within government in Australia, there often seems little more than a theoretical respect for what media are there to do: hold the elected representatives and institutions accountable and be the eyes and ears of the Australian people. Where this generates tension on the ground, it is generally not the fault of military practitioners down the chain—for example, the good men and women assigned as liaison officers for media teams during operational embeds. They are, to borrow a phrase, just following orders. As it translates in the military arena, this culture means that access to information is not treated as an assumed right; it is considered a privilege. The lines between maintaining operational security—the standard reason given for refusing media access—and avoiding embarrassment and reputational damage are still too often blurred.

Where Australians are involved in combat controversies, the investigation process is slow, public disclosure seemingly reluctant, and redaction often extensive. Journalists' efforts to conduct their own investigations and publish or broadcast the results are met by obfuscation, objection and ultimately a phalanx of lawyers. This is especially the case where journalistic endeavours might contradict the official version of events or challenge the hero status of anyone whose image has been co-opted to tell a shinier story. Logue's study focused on the media embeds conducted in Afghanistan in 2011, when the system of offering journalistic access to that conflict was at peak effectiveness for both the military and the media.

Undertaking a media embed role is a compromise and sometimes an uncomfortable one. Journalists enter a theatre of operations completely reliant on the ADF for transport, security, food and accommodation, and access to the conflict and its personnel. For the military, the PR risk lies in welcoming scrutineers who are not part of the family and who will be focused on what the public does not already know; who are programmed to look first—although not only—for what might not be quite as described

---

3 Lieutenant Colonel J. Logue, *Herding Cats: The Evolution of the ADF's Embedding Program in Operational Areas*, Working Paper 141, Land Warfare Studies Centre, Canberra, 2013, p. 5.

back at headquarters and what might be going wrong. Everything that journalists publish and broadcast during media embed trips should be seen in that overall context. Few would jeopardise their situation by running a mid-level gotcha story while they were still away. But they do have to file *something* to justify the investment in time and money and the risk to personal safety of sending them there. That does not—and should not—preclude them from filing non-time-sensitive stories of greater import when they get home. But it can make for some less exciting and sometimes overblown on-the-spot reportage when circumstances do not provide the fire fights and other action that viewers, readers and bosses are expecting.

Difficult choices sometimes must also be made. As a correspondent for SBS Television, I undertook three media embed trips to Afghanistan in 2007, 2011 and 2012. The first time was as part of a highly managed group visit involving several media organisations, colloquially known as a 'bus tour'. In the subsequent tours, we embedded separately. In those early days, the ADF leadership—or at least those running its communications strategy—appeared little interested in an intelligent or thoughtful media-led discussion about what Australia was doing in Afghanistan. It just wanted to show us its helicopters at Kandahar—replete with pilots who were not allowed to say anything about anything other than what they could do—and the trades training school it was operating on the base at Tarin Kowt. That school quickly became a running joke among embedded reporters in the years that followed, so regularly was it peddled as potential story fodder. Returning to the multinational base on each new visit, we were offered the same school tour and interviews with trainees. It was like *Groundhog Day* in camouflage.

That became symbolic of the ADF's failure to understand its own communications responsibilities, not only to the journalists it was hosting but also to the people of Australia. Why did they need to be shown the same pictures and told the same story over and over? The answer is that they did not. The ADF was just serving up something designed to occupy reporters on the spot and stop them from looking for and finding some actual news. Treating journalists as propagandists only serves to generate the very hostility the ADF seeks to guard against.

While concluding that a more sophisticated and less guarded (some might say paranoid) approach is more successful, Logue's study revealed an official benchmark that should be queried. He detailed a commissioned analysis of the coverage embedded journalists produced during 2011 that showed 'a strong correlation with the identified favourable messages of the ADF supporting its personnel, the military/personal conduct of ADF personnel as "beyond reproach" and that ADF operations were making progress towards strategic goals'.[4]

To define success as being the adoption of the ADF's talking points suggests that the exercise is not about letting Australians know what is *actually* going on but what the ADF wants to be known and the image it seeks to project. In those circumstances, it is very easy for the line between restricting journalists' activities for reasons of operational security and restricting them to limit embarrassment to become indistinct. The problem is that the tighter the hold the ADF seeks to exercise over the content of coverage, the more likely we journalists are to try to break free. If the objective is to avoid hostile coverage, what is the value in generating a hostile relationship?

Logue's interviews with senior ADF officers overseeing Australia's Afghan deployment from the Middle East Area of Operations in 2011 indicate that they appreciated the value of openness along with the risks. The Dubai-based joint task force commander at the time, then Major General and now Chief of the Defence Force General Angus Campbell, recognised both the obligation to inform and the operational value in doing so. 'As Australians, we live in a democracy and in that democracy, media agencies play a key role that has been acknowledged by the government and population we serve,' Campbell observed, noting the media coverage was often 'underwhelming' but would be worse if the ADF chose not to engage.

> There is an expectation, a reasonable one in our society, to engage with media. We have no choice but to do so ... What Army and the defence force really does, within the agreed bounds of operations security constraints, is 'media enabling' to assist media access to report independent perspectives on military operations in a contested and dangerous environment. Put simply, war is sustained through public support which, in turn, is enabled through regular and consistent contact with the media. It is simply unreasonable to not engage because to not do so will damage the campaign.[5]

---

4   Ibid., p. 27.
5   Ibid., p. 44.

The commanding officer of Mentoring Task Force 2, the then Lieutenant Colonel Darren Huxley, described a 'balancing game' of inviting strangers into the house. 'Obviously, in a liberal democracy it is absolutely correct for us to be open to scrutiny,' Huxley said. 'But it will never be easy to depart from a view that media embeds are generally looking for failure on which to report.'[6] The commanding officer of the task force that followed, the then Lieutenant Colonel Chris Smith, summarised succinctly the obligations of both the military and the media, and the implications of working side by side in a war zone:

> Military professionals ought to seek the truth no matter how awkward or uncomfortable it is and support the media in reporting that truth. If the truth is unfavourable then we should not be surprised by the unfavourable response of the public to such reports. Quite simply, if you want the media to report on success, be successful. If you are losing a war, then the media will try to identify why things are going wrong and report on the possibility of losing … If your soldiers are poorly disciplined, racist or misogynistic then this truth will be revealed sooner or later. It's all fairly simple. Work on getting real things right, invite the media in to see it and let them report what they see.[7]

Smith was the commanding officer at the time I undertook my 2011 embed. I reported some of what I saw but not all. In the final days of our visit, we stayed at Combat Outpost Mashal, in Uruzgan Province's Baluchi Valley. I had asked to visit Mashal as it had been the scene of a fatal attack on an Australian soldier—the base's cook, Lance Corporal Andrew Jones—by an Afghan colleague earlier that year. It would become the first of many such incidents.

I wanted to gauge the impact on the Australians who had been deployed soon after the attack and were living there alongside Afghan army personnel. On arrival something caught my eye—and raised an eyebrow—in the soldiers' mess. The dining tables were laminated with pictures of naked women. There were no women living at the base and few passing through. I was tempted to highlight this in a news report as it did not seem to align with Defence's policies on equality and respect. But I knew that if I did, the story I had gone to Mashal to report—about how young Australian soldiers were managing the stress of working with Afghan trainees who

---

6   Ibid., p. 45.
7   Ibid., p. 47.

might turn on them—could not be written. If I called them out on their sexist pictures, nobody would speak to me. Not then and possibly not in future. When I sat down to speak to a soldier at one of the tables, he apologised unprompted for the images, despite having had no role in putting them there.

Perhaps Chris Smith did not know about the pictures. More likely, he took a decision that there were bigger battles to fight. And so did I. Although the images were clearly visible in what we put to air, I chose not to draw particular attention to them. It is perhaps an example of what Logue describes as 'self-censorship'.[8] It is not a term that sits comfortably with any journalist, and others might criticise the decision I took. Some other feminists certainly would. But it was a choice I made with a longer-term investment in mind: the investment in relationships that would build trust and enable bigger, better and arguably more important stories to be told in future.

In his interview with Logue, Campbell singled out those same trust relationships as the by-product of embedding that had greatest value for all concerned. 'From my perspective, the opportunity to inform and educate on our military operations is a key benefit of the media embed program,' Campbell said. 'In fact, it is this enhancement of the journalist's understanding which endures well after the journalist has left the theatre that I believe is the most important aspect of the program.'[9]

In his book, Foster interprets Campbell's comments more cynically, suggesting that they reveal an 'unwanted propinquity with the fourth estate'.[10] Foster correctly notes some failings in the embed system and the influence of restrictions on the standard of coverage.

The system remains vulnerable to individual whims in the field, as demonstrated in 2012 when my cameraman colleague Jeff Kehl and I were subjected to repeated sets of unnecessarily intensive vetting of images. This degree of vetting, undertaken by young officers seeking to exert their authority, had not been deemed necessary on previous, higher-tempo visits. We had filmed nothing out of bounds—by our third visit, we knew what was and was not allowed and had no interest in jeopardising anyone's security, including our own—and these young officers were

---

8   Ibid., p. 33.
9   Ibid., p. 43.
10   Foster, *Don't Mention the War*, p. 33.

acting beyond their remit. But I would argue that Foster's analysis is missing some context that affected the nature and quality of reportage, including the implications for embedded journalists as Australia's role in the conflict changed.

Singling out some of my own in-country reports from 2012 for criticism, Foster observed that they included a descriptive feature story on bomb detection dogs and a piece on the use of blast-proof underwear. He did not ask why. The answer goes to the heart of the challenges embedding presents to both dispatcher and dispatched. For a television news journalist on a military embed at war, two imperatives come into direct conflict: the logistically heavy broadcast medium's requirement for anticipation and—wherever possible—advance planning and the situational requirement for spontaneity and maximum ability to change course at short notice.

Arriving in 2012, it became clear that the activities we had hoped to conduct were not going to be possible. It was not like the previous year, when we had stayed among Australian soldiers at Forward Operating Base Mirwais and Combat Outpost Mashal and been properly embedded in their routines. Then, we had joined them on foot patrols through the town of Chora and the valleys beyond.[11] In the shared compounds, we had access to Afghan soldiers and their commanders—albeit using ADF and ISAF interpreters—who were then working under coalition leadership. But by late 2012, the Afghan National Army was taking the lead on the ground. The Afghans decided who did what, who went where and whether anyone went anywhere at all. That had a material influence on what was possible as an embedded Australian journalist. At Forward Operating Base Hadrian, near Deh Rawood, the patrols we were to join were cancelled without explanation.

The Australians were preparing to pull back to the main base within a fortnight, before ending their mission in Uruzgan altogether, so operations were winding down. The so-called green-on-blue attacks had become so prolific that the forward bases had been segregated and relations were strained by suspicion, resentment and grief. Beyond reporting that situation—which we did—there were only two choices. We could be the network's chief political correspondent and cameraman who spent three

---

11   K. Middleton, 'Shadow of the Towers', Part II, *Dateline*, SBS, 11 September 2011, www.youtube.com/watch?v=VW12K3cFGcU&t=3s (retrieved 1 April 2020).

weeks away and produced next to nothing until we got home, or I could generate some ideas for fall-back, fill-in pieces that were not what we had hoped for but were also not entirely irrelevant. I chose the latter course.

I was not going to inspect the trades training school again, so we produced stories that might at least be interesting to viewers, if not exactly herald the unconditional surrender of the Taliban and cessation of international hostilities for all time. This is one of the risks of agreeing to embed: no control over what might happen outside the wire and little more over what the ADF—or Afghan National Army—will allow. In cases like this, the downside for media embeds is obvious, the longer-term upside less so.

What is harder to quantify is the impact on the depth and quality of reporting and analysis produced upon returning home and into the future. I am convinced that among non-specialist and specialist journalists alike, and despite those compromises, the media embed experience fosters a more sophisticated understanding of a conflict than does reporting from afar without it. It is in the interests of the ADF, journalists and the public to continue to foster those trust relationships. Thus far, the ADF has made an effort to do so. But, again, more could be done.

While fair criticism of media coverage is to be encouraged, Defence might contemplate the implications of discrediting the traditional news media generally. With the advent of the concept of 'fake news', the role of professional, credible media is more important than ever. Propaganda is no longer the sole purview of the security apparatus and all kinds of players—including whole states—are weaponising information in the non-military arena. The emergence of information-sharing social media platforms that empower individuals as 'influencers' and spawn 'citizen journalists' has meant that news consumers disillusioned with superficial trash from traditional sources or suspicious of commercial motives—or both—now feel like they have alternatives. They can bypass the regular news media and access information—if often echo-chamber opinion masquerading as fact—from other apparently independent sources. The eagerness to look to those alternatives and willingness to trust them, in some cases in preference to professional media, has created the perfect climate for disrupters-with-intent. Clever propagandists have been able to co-opt the credibility of some traditional media by mimicking their presentation.

Suddenly, it is harder to know what is real online and what is invented. The explosion in the use of social media means stories that look as if they come from reputable sources can have instantaneous, widespread distribution. As allegations of Russian interference in the 2016 US presidential election demonstrate, this is a potentially dangerous development that threatens the operations of democracy and the institutions within it, including the military. While diversity of news sources is essential, so is credibility. Above all, so is fact.

Strengthening engagement and trust between the military and the media and ensuring that the truth is told should further the credibility of both parties in the eyes of a disillusioned public. Contrary to its PR mission as explained by Logue, the ADF should not strive to be described as beyond reproach. As Chris Smith suggested, it should strive to operate in ways that make reproach unnecessary. And we in the media should do the same.

13

The Australian Federal Police in Afghanistan, 2007–14

Col Speedie and Steve Mullins

The humanitarian work undertaken in support of civil society and non-government organisations described earlier was complemented by the work of the Australian Federal Police (AFP), notably in Afghanistan. This chapter examines this police dimension to Australia's war in Afghanistan.

The AFP commitment to Afghanistan commenced in October 2007 with four officers deployed to Kabul and Jalalabad, growing to 28 officers per deployment by the time it finished in 2014. These officers were deployed to Kabul, Kandahar and Tarin Kowt. This effort is not widely known outside those government agencies and foreign partners involved in Afghanistan, and in general prompts the question of why they were there and what were they doing in a high-risk, warlike environment. The answer is that Australian civilian police have been engaged in expeditionary policing[1] since 1964 with the United Nations Peacekeeping Force in Cyprus (UNFICYP), which saw the deployment of 40 police officers from several Australian police services. The term 'expeditionary policing' is used to define the role of civilian police who are increasingly deployed abroad to support peace operations.

---

1   'Expeditionary policing', a term defined by the author, best describes the activities of civilian police deploying to an international foreign jurisdiction, to conduct domestic policing activities as they would in their home jurisdiction. This usually includes the application of executive police powers of that foreign jurisdiction, as generally happens on Chapter 7–mandated UN peacekeeping operations. 'International policing' differs in the application of effort.

Since that first deployment to UNFICYP, the AFP has deployed officers in an expeditionary role to Cambodia, Mozambique, Somalia, Sudan, Haiti, Timor Leste, Bougainville, Solomon Islands, Papua New Guinea and Afghanistan. The Solomon Islands deployment, also known as the Regional Assistance Mission Solomon Islands (RAMSI), is distinctive for two reasons. First, it was as an Australian-led regional mission rather than United Nations one, and second, that, within the umbrella of overall civilian leadership, it was police-led with a robust military component in support, rather than the reverse, which was historically the case in UN peacekeeping missions.

Each peacekeeping or police capacity development mission is different, and Australia's international policing experience has shown that the dangers posed to police are very real and quite varied. The deployment of AFP members to Afghanistan certainly presented unique challenges that had not been present in other missions. The majority of the Afghan battle space was dominated by an insurgency that was actively involved at the epicentre of the global opium trade. The capital, Kabul, was under regular complex attacks,[2] which included the use of vehicle-borne improvised explosive devices (VBIEDs). So, with this in mind, the AFP Commissioner at the time declined requests that AFP members be employed in 'outside the wire' mentoring duties in Uruzgan Province until such time as the environment permitted civilian police to do so.

The first deployment

The first contingent of four AFP officers deployed to Afghanistan in October 2007. Two members were embedded[3] within the Combined Security Transition Command – Afghanistan (CSTC-A) at Camp Eggers as mentors; one as Senior Mentor to the Afghan National Police (ANP) Chief of Criminal Investigations Department and the second as a police adviser to the CSTC-A Deputy Commanding General for Police Development. The remaining two members were deployed to Jalalabad to focus on counter-narcotics intelligence. This city, to the east of Kabul, straddled the significantly strategic road to Peshawar. The police also

---

2   'Complex attack' is a military term for a multiple, simultaneous and multi-locational attack, although, in the case of Afghanistan, this usually involved use of vehicle-borne improvised explosive devices (VBIEDs), placed IEDs and/or suicide bomb attack by armed fighters who attack the target post blast and as a final act detonate a suicide vest they are wearing.
3   An embed in this context was the deployment of a military, police or civilian officer into a foreign military unit; in this case, an Australian police officer into a US Army unit.

mentored the Afghan Counter Narcotics Police (CNPA) in that location. This is the only time when AFP members were working and mentoring ANP 'outside the wire'.

This first deployment was under the auspices of a government-to-government agreement separate from the same status of forces agreement covering the ADF or NATO. Hence, each year, a new agreement for the deployment of Australian police to Afghanistan had to be negotiated and signed before a new contingent could be deployed. This agreement approved the carriage of firearms, movement into and out of the country, specific armed and armoured private security, and life support services for the AFP in Kabul and Jalalabad.

Midway through this first deployment, the two AFP members deployed to Jalalabad had to depart that city owing to specific significant threats against them. Their increasing success in the mentoring of the CNPA there, culminating in the public destruction of a few thousand kilograms of illicit narcotics, upset some significant players in the illicit narcotics industry. Those in Kabul were equally successful, with the AFP Commander Afghanistan Mission responsible for writing the highly significant ANP Criminal Investigations Department development and training program, which was eventually adopted by the European Union Police Mission in Afghanistan as the foundation development and training program for criminal investigations in Afghanistan. The second member was appointed as a senior police adviser, working within the staff of the Commanding General of CSTC-A.

Operation CONTEGO

In 2008, the Australian Government National Security Committee of Cabinet (NSC)[4] approved a new AFP Concept of Operations for the mission. The strategic guidance of the mission was defined thus:

> The Government of Australia intends to enhance support for international stabilization operations in Afghanistan through the deployment of policing expertise to Australian whole of government activities in southern Afghanistan and other international efforts based in Kabul. The AFP contingent will focus on counter-narcotics and criminal intelligence.

---

4   The NSC is chaired by the Prime Minister and is the focal point for decision-making on national security.

On 15 October 2008, the Prime Minister of Australia further outlined government policy as it related to the strategic engagement with Afghanistan as follows:

> To get a long-term solution to Afghanistan's internal tension (both in Uruzgan Province and nationwide), there will need to be a carefully integrated civilian, political and military strategy. Our Afghanistan policy is a comprehensive one. We have a strong military commitment—one that includes training and mentoring as key roles. We have a broad development assistance program—one that helps to build skills and soft and hard infrastructure. We will subject our commitment to annual review against the mission we have set for ourselves, against the integrated civilian and military strategy agreed with NATO and against the application of those strategic objectives to our particular charge in Uruzgan Province.[5]

Also supporting the intent of this concept of operations General Stanley McChrystal, the new Commander of the International Security Assistance Force (COMISAF), stated in 2009:

> The insurgency is fuelled by a number of enabling factors, including a thriving narcotics industry, illicit finance, corruption at all levels of government, and a variety of other criminal enterprises. The narcotic industry dominates Afghanistan's economy and has a chokehold on the country's other major industry, agriculture. Narcotics are a significant source of funding for the insurgency of an estimated 3 to 4 billion dollars a year in drug revenue. These factors form a nexus that undercuts population security, legitimate governance, rule of law, licit agriculture, and sustainable development.[6]

However, as the war against the insurgency in Afghanistan was still within the armed conflict phase of operations, the mission could not be defined as a traditional peacekeeping mission as the parties had not yet ceased military operations. Nor could the mission be defined as a traditional or contemporary police capacity-building mission at that stage for the same reason.

---

5   K. Rudd, Prime Minister of Australia, 'Australian Policy in Afghanistan: Address to the C.E.W Bean Foundation Dinner', speech, 15 October 2008, Australian War Memorial, www.pm.gov.au/node/5517 (retrieved 1 May 2010).
6   S. McChrystal (COMISAF 2009), *United States Government Integrated Civilian and Military Campaign for Support to Afghanistan*, Commonwealth Institute, www.comw.org/qdr/fulltext/0908 eikenberryandmcchrystal.pdf (retrieved 5 May 2010).

During October and November 2008, the new mission, called Operation CONTEGO, deployed personnel to intelligence and strategic advisory roles, to shape counter-narcotics and law enforcement activities that would contribute to whole-of-government and international efforts to debilitate illicit narcotics activities in Afghanistan. The deployment for Operation CONTEGO involved the new AFP Commander of the Afghanistan Mission deployed to Kabul as an embed in the Combined Security Transition Command – Afghanistan. The appointment was for him to continue as Senior Mentor to the Chief of the ANP Criminal Investigations Department while also responsible to further leverage stakeholder and partner agency influence from a whole-of-country perspective in respect of the narcotics industry. These stakeholders and partners included the country managers of the US Drug Enforcement Agency, the UK Serious and Organized Crime Office (now called the UK Crime Commission), senior ISAF members, the Australian defence attaché in Kabul, the Australian ambassador to Afghanistan and the head of the European Union Police Mission.

Three AFP members deployed to Kandahar airfield to leverage military intelligence resources located at ISAF Regional Command South Headquarters. Three members deployed to Tarin Kowt to support ADF assets who shared joint responsibility with Dutch forces for ISAF security within Uruzgan. A criminal intelligence officer deployed to the joint US–UK Interagency Operations Coordination Centre (IOCC)[7] in Kabul to support the ISAF criminal intelligence collection effort undertaken to combat the Afghan narcotics trade.

All life support and protection for the AFP mission members deployed to Kandahar and Tarin Kowt were provided by the ADF. Members in Kabul were provided with life support and personal security via a commercial contract arrangement with Armour Group, who were eventually taken over by the security firm G4S.

---

7   The AFP had a strategic partnership with the IOCC and its parent organisation, the Joint Narcotics Analysis Centre (JNAC). The IOCC, the tactical arm of the JNAC, provided criminal intelligence and law enforcement fusion in Afghanistan. The IOCC fuses the strategic intelligence capabilities of the US and UK military and law enforcement agencies—the DEA and SOCA respectively—which had the lead role in narcotics interdiction within Afghanistan.

Afghan artillery soldiers fire their D-30 Howitzer as the Australian mentors watch on at the heavy weapons range in Tarin Kowt, Afghanistan, 2010.
Source: Courtesy of the Department of Defence.

Apart from the continuing international engagement stakeholder tasks in Kabul, three important projects emerged early in the deployment that would set the scene for significant strategic impacts on the rule-of-law environment.

First, Col Speedie, who was AFP Commander of the Afghanistan Mission, was deeply involved in the initial establishment of the Senior Police Advisers Group in Kabul. Attending a meeting at the United Nations Assistance Mission Afghanistan (UNAMA) in October, the AFP Commander of the Afghanistan Mission noted that the lack of coordinated effort in the law and justice space directly affected the development of the ANP. Despite the many projects underway by various NGOs, no one was coordinating the projects to ensure that there was no duplication of effort or any negative impact from competing groups. Discussing the problem with the International Police Liaison Officer assigned to the CSTC-A (a full colonel from the US Army Military Police), the AFP Commander suggested a coordination group of the heads of the many police missions in Afghanistan to deconflict and synergise police development projects. This body would also act as a strategic police development think tank for the International Police Coordination Board. The board was chaired by the Minister of the Interior and attended by the ambassadors of countries contributing financially to police development, as well as the Commanding General of the CSTC-A and the head of the European Police Mission in Afghanistan.

The main purpose of the Senior Police Advisers Group was to have the most senior foreign police officers in Afghanistan feed organisational development advice to the Minister of the Interior and to the International Police Coordination Board, in a coordinated manner, and coordinate police development projects across all the regions. Importantly, it also had as a member a senior police officer from the Office of the Minister of the Interior. In order to bring the Senior Police Adviser (SPA) of UNAMA into the project, it was decided to offer the chair of the Senior Police Advisers Group to the SPA for the first three months, and after that it would rotate between the members. Meetings were hosted at the European Police Mission camp in Kabul.

The second project the AFP Commander led in Kabul was the establishment of the Afghan Major Crimes Task Force. This was a joint task force of the ANP and the National Directorate of Security designed to combat kidnapping, organised crime and corruption. Crimes of these types were strongly linked across the country and had a nexus with the illicit narcotics industry. The project commenced with the development of the Kidnapping Investigation Unit. Kidnapping of Afghan nationals was on the increase in Kabul, along with the alarmingly high rate of kidnapping of foreign journalists and aid workers. Owing to concerns that certain members of the ANP might have been behind some of the kidnappings,[8] a US Army colonel tasked as mentor to the Afghan Counter Terrorism Police ensured that a highly vetted police unit was established within the ANP that could be trusted to combat kidnapping. His plan was to have the unit mentored by anti-kidnapping experts from the FBI and to have all members polygraphed to ensure that they were not involved in crime, nor linked to it through family members.

---

8   Intelligence was being received at that time that a small cadre of senior and highly placed Afghan police officers were engaging their own officers to carry out the kidnappings of the foreign nationals and then both negotiating and delivering the ransom money in cash for their release.

Unfortunately, the colonel was in the final stages of his deployment and asked that the AFP Commander take over the project as the new Senior Mentor of the Kidnapping Investigation Unit. AFP management back in Australia granted permission and, as part of the process, the AFP Commander was also able to hand over his duties as Senior Mentor to the Chief of the Criminal Investigations Department to the Chief of the European Police Mission in Afghanistan (EUPOL). EUPOL was eager to take on this role and could provide up to seven more members as the new development team to the Chief of the Criminal Investigations Department. This handover was considered a win for both the European Police Mission and CSTC-A. Just before the departure of the colonel, the first of the FBI Kidnapping Investigation Unit mentors arrived in country to commence work on first recruiting and vetting the new members, then training them, all while commencing actual operations as the kidnappings continued to occur. This unit had a direct line of communication to the Minister of the Interior, HE Mr Hanif Atmar, who was exceptionally supportive. As Senior Mentor for the Kidnapping Investigation Unit, the AFP Commander was responsible for its development at the political and organisational levels.

In harvesting more intelligence on kidnappings from various foreign sources in Kabul, the AFP Commander of the Afghanistan Mission confirmed the suspected nexus between kidnapping, organised crime groups and corruption within the police, justice sector and Afghan government. Combined with the problem of the lack of coordinated effort within these sectors, the AFP Commander of the Afghanistan Mission moved to overcome these issues by expanding the Kidnapping Investigation Unit into a major national law enforcement task force to combat kidnapping, corruption and organised crime. With its own intelligence and prosecutions teams, it would be able to develop in secret criminal target packs with information provided by foreign and local intelligence sources, then investigate, arrest and finally prosecute those arrested in court, in front of a vetted judge.

The Afghan Major Crimes Task Force would be an Afghan-led, joint ANP and National Directorate of Security unit being (initially) mentored and trained by a multinational law enforcement mentoring team from the United States, the United Kingdom, Canada and Australia. As the scope of the project involved a great deal of financing and the deployment of more FBI agents, the full support of the US Government was required. The AFP Commander of the Afghanistan Mission negotiated the project through both the CSTC-A and US Embassy law enforcement contacts in order to gain that commitment before briefing the Minister of the Interior. During the following months, the Kidnapping Investigations Unit was very successful, with some 40 national and foreign kidnap victims safely recovered and more than 140 persons involved in the kidnappings arrested. By July 2009, the Afghan Major Crimes Task Force project was fully operational with US$30 million in funding from CSTC-A and the further deployment of FBI members who assumed control of the project on their arrival. The AFP Commander of the Afghanistan Mission remained the Senior Mentor to the Afghan Major Crimes Task Force (AMCTF), representing the interests of the Commanding General of CSTC-A.

The third project of the AFP Commander of the Afghanistan Mission was to have three AFP members embedded within the Kandahar Intelligence Fusion Cell situated at Kandahar airfield to gather and process counter-narcotic intelligence that could then be used as evidence. Before deployment, the ADF asserted that it would take the lead for securing the engagement of the 'Four Eyes' (i.e. the Five Eyes, less New Zealand, which was not involved) military intelligence community within Regional Command – South (RC-South). From October 2008 until late February 2009, the ADF was unable to secure that support and subsequently advised that the AFP would have to engage each individual country's intelligence community on a bilateral basis to gain access to the facility and the material within. This surprising roadblock was eventually overcome in no small way thanks to an AFP officer embedded within the ISAF headquarters of the IOCC in Kabul. The general work of this officer involved developing law enforcement and prosecutorial target packages for those involved in the illicit narcotics industry, with the great spin-off that the AFP would be exposed to the best daily intelligence on the Afghan illicit narcotics industry. Another advantage was that this presence strengthened the relationship between the AFP Commander of the Afghanistan Mission and the head of the IOCC. As good fortune would have it, this head of the IOCC reported directly to Commander of ISAF, who was then General David D. McKiernan, and had an excellent working relationship with him. It was this relationship that was positively exploited in February 2009 by the AFP Commander of the Afghanistan Mission in order to place three AFP members in the Kandahar Intelligence Fusion Cell.

In March 2009, the new US administration changed its counter-narcotics strategy from one of large-scale poppy eradication to a more targeted policy that combined a more cohesive military–civilian plan to attack the nexus of the insurgency, narcotics and government corruption. To implement this new policy, the US administration, through ISAF Command, directed that a new joint military–civilian task force be established at RC-South, known as the Combined Joint Interagency Task Force – Nexus (CJIATF-Nexus). It was tasked to develop a counter-narcotics intelligence collection, counter-narcotics campaign planning, assessment, targeting and fusion capability, and support the London-based Joint Narcotics Analysis Centre to conduct strategic-level analysis, studies on effects of the narcotics trade on security and governance, and provide reach-back support to the IOCC situated at ISAF headquarters in Kabul.

Fortuitously, the AFP team had just been accepted into the Kandahar Intelligence Fusion Cell and was now in the best position to be part of this new unit. Very quickly after the announcement of the creation of the CJIATF-Nexus, as the IOCC representatives in RC-S, the AFP was quickly invited to join it as a senior partner, and was tasked with a leading role in its development.

The AFP mission was now placed at the centre of the implementation of the new ISAF Civilian–Military Plan as it related to counter-narcotics within the country. In the weeks that followed, the CJIATF-Nexus undertook a comprehensive harvest of all known military and criminal intelligence from within the Afghan battle space. This intelligence environment scan identified most, if not all, of the criminal syndicates that were operating in and out of Afghanistan. Unfortunately, none of this intelligence reporting could be disseminated to Afghan law enforcement as all of the military intelligence was highly classified. Also, Afghan law enforcement, in particular the ANP and the Counter-Narcotics Police of Afghanistan, had serious allegations of corruption to confront, as it appeared that a number of the criminal syndicates identified in the intelligence scan had strong links to serving senior executive officers of the Counter-Narcotics Police of Afghanistan.

This new cell was able eventually to deliver criminal intelligence solutions to the ISAF battle space managers in direct support to non-lethal military counter-narcotic operations. What this means is that the AFP, through its involvement with the CJIATF-Nexus, was now able to provide a non-kinetic means of removing significant players from the battlefield, through a rule of law path that, when done, had a positive impact on the general population and on the government of Afghanistan.

Proof of the success of this joint police–military initiative came in July 2009. The Aghan Major Crimes Task Force enabled with sanitised CJIATF-Nexus criminal intelligence and supported by US Drug Enforcement Agency and mentors from the UK Serious and Organized Crime Office arrested the Argestan Provincial Border Police Chief, Colonel Shar Shahin, with 4,300 kilograms of hashish and 90 kilograms of pure Afghan brown heroin. While Shahin was subsequently sentenced to 20 years imprisonment, this operation caused significant anxiety with certain members of the government of Afghanistan and police as it was the first time some felt truly exposed to the coming tide of high-profile arrests and criminal prosecutions that would be the inevitable result of such a successful multinational–Afghan military–police partnership.

In May 2009, when the sterile corridor concept (for evidentiary integrity) was being cemented within the operations, the CJIATF-Nexus team, as well as its executive team (including AFP), briefed the US Defence Secretary of Defence, Robert Gates. They outlined the capabilities being realised through the fusion of military intelligence and international law enforcement criminal intelligence inside the CJIATF—-Nexus. These were in direct support of both ISAF battle-space owners and the potential positive outcomes utilising Afghan rule of law outcomes. Gates checked out the intelligence, surveillance and reconnaissance capabilities— which he pushed to increase in both Afghanistan and Iraq, at a classified intelligence fusion centre. He emphasised the importance of this effort to operations underway in Afghanistan, with the 'fusion of intelligence and operations in a way that has never been done before in warfare'.[9]

Operation SYNERGY

Moving on through this very busy period, in August 2009, the AFP deployed a further contingent of police to Tarin Kowt under the banner of Operation SYNERGY. These members were to work in partnership with

---

9   D. Miles, 'Gates wraps up Afghanistan visit with new insights', 8 May 2009, United States Department of Defense, waronterrornews.typepad.com/home/2009/05/gates-optimistic-on-afghanistan.html (retrieved 3 May 2010).

the Dutch police from the European Union Police Mission in Afghanistan; however, not long after their arrival, the Dutch police withdrew, allowing the AFP essentially to take over full management of the police training facility. Their main focus was to train all ANP recruits who were deployed to Uruzgan. They were also able to develop new training programs for leadership and specialist operations, which was a hugely successful project that eventually provided training for more than 2,500 police officers in basic police patrol officer courses and other police specialist and leadership programs.

Operation ILLUMINATE

In 2010, Operation CONTEGO and Operation SYNERGY were combined into Operation ILLUMINATE. From this point on until its withdrawal in 2014, the AFP continued to be engaged mostly in the training of ANP, but in a broader sense that also included training members of the Afghan Major Crimes Task Force, and conducting other police specialist training programs in Kabul. Further development of the AFP contribution to Afghanistan from that point witnessed senior members of the AFP deployed to significant positions within ISAF headquarters as advisers.

Conclusion

This historical study has highlighted one of the more distinctive roles of the AFP in undertaking capacity-building efforts in support of both indigenous law enforcement and international stabilisation efforts in Afghanistan.

The mission provided tangible solutions to ISAF senior officials who continue to enable and support international stabilisation operations in Afghanistan. The mission, via its direct involvement in establishing both the AMCTF and the CJIATF-Nexus, further delivered law enforcement solutions that enabled the movement of sanitised classified military intelligence to the Afghan law enforcement criminal intelligence domain. This then allowed vetted and credible Afghan law enforcement teams (specifically the AMCTF) to target, disrupt and dismantle those criminals operating in the nexus between insurgency, narcotics and corrupt operations within the Afghan Government. Through its involvement in the initial establishment of the Senior Police Advisors Group in Kabul, the AFP supported the strategic development of the ANP in both policy and training.

In the initial stages of the AFP contribution, three key developments were successfully undertaken by the AFP that aligned to support the international stabilisation efforts in Afghanistan. These were, first, to develop an operational national law enforcement unit of integrity to combat kidnapping, corruption and organised crime (the Afghan Major Crimes Task Force); second, to develop a robust, internationally supported national criminal intelligence unit (CJIATF-Nexus) to support the Major Crimes Task Force; and last, to assist in developing a Strategic Police Advisory Group to shape and influence ANP policy and training development. Following on from this, the AFP then expanded its mission fully and successfully to conduct and manage the training of Afghan police who were involved in many varied policing disciplines.

The Concept of Operations was developed to support the deployment of the mission in a way that was broad enough to allow for the realignment of the mission towards capacity building of the government of Afghanistan and Afghan law enforcement, should the opportunity arise. This flexibility was crucial to the mission outcomes and ensured that opportunities could be harnessed in support of wider strategic objectives, such as in 2009 and later in regard to the training effort from 2009 to 2014.

The AFP withdrew its mission in 2014 after maintaining a presence in Afghanistan for seven years, successfully deploying some 103 members in various roles in four locations. Over those seven years, the significant outcomes included:

- The writing of the complete training and development package for the ANP Criminal Investigations Department.
- The initial establishment of the Afghan Major Crimes Task Force, which saw great success initially in the rescue of 40 kidnap victims in Kabul, and the arrest of some 140 persons involved in those kidnappings.
- The initial establishment of the Senior Police Advisers Group in Kabul, a strategic police development think tank hosted by the European Union Police Mission in Afghanistan and led initially by the UNAMA Senior

Police Adviser, which included representation from the ANP. Its purpose was to feed organisational development advice to the Minister of the Interior and the International Police Coordination Board.

- The establishment of the CJIATF-Nexus in Kandahar, which designed and implemented the first sterile corridor intelligence pathways that allowed information gathered by the military to be used for police intelligence on the narcotics industry and high-level corruption by public officials. This type of information was later fed to the Afghan Major Crimes Task Force and resulted in the first, very public arrest of a senior Afghan Police Colonel, Shar Shahin, for the possession and transport of more than 1,000 kilograms of illegal narcotics.

Within five years from late 2009 until 2014, the AFP trained:

- 2,194 ANP patrolmen
- 259 non-commissioned officers
- 98 evidence collection officers
- 570 investigators for the Afghan Major Crimes Task Force
- 65 surveillance officers
- 13 police trainers
- 96 police officers on leadership and development programs.

The AFP also held significant police advisory positions on the International Police Coordination Board, in the Office of the Commander ISAF, and as Senior Mentor to the Deputy Minister for Security. Members were also deployed to the European Union Police Mission.

The seven-year AFP Afghanistan Mission was a highly risky and expensive endeavour that saw 103 AFP members deployed to harsh and dangerous conditions. Numerous rocket and mortar attacks at Tarin Kowt and Kandahar airfield took the lives of soldiers and civilians alike. In Kabul, numerous complex and VBIED attacks were carried out against ISAF camps and convoys. Camp Eggers, which was the headquarters of CSTC-A, where the AFP Commander of the Afghanistan Mission worked, and the front gates of ISAF headquarters, where the AFP IOCC member worked, were both subject to a VBIED attack that resulted in the deaths and injuries of ISAF personnel. In addition, a convoy of civilian staff from the IOCC was attacked by a VBIED at the military entrance of Kabul International Airport, resulting in a loss of life and severe wounding of civilians in armoured vehicles, the same type as used by the AFP.

13. THE AUSTRALIAN FEDERAL POLICE IN AFGHANISTAN, 2007–14

There was the constant threat and fear of green-on-blue attacks whereby rogue ANP officers or soldiers would target their ISAF mentors and trainers, at times preventing AFP members from attending ANP buildings or the headquarters in Kabul. The Ministry of Justice was the subject of a complex attack while a member of the UK prosecutions mentoring team was there, luckily escaping thanks to the excellent quick extraction reactions of his Close Personal Protection Team supplied by Armour Group, the very same company that provided protection for the AFP in Kabul. The back road to the military airport that was used as an alternative route for AFP members in Kabul came under sustained sniper attack, preventing its further use and thereby forcing the AFP to use Jalalabad Road, nicknamed 'Bomb Alley', as the only route they could take to get to and from work each day. All of this and more happened just in 2008–09, with no reduction in the threat at any time throughout the entire seven years the AFP was deployed to Afghanistan.

With this as the working environment for AFP members, special recognition is given to all of them for achieving so much in such a short period, in such conditions that civilian police are neither conditioned, trained nor fully mentally prepared to work in. It takes personal resilience and boldness to achieve anything in this environment, and all participating AFP members should be rightfully recognised for their excellent and dedicated contribution. Not all returned to Australia without scars. Not all returned the same as when they left. While this narrative contributes in some small way to tell the story of the AFP's highly successful contribution to Afghanistan, it certainly fails to tell the human story, which only those who served there can tell in their own words and perhaps in their own time. I hope, however, that in some small way, this chapter can at least describe in general terms just how successful the seven-year AFP contribution to Afghanistan was, and that there were 103 AFP officers who, with immense dedication and at great personal risk and, in some cases, personal cost, fully contributed in striving to succeed.

14

AusAID stabilisation

David Savage

When thinking about Australia's role in Afghanistan, most automatically gravitate towards the work of the Army in particular, and the Air Force and Navy in support. The last few chapters have made clear that Australia's engagement, while constrained, was multifaceted. Yet another facet of that engagement concerned the provision of support to the local people through aid and development projects.

This chapter presents a snapshot of the role that officials from the Australian Agency for International Development (AusAID) undertook in Uruzgan Province, Afghanistan, as part of Australia's whole-of-government effort.

The chapter focuses largely on my personal experiences as a stabilisation adviser (STABAD), and on impressions of Australia's response, including the challenges faced, what worked and what did not, and why. The details and achievements hereafter are those up to the withdrawal of Department of Foreign Affairs and Trade (DFAT) and AusAID personnel in late 2013.

Background

Australia's mission in Afghanistan was one of foreign policy, and the DFAT is the department primarily responsible for setting Australia's foreign policy. The then Australian Agency for International Development[1] had responsibility for Australia's aid budget globally, and of course this included in Afghanistan.

---

1   In November 2013, AusAID formally became part of the Department of Foreign Affairs and Trade.

Australia has been committed to international operations in Afghanistan since 2001 in the areas of military operations, diplomacy and development. Since 2006, Australia has been operating a diplomatic mission in Kabul with a small DFAT staff and representatives from other government agencies. With the return of the ADF, and Australian operations focusing on Uruzgan in 2009, we identified that it was necessary to have the relevant civilian arms of the government also operating in Uruzgan. The United States already had a joint civilian–military approach in Afghanistan, and the Dutch, who had primacy in Uruzgan at that time, also had a combined civilian–military team.

Australia had previous experience in civilian–military operations in the non-warlike operations undertaken in Bougainville[2] and in Solomon Islands.[3] However, in the high-risk conflict zone of Afghanistan, Australia was presented with a new challenge, and one that had not been envisaged.

The ADF force elements that deployed were well trained, well equipped, focused and highly effective in fighting the insurgency and building the capacity of Afghan National Security Forces (ANSF). However, as we know, winning wars in the 21st century requires more than a purely military approach. The military alone cannot ensure the defeat of the insurgency; it is a complex political, ethnic and tribal issue requiring an equally complex, measured and wide-ranging response to it.

To be fully effective in nation-building and strengthening fundamental elements of the fabric of society required a holistic approach, with diplomats working alongside, mentoring and supporting their Government of the Islamic Republic of Afghanistan (GIRoA) counterparts in all aspects of governance, accountability and human rights. It required AusAID working in partnership with the Afghan government line directors and implementing partners on development and capacity-building of Afghan government employees and institutions. The view was taken that only by adopting this approach could military gains be made enduring and the reach of GIRoA in the province and with the people be strengthened.

The road to transforming Afghanistan from a fractured, war-ravaged country, where institutions were either broken or non-existent, to a functioning self-governing democracy, is strewn with many obstacles. To have any hope of

---

2   The Truce Monitoring Groups and subsequent Peace Monitoring Groups after the cessation of hostilities in the civil war.
3   International Peace Monitoring Team and then Regional Assistance Mission Solomon Islands (RAMSI).

effective and sustainable development, several key ingredients had to be present. This was especially critical in a multi-donor and multi-mission environment.[4] These key factors included early intervention, long-term government commitment,[5] and donor coordination. However, all three of these factors were absent in whole or in part from all contributing nations.

Diplomacy and overseas development assistance is difficult even in the most permissive of environments; however, operating in the warlike setting of Afghanistan was undoubtedly the most difficult environment faced by the Australian Government in recent memory.

With the ADF focused on its area of operation, most ADF reporting and analysis was based on supporting their activities. Australia needed to have an overall vision of what was happening, especially politically, economically and in terms of the rule of law. We needed an understanding of the complex tribal dynamics that affected everything occurring within the province and beyond, including nationally and internationally. With the right tone and vision, this would enable Australia to form a strategic view for short-, medium- and long-term goals.

DFAT was and remains the most appropriate source of that reporting, as this is their 'bread and butter'. AusAID played a crucial role in support, identifying how to assist the community and overseeing project delivery, ensuring that Australia's and GIRoA's best interests were served.

A report of the Australian Civil-Military Centre (ACMC) stated that other coalition partners such as Canada and the Netherlands have long since used this combined team approach 'in together-out together':

> Civilian and military personnel participated in mission preparation activities together, including security and safety training, as well as headquarters-level exercises and simulations designed to strengthen relationships and understanding between participating agencies.[6]

---

4   Donors included the United States, European Union and the Organisation for Economic Cooperation and Development as well as local and international non-government organisations. Missions covered included the work of the NATO, the UNAMA and the ISAF.
5   Commitment needs to be in tranches of five to 10 years, not the frequent maximum of one to three years. As we have seen, it takes generations to repair decades of war, corruption and neglect.
6   Australian Civil-Military Centre, *Afghanistan: Lessons from Australia's Whole of Government Mission*, ACMC, Queanbeyan, 2016, p. 40.

As the ADF and government agencies have distinctive cultures and can be somewhat insular, training and preparation together breaks down these internal constraints so that they can work together for the same goal. I hope that this will be the approach adopted for future missions.

The rest of this chapter sets out to examine how this approach was implemented.

Mission

DFAT's policy advisers, or POLADs, were responsible for offering advice to their military counterparts on matters ranging from governance, detainee visits, human rights and the rule of law. In Afghanistan, AusAID's mission statement for the development advisers was building resilience and supporting at-risk populations, empowering women and girls by addressing barriers to their social, political and economic participation, and supporting the Afghan Government to maintain economic growth and institute more effective and accountable governance.

Often enough, the provision of aid is the easiest part. The real challenge is ensuring that the aid is what is really required, is compatible with the mission, is not supporting the insurgency, and is both viable and sustainable over time. Indeed, aid that is poorly delivered can often be worse than no aid at all, as it can create or exacerbate tribal or community conflicts and power imbalances and even ruin economies.

Before going further, it is important to note that AusAID itself does not implement aid. Instead, AusAID focuses on institutional strengthening, so that development is sustainable and enduring. In Afghanistan, AusAID identified community needs in concert with GIRoA and communities. It identified the implementing partners required to construct infrastructure and to deliver and fund projects either independently or in partnerships. These partner organisations ranged from UN agencies, international non-government organisations such as the International Committee of the Red Cross (ICRC), and non-government organisations (NGOs) such as Red Crescent, Save the Children, World Vision and other national NGOs.

In line with the mission, the projects in Afghanistan ranged from vaccinating children against preventable diseases, water, sanitation and health (WASH) training and distribution of sanitation packs, construction of schools and health facilities, the training of nurses and midwives, agriculture, rural development, governance and capacity-building, to name a few. These projects were designed to support the coalition's counter-insurgency focus, by extending the reach of GIRoA into the community and encouraging the community to support GIRoA and distance of themselves from the insurgents.

Challenges

It will not surprise the reader to know that implementing these projects had their challenges. International interventions and support requirements do not end when the conflict ends; they need to continue to strengthen government and institutions, building capacity to make it resilient to challenges, and to prevent it reverting to its previous state. In the post-conflict environment, there are several schools of thought that seek to benchmark when a country can operate largely independently, although with a level of continuing support from the international community. Often the benchmark is successful free and fair democratic elections. However, the assessment of what constitutes 'free and fair' can be rather subjective, and of course can be used as a convenient metric for donors seeking justification to withdraw. Another approach is suspicious of the electoral benchmark and focuses more on economic factors as being indicative of community confidence and stability. These factors include economic growth, flow of currency into or out of the country, good governance, transparency, anti-corruption strategies and adherence to the rule of law. Going by these realistic measures, progress becomes more difficult to discern.

The reality

The reality faced was that Afghanistan was a country that was still at war, had a highly dubious electoral process, and was performing poorly against other benchmarks. Out of 180 countries on the Transparency International scale of corruption, it rated 179th.[7] This made it clear that a resolution to any of the governance or development challenges was never going to be quick or easy. Afghanistan required a long-term, scalable commitment.

---

7   Civil-Military Fusion Centre, *Corruption and Anti-Corruption Issues in Afghanistan*, Civil-Military Fusion Centre, Norfolk, VA, 2012, p. 6.

For more than 30 years Afghanistan has barely been able to draw breath between conflicts, and an estimated 9 million of its people are illiterate. In the largely Pashtun, highly conservative and less progressive province of Uruzgan, the literacy rates were estimated to be as low as 2 per cent. Illiteracy and lack of formal education fed into the insurgency and made the community vulnerable to misinformation and recruitment; hence the Taliban opposed education except in places where they could control the content. When the coalition moved into the province, few schools existed, and almost no female students were able to attend those schools that did exist. Infant and maternal mortality was high, medical facilities, midwives, clinics and so on were either not available or not operating. Knowledge and understanding of basic principles of WASH were largely absent. Agriculture was primitive and undertaken in the same manner as it had for centuries, and opium production was the major cash-crop. The continuing war, complicated by political, tribal and ethnic conflicts, made the delivery of aid risky.

Just as with a doctor, the first principle of delivery of overseas development assistance is 'Do no harm'. It is easy to trigger jealousies, increase divisions between communities, inflame conflict, encourage corruption and create unrealistic community expectations. This not only affects the community and aid deliverers but can also undermine the coalition and GIRoA. The risk and impact in Australia of poor overseas development assistance can be about both loss of reputation and loss of trust, which in turn can affect funding.

The situation on the ground was all the more complicated as the insurgents were operating a parallel government in order to legitimise their standing and to undermine GIRoA and the coalition. They created doubt in the mind of the community as to the legitimacy of the central government and the long-term commitment of the coalition, resulting in a reduction of community support for the ANSF.

We strove to counter this by mentoring and encouraging GIRoA officials to leave the security of their blast walls and razor-wired office compounds and go out into the community to extend the reach of GIRoA, not just from outside Tarin Kowt, the provincial capital, but also to the district centres and beyond into villages. We encouraged district government representatives to interact with the community and improve their standing by having aid delivered through the prism of GIRoA, rather than through the donors.

Just as it was critical for security, counterinsurgency and development to spread out from Kabul into the countryside and into the provinces, it was just as critical that it spread out from provincial capitals into the districts and smaller villages. These were the areas that were either supporting insurgents or were vulnerable to joining their support base if they doubted the capacity of GIRoA to support them. In short, development and security goals sat side by side in Uruzgan, and they were not incompatible.[8]

Effective aid delivery needs to be coordinated at both the national and provincial levels. Cooperation between donors is necessary to prevent duplication, competition and gaps. However, even in Afghanistan the aid world is crowded, often with various donors working to their own agendas and mission statements to the detriment of the overall objective; in this case, the provision of assistance to the Afghan people. The lack of coordination at national and provincial levels severely hampered aid delivery and effectiveness, with duplicate, overlapping and inefficient application of uncoordinated efforts often leaving little in terms of a long-standing legacy.

In 2008 there was still some hope that such coordination could be put into effect. That was when the Afghan Government approved the Afghanistan National Development Strategy for security, governance, economic growth and poverty reduction.[9] It expressed a strong preference for aid to be channelled through the central government. While it was understandable for a sovereign nation to want ownership of development and to coordinate development assistance to its people, the reality is that GIRoA did not possess the necessary capacity to do so. Nor were effective systems in place to enable funding from a national level to reach projects, or even line ministries. In addition, there was a distinct shortage of the experience needed to understand the basic principles of aid delivery.

Whether unintended or by design, this level of dysfunction promoted and enabled large-scale corruption and diversion of critical funds from projects and the people of Afghanistan into the hands of individuals. Doubtless, some of those funds would have found their way into the very hands of the insurgents our forces were fighting.

---

8   ACMC, *Afghanistan*, Chapter 3.
9   Ibid., p. 35.

Implementation

Notwithstanding these concerns, considerable effort was made in an attempt to pursue the government's national development strategy. The civilian contribution was based within the PRT in the Multi-National Base — Tarin Kowt. Effective overseas development aid and diplomacy cannot be conducted behind the wire. Face-to-face meetings between provincial government line directors were critical to build relationships, engender trust and identify common goals. Consultation with communities was necessary to determine what kind of assistance was required, along with requirements for due diligence and the mentoring of partners for the implementation of this program. To achieve this level of interaction with the provincial government, the coalition military had to support all civilian movements. The ADF formed the Other Government Agency (OGA) Platoon to provide security for 'outside the wire' missions in and around Tarin Kowt. In other districts where either AusAID or Australian Civilian Corps members were working, security was undertaken by US members of the PRT.

Regular meetings took place in Tarin Kowt at either the governor's office or PRT House between DFAT and AusAID officials and their Afghan counterparts. This ensured the development of relatively strong working relationships and productive partnerships. This also made certain that provincial officials knew that they were getting the necessary support, and allowed us to have a good view of what was occurring within the government in order to structure our responses accordingly.

During the next few years, the civilian contingent grew in number as the aid projects increased. This formed a key component of the PRT, in both the provision of their projects and in supporting military reconstruction projects with technical and other advice.

In early 2011, the Australian Civilian Corps was created as a branch within AusAID by the then prime minister Kevin Rudd. I was selected for the first Australian Civilian Corps deployment to Afghanistan as a stabilisation adviser. There were six stability advisers deployed in two rotations. One deployed to Tarin Kowt, another to nearby Deh Rawud, and I was based in Forward Operating Base Mirwais, in the neighbouring Chora District. My colleagues and I arrived in early September 2011, and we were due to finish our deployment at the end of October 2012.

Unfortunately, the decision to deploy stability advisers to Uruzgan coincided with the announcement by US President Obama of the drawdown or end date of the US mission in Afghanistan.[10] Without the military to provide security, there were questions as to how civilians could undertake institutional strengthening, development and anti-corruption roles.[11] Australian Prime Minister Julia Gillard also announced that Australia would be withdrawing from Uruzgan between 2012 and 2014.

The announcement of the coalition forces' withdrawal from Uruzgan (and Afghanistan) worked directly against our goals, one of which was to persuade the community to support the Afghan Government instead of the insurgents. The community, especially in contested areas, were going to support whoever they believed would be in control of their village, district and province when the coalition forces withdrew and, at best, were understandably going to have a bet each way.

As stabilisation advisers, our new role was largely undefined, and identifying how we worked with the PRT was not clear. We came from the Australian Civilian Corps roster. The Australian Civilian Corps members came from a wide range of backgrounds, which included NGOs, the United Nations, consultants, contractors, police and military. I was the only civilian who came from either DFAT or AusAID, although most of my career had been with the United Nations, NGOs and the AFP. The stabilisation adviser role had a multitude of responsibilities: part diplomat, part development and mentoring, and an advising, training and trouble-shooting role within the Afghan communities. Although civilians had been at forward operating bases previously, it was the first time that they were permanently based there.

After a brief induction at Al-Minhad Air Base in Dubai on the way to Afghanistan, my colleagues and I arrived in Multi-National Base — Tarin Kowt. My concerns, first raised in Dubai, that the ADF did not quite understand that civilians were *really* being deployed outside the base at Tarin Kowt to forward operating bases and all that this entailed, were confirmed in Tarin Kowt. After only a day and a half in Tarin Kowt,

---

10   CNN Wire Staff, 'Obama announces Afghanistan troop withdrawal plan', CNN Politics, 23 June 2011.
11   J. Dougherty, 'What happens to "civilian surge" as military surge ends', CNN, 22 June 2011.

I was deployed to Forward Operating Base Mirwais in the Chora Valley. It was clear that civilians were tolerated, but war-fighting was what it was all about, and assets for civilians were pretty much last on the priority list.

I was set down at the flight line unaccompanied by security, awaiting my flight on a Chinook helicopter. When it arrived, I struggled across to it with my (excess) luggage and managed to climb aboard. The flight was soon full of soldiers, and as no one else was heading to Forward Operating Base Mirwais, I asked the loadmaster to let me know when I arrived, so that I could know when to get out. We soon lifted off and began flying from base to base. The soldiers alighted at the various bases, until I was the last passenger left on the flight. The loadmaster then came up to me and yelled in my ear: 'We are just pulling up now. The base is uphill. When we stop, get out and run like hell.' He then emphasised: 'This is Injun country!'

As instructed, this unarmed civilian jumped out and grabbed all of his gear for the next year. The loadmaster pointed up a steep incline to a small HESCO'ed base (i.e. surrounded by HESCO walls) with a metal door about 80 metres away. I started running uphill towards the base in the oxygen-deprived air, in my PPE, and dragging enough jack rations to last me 14 months.[12] I bashed on the metal door, and after a few moments it was opened by a soldier who just looked at me.

I said, 'Hi, I am the new STABAD [stabilisation adviser] from AusAID.' Answering in a strong southern US drawl after a rather pregnant pause, the man at the door said: 'OrzAID? Never heard of 'em, but get in here real quick.' Yes, I was not at Mirwais but a small combat outpost. After the mistake was realised, I was quickly collected and taken to the more substantial Mirwais. My departure from Afghanistan was also rather different from what I would have liked.

---

12   PPE: Personal Protective Equipment—ballistic vest, helmet and glasses. Jack rations are civilian food taken to the field to enliven standard issue rations.

14. AUSAID STABILISATION

Lieutenant Christian Johnston, Afghan mentor team leader for Combat Team B, 5th Battalion, the Royal Australian Regiment, looks on as his Afghan National Army counterpart speaks with an Afghan community member near Patrol Base Mohammed, Uruzgan province, Afghanistan, 2010.
Source: Courtesy of the Department of Defence.

I think it is fair to say that the in-country civilians from DFAT and AusAID did not see the need for stabilisation advisers to be deployed. Initially they were not as enthusiastic about our deployment as one might have expected. I put it down to concern that we were encroaching on their patch, but in reality, there was much for all of us to do and scope to assist each other. However, when I arrived at Mirwais I was warmly welcomed by the ADF, perhaps since I had served with several of them on previous peacekeeping missions. Although many did not know or understand what I could add to the mission, I was housed in a tent along with the US PRT members and National Guard Security Detachment. I then decided that I would invite a different soldier into each of my meetings with the community and district officials, so that they could see and understand what they were risking their lives for.

The challenges were something I had not confronted in more than 20 years of working in developing countries, including in the north of Afghanistan in 2009. It was not just the security issues. There were tribal rivalries; communities lacked the fundamentals of basic hygiene and education;

and, in the words of the famous Fred Smith song, 'And the Education Minister can neither read nor write, and the Minister for Women runs the knock shop there at night'.[13] It truly was another world.

Security

The greatest impediment to undertaking my role was the lack of security. Not only could I not move outside the base without a security detachment, but it also took enormous planning, and approvals had to be sought. This meant that ad hoc movements or meetings were almost impossible. The result was that our ability to respond to issues in real time was severely hampered. Owing to security concerns, we could not inform either government or tribal leaders of our intentions to meet them, which meant that we would arrive at offices only to find them vacant. It was very frustrating for all of us.

I also found that I was not granted permission to travel to villages where it was important to show the flag due to security concerns. This meant that those villages that were vulnerable to Taliban influence often did not receive the support from the coalition or GIRoA officials that might have helped them resist the insurgency. It was a vexed issue, as failing to assist these villages could have reinforced their view that the government did not care about them or favoured other villages over them.

Achievements

Although the challenges were enormous, there were equally numerous achievements of which Australia, the coalition and the PRT can be justifiably proud, improving the quality of life for a significant portion of the Uruzgan population. These include:

- A functioning hospital in Tarin Kowt, with a women's wing and surgery unit.
- Health facilities increased from nine in 2006 to 29 facilities in 2013, and 322 health posts in operation throughout the province, staffed by 106 healthcare professionals and 493 volunteer community health workers.

---

13   See www.asiaeducation.edu.au/docs/default-source/curriculum-resources-pdf/dust-of-uruzgan.pdf?sfvrsn=4.

- Improved maternal health care—up to 80 per cent of women received at least one antenatal visit, up from 50 per cent in 2007, and 24 new midwives and 26 nurses were trained.
- Lessons in hygiene and health were delivered to 4,400 children.
- Between January and June 2013, 12,470 health consultations were provided.
- More than 8,700 children under five screened for malnutrition, and more than 300 children with severe malnutrition were referred to treatment centres and counselling.
- The number of schools increased from 34 in 2006 to around 200 active schools in 2013, including 26 girls-only schools and 19 co-ed schools.
- An all-year, commercially capable civil airfield was opened.
- More than 320 kilometres of roads were improved, including 200 kilometres of paved roads across the province.
- Several government buildings were constructed.
- Agriculture production slowly improved and passed pre-conflict levels.
- Rural infrastructure was improved to protect against floods, droughts and other disasters.

Although we were supposed to give prior warning of our intention to visit schools, we often took the opportunity when nearby to see if they were being utilised. Some schools were not but many more were, and it was heartening to visit a school in a remote area and to see a classroom crammed with young girls embracing the opportunity to learn.

Challenges

It would be disingenuous of me to pretend that our programs were delivered without problems or that we were not taken advantage of, and we found ourselves often in the middle of tribal disputes, delivering aid to areas that did not need it and failing others that did.

Communities like those in the Chora Valley have been through extended periods of war, and in the absence of the rule of law, they become survivors, trusting no one, and understandably willing to try to get anything they could to assist their family and community. Promises by GIRoA and foreigners are easily made and often broken, and those who make them are soon gone, either rotated out or the mission completely withdrawn. In this environment, achieving effective aid delivery requires strong cooperation between all donors and implementing partners, showing a unified face to the community to avoid governments, NGOs, the United Nations and so on from being played off against each other. It is often the case that many problems were already entrenched before Australia's arrival, the situation being no different in Uruzgan.

With the need for quick results, it became clear that little or no due diligence had been undertaken, and mistakes were made. This was also in part due to the military trying to get quick runs on the board with the community, with quick impact projects and the US Commanders Emergency Reserve Program (CERP) funding.[14] Joint pre-deployment training between ADF, PRT and civilian members could have mitigated these issues, resulting in a more coordinated approach between the military and civilian elements from the pre-deployment phase throughout the mission.

When I arrived in Chora, there was no district governor and the head of the 2nd Kandak of the Afghan National Army[15] was acting in the role. This was problematic, as several suspect tribal leaders whom he had dealings with in the security context were hostile to him, and this was having a negative influence on community trust in his role representing the Afghan government. I was tasked with finding a suitable successor, but no one wanted the job. Although a salary was attached, it was very rarely paid, so the only way of supporting oneself, it appeared, was through graft and corruption. The position also came with a target on one's head, as the Taliban regularly executed GIRoA officials.

The first thing I had to do was negotiate a number of problems created by the well-meaning US PRT members. They had paid for a tube well, taking assurances from a village leader on face value, so they had not undertaken any due diligence. The tube well was sunk on private property, which was then walled off. The owner then commenced charging the community for water. This angered the villagers and had the potential to provoke animosity towards the PRT. As a solution, the PRT agreed to pay for three additional tube wells in the village at $5,000 each. However, being paid in advance, the contractor was never seen again, and neither were the

---

14   The purpose of the CERP program is to enable commanders to respond to urgent humanitarian relief and reconstruction requirements within their area of responsibility by carrying out programs that will immediately assist the indigenous population.
15   Kandak is equivalent to an Afghan brigade. Lieutenant Colonel Gul Agha acted in both roles.

tube wells. Basic understanding of contracting practices, using AusAID civilians as a resource, and working through government officials might have prevented this.

The actual cost of goods and services in the community was not known to the PRT. This made it difficult to ensure due diligence when awarding contracts even for projects as simple as a tube well, and this problem was multiplied exponentially for major constructions. Tube wells that should have cost between US$800 and US$1,000 were often charged US$5,000 to coalition forces, and on occasion several times more. Once precedence of prices had been set, very few Afghan contractors were willing to do work for a lower price, thereby reducing the number of projects that could be implemented and communities assisted, and decreasing the effectiveness of the mission. Often quotes had to factor in illicit payments to various government, police and tribal leaders to allow projects to proceed.

We were travelling 'outside the wire' five to six days per week, visiting community and tribal leaders and district government officials. However, they were rarely in the district governor's office, and we could not forewarn that we were visiting owing to security concerns, leading to lots of wasted time. However, it became clear that, as most government employees, including teachers and police, rarely received any salary, they had an understandably relaxed attitude to work.

The issue could not be resolved at district or provincial level because donors would contribute funding to the government or specific ministries at the national level. However, by the time funds trickled down from government ministers, to ministries, to provincial and then to district level, with each taking a share, there was little or, on many occasions, nothing left for the actual employees to receive.

Eventually a new district governor was appointed. He came from another district in Uruzgan after being removed from his previous role … yes, for graft and corruption. He quickly aligned himself with a powerful warlord, and I spent a great deal of my time trying to prevent the two of them from taking control of a large AusAID-funded flood mitigation project, which was designed to provide employment to representatives of each tribe.

Members of other tribes and villages marched in protest against them. Without the intervention of the ANSF and the coalition, it would have resulted in a violent confrontation. After some tense mediation, the original work-sharing agreement was upheld and the status quo was maintained—

for a while. I spent a considerable amount of time mentoring the district governor on basic principles of good governance, and for the rest of my deployment he was relatively cooperative. Emblematic of the lack of stability in government, the district governor was later removed, and the tribal leader disappeared after being linked to the insurgents. The lack of continuity in positions, owing to corruption or political interference, continually undermined the effectiveness of our capacity-building and institutional-strengthening efforts.

When Australia took control of the province and the PRT, we inherited several large, incomplete projects from the Dutch. AusAID had to oversee the final implementation phases of these projects, in concert with Kabul-based Dutch representatives. One of these was the much-lauded Tarin Kowt–Chora road. Initial planning had been for no culverts along the route, because we knew that insurgents would use them to deploy improvised explosive devices (IEDs). Where watercourses intersected the road, there were to be dips or wash-aways instead. However, owing to the failure in ensuring oversight of the project, the 30-kilometre roadway had some 120 culverts constructed by the time we took control. Several days before the road's opening, the security contractor withdrew his services and sought increased funding to re-secure the road. This was not forthcoming, leaving the length of the road vulnerable to insurgents or others.

Within an hour of the official opening of the road in Chora by the Dutch ambassador and minister, the first insurgent-placed IED blew a culvert. As a result, the official party had to be flown back to Tarin Kowt, as it was deemed too dangerous for them to travel back along the newly opened road. This, of course, resulted in a major embarrassment and loss of face for the ANSF, which could not maintain security, and for the coalition, even though the Dutch had built it.

Nearby communities knew that insurgents were placing IEDs; however, they decided, on the basis of their long-term survival prospects, not to inform on them to the ANSF or coalition. Within five months, most of the 120 culverts along the road had been blown, usually as coalition or ANSF vehicles passed. The result was that no Afghans would use the road, choosing to travel through the *dasht* (desert) instead.

Construction of projects that communities did not want was also problematic. In Chora, for instance, the Dutch constructed a new commercial hub of shops and a market, known as the Caravanserai, opposite the district government buildings. The only problem was that none of the shopkeepers wanted to move their businesses from the newly sealed road in the centre of town to the Caravanserai, especially when they found out that they would have to pay rent for the privilege. As a result, the Caravanserai was never inhabited, and its shoddy construction meant that within six months of opening, it was already falling apart.

In an area where two villages coexisted amicably, side by side, the construction of a dam almost brought them into conflict. Awi 1 and Awi 2 were two villages that shared a common water supply, which had never dried in living memory. Someone decided that the construction of a dam to capture this water would be of benefit to the community. Both villages agreed, and construction had taken place by the time I arrived in country. I was tasked with finalising the contract between donor and contractor. The villagers were refusing to allow the dam to be filled, yet without ensuring that it worked we could not make the final payments. With many visits backwards and forwards taking up a huge number of soldiers and assets, we finally identified the problem. The villagers did not actually understand what a dam was. They had never seen one, and it had never been discussed with them during the planning. By this time, they were using the dam as a public lavatory and did not understand the nexus between this and the fouling of their drinking water. We finally managed to persuade them to divert the water to fill the dam, which thankfully held. The contractor was paid; however, on our next visit the dam had been drained, and to my knowledge was never used again.

Nevertheless, we then received many requests from villages for dams, and we subsequently identified that each village was hoping for the same pay-off as Awi from the contractor, which was some US$20,000, and a similar amount to the district police chief to allow construction workers safe passage along the road. We could not instigate any action against the police chief, as he was killed shortly after by an insurgent IED.

In another instance, an Afghan police officer requested us to provide a dam to drought-proof the water supply of his remote village. We travelled to the village to undertake an assessment; however, after a community meeting, we discovered that the land where the dam was to be located was owned by the head of the Afghan National Police (ANP) in the area, which he had failed to disclose. The dam would have meant he controlled the village water supply, which could have resulted in instability and the village turning against the police. We declined to fund the dam, and instead funded the extension and construction of the existing concrete holding tanks situated on communal land in the centre of the village. Attending these locations is the only effective way of ensuring that appropriate aid that does not destabilise communities, but this came at a cost in resources and time.

Investigating the cause of a mobile phone tower being non-operational after 5 pm every day until sunrise, we discovered that the operators had been coerced by insurgents to limit hours to daylight only, preventing the population from reporting the insurgents operating at night in the district. The operators had complained to the local police post only some 500 metres away. The ANP replied that as they did not receive any salary, they had essentially made a non-aggression pact with the Taliban. So, to prevent the Taliban attacking them, they would allow the Taliban to control the towers' transmission hours.

These few examples are symptomatic of the challenges confronted by the coalition, ANSF and, provincial and district governments when there is limited support from the central government.

The civilian–military coordination in the province improved when Australia took the lead, and many of the problems between the ADF and civilian actors were mitigated by joint training, exercises and coordinated deployments. In these circumstances, the joint leadership model worked well.

What this review has shown is that, in all probability, there will always be challenges with deployments to environments like Afghanistan given the low base level of education, transport and communications. Developing people and infrastructure requires a long-term commitment in order to overcome generations of neglect. Once the announcement was made that the coalition was withdrawing, it was an uphill battle to persuade the population to reject the insurgents and support the ANSF, especially in areas where they had not received significant development assistance.

The real risk with short-term engagements such as in Uruzgan is that instead of strengthening institutions, we develop and strengthen individuals. In the case of Afghanistan, this often leads to an imbalance of power, corruption and even further conflict. We saw examples of this in the coalition's interactions in Uruzgan. The other side effect of concentrating power in individuals is that it creates a target for both insurgents and their rivals. Removing the individual by undermining them or, in the Afghan scenario, by killing them was a common and effective practice in Uruzgan. On 26 March 2011, while returning from a meeting with the district governor, my PRT patrol was attacked by a 12-year-old child suicide bomber and as a result I and three US soldiers were critically wounded, effectively ending the work of the PRT in Chora.

In closing, the unique nature and circumstances of the commitment to Uruzgan limited a long-term and sustainable approach to assist the Afghan Government to develop and strengthen the institutions. The need to deliver aid to assist securing community support and to assist coalition forces resulted in short-term gains, with some possible longer-term benefits being drawn from individuals who received training and education from Australian official development assistance. There was little long-term benefit in the capacity-building of individuals versus institutions, as many of those individuals were targeted and killed or subsequently left their positions. The increased spread of the insurgency throughout the province after the withdrawal of coalition forces had deleterious effect on many of the completed projects. Insurgents gained control of most of Uruzgan.

On balance, I do not think that we can judge the effectiveness of our intervention at the time of our departure. Instead, the sustainability of our efforts needs to be evaluated several years after our withdrawal. This would identify whether or not the seeds sown have been allowed to grow, mature and bear fruit.

15

The gender dimension

Elizabeth Boulton

An historically significant aspect to Australia's involvement in the Afghanistan and Iraq wars from 2001 to 2014 was the emergence of the so-called gender dimension. There are two broad components to consider: *internal* issues—the changing nature of the ADF's own troops; and *external* issues—the character of these wars, such as the 'war among the people' and counter-insurgency dimensions, in which gender issues became more prominent. This chapter draws on contributions from a range of ADF members and is divided into two parts corresponding to the two types of issue.[1]

Internal issues—own troops

The Afghanistan and Iraq wars were notable for seeing the first mass deployment of women in warlike operations in combat-related roles in Australian history. Although it might seem obvious to state, the most significant story to emerge is that women were well integrated into teams and well trained, and that they performed under pressure. This story is less well known, and is the focus of this chapter.

---

1   Contributions by Kellie Brett, Deb Butterworth, Fiona Grasby, Leanne Iseppi, Paula Ivanovic, Amanda Johnston, Marija Jovanovich, Bevan McDonald, Stacey Porter, Grant Prendergast, Janelle Sheridan, Donna Sill, Kelley Stewart and Jasmine Young.

However, a second, parallel and more negative story of gender and the ADF during this period must also be recorded. External inquiries into ADF culture around 2012–14 identified and sought to remedy a range of discrimination and abuse problems that had occurred from the 1960s onwards.[2] It was found that for both genders, the severity of abuse was much decreased between 2001 and 2011 compared to earlier periods; however, proportionally, rates were still higher for females.[3] These cultural difficulties likely affected female retention during the 1990s, something that was already challenging to maintain owing to general societal attitudes about gender and vocational choices. Operationally, this meant that there were low numbers of women in the ADF, just as the 'war among the people'[4] and counter-insurgency aspects of modern warfare came to the fore, and thereby, militarily, gender issues also became more important. Although these abuse issues internal to the ADF are deeply troubling, they need to be placed in context; similar problems occurred in wider Australian society at the same time, reflecting the influence of broader sociocultural factors.[5]

A finding that immediately emerged from my initial inquiry into 'own troops' is that data capture and analysis of this area is limited. Accordingly, this account relies on select voices from the field to illustrate the types of lesson that arose and does not claim to be a definitive, all-encompassing account.

---

2   Defence Committee, *Pathway to Change: Evolving Defence Culture—A Strategy for Cultural Change and Reinforcement*, Department of Defence, Canberra, 2012, and Defence Abuse Response Taskforce, *Report on Abuse in Defence*, Commonwealth of Australia, Canberra, 2014.
3   Defence Committee, *Pathway to Change*, pp. 288–9.
4   'War among the people' refers to conflict scenarios in which there are no clear delineations of combat zones or safe rear echeons. Armed violent individuals or groups and/or military forces undertake operations in urban or rural areas, where civilians live and work. An example is bombing of a busy marketplace. The widely used term is attributed to British General Rupert Smith, who introduces it in his book, *The Utility of Force: The Art of War in the Modern World*, Penguin, London, 2012.
5   R. Knowles, H. Szoke, G. Campbell, C. Ferguson, J. Flynn, J. Lay and J. Potter, 'Expert Advisory Group on discrimination, bullying and sexual harassment: Report to Royal Australasian College of Surgeons', Royal Australasian College of Surgeons, Melbourne, 2015, www.surgeons.org/-/media/Project/RACS/surgeons-org/files/operating-with-respectcomplaints/expert-advisory-group/background-briefing-16-june-15-final.pdf?rev=7b721c1d5a264a5983f715783a3ab18f&hash=DE07ACB50DC25A6D5C8400405C164B43 (retrieved 20 October 2020), and Australian Human Rights Commission, *Change the Course: National Report on Sexual Assault and Sexual Harassment at Australian Universities*, Australian Human Rights Commission, Canberra, 2017.

15. THE GENDER DIMENSION

Women in ADF operations in the Middle East: Business as usual

Interviews that I conducted with senior female regimental sergeant major (RSM) equivalents of each service found that women characterised the Middle East deployment as 'business as usual'. Areas like logistics, intelligence, communications and medicine had long been gender-integrated. Operational expertise had been steadily built from the late 1980s, for example, from Fiji in 1987, to the First Gulf War in 1990, and various deployments during the 1990s such as in Rwanda, Somalia and Timor Leste. It was the actions undertaken in the 1990s—the long investment in mainstreaming women into units, training regimes, posting cycles and selection for deployments—that allowed women to develop the requisite experience to perform in the Middle East.

In the RAN, ships had already long examined and resolved a range of pragmatic gender-related issues, such as sleeping quarters arrangements, and whether women should wear head scarves when ashore in some locations. RAN women were exposed to more hostile action, collectively, than seen before. For example, HMAS *Stuart* was part of a multinational naval security force in the Persian Gulf when, on 24 April 2004, hostilities erupted. There were two concurrent attacks: a dhow acted as a suicide bomb against a USS *Firebolt* boarding party, killing three crew members, while shortly after, an insurgent speedboat, laden with explosives, attacked an offshore oil rig. Commander (now Commodore) Michele Miller was the Executive Officer (XO) at the time and played a key role in leading the HMAS *Stuart* response.[6]

In the Army, the Centre for Army Lessons database reflects that army women's employment in standard non–arms corps environments has been uneventful. Nonetheless, soldiers indicated that they required additional focus and strategies to fit in when attached to combat arms corps units. Cognitive bias might have influenced the inclusion of women in some operational activities (such as tactical reconnaissance activities), typically required for the conduct of their roles. Generally, like their male peers,

---

6   D. Ellery, 'Captain Miller has a firm grasp of the Navy's tiller', *Sydney Morning Herald*, 14 October 2011, www.smh.com.au/politics/federal/captain-miller-has-a-firm-grasp-of-the-navys-tiller-20111014-1v6i8.html (retrieved 1 April 2020).

women filled new functions needed to suit operational needs. For example, Lieutenant Colonel Amanda Johnston worked on Taliban reintegration programs throughout the provinces.

The 'no women in combat' rule for the Army was not lifted until 1 January 2013; hence women were not employed in direct land combat roles in Iraq and Afghanistan. Nevertheless, the blurring lines of where the battlefield began and finished saw many women working in locations where they were under mortar fire, such as the Force Level Logistic Asset – Baghdad. Others experienced incidents involving improvised explosive devices during convoys and the like. One radio operator in Iraq provides an interesting anecdote:

> Her contingent received sporadic indirect fire, and they did not have an indirect fire warning system. To cope with the pressure, the corporal would listen to music … As section commander, she would talk to her team and check on matters like if they were getting enough sleep and they were communicating with people at home.[7]

Female soldiers kept their sense of humour, as shown through feedback on the resupply system for basic items: 'The full briefs that are only worn by grandmas need to be replaced with standard black underwear otherwise they will only be used for rifle pull-throughs.'[8]

This was regarded as a routine part of army deployment for many. Some individuals sought to apply the 'no women in combat rule' to prevent women from visiting units like the Security Detachment in Baghdad and other 'red zone' areas. However, generally, operational imperatives required this rule to be broken. It became obvious that with modern war, where there is no front line, such rules lacked relevance and often ended up being ignored.

By the time of the Afghanistan and Iraq wars, women had become so integrated into the Australian Army's approach to land operations that Australian policies on women in combat lagged behind reality. Although this issue had been long realised on preceding operations, it had not precipitated any consequent review of policy or force structure before Middle East operations. This suggests a gender blind spot in national security strategic planning forums and post-operational analysis activities.

---

7   Anonymous comment found in 'Centre of Army Lessons' database for Middle East deployments.
8   Anonymous comment found in 'Centre of Army Lessons' database for Middle East deployments.

Despite this lag, Army women gained substantial senior leadership experience during operations in Afghanistan and Iraq, which bodes well for the development of the future force. It is also historically significant. The first female RSM appointment in the Middle East, Warrant Office Class 1 Lynne Foster, occurred in 2006. By 2014, the Army had 12 female RSMs in total, and six of these had also served in an RSM capacity on operations in the Middle East. At the officer level, women also filled more senior operational leadership roles than seen before. For example, Major General Simone Wilkie served as both Assistant Chief of Staff on the Headquarters Multi-National Force – Iraq (MNF-I) in 2007 and as Assistant Commander, Joint Task Force (JTF) 633 in Afghanistan in 2011–12. Major General (then Colonel) Sue Coyle also served as a deputy commander of the JTF 636 Afghanistan in 2014.

When it comes to the Air Force, aside from long-standing roles in such areas as communications and logistics, Air Force women played critical operational roles. This was particularly so in the Air Traffic Control element at Baghdad airport in the early phase of the Iraq War. Others also worked in military policing roles among the population.

What was new about the Middle East deployment was the more extensive role women played as aircrew. For example, Warrant Officer (then Flight Sergeant) Paula Ivanovic was a loadmaster on C-17 Globemaster aircraft for 21 missions in Afghanistan, from 2007 to 2010. Before the Middle East conflict, this was a role almost exclusively performed by men. AP-3C Orion aircraft pilot Squadron Leader Marija Jovanovich completed three tours, in total, flying more than 100 missions. Her crew provided overland intelligence, surveillance and reconnaissance support to coalition troops in Iraq and Afghanistan and maritime surveillance in the Persian Gulf and the northern Persian Sea, and conducted counter-piracy operations off the coast of Somalia and in the Gulf of Aden.

Flight Lieutenant Jasmine Young, a weapon systems officer on the F/A-18F Super Hornet fighter aircraft, was the first female Australian deployed to air combat operations. She executed pre-planned and dynamic strike missions against Daesh in Iraq from 2014 to 2015. Aircrew also includes those working with the IAI Heron remotely piloted aircraft, such as sensor operator Flight Lieutenant Janelle Sheridan. While the Air Force had some female air combat officers qualified for fast jets, these aircraft did not deploy to the Middle East during the 2001–14 period.

An RAAF C-17 Globemaster prepares to land at Tarin Kowt, 2012.
Source: Courtesy of the Department of Defence.

On being interviewed about her experiences as aircrew, Squadron Leader Marija Jovanovich agreed with the 'business as usual' concept:

> Although there are not many of us, female aircrew are fully integrated into 92 Wing. Both as a co-pilot and as a captain, I always felt like I belonged and my gender was never an issue. I also had a highly competent female navigator on my crew for the 2010 tour, and the same applied to her.[9]

One minor problem was that sometimes separate sleeping locations were created for female aircrew. This arrangement was not ideal as it meant that the women's sleep was disrupted by other women working different shifts. When mixed-gendered aircrew were accommodated together, no problems were experienced.

Beyond the service-specific experience of women outlined so far, some other interesting leadership and teamwork dimensions are worth reflecting upon. The above descriptions indicate that there are many positive aspects about the way in which women had been mainstreamed into the ADF's various units by the time of and during Middle East operations. Part of this success might also relate to the idea that, regardless of service, the

---

9 Conversations with author.

mentality of 'a soldier is a soldier' (a sailor is a sailor and so on) was pre-eminent. Primarily, ADF members regarded themselves as members of a team, in which gender was not a conspicuous issue. However, the preference for the 'soldier is a soldier' approach meant that sometimes gender aspects were not considered when they needed to have been. For example, initially combat body armour did not fit women well, while pre-embarkation training did not address the risk of rape, for both men and women, on some deployed bases. As highlighted elsewhere, research insights from the new field of 'men's studies' might have helped the ADF to better support deploying men.[10]

One insight to emerge was that, when it came to resolving gender-related issues on deployment, the critical point was the person's chain of command. This has implications for the focus of gender policies; specifically, investment in leaders' knowledge, skills and behavioural repertoires to manage diverse teams might be the key to success.

Despite external review findings that some men made women's service life difficult, history must also record that there were many other ADF men who played a positive role in this story. From the 1990s onwards, it was a numerical reality that many ADF men were responsible for training, mentoring and developing these pioneering women. It should be noted that some of these men showed more acceptance towards military women undertaking a non-traditional work role than was seen in wider Australian society. In many units, strong teams and collegial connections developed over a sense of shared purpose. The success of this varied by unit and type of function; however, it suggests those areas of the ADF that achieved cohesion might have excellent lessons to offer other units still embarking upon this task.

In addition to issues of leadership and teamwork, the issues of parenthood had to be managed as well. Although the ADF has long had measures and systems in place to support deploying fathers, it is likely that some of the thinking around this had become dated. For example, societal shifts involve more dual-income families. Additionally, the 'longest war' nature of the Iraq and Afghanistan wars might have had particularly harsh consequences for fathering duties, which might not be properly understood and might require further analysis.

---

10   E.G. Boulton, *Teaming: An Introduction to Gender Studies, Unshackling Human Talent and Optimising Military Capability for the Coming Era of Equality: 2020 to 2050*, Australian Army, Canberra, 2017.

The report 'Mothers in the Middle East Area of Operations (MEAO)'[11] found that women greatly valued their deployments from a professional perspective, and were creative and resourceful in finding ways to constructively manage separation from children. Nonetheless, although ADF women achieved this, they sometimes also faced harsher criticism over their decisions than fathers might have experienced. Wing Commander (then Squadron Leader) Kelley Stewart, OIC Medical, Task Group 633.2, in 2006 summed up the sentiment here, when she wrote:

> The main issue for me ... is Mother Guilt with a capital 'G'. There can be a lot of pressure applied or inferred ... You often feel the urge to justify why you want to leave them all to deploy operationally. Why? Because this is our job and it's what we joined up to do ... Another mother at school had said, 'There is no mother' about my family. Luckily, the Family Day Care mum set them straight.[12]

Generally, mothers required additional time before deployment to make various family support arrangements while for others it was the post-deployment phase that was most difficult. As Wing Commander Stewart observed, '[O]n returning from deployment to Afghanistan, she was informed that she would be involved in three major training exercises after returning from operational duty. She was heartbroken over how she was going to tell her family ...'.[13]

Women's partners and husbands (whether civilian or also serving in the military) were a new demographic that, initially, might not have been well understood by ADF units and the Defence Community Organisation.

A related issue was that the Australian population, in general, was largely oblivious to the changing role of women in the ADF. This particularly affected female veterans. A study in this area found that female veterans perceived that they were not regarded as (and were not treated as) 'real' veterans.[14] However, male veterans also reported this experience, especially

---

11   E. Lawrence-Wood, L. Jones, S. Hodson, S. Crompvoets, A. McFarlane and S. Neuhaus, 'Mothers in the Middle East Area of Operations (MEAO): The health impacts of maternal deployment to an area of operations', Applied Research Program, Department of Veterans' Affairs, Canberra, 2014.
12   K. Stewart, 'International Women's Day 2006—inspiring potential', *Newsletter*, Defence Community Organisation—South Australia, 8 March 2006.
13   Ibid.
14   S. Crompvoets, *Health and Wellbeing of Female Vietnam and Contemporary Veterans*, Department of Veterans' Affairs, Canberra, 2012.

the younger ones. Arguably, though, the challenges faced internal to the ADF have not been nearly as challenging as those external to the ADF, as the rest of this chapter sets out to illustrate.

External issues—a gendered area of operations

Although women within the ADF were ready—that is, well trained and integrated into teams—arguably neither the coalition nor the ADF were ready for a gendered battlefield. Gender became significant in Iraq and Afghanistan for three reasons.

First, 'rescuing Middle Eastern women' was a conspicuous part of the narrative that accompanied the rationale for both wars. For instance, at a press conference two weeks before the US-led invasion of Iraq, Paula Dobriansky, then Undersecretary of State for Global Affairs, flanked by four members of a group called Women for a Free Iraq, declared: 'We are at a critical point in dealing with Saddam Hussein. However, this turns out, it is clear that the women of Iraq have a critical role to play in the future revival of their society.'[15]

In their book *What Kind of Liberation?*, Nadje Al-Ali and Nicole Pratt argued that 'women's causes' became part of an empire-building approach that backfired on Iraqi women and undermined their own sense of agency. They insisted that the most damaging impact to women in Iraq came from the degradation of the security environment. Women's rights and how this was progressed was a significant part of these conflicts. At times this became at least an ideological battleground, and at worst it influenced targeting choices made by al-Qaeda, the Taliban and later Daesh.

The second reason gender became important in Afghanistan and Iraq is because, although this varied by geography and time, one of the features that did emerge was that of 'war among the people', at other times described as the 'three-block war' phenomenon. This concept, articulated by US Marine Corps General Charles Krulak in the late 1990s, envisaged the close relationship between combat operations, peacekeeping and humanitarian assistance undertaken simultaneously within the space

---

15   N. Al-Ali and N. Pratt, *What Kind of Liberation? Women and the Occupation of Iraq*, University of California Press, Berkeley, 2009, p. 56.

of three neighbouring city blocks. In this context, women, children and communities were integrated into battlefield and conflict zones to an extent not seen by the ADF or modern Western militaries in living memory.

Third, there was a new international legal framework influencing security and military operations. In 2000, United Nations Security Council Resolution 1325 (UNSCR 1325) on Women, Peace and Security (WPS) was adopted by the UN Security Council, followed by a wave of other WPS-related Security Council resolutions . UNSCR 1325 'reaffirms the important role of women in the prevention and resolution of conflicts … and stresses the importance of their equal participation and full involvement in all efforts for the maintenance and promotion of peace and security'.[16]

To explore lesson learned, five aspects will be considered: female engagement teams (FETs); gender advisers (GAs); Australian commanders' perspectives; the strategic approach to WPS; and general lessons.[17]

Female engagement teams

In response to the 'war among the people' dimension, the United States raised FETs in Iraq, most notably though its Lioness program.[18] An early lesson was that the women were not adequately trained in crew-served weapons systems and patrolling techniques used by the Marines, which differed from those taught by the US Army in basic Infantry Minor Tactics training.[19]

ADF members became involved in FETs as part of a larger approach managed by the NATO International Security Assistance Force (ISAF) in Afghanistan. Australian Major Grant Prendergast was the FET Commander for ISAF from March to October 2012. He introduced new initiatives, such as requiring completed FET patrols to produce a 'quad-slide' summarising key insights and learnings from each patrol within 24 hours, synchronising efforts of FET patrols, and facilitating

---

16 Office of the Special Adviser on Gender Issues, 'Landmark resolution on Women, Peace and Security', United Nations, New York, www.un.org/womenwatch/osagi/wps (retrieved 25 March 2020).
17 The analytical time-period has been extended from 2014 to 2017 to capture WPS lessons, which were pertinent to the Middle East yet did not begin to be progressed by the ADF until around 2012.
18 M. McLagan and D. Sommers, *Lioness* (documentary), Roco Films/Public Broadcasting Service, USA, 2008
19 M. Mackenzie, *Beyond the Band of Brothers: The US Military and the Myth that Women Can't Fight*, Cambridge University Press, Cambridge, 2015.

a process whereby they could all collectively learn from each other. FETs were given formal orders, end-states and detailed information messaging guidance.

Through these more structured and regular FET activities, nascent standard operating procedures emerged. Major Prendergast concluded that FETs were effective in aiding in situational awareness, for example on Taliban presence; however, great care was required when planning how and when to employ FETs owing to risks to local women and FET members. Sometimes the risks were so high that it was not worth employing FETs directly. FETs were created in theatre, and women were drawn from existing units undertaking a 55-hour certification course while deployed. RAAF Warrant Officer Fiona Grasby was the second in command of the Force Protection and Security Section Multi-National Command, Tarin Kowt, from July 2012 to January 2013. She observed:

> We searched the women and children in a partitioned area at the Main Entry Control Point, away from the men, and would then monitor them until … we were required to escort them to the flight line. We were cognisant not to be too familiar with women who visited regularly (in the view of others), as they may have then been used to target us. Behind the safety of the screens, though, there were hugs and food swapping and gift giving. Being aware of the atmospherics was paramount.[20]

Australian special forces also experimented with FET patrols in Afghanistan, using medics and local contractors. However, it was assessed that these were not well integrated into what was called 'human terrain analysis' or intelligence collection plans. There were various attempts to recruit Afghanistan nationals for indigenous FETs; however, these attempts failed.

The Australian Civil-Military Centre conducted some analysis on FETs, but noted a key problem was that there was not enough data or knowledge about FET activities to draw definitive conclusions. Nonetheless, they assessed that, on the basis of limited knowledge, FETs appeared to be a 'useful operational tool that ought to be integrated into future operational planning'.[21]

---

20   Conversation with author.
21   H. Studdert and S. Shteir, *Women, Peace and Security Reflections: From Australian Male Leaders*, Australian Civil-Military Centre, Canberra, 2015, p. 58.

Gender advisers

Apart from FET, another category of engagement for women was as gender advisers (GAs). The ADF deployed a number of GAs into Iraq and Afghanistan. The role of the GA varied greatly, reflecting that some were deployed when such initiatives were in start-up phases—whereby obtaining funding and agreements was a large part of their tasking—while later GAs could focus upon pragmatic operationalisation of WPS objectives.

Over several rotations some WPS objectives were progressed, despite the extreme difficulties involved. For example, a girls' school was established in Tarin Kowt, and Afghan women were trained as police officers and army officers. A 'soldiers' card' on WPS was developed, and briefings were incorporated as part of the mainstream component of the Force Preparation and Reception, Staging, Onward Movement and Integration (RSO&I) processes.

GAs were well prepared for their roles through being sent on a variety of specialised training courses, such as those conducted at the Nordic Centre for Gender in Military Operations in Sweden, and other NATO-sponsored courses. Additionally, GAs were considered to be highly collegial, allowing informal learning to occur in addition to the formal programs.

What emerged is that the GA role is complex and required understanding a wide range of legislation and policies from the United Nations, NATO, coalition forces, the ADF and the relevant countries within the area of operations. Given the significant challenges in unravelling various levels of rulings, GAs did not have formal authority, but relied upon their ability to persuade and influence to make a difference. An example of this circumstance is the experience of Captain Stacey Porter, RAN.

Captain Porter was assigned as the senior GA to the Commander, Resolute Support Mission, Afghanistan, from April 2016 to February 2017. She observed that while the gender training was largely tactical in nature and about instilling a gender perspective in all aspects of operations, this was not strictly what she did; instead, she was working at a high level in collaboration with ministerial, political, civil society, international community and vice-regal actors.

Afghanistan launched its National Action Plan (NAP) on 13 June 2015, but during Porter's time she observed that, on the ground, very little work was being done to implement many of its actions. She attributed this slow progress to three factors. First, the immediate problem that Afghanistan was still largely a country at war; the Afghans continued to fight the Taliban and the 14 other terrorist groups that existed in their country, so it was not surprising that other issues took precedence at the ministerial level.

The second reason for the slow traction on the NAP was the backlog of legal and legislative issues to be resolved. For example, much work was being conducted on trying to get approval for the draft penal code, which sought to address challenges like the incompatibility of Afghan law with Afghanistan's obligations under international treaties (including that of human and women's rights, which was not ratified). Other work was concentrated on the High Peace Council, a body appointed by President Karzai to negotiate reconciliation with the Taliban.

Finally, there were cultural issues. Women's political marginalisation and other forms of gender discrimination were the norm. Explaining this, Porter remarked: 'While I was deployed, a six-year-old was married off to a 60-year-old in exchange for a goat, a bag of flour, and a jar of ghee … When these norms exist, you can appreciate the uphill battle we had.'

Porter reflected that, at the end of the day, NATO was institution-building in Afghanistan. To do so, NATO concentrated on advising the Afghans how to become independent and self-reliant. The view was that any solutions had to be Afghan-led and process-based. However, by the time Captain Porter left some nine and a half months later, she observed, 'NATO was starting to realise that this approach was going to take a lot longer than they realised'.

Porter commented that the biggest challenge was encouraging the move from merely increasing recruiting figures to advising the Afghans on the development of a human resource strategy for women in the security forces. Crucial to this was having females assigned to positions on the manning document, or *Tashkil*, so that adequate specialised training and career management could be achieved.[22]

---

22   Written account by Captain Porter and subsequent conversations with author.

Australian commanders' perspectives

Australian commanders, from tactical to strategic levels, provided further useful insights on WPS. For instance, at the tactical level, an Air Force ground defence officer made this observation:

> Women still were not allowed to join as [Air Defence Guards/Ground Defence] when we were in Iraq, and for most of our time in Afghanistan. I remember it was an issue when I was attached to [the Royal Air Force] and we were patrolling [the area] around Kandahar because we couldn't enter any compounds with women in them and I remember wishing we had some girls so that they could access certain areas that otherwise we could not. About this time [the US Marine Corps] started using female platoons for that exact purpose. Beyond that, small numbers of female dog handlers and security police performed security (as opposed to 'combat') roles, at bases such as [Al-Minhad Air Base].[23]

At the operational level, Bernard Philip, from DFAT, headed the Provincial Reconstruction Team (PRT) in Uruzgan from 2010 to 2011. Considering WPS, Philip's reflections capture the immense difficulty of engaging women in Uruzgan—Taliban heartland. He decided to avoid direct action on gender issues, explaining that this decision was 'the product of an intuitive judgement that a direct approach to gender equality would be counter-productive and constitute a red line for the male leaders of Uruzgan'.[24]

He therefore pursued indirect methods such as aid programs to support children. Of these indirect methods, Philip assessed that perhaps the most enduring was the example of gender inclusion the PRT provided, especially in allowing Afghan men to experience it. Male Uruzghani leaders were enthusiastic about meeting Prime Minister Julia Gillard and Major General (then Brigadier) Simone Wilkie on her visits, and they worked well with female leaders within the PRT. Philip noted that, somewhat ironically, PRT civilian female diplomats and advisers

> enjoyed some of the closest and most productive relationships with key tribal and government leaders. I remember one of our female diplomats being especially effective in strengthening the resolve of a key tribal leader to remain engaged with the government and to discourage his tribe from supporting the Taliban.[25]

---

23 Conversations between an anonymous male RAAF ground defence officer and author.
24 Studdert and Shteir, *Women, Peace and Security Reflections*, p. 50.
25 Ibid.

At the strategic level, Major General Fergus McLachlan was a senior military planner with the International Security Assistance Force in Afghanistan from November 2012 to November 2013. He assessed that the overall mission would have been better positioned to address WPS issues if they had been integrated into earlier ISAF planning activities.[26] Another lesson is the deeper insights into Taliban strategy. McLachlan notes that the Taliban sought to attack the social cohesion of the Afghan community and that one way to do so was through targeting women and girls. Their cold-bloodedness in pursuing this strategy was evident in such incidents as the bombing of a busload of women and girls. This led McLachlan to observe: 'We have an increasingly sophisticated understanding that we must also defeat the enemy across their range of objectives, including their deliberate targeting of women and girls.'[27]

To counter this, the ISAF sought to shift responsibility for town security to police forces, so that military forces could be freed up to pursue the Taliban outside the township. McLachlan, again, commented:

> We made gains for the security of women and girls in Afghanistan by moving the violent clashes between the Taliban and the security forces away from the population centres ... In Kabul and Kandahar, Afghan police chiefs gained control of their cities—the two largest cities in the country became increasingly safe places for women and girls—but only as a subset of broader security gains.[28]

The strategic approach to Women, Peace and Security

Reflecting on the issue of WPS and whether there was a strategic approach and analysis, various GAs and commanders agreed that the ability to progress WPS objectives was extremely difficult, mostly owing to the cultural contexts of Iraq and Afghanistan, but also owing to the existence of a war. However, it is also possible that progress was hindered by the way WPS was conceptualised and managed. As Captain Porter observed, 'Effectively, NATO forces are conducting what we term non-combat operations in a combat environment.'[29]

---

26 Ibid., pp. 55–61.
27 Ibid., p. 61.
28 Ibid., p. 60.
29 Conversations with author.

Initiatives seemed burdened by bureaucratic paperwork, legislative tasks, transferring WPS objectives into policy, and then funding cycles. Part of this was because WPS was not treated as an operational matter but rather an administrative one. For example, if the key present hurdle in Afghanistan is the legislative backlog, the logical solution would be to bolster legal and policy support. It is not clear, however, that such a reorientation of effort was considered, let alone implemented. In general, one wonders where the role of creative or transformative thought exists in the WPS space—for example, the application of design thinking to the problem, or the conduct of large multidisciplinary problem-solving workshops and conferences, as have occurred for other intractable security dilemmas. It was not apparent that any agency had either the mandate or the resources to undertake this task. Government progress reports during this period focused on compliance rather than effectiveness, and seemed to paint a universally 'good story', which did not identify problems or opportunities to improve a new initiative in its critical start-up, growth phase.[30]

Perhaps related to the lack of strategic analysis has been the issue of lukewarm attitudes towards WPS activities by some within the security sector. GAs had quite different perspectives on this, several noting excellent support, especially from command levels. Others thought it was personality dependent, while another noted that what she called the 'middle management level' of the ADF could be sceptical. This often related to people not understanding what WPS was about, or getting it confused with general internal institutional equity initiatives. One GA speculated as to whether the impact of external investigations into the ADF on gender issues during 2012–14,[31] which involved some painful revelations and sudden changes, have indirectly undermined some people's enthusiasm for WPS initiatives. Porter, for instance, in her role as senior GA to the Commander, Resolute Support Mission, in Afghanistan in 2016, observed:

> I was quite unprepared for the comments that came from within RSM [Resolute Support Mission] such as 'what about the men?' and 'why are we putting gender before the fight?' … I had to remain diplomatically stoic in the face of not only Afghan cultural and organisational resistance but that of coalition complaints.[32]

---

30   Commonwealth of Australia, *2016 Progress Report on the Australian National Action Plan on Women, Peace and Security: 2012–2018*, Commonwealth of Australia, Canberra, 2016.
31   Defence Abuse Response Taskforce, *Report on Abuse in Defence*, and Defence Committee, *Pathway to Change*.
32   Conversations with author.

Similarly, Lieutenant Commander Donna Sill, GA to Commander JTF 633 in 2017, observed: 'The most regular question has been "but how is this relevant to my job?" The gender adviser role is primarily about developing awareness of gender-related issues and developing tools that allow others to answer this question themselves.'[33]

The impact of some of this disinterest or doubt subtly slowed the ability of GAs to progress WPS initiatives, while others would argue that dealing with such attitudes was and remains part of the GA role. Some people's ambivalence towards WPS initiatives could reflect deeper general Australian cultural attitudes to traditional gender roles and activities of the military. Addressing such attitudes will require broader approaches before further progress can be achieved.[34]

General lessons

Overall, in relation to the gender dimension of the Afghanistan and Iraq wars, and how the coalition and ADF responded to it, four key lessons have been identified. The first and most important lesson is that there were opportunity costs of 'gender ignorance' or inadequate analysis before the outbreak of the Iraq and Afghanistan wars and during the conflicts. Coalition operations could have benefited from a greater understanding of gender-related issues in the early framing, conceptualisation and planning phases of operations. In addition to those already discussed, there are a number of additional aspects, which I will just touch on here.

The first is masculinity studies, which could have aided analysis of the human dimension. See, for example, work on Afghan men by Echavez, Mosawi and Pilongo, who analysed views of masculinity by different groups in Afghanistan, finding that the prevailing view was that men were *nafaqah* providers, responsible for family security, safety and all 'living support' and financial needs.[35] Second is pedophilia and especially *bacha bāzī* (or 'boy rape', as it is commonly referred to in Afghanistan). The high-profile case of US Sergeant First Class Charles Martland, who in 2011 assaulted an Afghan police officer who had raped a 12-year-old boy, brought to

---

33 Conversations with author.
34 Boulton, *Teaming*.
35 C.R. Echavez, S. Mosawi and L.W.R. Pilongo, *The Other Side of Gender Inequality: Men and Masculinities in Afghanistan*, Afghanistan Research and Evaluation Unit, Kabul, 2016, p. 19.

global attention the lack of adequate coalition policies to deal with such incidents.[36] Third is counter-insurgency and gender; other analysis suggests that counter-insurgency efforts would have been improved had greater efforts been made to incorporate women.[37] Fourth is the issue of women in special forces and arms corps functions. If women had been employed more strategically, it is possible they might have helped with situational awareness, thereby improving planning and benefiting the entire force. There are many unknowns about Iraqi and Afghan women's perspectives and experiences at critical moments of the campaigns. Although these details might have been included in post-mission reports, they have been less visible in mainstream military accounts in the public arena. This leaves a knowledge vacuum, potentially limiting strategic discourse. Fifth is the issue of people who identify as LGBTI. Greater attention to lesbian, gay, bisexual, transgender and intersex (LGBTI) issues might have allowed early warning on the extreme vulnerability of LGBTI locals to violent attack and executions by groups like Daesh,[38] and to have enacted warnings proactively or to have initiated other protective strategies.

The second lesson is that the ADF conducted WPS-type activities before Australia adopted UNSCR 1325 but used different language to describe them. For example, in 2003–04, the Security Detachment in Baghdad was heavily involved with the kindergarten in their area of operations, and they connected to the entire community in layered ways. This approach was often considered standard practice, sometimes managed through civil–military cooperation constructs.

Colonel Studdert's quite amazing account of how he used an understanding of gender dynamics to achieve operational outcomes, as part of the United Nations Transitional Authority in Cambodia in 1992–93, is another example.[39] These instances demonstrate that the stereotype of military males being ignorant about such issues might not be fair. It is possible that this type of existing expertise, which relates to the WPS task within conflict zones, has not been properly acknowledged nor harnessed.

---

36 K. Jahner, 'Green Beret who beat up accused child rapist can stay in Army', *Army Times*, 28 April 2016.
37 M. Anderson, 'Where are the women? The unfortunate omission in the Army's COIN doctrine', Modern War Institute, United States Military Academy, West Point, 2017.
38 J. Stern, 'The UN Security Council's Arria-formula meeting on vulnerable groups in conflict: ISIL's targeting of LGBTI individuals', *NYU Journal of International Law and Politics*, vol. 48, pp. 1191–8, 2015, nyujilp.org/wp-content/uploads/2010/06/NYU_JILP_48_4_Stern.pdf (retrieved 30 April 2020).
39 Studdert and Shteir, *Women, Peace and Security Reflections*, p. 7.

The third lesson is that gender lessons from Iraq and Afghanistan should not drive conceptual development. Although the Iraq and Afghanistan experience provides valuable WPS lessons, it might be unwise to use this experience as a template for future planning. In other regions, such as the Asia Pacific or Africa, women have far different, often considerably more influential roles in their societies. Such environments might demand greater resources and a more comprehensive approach than was possible in Afghanistan and Iraq.

The fourth lesson is that Australian national policy setting on WPS is slow. For instance, the UN Security Council adopted UNSCR 1325 on WPS in 2000; however, Australia did not commit to implementing it until 2015. This 15-year delay meant that the ADF did not have WPS policy and a developed WPS capability in place in time for the wars in Afghanistan and Iraq.

Conclusion

This chapter has outlined a range of gender-related issues as they concern ADF operations, both internal to the ADF and external. The activity that occurred from the late 1980s to expand women's military roles and mainstream women into standard military units was at times difficult and flawed, with recurrent scandals prompting external reviews. These received immense media attention and dominated the Australian public's perception of women and the military. However, a 'good story' quietly paralleled this period as well.

By the time the Afghanistan and Iraq wars commenced, in many areas of the ADF women were well integrated into teams, were well trained, and had the requisite experience to perform well under pressure. Although both wars had tragic outcomes, ADF women gained invaluable operational experience and a depth of expertise that increased as the wars progressed. It is unfortunate that the Australian community, during the conduct of the wars, were largely kept ignorant of the brave, resourceful and historically significant feats of various ADF women, instead receiving an almost ceaseless and unbalanced story of ADF women as victims. Another untold story is that, owing to numerical realities, in the main, it was ADF men who effectively trained and developed these pioneering women, from the late 1980s onwards.

To be sure, there was a distinction between the vast bulk of ADF units and specialities that were long used to working in mixed-gender teams and those units for which mixed-gender teams was still a novel experience. Not surprisingly, leaders from generally mixed units had solid repertoires of skills for managing minor gender issues that might arise and were able to set command climates that supported cohesion. For mothers, some flexibility was often needed, and the chain of command was the critical point that determined how possible and successful their deployment was. The impact of the 'longest war' on fathering duties requires analysis.

Like most Western military forces, the ADF was not ready for a gendered battlespace at the start of the century. New capabilities were often developed in theatre and then, perhaps owing to culturally related trepidation or a lack of expertise, were not properly analysed or developed. The setting up of capability to address WPS was unfathomably slow compared to responses to other new dimensions, like IED, cyber or drone warfare. Indeed, the promise of WPS has not yet been realised.

There were six inquiries into aspects of ADF culture during the period 2011–14 (with gender issues being prominent). It is possible therefore that gender issues became associated with pain and shame. This might have subtly influenced some individual, and possibly institutional, support for WPS activities. In essence, the effect of this is that WPS issues remain underanalysed and could suffer from being segregated from mainstream capability development and operational planning processes. In general, limited data capture or inclusion of the gender dimension in multiple routine post-operational review and analysis activities hinders the ability of the ADF to understand the gender dimension in a sophisticated way. This, in turn, limits the ADF's collective ability to refine methods and exploit emerging opportunities.

Without women in arms corps or special forces, it is likely that the ADF lacked certain unique capabilities that could have been advantageous. Although three Victoria Crosses were awarded to men, no Nancy Wake equivalent emerged, nor had the opportunity to emerge, in these conflicts. Other opportunities were also likely to have been lost through ignorance of other issues such as masculinity studies.

As a final point, a key lesson is that national strategic security planning needs to be forward-looking regarding demographic and societal changes, which affect not only our own troops but also the external operating environment.

PART 4: LESSONS AND LEGACIES

16

Lessons and legacies of the war in Afghanistan

William Maley

In 1897, Rudyard Kipling penned some verses to mark Queen Victoria's Diamond Jubilee. Kipling is often seen as virtually the poet laureate of British 19th-century imperialism, but his words on this occasion, a poem called *Recessional*, offered a warning against the sin of hubris:

> Far-called, our navies melt away,
> On dune and headland sinks the fire,
> Lo, all our pomp of yesterday,
> Is one with Nineveh and Tyre!
> Judge of the Nations, spare us yet,
> Lest we forget—lest we forget.

It is quite common at conferences dealing with Afghanistan to hear some speaker quote Kipling's words about that country, although Kipling never set foot in Afghanistan, and images of Afghanistan in the 19th century offer a poor guide to the complexities of Afghanistan in the 21st century. Kipling's *Recessional*, however, does have some lessons to offer. One is that military power can be a crude tool for realising political objectives. Another is that well-intentioned actions can have unintended consequences. But a third, perhaps not intended by Kipling, is that how one assesses particular actions might crucially depend upon the point in time at which one attempts an assessment. This was captured in Hegel's famous comment that the Owl of Minerva spreads her wings only when dusk is setting, and in the remark of Zhou Enlai, who, when asked what he thought was the main consequence of the French Revolution, responded that it was too soon to tell. Today there is no shortage of works, some of high quality, proclaiming the international enterprise in Afghanistan after 2001 to have been a failure.[1] This judgement, however, might be premature. While no one would dream of pronouncing it a dazzling success, the jury is ultimately still out, and large numbers of Afghans have no desire to return to the environment that confronted them before Operation ENDURING FREEDOM overthrew the Taliban regime in October and November 2001.

In seeking to draw lessons from experience in Afghanistan, inevitably different observers will come up with different conclusions. This is in part because various actors involved in the Afghanistan theatre became engaged on the basis of different interests and values. But that said, it is worthwhile to pay some attention to the attitudes of ordinary Afghans, whose perspectives are almost always omitted from explorations of this kind. Yet we have clearer windows into their thinking than we often have into the policy processes of Western countries that became involved in Afghanistan. Since 2004, the Asia Foundation has been conducting rigorous surveys of mass opinion in Afghanistan, and the results are quite illuminating. An enduring question has related to the mood in Afghanistan, with respondents being asked whether they thought things in Afghanistan were going in the right direction or in the wrong direction. In 2004, the mood was one of optimism: 64 per cent responded positively and only 11 per cent negatively. There was a stark shift by 2006; the percentage responding positively had dropped to 44 and the percentage responding negatively had risen to 21. From 2008, perceptions steadily improved, with those positively inclined rising from 38 per cent in 2008 to 58 per cent in 2013, although the percentage with a negative view also rose, from 32 per cent to 37 per cent. With the substantial withdrawal of foreign forces, however, the national mood again took a turn for the worse: in 2017, fully 61 per cent concluded that things were going in the wrong direction, with only 33 per cent of the view that things were going in the right direction.[2]

---

1   See for example N. Coburn, *Losing Afghanistan: An Obituary for the Intervention*, Stanford University Press, Stanford, 2016; F. Ledwidge, *Losing Small Wars: British Military Failure in the 9/11 Wars*, Yale University Press, New Haven, 2017; and A.B. O'Connell (ed.), *Our Latest Longest War: Losing Hearts and Minds in Afghanistan*, University of Chicago Press, Chicago, 2017.
2   Asia Foundation, *Afghanistan in 2017: A Survey of the Afghan People*, Asia Foundation, Kabul, 2017, p. 203.

16. LESSONS AND LEGACIES OF THE WAR IN AFGHANISTAN

Major General Abdul Hamid, Commander 205th Hero Corps, Afghan National Army, addresses tribal elders at a Shura held at an Afghan National Army base in Chah Chineh, Afghanistan, 2013.
Source: Courtesy of the Department of Defence.

Interestingly, the two main plunges in confidence took place when international attention shifted away from Afghanistan, with the deterioration of the US position in Iraq in 2005–06, and with the completion of transition in Afghanistan at the end of 2014. Whether this represented causation or merely correlation is difficult to tell, but it does suggest that when international forces substantially withdrew from Afghanistan, ordinary Afghans were not cheering the process.

In the remarks that follow, my aim is to focus on some specific lessons for military deployments that might be of value to the Australian Defence Force (ADF) in the future, as well as on the ongoing problem of insurgency and on questions related to where Afghanistan might go from here. Before doing so, however, there are two overarching observations about the situation in Afghanistan that are potentially relevant to other conflict zones in which Australian forces could be deployed.

First, Afghanistan since 2001 has been exposed to the forces of globalisation to a greater extent than virtually any other country in the world. The effects have been all the more dramatic because of the extent of the isolation of the country during the period of Taliban rule following the fall of the Afghan capital in September 1996.³ Opening Afghanistan to the wider world has been one of the greatest achievements wrought by the international presence in the country. With 70 per cent of the settled population under the age of 30,⁴ the scope for the Afghan population to prove receptive to new ideas and new ways of proceeding might be somewhat greater than is often thought. The crucial point to note here is that military deployments do not take place in an environment that is frozen and fixed. On the contrary, the context of deployments is almost always one that is subject to dynamic forces at a number of levels. From a longer-term point of view, societies are in a process of near-constant change and adjustment while, on a day-to-day basis, individual actors are routinely reconfiguring and renegotiating their relationships and recalculating what kind of alignments will best serve their interests in the absence of the kind of certainties that the existence of a consolidated state can offer.

Second, the *psychology* of the situation in a fraught environment such as that of Afghanistan could be absolutely central to the success or failure of international interventions.⁵ Put bluntly, it does not pay to be on the losing side if one is an ordinary Afghan, and the importance of military deployments might lie not so much in what they physically achieve but in the wider psychological climate that they foster. This, in turn, will depend to some extent on how well international militaries understand the minutiae of their operational environment. Given the complexity of Afghan society, mastering such detail would be no easy task,⁶ but failure in this sphere can lead to misdiagnosis of conflict formations, with serious ramifications for the effectiveness of both kinetic operations and reconstruction activities.

---

3 See H. Mohammadi, *Tasir-e jahanishodan bar farhang dar Afghanistan*, Entesharat-e Farhang, Kabul, 2014.
4 Central Statistics Organization, *Afghanistan Statistical Yearbook 2016–17*, CSO, Kabul, 2016–17, p. 5.
5 W. Maley, 'Afghanistan on a knife-edge', *Global Affairs*, vol. 2, no. 1, 2016, pp. 57–68.
6 See W. Maley, 'Studying host-nationals in operational areas: The challenge of Afghanistan', in *Routledge Handbook of Research Methods in Military Studies*, ed. J. Soeters, P.M. Shields and S. Rietjens (eds), Routledge, London, 2014, pp. 53–64.

Some lessons for military deployments

There are a large number of lessons one might potentially extract from the international deployment in Afghanistan from 2001, and different analysts will likely produce different lists. The following seven points therefore are in no sense definitive; they simply reflect what this writer considers worth canvassing with an interested audience.

First, military deployments always need to be linked to a *political* strategy. One of the enduring criticisms of the international involvement in Afghanistan after 2001 was that, following the overthrow of the Taliban regime, the precise aims of international action were relatively unclear, leading to improvisation on the ground and contradictory assertions at the higher policy level as to the purpose of the mission.[7] This does not foster the confidence on the ground on the part of locals that should be central to any such mission to encourage, and it can lead soldiers to be deeply frustrated at the wilderness of mirrors in which they seem to be living. This of course is not a problem that militaries can resolve on their own; rather, it depends upon the willingness and ability of senior political leaderships to develop a coherent image of what they are seeking to do. Great wartime leaders, such as Winston Churchill, are almost always individuals who prove capable of articulating and driving a grand strategic vision that offers a pathway for achieving defensible and desirable goals. In the Afghanistan case, part of the problem was that there was no Churchill on hand to perform this task, and another was that the countries contributing forces to Afghanistan did not see themselves as being on a war footing.

Second, it is not possible to stabilise a disrupted state such as Afghanistan on a province-by-province basis. The Provincial Reconstruction Team (PRT) approach that took shape in Afghanistan provided some opportunity to do good for some people, but it neither constituted a coherent model for reconstruction activity nor supplied a workable framework for addressing the problem of ambient insecurity. The 'ink spot' theory positing that local stability, created by the deployment of a PRT to a particular area, might then spread more widely proved to be ill founded for several reasons. On the one hand, while Afghans are not ingrates, they are also not inclined to align themselves politically on the basis of gratitude for what

---

7   See S. Rynning, *NATO in Afghanistan: The Liberal Disconnect*, Stanford University Press, Stanford, 2012; and D.P. Auerswald and S.M. Saideman, *NATO in Afghanistan: Together, Fighting Alone*, Princeton University Press, Princeton, 2014.

has been done for them in the past rather than on the basis of a rational calculation of what is likely to happen to them in the future. On the other hand, there is evidence that in areas that were already contested between the government of Afghanistan and the armed opposition, aid was more likely to aggravate conflict than defuse it, providing 'soft' targets for attack and inspiring the enemy to concentrate its firepower.[8] Both of these considerations worked against aid delivery producing a significant political dividend.

Third, in a number of further senses, aid can act as a fuel for conflict rather than function as a flame retardant. In many parts of Afghanistan, there are long-standing, ongoing conflicts that do not fit easily into a simple model of enmity between the Afghan Government and the Taliban.[9] International actors might inadvertently find themselves injecting resources into conflicts of this kind, conflicts of the dynamics and dimensions of which they are blissfully unaware. For example, the Helmand Food Zone Programme, trumpeted as a major counter-narcotics endeavour, ended up feeding the patronage networks of the provincial governor,[10] in a way that was profoundly corrupting of Afghanistan's wider state-building enterprise.[11]

Fourth, 'stability' can prove remarkably tenuous. The classic example of this was the fall of the town of Kunduz to Taliban forces for a fortnight from 28 September 2015. Kunduz was not a hamlet in the middle of nowhere. It was a strategically important urban centre where a German PRT had been deployed for a considerable period of time.[12] Through much of 2015, the situation in the vicinity of the town had been deteriorating, but this meant that when it eventually did fall to the Taliban, it was hardly an event that came out of the blue.[13] The human consequences for

---

8   R. Sexton, 'Aid as a tool against insurgency: Evidence from contested and controlled territory in Afghanistan', *American Political Science Review*, vol. 110, no. 4, 2016, pp. 731–49.
9   M. Martin, *An Intimate War: An Oral History of the Helmand Conflict*, Hurst & Co., London, 2014.
10 D. Mansfield, *A State Built on Sand: How Opium Undermined Afghanistan*, Hurst & Co., London, 2016, pp. 225, 242.
11 S. Chayes, *Thieves of State: Why Corruption Threatens Global Security*, W.W. Norton, New York, 2015, pp. 59–60.
12 See W. Maley, 'Civil–military interaction in Afghanistan: The case of Germany', in *Reconstructing Afghanistan: Civil–Military Experiences in Comparative Perspective*, ed. W. Maley and S. Schmeidl, Routledge, London, 2015, pp. 98–109.
13 M. Kamal, 'L'offensive de Koundouz: Le contexte militaro-stratégique', *Les Nouvelles d'Afghanistan*, vol. 151, pp. 7–11.

ordinary Afghans were devastating,[14] and the psychological effect in other parts of Afghanistan proved considerable, even though government forces managed to reassert control over the town from 13 October. The same was true of the fall of the strategic town of Ghazni in August 2018, an event for which the Afghan Government and its backers were not prepared despite clear warning signs, and which sent reverberations through many other parts of Afghanistan.[15]

Fifth, while it might be convenient in the short run to ground one's engagement with the local population in friendships struck with those who appear to be 'strongmen', in the long run this tends to be at the expense of sustainable institutional development. A crucial point to bear in mind in Afghanistan is that when you make a friend, you can also make an enemy. Much political activity in Afghanistan is based on networks, and different networks can be in brutal competition with each other.[16] But network relations are also in a process of constant renegotiation, and cannot be taken for granted. In 2010, a senior Australian general described the police chief in Uruzgan, Matiullah Khan, as 'our guy'.[17] This observation was alarming in two critical respects. In Afghanistan, *no* political actor is *ever* 'our guy'. Local actors, quite understandably, almost always have objectives of their own that need not coincide with those of their international backers,[18] and Matiullah certainly had his own agenda.[19] In addition, individuals are not institutions, and can be eliminated quickly once they have acquired the wrong enemies. This was what happened to Matiullah, who was assassinated in Kabul in March 2015.[20] A cynic might say that by this time, he had exhausted his usefulness to the ADF; but of course, the relationship between the ADF

---

14 UNAMA, *Human Rights and Protection of Civilians in Armed Conflict: Special Report on Kunduz Province*, United Nations Assistance Mission in Afghanistan and United Nations Office of the High Commissioner for Human Rights, Kabul, 2015, pp. 13–18.
15 See N. Azadzoi and R. Nordland, 'Afghanistan says it controls key city, but ravaged streets show otherwise', *New York Times*, 12 August 2018.
16 See T. Sharan and S. Bose, 'Political networks and the 2014 Afghan presidential election: Power restructuring, ethnicity and state stability', *Conflict, Security and Development*, vol. 16, no. 6, 2016, p. 616; and T. Sharan, *Dawlat-e Shabakahi: Rabeteh-i Qodrat wa Sarwat dar Afghanistan Pas az Sal-e 2001*, Vazhah Publications, Kabul, 2017.
17 D. Oakes, 'General defends Afghan warlord ties', *Sydney Morning Herald*, 7 December 2010.
18 See W.C. Ladwig, *The Forgotten Front: Patron–Client Relationships in Counterinsurgency*, Cambridge University Press, Cambridge, 2017.
19 S. Schmeidl, *The Man Who Would be King: The Challenges to Strengthening Governance in Uruzgan*, Netherlands Institute of International Relations Clingendael, The Hague, 2010.
20 A. Ahmed, 'Powerful Afghan police chief is killed in targeted suicide attack', *New York Times*, 20 March 2015.

and Matiullah had wider implications for the long-term effectiveness of what Australia had been attempting to achieve in Uruzgan.[21] The dangers of dependence on individuals is a pervasive one, and was again illustrated with the assassination on 18 October 2018 of the 'strongman' of Kandahar Province, the 39-year-old police chief General Abdul Raziq.[22]

Sixth, time is the ultimate scarce commodity, and it is often in short supply in undertakings such as that in Afghanistan. April 2018 marked the 40th anniversary of the communist coup in Afghanistan that tipped the country into disorder, and it has not enjoyed much serenity since that disastrous event. When a country has experienced four decades of dislocation, it is naïve in the extreme to think that it will be able to rapidly recover from all the accumulated consequences. Yet the time frames of international missions, let alone the domestic politics of the states contributing to them, rarely make much allowance for this, and the consequence can be a neglect of sustainability, a focus on 'quick impact projects', and a reluctance to engage in relationship-building except with what might appear to be existing powerholders.

Seventh, exercises of the kind in which the ADF engaged in Afghanistan might from the point of view of political leaders be almost entirely unrelated to the needs of the people whom nominally one is helping. This is not for one moment to challenge the genuine commitment of Australian personnel at the operational level to aiding the local population of Afghanistan, but simply to recognise that Australia's strategic narrative—to the extent that it had one of its own at all—was not focused on aiding Afghans but on preventing Afghanistan from being used as a terrorist base for attacks on other peoples, and on consolidating Australia's alliance relationship with the United States.[23] These are not trivial objectives, and might well have been formulated as they were in order to make the deployment to Afghanistan more palatable to the general public in

---

21 See also C. Masters, *No Front Line: Australia's Special Forces at War in Afghanistan*, Allen & Unwin, Sydney, 2017, pp. 262–3.
22 T. Shah and M. Mashal, 'Taliban assassinate Afghan police chief ahead of elections', *New York Times*, 19 October 2018.
23 See W. Maley, 'PRT activity in Afghanistan: The Australian experience', in *Statebuilding in Afghanistan: Multi-national Contributions to Reconstruction*, ed. N. Hynek and P. Marton, Routledge, New York, 2011, pp. 124–38; and W. Maley, 'The war in Afghanistan: Australia's strategic narratives', in *Strategic Narratives, Public Opinion and War: Winning Domestic Support for the Afghan War*, ed. B. de Graaf, G. Dimitriu and J. Ringsmose, Routledge, New York, 2015, pp. 81–97.

Australia. However, in treating assistance to the people of Afghanistan simply as a means to some other end, it ran the risk of devaluing them, an experience with which they are all too familiar.

The problem of insurgency

The great failure of the international enterprise in Afghanistan from 2001 to 2014 was that it at no time came effectively to grips with the principal factor driving ongoing insurgency, namely the availability to the Taliban of operating bases and support in Pakistan.[24] As recently as 1 March 2016, the Pakistani Adviser to the Prime Minister on Foreign Affairs, Sartaj Aziz, admitted in a presentation to the Council on Foreign Relations in Washington, DC, that the 'leadership' of the Afghan Taliban 'is in Pakistan'. The attack on Kunduz in 2015 was not carried out by a rag-tag peasant army but by what David Kilcullen has called 'professional full-time fighters, put through rigorous training by experienced instructors in the camps in Pakistan, with uniforms, vehicles, heavy weapons, encrypted radios, and a formal command structure'.[25] Afghanistan has serious problems of poor governance, but what makes them critical is the ongoing 'creeping invasion' by its neighbour to the east, using surrogates as a tool to try to deny influence in Afghanistan to Pakistan's great regional and geopolitical rival, India.[26] This problem is not one that Afghanistan is in a position to confront on its own, and nor is it one for the militaries deployed to Afghanistan to solve. Unfortunately, it is also not one that most leaders of states that have contributed forces to Afghanistan have been prepared to take up either, although President Trump has now begun to address it.[27] The result has been to put Afghanistan in a kind of holding pattern, which it will most likely continue to occupy unless and until diplomatic and political pressure is brought to bear on Islamabad to cease its destructive activities. Ironically, there is a strong interest-based case for Pakistan to do so, since its nurturing of the Afghan Taliban predictably led to the emergence of a Pakistani spin-off that has brought terror and grief

---

24 See C. Gall, *The Wrong Enemy: America in Afghanistan, 2001–2014*, Houghton Mifflin Harcourt, New York, 2014.
25 D. Kilcullen, *Blood Year: Islamic State and the Failures of the War on Terror*, Black Inc., Melbourne, 2016, p. 77.
26 W. Maley, *Transition in Afghanistan: Hope, Despair and the Limits of Statebuilding*, Routledge, New York, 2018.
27 Z. Khalilzad, 'Why Trump is right to get tough with Pakistan', *New York Times*, 23 August 2017.

to different parts of Pakistan. But regrettably, senior Pakistani generals tend to be insulated from the ill-effects of the actions undertaken by their forces.

The consequences within Afghanistan have been dire. Kabul has become an increasingly dangerous place for ordinary Afghans. On 23 July 2016, a peaceful demonstration, largely comprising members of the historically marginalised Hazara ethnic minority,[28] was struck near Deh Mazang by bombers, and more than 80 participants in the protest were killed. In August 2016, Taliban terrorists attacked the campus of the American University of Afghanistan, killing students and faculty members.[29] On 8 March 2017, gunmen attacked the Sardar Daud Khan hospital in Kabul, killing doctors and patients. And on 31 May 2017, a massive explosion was triggered near the German embassy in Kabul by a suicide bomber, killing more than 90 people and wounding nearly 500.[30] Bombings since then have continued to claim lives, especially those of Hazaras. Rural Afghanistan has become even more dangerous, with Hazaras at particular risk when attempting to travel from one part of the country to another. The specific targeting of civilians makes these attacks not just acts of terrorism but also war crimes. It is by no means clear how all this will end.

Where to from here?

Given the reluctance to confront Pakistan over its meddling in Afghanistan, Western powers have gone down a rather different path, floating instead the idea that Afghanistan can be stabilised through an agreement with the Taliban. A number of the more notable writings of this ilk carry a distinct whiff of fantasy. For example, in March 2017, a former US ambassador to Pakistan, Richard G. Olson, wrote:

> Pakistan's cynical support for the Taliban is merely the most visible of the hedging strategies that various neighbours, including the Iranians and the Russians, have adopted to ensure that they

---

28   N. Ibrahimi, *The Hazaras and the Afghan State: Rebellion, Exclusion and the Struggle for Recognition*, Hurst & Co., London, 2017.
29   M. Mashal, M.F. Abed and Z. Nader, 'Attack at university in Kabul shatters a sense of freedom', *New York Times*, 26 August 2016.
30   M. Mashal, F. Abed and J. Sukhanyar, 'Deadly bombing is among worst of Afghan war', *New York Times*, 1 June 2017.

have some armed Afghan faction beholden to their interests. A comprehensive political settlement would remove the security dilemma that drives these counter-productive interventions.[31]

This argument is radically misconceived on three fronts. First, there is no real equivalence between the massive and decisive support that Pakistan provides to the Taliban and the petty meddling in which various circles in Russia and Iran have occasionally engaged. Second, Pakistan's behaviour cannot be understood simply in terms of the idea of a security dilemma: its actions involve more than a response to the structural features of the international system that can generate security dilemmas in their classic form.[32] Third, a 'comprehensive political settlement' of the kind that Ambassador Olson advocates would need to address not just the situation in Afghanistan but also the bilateral rivalry between India and Pakistan over Kashmir, a rivalry that has defied all endeavours to overcome it since the partition of the subcontinent in 1947. The belief that the Kashmir conflict is ripe for resolution verges on the delusional.

An even more remarkable article on negotiations was penned by another former US official, Laurel Miller, who defined the problem as 'vested interests on all sides in continuing the war', and argued that the United States could influence the Taliban's calculations through 'applying military pressure and offering political opportunity' and 'using our leverage with the Afghan political elite to ensure their commitment to negotiating'.[33] But there is far more to the conflict in Afghanistan than simply vested interests. The Taliban continue to embody a vision of social order that is anathema to the very groups whose emergence since 2001 the United States and its allies have celebrated, such as educated women, who fear that their gains could be sacrificed as part of a negotiation.[34] The conflict here is much more one of values than of interests. Furthermore, after the Taliban's abominable behaviour in Kunduz in 2015 and Ghazni in 2018, few Afghans are under any illusions about what creating space for the Taliban might involve, and many would be affronted by the suggestion that the United States has any right to offer 'political opportunity' to the Taliban, especially when the 2017 Asia Foundation survey found

---

31 R.G. Olson, 'The art of a deal with the Taliban', *New York Times*, 29 March 2017.
32 See N. Motwani, 'Afghanistan and the regional security contagion', in *Afghanistan—Challenges and Prospects*, ed. S. Bose, N. Motwani and W. Maley, Routledge, London, 2018, pp. 219–40.
33 L. Miller, 'A peace "surge" to end war in Afghanistan', *New York Times*, 23 July 2017.
34 E. Cameron and and J. Kamminga, *Behind Closed Doors: The Risk of Denying Women a Voice in Determining Afghanistan's Future*, Oxfam International, Oxford, 2014.

that 80 per cent of Afghans had 'no sympathy at all' for the Taliban.[35] The United States, unfortunately, brings some baggage to the table on this issue: on 3 October 1996, the US Assistant Secretary of State for South Asia, Robin Raphel, notoriously stated in an interview for the BBC that 'We have no quarrel with the Taliban in terms of their political legitimacy or lack thereof'.[36] Talk of 'talking to the Taliban' has now been around for more than a decade,[37] and nothing of substance has come of it. This alone should make one wary of overestimating what negotiations of this kind are likely to deliver. If diplomacy has a role to play, it is in bringing concerted pressure to bear on Pakistan to cease its destabilisation of Afghanistan and to act as a responsible member of international society.

It is highly unlikely that the Taliban could overthrow the Afghan Government by a grinding military campaign of the kind that Soviet forces mounted from 12 January 1945 to seize Berlin. That has never been the main danger that the Afghan Government faces, and it is not in general the way that regimes in Afghanistan change. The danger for the Afghan Government is more insidious. It is that simultaneous threats to a number of towns such as Kunduz and others of similar significance could trigger a 'cascade',[38] in which actors who did not like the Taliban might nonetheless calculate that the Taliban were well on their way back to power and that it would be opportune to switch sides. It was cascades of this kind that brought about the collapse of the communist regime in late April 1992 and the fall of the Taliban in November 2001. This is where a continuing foreign presence could be psychologically critical. As long as international actors affirm a commitment to the survival of the post-2001 political order and retain forces on the ground that make such a commitment seem credible, a cascade is unlikely on the whole to eventuate.

In conclusion, is Afghanistan, now, of anything more than academic interest to most Australians? Perhaps not, but there are some rather good reasons why Australia should retain a focus on what is happening in the country where so many ADF personnel served and precious lives were lost. No one should underestimate the dangers that could flow from a spreading perception that the international enterprise in Afghanistan after 2001 had

---

35   Asia Foundation, *Afghanistan in 2017*, p. 228.
36   Cited in W. Maley, *The Afghanistan Wars*, Palgrave Macmillan, New York, 2009, p. 90.
37   W. Maley, 'Talking to the Taliban', *World Today*, vol. 63, no. 11, 2007, pp. 4–6.
38   C.R. Sunstein, *Laws of Fear: Beyond the Precautionary Principle*, Cambridge University Press, Cambridge, 2005, pp. 94–102.

failed. At the very least, refugee movements out of Afghanistan, already very substantial,[39] could be expected to increase. Much more dangerously, just as the Soviet withdrawal from Afghanistan in 1989 prompted radical Islamists to claim that the lesson was that religion was a force multiplier that could defeat even a superpower, so a perceived Western failure in Afghanistan in the 21st century could easily inject similar claims into radicals' discourse directed at impressionable ears. But perhaps most dangerously of all, extremist groups in Pakistan such as Lashkar-e Toiba might well be tempted to try another major terrorist strike against India, comparable to the November 2008 Mumbai attacks. Were this to occur, no one could be sure exactly how India under Prime Minister Narendra Modi might react. The risk of a serious escalation in conflict between India and Pakistan could certainly not be ruled out.

---

39 W. Maley, *What is a Refugee?*, Oxford University Press, New York, 2016, p. 1.

17

American and British experience in Iraq and Afghanistan, 2001–04

Dan Marston

The experience of the US and British militaries in the recent wars in Afghanistan and Iraq can be understood in five core lessons identified.[1] From my perspective, these are:

- There was a lack of clear and realistic strategic debates for use of force by both countries.
- There were breakdowns in civilian–military relations in both countries.
- There were breakdowns in trust between the two key allies: the United States and United Kingdom, especially in Iraq.
- There was tactical-level reform on the battlefield by both the United States and United Kingdom; however, winning tactically on the battlefield does not equate to strategic victory.
- There were problems created by ignoring the 'mosaic of the battlefield' and attempting to apply simplistic narratives and solutions to complex scenarios.

---

1   Lessons are identified but not necessarily analysed, and then disseminated to the proper levels in most wars.

Why is there a need for a critical and deep assessment of the wars? We have fought difficult wars that need to be properly analysed. All experience of war needs to be analysed and the lessons identified disseminated properly. Afghanistan and Iraq are wars, and the key lessons to take away from them are timeless and relevant to both the United States and United Kingdom for future war.

As we all know, war is extremely difficult, complex and ugly, and it always has been. The last two decades of war in Iraq and Afghanistan have been difficult, but no more complicated, I would argue, than the Roman invasion and occupation of Gaul. This chapter is based upon my work and research with US and UK officers, non-commissioned officers and soldiers, from 2006 to the present in Iraq and Afghanistan, where I engaged with 65 battalions, 27 brigades, 14 divisions, 10 corps and multiple command generals of the Multi-National Force – Iraq (MNF-I), Commander ISAF and Operation IRAQI RESOLVE. In the end, more than 80 per cent of these men and women understand and understood the need for analytical debates that dealt with the width, depth and context to understand the war they were and are engaged in.

Lack of strategic debates

The decision-making and debates for the use of force in both Afghanistan and Iraq have not been as robust as they should have been. National interest was never clearly defined by either the United States or United Kingdom throughout either campaign. Most politicians and senior military commanders did not ask the difficult questions supporting the key question: to what end? They did not consider worst-case scenarios in terms of the potential sacrifice of both the countries, as well as considering the potential destruction of the enemy and the countries we were invading. We did not honestly consider the reality that when a country uses force, it will probably mean a bloody exercise and that, for all the technological advances of weapons, people are going to be killed and maimed— including our own soldiers, sailors, marines and airmen as well as the enemy. The silver lining to this bleak assessment is that many US and UK officers, from all levels of command, are asking key questions informed by their experiences, such as: can we define the national interest? Why have we deployed forces? Do we have a coherent strategy that is tied to national interest and to the overall question of 'to what end?' This is a key lesson identified from the experiences of the wars in Afghanistan and Iraq.

Civilian–military issues

In both the United States and United Kingdom, civilian–military relations have broken down at different times, owing to the strain of the war and lack of clarity over strategic end states. Many within the political and military leadership blamed one another for the apparent quagmire that occurred in the summer of 2003 in Iraq. Most of the leadership on both sides of the Atlantic did not engage in robust debates before launching these wars and, by 2004, we started to see some rifts within the leadership as the war in Iraq did not go to plan and Afghanistan appeared to be losing momentum.

By 2006 and early 2007, many policy-makers and military leaders were questioning the commitment to the wars, especially in Iraq. This was also a period where many people would accuse some of the military leadership in both countries of giving politically aware advice to policy-makers, instead of sound military advice. This was especially true in the context of the British experience in Iraq in 2007.[2]

There are two high-profile examples that illustrate the apparent breakdown in relations. The first occurred in 2010, when General Stanley McChrystal resigned from his post in Afghanistan as Commander ISAF. This example highlighted an evident breakdown in communications between senior military and political leaders within the United States. The other example is from the United Kingdom, when then Chief of the Defence Staff, General Sir David Richards, had an open debate with the then British Government and people regarding the 'covenant' and the role of the military in society.[3]

Although many people in Britain have applauded the establishment and findings of the Chilcot (or Iraq) Inquiry, other observers point to a lost opportunity.[4] Many journalists and commentators have focused

---

2   See some the following recent studies by Brigadier (ret'd) B. Barry, which cover some key issues for British experiences in both Iraq and Afghanistan: 'Bitter war to stabilize southern Iraq—British Army report declassified', Adelphi Series, International Institute for Strategic Studies, vol. 56, issue 461, London, 10 October 2016; and *Harsh Lessons: Iraq, Afghanistan and the Changing Character of War*, International Institute for Strategic Studies, London, 2017. See further H. Strachan, R. Iron and J. Bailey (eds), *British Generals in Blair's Wars*, Ashgate Publishing, Farnham, UK, 2013, for more detailed discussions of these issues.
3   See the following article, which hints at the tensions: C. Coughlin, 'A last salvo from General Sir David Richards', 17 July 2013, www.telegraph.co.uk/news/uknews/defence/10185613/A-last-salvo-from-General-Sir-David-Richards.html (retrieved 2 April 2020).
4   Sir John Chilcot, *The Chilcot Inquiry*, House of Commons Library, 1 July 2016, at commons library.parliament.uk/research-briefings/sn06215/.

exclusively on the decision-making regarding the invasion of Iraq in 2003 while failing to address the more damning evidence relating to the difficult civilian–military debates in the post-2003 phase of the war and the many tensions and lessons identified during this period. The US debates in late 2006 and early 2007, regarding whether to 'surge' or 'not surge' in Iraq, offer a similar level of lessons and debates from which much could and should be learned.

Breakdown in trust with allies

Another major issue that occurred was the breakdown in trust between the two key allies, the United States and United Kingdom. Much of this breakdown came down to arrogance: both countries were guilty of not understanding the long-term impact of invading and occupying two different countries, Afghanistan and Iraq. Both countries discounted the impact of using force with no clear end state in either country.

Both countries were also arrogant regarding the perceived response from their respective populations. Many of the policy-makers and military commanders expected that the populations would see their militaries as liberators—an assumption in which we were very much mistaken.

The levels of arrogance and distrust between the United States and United Kingdom reached the high-water mark in Iraq. Although Britain agreed with the initial planning of the campaign, it quickly distanced itself from the breakdown of the security situation in Iraq. The British hunkered down in Multi-National Division – South East (MND-SE) and attempted to withdraw from the war as quickly as possible. As the US military and civilian organisations in Baghdad attempted to come to terms with the rise of violence from the summer of 2003, there was a growing disconnect between the two allies. The level of arrogance started to permeate the British policy and military leadership as they claimed to have pacified MND-SE and Basra in particular. Senior British military officers specifically stated that the US military had much to learn from the British expertise when dealing with the rising insurgency.[5]

---

5   An example of this: BBC News, 'UK general attacks US Iraq policy', news.bbc.co.uk/2/hi/6973618.stm (retrieved 3 April 2020).

Major Cootes, Chief of Engineers on Multi-National Corps — Iraq, in 2005 surveying a bridge that was partially destroyed by a VBIED attack in 2004.
Source: Courtesy of the Department of Defence.

In 2005–06, both militaries were trying to come to terms with the occupation. Many within the British junior and mid-level leadership questioned both so-called British expertise and criticism of US efforts. Nevertheless, British media commentators and policy-makers in London continued to follow this simplistic narrative, and by 2006 the two allies were on divergent paths in Iraq. This was particularly ironic as the US military had been undergoing a major transformation to deal with the reality of the conflict they were facing. Meanwhile, British arrogance would come back to hurt them by 2008.

Many American and British senior officers in MNF-I were doubtful about the validity of reporting from Basra by late 2007 and early 2008. They understood that most of the 'dishonesty' coming through could be attributed to the disconnect within the British Government and the pressure to withdraw from an unpopular war.⁶ The issue is that many professional soldiers, NCOs and officers in the British Army understood that the previous narrative of 'expertise' had been incorrect, and felt that their senior command was not being honest with their US allies. In February 2007, I wrote a report after my second visit to Iraq in six months, in which I stated:

> I was upset with what I saw and heard in Basra. This may sound a bit over the top, but the honour of the British Army and its reputation [are] at stake. Overall, the mood amongst many British officers is frustration. They want to be boots on the ground 24/7, like they perceive the Yanks are in the north … Allow the boys on the ground to storm back into Basra, start up company bases with embedded Iraqis and think long term … get the British Army thinking more about long term and less about force protection. The last thing we need is for a USMC regiment or US Army Brigade to come south in the future to do the job. Such an eventuality would be humiliating for the British Army.⁷

The end result was a complete breakdown between the British and Americans in Iraq. The British were withdrawing, based not upon the situation on the battlefield but upon political requirements in London.⁸ The culmination of this breakdown and distrust came to a head in March 2008, during Operation CHARGE OF THE KNIGHTS (CoTK). As a senior British officer stated:

> The opening moves of Operation CoTK did indeed expose our lack of situational awareness and lack of resources to take the fight to the enemy. This led to the Iraqis and the Americans doubting our commitment and ability, and tarnished our reputation.⁹

Luckily, after this breakdown, interactions and coordination improved for the war in Afghanistan, for later operations in Iraq, and for Syria and beyond.

---

6   See the findings of the Iraq Inquiry for an in-depth discussion of the breakdown between the United Kingdom and the United States and the disconnect with the policy-makers in London and the field commanders in Iraq. For further details, see webarchive.nationalarchives.gov.uk/20171123123237/http://www.iraqinquiry.org.uk (retrieved 3 April 2020).
7   Report to MNF-I and MND-SE, February 2007 (copy held by author).
8   Daniel Patrick Marston, 'Operation TELIC VIII to XI: Difficulties of twenty-first-century command', *Journal of Strategic Studies*, 2019, doi.org/10.1080/01402390.2019.1672161.
9   Comments from senior British officer from Operation CoTK, 2008.

There was also some arrogance from US Iraq War veterans after 2008, notably when they deployed to Afghanistan. Many assumed that they could apply the same tactics, techniques and procedures to the very different war in Afghanistan. Luckily, we were able to limit the influence of these attitudes and avert any serious damage. A US Marine Corps report from early 2007 was blunt in its message to Iraqi veterans:

> Afghanistan is not Iraq. The people, culture, terrain, and climate, and the nature of the enemy differ greatly between the two geographic areas. Units are responsible for substantial operating areas and as a result their influence can span all the war-fighting functions as is noted by Operation Enduring Freedom veteran units ... than that found in Iraq.[10]

Tactical reform

One key lesson of these conflicts was that tactical reform did occur on the battlefields of Iraq and Afghanistan, for both US and British forces. Reform was generally bottom up and was slowly tied to home stations and systems, and followed time-honoured traditions of staring defeat in the face, learning from the battlefield, and wanting to win—all of which provide key lessons for the future. The process supported a transformation of units and formations to defeat the enemy—whoever that may be. The US Army, US Marine Corps and British Army tactically adapted to a war—it was not a counter-insurgency moment.[11]

Reform in Iraq and Afghanistan occurred within the US Army and US Marine Corps before the arrival of General David Petraeus and the publication of the US Army counter-insurgency field manual, *FM 3-24*. For some units and formations, it began in 2003, on the road to Baghdad.[12] The Petraeus and 3-24 moment provided the needed 'top cover' for units, formations and commanders in both theatres—leading to a post-war narrative that is somewhat different from the reality on the ground. As many officers, non-commissioned officers and soldiers

---

10   Internal USMC report, 2007.
11   See my article 'Smug and complacent? Operation TELIC: The need for critical analysis', *British Army Review*, vol. 147, 2008, pp. 16–23, for a more detailed discussion.
12   Headquarters, Department of the Army, FM3-24 & MCWP3.3-33.5 *Insurgencies and Countering Insurgencies*, Washington, DC, May 2004. One need only to look at the 1st Marine Division and 3rd Infantry Division reporting and after-action reports to see that the soldiers, NCOs and officers were quite critical of problems that occurred and the need for constant adaptation.

attempted to come to terms with the wars in front of them, they were quite open to new ideas. The following two examples from a British officer and an American officer, both veterans of the Afghanistan war, highlight the constant assessment and debates needed within a military organisation to deal with the complexity of war.

The British officer, a veteran of the first Herrick operation (involving the deployment of British forces in Afghanistan in 2002) in Helmand Province, stated in 2006:

> We must also avoid dressing COIN [counter-insurgency] up as something fundamentally new. We must be wary of losing sight of the lessons from previous campaigns ... [A]dditionally, as in previous COIN campaigns, WARFIGHTING is an element of COIN ... Many of the lessons learned from the battlegroups resulting experiences are not new. Common themes from previous UK COIN campaigns and conflicts were all evident in the operations conducted in Helmand Province. The key lesson is that we ignore previous experience of such campaigns and those of our allies at our peril.[13]

The US Army officer, a veteran of Regional Command East, stated in 2007:

> While a population focused strategy relies heavily on non-kinetic means, it increases kinetic operations as well. 'Planting the flag' in the heart of known enemy sanctuaries dislocates the enemy both physically and psychologically. He must fight back or lose. Task Force Spartan experienced a sharp rise in combat over previous rotations, but thanks to the close combat skill and firepower of American units, killed exponentially more enemy than suffered friendly casualties. The metric of enemy dead is not useful in gauging COIN success, but it does provide insight into the degree to which a unit has separated the enemy from the populace. Killing, capturing, forcing to flee, or convincing the enemy to reconcile are all ways to achieve separation.[14]

These quotes give some indication that the US and British militaries were learning institutions over the course of these two wars, and could be proud of their abilities to adapt, as their fathers, grandfathers and

---

13   Comments from a British officer, 2008.
14   Comments from a US Army officer, 2007.

great-grandfathers had done since the First World War. The question that remains is: have they taken these experiences and dived deep enough with critical analysis to draw some key themes for future wars?

Mosaic of the battlefield

This final theme or lesson is linked heavily with the previous lesson. Throughout the wars in Iraq and Afghanistan, there were times when policy-makers and military commanders attempted to apply 'blanket solutions' and/or narratives for the various districts and provinces in Iraq and Afghanistan and each year of the campaign without understanding the need for context. As many veterans were aware, Basra was different from Al-Anbar, which was different from Mosul in Iraq; in Afghanistan, Regional Command (RC) South was different from RC South-west, which was different from RC East. Each year of the war in Iraq and Afghanistan was different from the previous and subsequent years. This is true in all wars—a fact that many have failed to recognise when they create their narratives or so-called lessons learned.

I made this point clear to the Commanding General, International Security Assistance Force (COMISAF) in Afghanistan in 2010:

> While this concept may be obvious at the COMISAF level, there is a need for clear and consistent recognition that each battalion's area of operation (AO) will have different solutions … [a]nd that the commanders need to be allowed to develop these different solutions and pass along their knowledge. It must also be recognised and made clear that all lessons may not be applied everywhere. Each area of operation needs to be allowed to come up with their own solutions in order to succeed. There is a need to share information and lessons, but all commanders understand that [there] is no silver bullet … Clarity in communication is essential, with due respect for the chain of command, the commanding officers of the AOs need to feel confident that they are right to use their judgement in tailoring solutions for their AO.[15]

---

15   Report to COMISAF, October 2010 (copy held by author).

Final thought

The five themes or lessons outlined here still need to be analysed and debated among the US and British policy and military leadership—before people move on to the next perceived threat. These five issues are sure to rear their heads on the next battlefield, wherever it may be, as they are timeless in history. The core reason why they need to be debated was best summed up by a former US Army General, William Sherman, who stated in 1872: 'There is many a boy here today who looks on war as all glory, but boys, it is all hell.'

18

Lessons and legacies of the use of force

Peter Leahy

The lessons and legacies from Australia's wars in Afghanistan and Iraq neither start in 2001 nor finish in 2014.

The Australian Defence Force and the Australian Army were not ready for the war in Afghanistan, and consequently there were severe limitations on what could be done in both deployments. The ADF arrived at this situation because of decades of errant strategic guidance and an underinvestment in defence capabilities, especially the Australian Army, in the last quarter of the 20th century.

Today, there are still lessons to be learned and legacies to be realised as Australia remains engaged in both Afghanistan and Iraq. These current lessons and legacies will continue to shape the ADF of the future, but only if there is the wit and wisdom to recognise them and do something about them.

Aim

The aim of this chapter is to highlight the major lessons and legacies for the Australian Army from the deployment to the Middle East from 2001 to 2014. The chapter will propose nine lessons at the strategic and operational levels and three legacies, which have yet to be fully realised.

Apart from acknowledging significant improvements in equipment, collective training, combined arms cooperation and the development of defensive measures against improvised explosive devices (IEDs) at the tactical level, these lessons will not be covered in any detail. Overall, care must be exercised in making tactical judgements because, as many have said, it is a poor practice to benchmark your tactical prowess against adversaries such as the Iraqi Army in 2003, and the Taliban throughout the duration of the fight in Afghanistan. In summary, the lessons and legacies to be covered are highlighted here. The nine lessons are:

- Be ready for the most likely conflict.
- Have a strategy.
- You can't go to war quickly without introducing risk.
- You can't make a flexible and versatile force out of nothing.
- Equipping the force is difficult, expensive and time consuming.
- Doctrine is important.
- When designing the force, a clear mission is essential.
- 'Whole of government' should mean whole of government.
- A combined arms approach is essential.

The three legacies are as follows:

1. any decision to go to war should be subject to parliamentary debate and vote
2. the alliance with the United States is important but it is not the only reason to go to war
3. a new community-based approach to caring for our wounded is emerging.

Lessons from the British and US experience

Several official and unofficial publications have highlighted various lessons from the perspective of the United Kingdom and the United States.

In the case of the United Kingdom, the principal report was the Iraq Inquiry, chaired by John Chilcot, which examined the UK's policy on Iraq from 2001 to 2009. The inquiry sought to answer two questions: whether it was right and necessary to invade Iraq in March 2003; and whether Britain could—and should—have been better prepared for what followed.[1]

The inquiry covered an enormous amount of material, and almost exclusively dealt with Iraq. However, the value of the inquiry report is that, like Australia, Britain was a junior partner of the US-led alliance in Iraq and has had a long-term security relationship with the United States. The British lessons are therefore useful when considering the Australian position. For those who might be wondering, a similar Australian inquiry is not necessary. It would no doubt come to very similar conclusions as those reached in Britain's Iraq Inquiry.

In a very British manner, the Iraq Inquiry concluded: 'The Iraq of 2009 certainly did not meet the UK's objectives as described in January 2003: it fell far short of strategic success.'[2] Another, now obvious and striking, lesson is found in the conclusion of the inquiry: 'It is now clear that policy on Iraq was made on the basis of flawed intelligence. The flawed premises were not challenged and they should have been.'[3]

Linking the campaigns in Iraq and Afghanistan, the inquiry observed:

> From 2006, the UK military was conducting two enduring campaigns in Iraq and Afghanistan. It did not have sufficient resources to do so. Decisions on resources for Iraq were affected by the demands of the operation in Afghanistan.[4]

The Iraq Inquiry also determined that the United Kingdom chose to join the invasion of Iraq before the peaceful options for disarmament had been exhausted. It judged that 'military action at that time was not a last resort'.[5]

---

1   J. Chilcot, 'Statement by Sir John Chilcot', in *Report of the Iraq Inquiry*, 6 July 2016 [hereafter Chilcot, 'Statement'], p. 1, webarchive.nationalarchives.gov.uk/20171123123519/http://www.iraq inquiry.org.uk/media/247010/2016-09-06-sir-john-chilcots-public-statement.pdf (retrieved 3 April 2020).
2   Executive Summary, *Report of the Chilcot Inquiry*, 6 July 2016, p. 109, webarchive.nationalarchives. gov.uk/20171123122743/http://www.iraqinquiry.org.uk/the-report/ (retrieved 3 April 2020).
3   Chilcot, 'Statement', p. 6.
4   Ibid., p. 10.
5   Ibid., p. 1.

In relation to the preparation for what might follow the intervention, it concluded: 'The Government's preparations failed to take account of the magnitude of the task of stabilising, administering and reconstructing Iraq, and of the responsibilities which were likely to fall to the UK.'[6]

The Economist magazine, when reporting on the inquiry release, observed that Tony Blair was not a liar or a war criminal. However, *The Economist* also observed that Tony Blair was a man steered by a fatal combination of hubris, wishful thinking and moral fervour into an ultimately disastrous course of action.[7]

Another crucial finding from the Iraq Inquiry was: 'Above all, the lesson is that all aspects of any intervention need to be calculated, debated and challenged with the utmost rigour.'[8]

Now let us turn to the lessons from the perspective of the United States. One provocative article by Stephen M. Walt, in *Foreign Policy*, provides a guide to what some have proffered as lessons learned in Iraq from a US point of view.[9]

The first observation from Walt is that the United States lost in Iraq. Walt then notes, in a series of statements: be careful which wars you choose; boneheaded decisions follow when there is no open debate about what to do; and the United States did not really understand Iraq and relied too much on 'ambitious exiles' for advice and intelligence. Walt also notes that the force must be prepared to adjust, that regional allies are required and that you should not assume that their interests are the same as yours. In yet another lesson, he records that 'winning a battle is easy when you have an overwhelming force and then, winning the occupation or the peace via a counter-insurgency campaign is a whole lot harder to do'.

In conclusion, Walt states, 'The real lesson of Iraq is not to do stupid things like this again.'[10]

---

6   Ibid., p. 9.
7   *Economist*, 'Iraq's grim lessons', 6 July 2016, www.economist.com/britain/2016/07/06/iraqs-grim-lessons (retrieved 3 April 2020).
8   Chilcot, 'Statement', p. 12.
9   S.M. Walt, 'Top 10 lessons of the Iraq War', *Foreign Policy*, 20 March 2012, foreignpolicy.com/2012/03/20/top-10-lessons-of-the-iraq-war-2 (retrieved 3 April 2020).
10 Ibid.

The time before 2001

In *America's First Battles*, the authors review such battles as Buna and Kasserine Pass in the Second World War, Task Force Smith in Korea and the Ia Drang Valley in Vietnam and conclude that the US Army was ill-prepared for all its first battles from 1776 to 1965. A similar conclusion could be made for Australia's first battles.[11]

In 2001 many in the Australian Army were veterans of what General David Hurley famously called the 'Long Peace'. Over this period, roughly from the early 1970s until the late 1990s, the Australian Army largely remained at home. Apart from a small number of UN postings and a brief burst of deployments around the early 1990s with operations in Cambodia, Somalia and Rwanda, about the only thing the Army did was get smaller.[12]

After these uncommon deployments, a few Army thinkers began researching the most likely nature of future wars. They were influenced by such authors as Robert Kaplan in *The Coming Anarchy* and Paul Kennedy in *The Troubled and Fractured Planet*.[13] These Army thinkers agreed with the judgements in successive Defence White Papers that a direct assault on the Australian continent was unlikely. In their view, the defence capabilities required were those with global reach to deal with wars among populations in distress away from Australian shores. These ideas took hold inside the Army but did not spread much further.

Instead, under the powerful 'Defence of Australia' policy, the Army was assigned the role of 'goalkeeper' against a mythical enemy. In the 'Army 21' review of the mid-1990s, the Army was given strategic guidance that its primary task was to defeat an understrength enemy raider battalion somewhere in the north of Australia. Predictably, these infamous 'thugs in thongs' never came. Strategic guidance, which favoured naval and air forces to interdict an invasion across the sea–air gap to Australia's north, was wrong. The Army languished, as a home-only force, without realistic guidance and an inadequate budget.

---

11 C. Heller and W. Stofft (eds), *America's First Battles, 1776–1965*, University of Kansas Press, Kansas, 1986.
12 From approximately 34,000 around the time of the withdrawal to around 25,000 around the time of the deployments to Afghanistan and Iraq.
13 T. Frame and A. Palazzo (eds), *On Ops: Lessons and Challenges for the Australian Army Since East Timor*, UNSW Press, Sydney, 2016, p. 64.

The 1994 Defence White Paper contained an assumption that the ADF would force structure for the defence of Australia. Resourcing for expeditionary tasks was to be in the 'margins'. The margins were tightly controlled and were estimated to be around 15 per cent. This was not enough to ensure that the Army was ready for the missions and tasks that would be required within the next decade.

After the change of government in 1997, the focus on continental defence began to change subtly and strategic guidance began to shift ever so slightly to an offshore role for the Army. However, the change in guidance did not permeate adequately through to strategic guidance, resourcing and capability development to result in meaningful and timely changes to force structure and preparedness of the ADF and Army before East Timor.

East Timor was a bit of a wake-up for the ADF. I say 'bit of a wake-up' because even by October 2001, when the deployment to Afghanistan began, the lessons of East Timor had not been fully understood, interpreted and implemented. The reality of East Timor was that the ADF struggled even when faced with such a geographically close and relatively benign task. There were significant deficiencies in strategic lift, communications, logistics over the shore, joint and combined operations, equipment stocks, coalition management, force preparedness and readiness. But at least East Timor did bring about a growing realisation that the defence force that faced the last battle of the 20th century was not the defence force needed to face Australia's first battles of the 21st century.

The reader might wonder about the relevance of this preamble, but it gets to the core issue of getting the strategy right. We in Australia have a patchy record on this account, but we are not alone. The British author and strategic thinker Basil Liddell Hart defined strategy as the calculation and coordination of ways and means to achieve ends. It is difficult to reconcile Liddell Hart's strategic equation with the situation in both Afghanistan and Iraq. Just what were the ends, and were the right ways and means applied?

Could anyone then and can anyone now answer three basic questions for both Afghanistan and Iraq: what is the shape of peace, what does victory look like, and what is the exit strategy?

The lessons of both Afghanistan and Iraq, at the strategic level, belong mostly to the United States. As Neil James from the Australia Defence Association states, Australia is a strategy taker, not a strategy maker. The United States took the policy lead in Afghanistan and Iraq at the beginning of both conflicts, and Australia largely acquiesced to the US strategy and narrative for both conflicts. Although Australia sought to contribute to the strategic discourse, it had limited influence. Indeed, how much impact can be expected from any individual nation in large coalitions such as those involved in Afghanistan and Iraq? The US-led anti–Islamic State or Daesh coalition has consisted of more than 50 nations—try finding consensus among that lot!

In October 2001, there was a clear objective in Afghanistan: kill al-Qaeda and their Taliban supporters in revenge for the 9/11 attacks and take away their sanctuaries and bases in Afghanistan. Vengeance might feel good, but it is not an adequate strategic objective.

In the years since al-Qaeda fled from Afghanistan across the border into Pakistan, after the battle of Tora Bora, it is difficult to identify a clear and constant strategy for Afghanistan. Instead, there has been a parade of missions and regularly changing force structures and force levels contributing little to an overarching and consistent strategy and a clear focus on an agreed and achievable end state.

As this chapter was being written, the overall situation in Afghanistan looked dire. In February 2017, in testimony to the Senate Armed Services Committee, the US commander in Afghanistan, General John Nicholson, warned that US troop levels were not adequate to prevent the Taliban from continuing to retake territory, especially in Helmand Province, the heartland of the insurgency. Senator John McCain at the same Senate hearing suggested that instead of playing 'not to lose', the United States needed a strategy to defeat the Taliban.

When it comes to Australia's lessons from the war in Iraq, the Australian defence official, Al Palazzo, has done the Australian public a service through his observations and conclusions in his report on Iraq, *The Australian Army and the War in Iraq: 2002–2010*. Although the report does not incorporate Cabinet and other high-level government documents, it is a good start to understanding Australia's involvement in Iraq and is an important contribution to the development of the lessons and legacies of Iraq. The journalist David Wroe, from the *Sydney Morning Herald*, when releasing the book, wrote:

> The report concludes that Howard joined US President George W. Bush in invading Iraq solely to strengthen Australia's alliance with the US … The result was a contribution that was of only modest military use and, in many cases, made little sense. Politically,

delivering the right force was secondary to the vital requirement of it just being there … yet frustrated commanders often asked what they were doing in Iraq and many took to writing their own mission statements. One commander wryly summed up his time in Iraq thus: 'We did some shit for a while and things didn't get any worse.'[14]

There is a problem with Australia's strategic approach to Iraq. The problem relates not so much to the initial decision to depose Saddam Hussein but with what happened after he was removed. Few predicted the development of a nationwide insurgency, nor did they foresee the unleashing of local and regional sectarian forces, which have led to turmoil and instability in Iraq and many regional states. The overconfidence and ignorance of local conditions of the American neoconservatives, who were the major cheerleaders for the invasion, led coalition forces into a morass from which it has been difficult to find any way out.

The Australian Army arrived at 2001 undermanned, underequipped and unprepared for what unfolded in the first decade of the 21st century. It was not ready for what became and remains a series of concurrent, competing and at times intense global missions.

On 10 September 2001, who would have imagined that Australian troops might soon deploy to Afghanistan? In October 2001, as Australian special forces deployed to Afghanistan, who would again have imagined that inside 18 months Australian special forces would launch into the western desert of Iraq? For both countries, there were many unanswered questions: who had the maps; how would the force get there; what language did the locals speak; was the right clothing and equipment available?

This quote from Palazzo states the situation very clearly:

> From the perspective of the stocks available the reality was that in mid-2002 little of the Australian Army's order of battle was readily deployable for a war with Iraq, even against an opponent that would prove as strategically, operationally and tactically inept as the regime of Saddam Hussein.[15]

---

14 D. Wroe, 'The secret Iraq dossier', *Sydney Morning Herald*, 25 February 2017.
15 Palazzo, *The Australian Army and the War in Iraq: 2002–2010*, p. 172, www.smh.com.au/interactive/2017/pdfview/ViewerJS/#../The_Australian_Army_in_Iraq.pdf (retrieved 3 April 2020).

Haunted by the memory of what happened to the unprepared Australian infantry units rushed into battle on the Kokoda Track in the Second World War, the ADF should know well the dangers of deploying inadequately equipped and prepared troops into combat. Troops should not be asked to accept this level of risk. The risk should be mitigated before conflict. The responsibility to address this risk lies with government and its fundamentally important dual functions of determining strategy and allocating appropriate budgets. Government is not entirely to blame as the military have not been particularly competent at articulating this risk to government. In part this is because the Australian Army has tended to focus on developing skills at the tactical level and up to the operational level of war. We have tended to leave the strategic level to others to manage.

The operational level of war is generally taken to be how a strategy is achieved by assigning missions, tasks, timings, geographic boundaries and resources. It is the ways and means portion of Liddell Hart's strategic equation. Important operational lessons for Australia from Afghanistan and Iraq are: demand, designing the force, equipping the force, doctrine and whole-of-government intent.

The hallmark for the period from 1999 to 2017 was the duration and consistency of the demand for combat forces. This showed that the force, as at 2001, was not large enough to sustain multiple operational deployments. Subsequent decisions taken, during the decade, to expand the force through such programs as the Hardened and Networked Army and the Enhanced Land Force have somewhat eased the pressure. However, there remain limits to what the ADF can do. Further expansions and force structure adjustments to all three services might still be necessary to cope with ongoing demands and future contingencies. One way of dealing with high demand is to adjust the duration of deployments. Longer deployments of individuals and formed bodies mean fewer troops are required. Of course, the situation has not been as bad as during the Second World War when troops went to war unsure of how long they would be away and when the Australian auxiliary forces included the equivalent of 14 divisions—a stark contrast to the far smaller Army of the early 21st century.

The initial deployments to the Middle East, in 2001 and 2003, were set at six months. This was on the basis that a prolonged campaign was not anticipated, the intensity of operations was not expected to be high, and six months was considered a reasonable time for individual and unit deployments. As pressure came on from other deployments in Bougainville, Iraq, Solomon Islands and East Timor, the immediate solution to concurrency pressures was to extend the duration of deployments and to limit the nature and type of tasks accepted from the coalition. This took careful management and explanation.

Multiple deployments to multiple theatres take a toll on individuals and their families. One significant aspect of managing demand for combat readiness since the start of the century is that there has been little respite for many elements of the ADF. Much has been asked of our soldiers, sailors and airmen and their families, and they have delivered magnificently.

Decisions to commit forces to an operation are taken at a political level. These decisions, while conscious of the need to deploy force, are not always conscious of the appropriateness and availability of the force. This was particularly so in the context of deployments to Afghanistan and Iraq. Designing suitable forces took a lot of negotiation, manoeuvring and management with government and with coalition partners. In the case of Afghanistan, in 2001, there was no realistic choice other than to send the SAS Regiment. This was also the case in the March 2003 deployment to Iraq. They were the most ready and appropriate forces for the assigned tasks. Beyond these initial deployments, an enormous amount of work was required to determine the task to be undertaken in follow-on phases and then prepare the appropriate forces.

It is no secret that the United States would have preferred that Australia offered more powerful, versatile, combat-oriented forces. The forces that deployed were a product of the available forces, their capability and the assessment of the risk. The Army was particularly concerned about the lack of armoured protected mobility and firepower available for deployment to Iraq in 2005. Once the task and appropriate force were determined, the force then had to be regrouped and prepared. The fact that the force eventually deployed to Al Muthanna as a combined arms group (made up of 52 different units), rather than an established unit, is a telling comment on the inappropriateness of the unit, regimental and corps structures of the day.

In the early days, the Army was not good at designing deployable forces. Things were often rushed and haphazard. Forces were 'going, ready or not'. It was only in later deployments that a system was developed that appropriately trained, prepared and assessed the force and formally handed it over for deployment to Joint Operations Command.

Any deployed military force should have the best equipment. In the early part of the deployments to Afghanistan and Iraq, the extant defence procurement system was unable to cope with the demands of the deploying forces. It was not responsive enough to match the rapidly changing requirements and too slow to deliver the necessary equipment. Peacetime procurement processes proved to be totally inappropriate. It was only with the introduction of a hastily developed rapid acquisition system that deployed forces began to be supplied with the right equipment in a timely manner.

In the early days of both deployments, there were many pronouncements about how these would be whole-of-government deployments whereby a range of government agencies beyond the Defence portfolio would engage and assist in accomplishing the assigned missions. But there was more talk than action. In the deployments to both Afghanistan and Iraq, AusAID was seldom seen in the field, and in Afghanistan AFP elements were largely confined to the base at Tarin Kowt. Things improved somewhat over the years, but issues of security, protection and capacity will always be a constraint on what civilian agencies can do. An exception was Australia's external intelligence agency, the Australian Secret Intelligence Service, which gave sterling support providing an intelligence edge to Australian soldiers in the field.[16]

Achieving the appropriate balance between security, stability and development will always be a difficult task. The military are clearly not the best force to be involved in the detailed work of development and delivering aid, but sometimes they are the only force available and able to do the task safely. One of the few official 'lessons learned' documents authored principally by Ric Smith and published by the Australian Civil-Military Centre was *Afghanistan: Lessons from Australia's Whole-of-Government Mission*. It is a rather narrow report, which by its own admission does not evaluate the effectiveness of the effort in Afghanistan but merely identifies

---

16 N. Warner, 'ASIS at 60', 19 July 2012, www.asis.gov.au/about-us/speech.html (retrieved 30 April 2020).

a number of areas worthy of consideration when planning and responding to future contingencies. It provides little tangible discussion to enhance the whole-of-government discussion. It acknowledges that it was not until April 2009 that the whole-of-government approach saw significant deployments of civil elements into the field—more than seven years after troops first deployed to Afghanistan following the 9/11 attacks. It also acknowledges that at the policy level, interdepartmental involvement was relatively light in the early period but intensified from 2006 until it acquired a more genuinely whole-of-government character by 2009.[17]

The report recorded 17 key lessons.[18] Included among them were the need to:

- involve all relevant departments and agencies in whole-of-government policy development and planning from the outset
- establish a senior-level, inter-agency group to oversee policy development and provide a high-level nexus with the National Security Committee of Cabinet and the Secretaries' Committee on National Security
- agree principles and protocols to be developed at the outset of the mission to define working relationships and responsibilities between different services and agencies
- establish a cross-agency public affairs capability to highlight the whole-of-government nature of the mission.

An area where commanders, in the field, were left with little support was in the development of doctrine. In both Afghanistan and Iraq, the campaigns rapidly morphed into a counter-insurgency effort with a constantly changing balance of tasks around the four-phased concepts shape, clear, hold and build. Commanders on the ground saw the need to support the local population and set about doing so on their own, but without adequate doctrine. Doctrine was eventually developed and was influenced by the experiences of those on the ground. Supporting this effort was an increased focus on immediate lessons learned, which were fed directly back into the force preparation cycle and mission rehearsal exercises.

---

17   Australian Civil-Military Centre, *Afghanistan: Lessons from Australia's Whole of Government Mission*, ACMC, Queanbeyan, p. 7.
18   Ibid., pp. 8 ff.

In many ways, the deployments were set-and-forget missions. By deploying, Australia had achieved the coalition aim: there were flags on the table. Commanders were certainly left to cope with changes to the operational environment without adequate strategic guidance. Commanders in the field stated that they received little strategic guidance on what their objectives were.[19] They were right to complain.

Moving beyond the issue of operational lessons lies the issues of legacies. A legacy is a gift or bequest handed down from those who have gone before. They are significant issues that shape the nature of the force and how it fights and how it is perceived by the public and the international community. The Anzac legacy of service and sacrifice is an example, and Australian forces deployed to the Middle East have proudly sustained and added lustre to the legacy of those who went before them.

It is too soon to identify clear legacies from the current experience of Australia's niche wars in Afghanistan and Iraq. However, there are three likely candidates: the decision-making process to go to war in the first place, the influence of the US alliance on Australian calculations, and the limitations in the treatment of wounded veterans.

Observations from the United Kingdom and the United States question the wisdom of the decision to go to war in Iraq. In Australia, where the prime minister reserves to him- or herself 'crown prerogative' on the decision to go to war, it is unacceptable, except in the case of a defence emergency, that the nation can be taken to war without parliament and the public being fully engaged.

Today, after nearly 20 years, Australia remains at war in Afghanistan and Iraq. For both locations, there has been very little public discussion or debate on the decisions to go to war and the daily repeated decisions to stay at war. Apart from relatively minor changes, Australia's strategy—what there is of it—in both places has remained the same. This is no way to make national security decisions. Such an approach is a disservice to the public and to those in the ADF required to deploy on multiple occasions to combat operations over such a long period.

---

19 Various conversations with the author.

As some express concern over the decisions President Trump might make, the historic and almost automatic response of Australia to become involved in the United States' wars is of concern. The United States, let alone the rest of the world, has yet to be convinced of the wisdom and maturity of Trump's foreign policy choices and actions. Where might a new US president take Australia, and is there any assurance that an Australian prime minister, in exercising crown prerogative, might not exercise similarly poor judgement?

There is cause to review crown prerogative. George Williams, Dean of Law at the University of New South Wales, in an opinion piece wrote:

> Parliament should pass a law requiring that it debate any proposal to commit Australian troops. A decision by the Prime Minister to go to war should also be subject to a veto by a majority vote of both houses of the federal Parliament. This would provide a much-needed circuit breaker, thereby reducing the possibility of Australia taking part in another inadvisable foreign conflict.[20]

Under a convention introduced in 2011, Britain is required to take deployment decisions to parliament for debate.[21] The United States has the War Powers Act, and in Russia, President Putin in 2015 asked the Russian parliament for authority to bomb in Syria. Australia is alone, among its major allies and world powers, regarding the decision to go to war. An initiative to engage parliament in decisions to go to war such as those proposed in the Defence Amendment (Parliamentary Approval of Overseas Service) Bill 2010 [No. 2] would be a fitting legacy of the Australian experience in Afghanistan and Iraq.[22]

The ANZUS Treaty is a key element behind the choices that Australia makes about going to and staying at war. Some argue that to guarantee continued benefit from the alliance, Australia needs to be involved in all US military activities. Their fear is that if requests from the United States for support are declined, then the United States might not respond to Australian requests for support in the event of a future defence or security emergency.

---

20 G. Williams, 'Why Australia must learn from our mistakes in the Iraq War', *Sydney Morning Herald*, 27 March 2017, newsroom.unsw.edu.au/news/business-law/why-australia-must-learn-our-mistakes-iraq-war (retrieved 24 April 2020).
21 C. Mills, 'Parliamentary approval for military action', House of Commons Library, 13 May 2015.
22 S. Ludlam, 'Debate on the War Powers Bill', 7 July 2011, scott-ludlam.greensmps.org.au/articles/debate-war-powers-bill (retrieved 3 April 2020).

There can be no disputing that the alliance with the United States is important to Australia. The ADF gains privileged access to intelligence, technology, armaments, logistics and strategic lift. The result is that Australia is more powerful and influential than it could ever expect to be without the alliance. However, a balance must be achieved between sustaining the alliance for capability and security reasons, and meeting Australia's sovereign national interests. This leads to the question: does Australia's level of dependency on the US alliance hinder its ability to make independent decisions based on its own national security interests?

Given the emerging judgements on the intervention in Iraq, and the apparent intractable nature of the conflict, questions must be asked about whether going to Iraq was the right thing to do. As with Afghanistan, the fundamental question is whether the Australian commitment was about supporting the alliance or acting to support its own national interests, be they security, moral or humanitarian.

It is a good thing that Saddam Hussein is gone, but while democracy and secularism have been introduced in Iraq, they have not taken a firm hold. The situation in Afghanistan is similar and becoming worse. Despite 16 years of a coalition presence in the Middle East, the terrorist base has expanded, democracy has not taken hold, there is unprecedented turmoil and Western influence has been diminished in part to be replaced by Russia, Turkey and Iran.

It is difficult to imagine the future circumstances in which US and Australian interests might not coincide, but Australia must be alert to the potential for our interests to diverge and be prepared to say no to any request from the United States to deploy forces to a conflict that is not clearly in our national interests.

During the 'Long Peace', the ADF, with tight personnel ceilings, had little room for those who were not able to meet fitness and readiness standards. Those with injuries were generally discharged quickly. As combat operations began and casualties occurred in both Afghanistan and Iraq, many quite rightly started to question these quick discharges. Surely those who were wounded in battle were owed time to recover from their wounds and, if possible, the option to continue their careers, to the best of their ability, in the ADF. Why would soldiers go forward into battle if they were not going to be looked after if they were wounded? The ADF was not adequately prepared to meet this obligation to its soldiers, sailors and airmen. The turnaround occurred but only after some solid prodding of the Defence bureaucracy.

There are three primary areas requiring improvement: the medical treatment and retention of the physically and psychologically wounded while in-service, the official government support provided to veterans after discharge, and the community support that can also be provided after discharge. Once the obligation to the wounded was recognised, the care and attention provided inside the ADF has been world class. One lingering area of concern is that those with psychological injuries tend to be discharged rather quickly, which means that injuries of this type are sometimes not declared and are therefore untreated or at least independently managed.

The Department of Veterans' Affairs does a commendable job of caring for the wounded once they are discharged. Regrettably, the department suffers from a less than desirable public image, but is aware of this and is pursuing internal reforms. These reforms need to be expedited. Everyone eventually leaves the military with most fitting back into the civilian community with little trouble. Some among the approximately 72,000 who have served in the ADF since 1990 with physical and psychological wounds find it more difficult to reintegrate into civilian life. For many, their recovery will be a lifelong journey during which they will need the support of their family, friends and the broader Australian community. In the last five to 10 years, a number of newly formed community-based organisations have been making a significant additional contribution to support veterans and assist in their successful reintegration to the country. These organisations should be encouraged as they develop a new community-based approach to caring for our wounded.

Conclusion

The Australian Army has been through a period of intense operational tempo over nearly two decades. Deployments have been global and continuous. They have varied greatly in nature and intensity. A great number of lessons have been learned, and their realisation has made the force more robust and combat ready and better able to cope with future demands.

Overall, the deployments have been handled adequately, and the Australian Army, although at times hard pressed, has provided government with manageable options and combat-ready forces. However, these forces were heavily restrained by the capabilities of the force in being in the early stages of both deployments. They remain so today. This means that the focus has been on protection, training, mentoring and support tasks rather than offensive missions.

Risk has been managed but, in the early stages of both deployments, was weighted towards the individual soldier rather than residing where it should be at government level. To mitigate this risk, government must provide realistic strategic guidance and adequate budgets. Neither were in place in 2001 and 2003 and, in many respects, are still not in place now.

The major lessons from the conflicts have been around honouring Basil Liddell Hart's strategic equation of the necessary ways and means to achieve the desired ends. This has not been done well, and there have therefore been considerable difficulties around articulating a strategy and assigning missions. So too were there problems in meeting the demands for combat forces, designing the force, equipping the force, developing relevant doctrine and providing a functional whole-of-government effort.

There are no clear legacies from these conflicts, but there are three candidates: first, the development of a parliamentary convention to debate and approve the commitment of ADF elements to conflict; second, the realisation that committing forces should not be based solely or even primarily on protecting the alliance but on clearly articulated Australian national interests; and third, an obligation to look after the wounded and a dedication to making them the best reintegrated generation of soldiers in our nation's history.

Although some lessons have been learned during the period 2001–14, there are more to be learned from current operations. As of mid-2020, the ADF remains in Afghanistan and Iraq, and the world order is under unprecedented strain. There is more work to be done, and Australia will be involved. The obligation to learn from the effort and sacrifice of our soldiers in Afghanistan and Iraq is a sacred one that must be honoured.

19

The Official History of Australian Operations in Iraq and Afghanistan, and Australian Peacekeeping Operations in East Timor

Craig Stockings[1]

Australia has commissioned official histories to record its experience on military operations five times over the last century: C.E.W. Bean in the First World War; Gavin Long and his team for the Second World War; Robert O'Neill for the Korean War; Peter Edwards for the Malayan Emergency, the Indonesian–Malaysian Confrontation and the Vietnam War; and David Horner for the peacekeeping, humanitarian assistance and other post–Cold War operations up to but excluding East Timor. I am humbled to be the next in line to carry this mantle, and this chapter outlines the scope and some of the challenges faced in writing this multivolume history.[2]

---

1   This chapter was written in 2018.
2   A version of this chapter was published as C. Stockings, 'A continuing tradition … but a whole new ballgame: The Official Historian of Australian Operations in Iraq and Afghanistan, and Australian Peacekeeping Operations in East Timor', in *Charles Bean: Man, Myth and Legacy*, ed. P. Stanley, UNSW Press, Sydney, 2017, pp. 215–28.

The effort to write the Official History of Australian Operations in the Middle East and East Timor has only just begun. Yet the history of this history project, even at this early stage, is important—for it frames what is a unique set of circumstances and contexts that surround this undertaking. There is no question that each of the five official histories that have preceded it have faced their own specific challenges and enjoyed their own individual advantages. At the same time, however, to me at least, the evolution of the process seems to have been incremental. I would put it to you at the outset that this series, dealing with a wide range of ADF operations both near and far from Australian shores, marks not a development or evolution of past experience so much as marking a new paradigm. Such a bold claim requires explanation—and I will certainly get there—but let me make one important early point. That is, this project is not, and cannot be, a repeat of past experience, updated for a new era. This is especially so in terms of the mechanics of research, and the environment in which my team labours. It is less so, of course, in terms of the tradition and philosophy behind past Australian official histories, which I seek to extend and enhance.

History of a history

Although talked about in a number of academic, public service and even political circles for some time, the real impetus for establishing a new Official History series came primarily through the tireless efforts of Emeritus Professor David Horner, the Official Historian of Australian Peacekeeping, Humanitarian and Post–Cold War Operations. Importantly, when Horner was appointed in 2004, Cabinet authorised the researching and writing of the history of all multinational operations and post–Cold War operations in which Australia has participated since 1947, excluding the recent operations in East Timor, Afghanistan and Iraq. Horner never stopped agitating for the inclusion of ongoing operations in Iraq, Afghanistan and East Timor to be taken within his or a subsequent Official History series. At every chance, including at the launch of the first volume of his peacekeeping series in April 2011, Horner spoke of the 'national disgrace' in the ongoing failure to capture and publicise the history of these operations.

At this point wheels began to turn once more. Kevin Rudd, then foreign minister, gave his support at the book launch, and Horner was commissioned by the Australian War Memorial in September 2011 to draft a feasibility study of the possibility of writing a new Official History series capturing Australian involvement in Iraq and Afghanistan. This was completed by the following March and turned into a Cabinet submission by the War Memorial. Three times this submission was put forth, containing options either to expand the peacekeeping series to include East Timor and other operations up to 2006, or to raise a new series for Iraq and Afghanistan. The first submission was set aside with the fall of the Gillard Government, the second time put on ice when Rudd called an election, and lost to Prime Minister Tony Abbott.

There were compelling reasons, argued in the submission, for a new Official History to capture the large-scale and ongoing operations in the Middle East. The proximity and sensitivities surrounding these operations, it was argued, ought not to preclude it; after all, Bean's first volume appeared in 1921. A new series, written as close as possible to the events they were chronicling, would provide a public so interested, yet so disconnected from these events, with an authoritative account of Australian involvement.

This was all well and good, but there soon emerged a rather obvious spanner in the works. If the peacekeeping Official History series traced ADF operations up to and including the first Iraq War, and the series proposed in 2012 picked up the story of Afghanistan and the second war in Iraq, what then of East Timor? The blunt answer was not, of course, that Horner or the War Memorial had failed to consider operations in this theatre from 1999 to 2012. Indeed, the expansion of the peacekeeping series to include East Timor had been a submission in itself, wrapped up in broader 'omnibus' Cabinet submissions that had also called for a new Official History of Iraq and Afghanistan. At the same time, political signals were such that it was pointless to press the issue. Horner had been 'warned off'. There were sensitivities and reputations mixed up in events in East Timor that were much closer to home than those in the Middle East—and this marks one of the challenges my project faces.

At last, in mid-2015, the government determined that a new multivolume Official History series should be produced to document Australian involvement in Iraq (2003–11), Afghanistan (2001–14) and East Timor (1999–2012). This then is the origin of my rather long title as

Official Historian of Australian Operations in Iraq and Afghanistan, *and* Australian Peacekeeping Operations in East Timor. The division still stands. I have oversight of a series dealing with the Middle East, and a separate series dealing with East Timor—all under the banner of the title above. It is worth remembering, however, that the nature of the Official History project over which I now preside was a function of the long, complex process undertaken by Horner and others designed to get the project approved by the government. Political considerations first and foremost—historical considerations a distant second.

My remit

The national significance of this project speaks for itself. Australia's involvement in the Middle East has been complex and long-running. As many as 40,000 Australian Defence Force personnel are believed to have served or supported these deployments over 13 years of operations. Forty-three Australians died on active service in these theatres, and hundreds were wounded. Equally, Australia's involvement in East Timor from 1999 to 2012 was an instrumental part of East Timor gaining its independence. The INTERFET deployment of 1999–2000 was Australia's largest mission conducted under UN auspices and the largest overseas deployment since the Vietnam War. Taken in total, these operations constitute an important part of Australia's recent past, and one that clearly needed to be chronicled in an analytical and authoritative manner.

The formal offer of the position of Official Historian was made to me via a letter from the Prime Minister. The task was made quite clear. 'You will be responsible for delivering the Official History by July 2022.' Importantly, my commission provided for full access to relevant government files and records, authorised under official access conditions as set out in the *Archives Act 1983*, subject only to national security requirements and restrictions. The letter closed with a reminder—not that one was required—that Australia has a long tradition of producing official histories telling the story of Australians at war. 'The role of Official Historian is one of great national significance,' I was told. The shadows of not only Charles Bean but also of Gavin Long, Bob O'Neill, Peter Edwards and David Horner perched on my shoulder. They are there still.

Governance

I did previously mention the significant differences between my project and those that have gone before. One key aspect in this regard is the type and level of governance imposed upon, and within, the project. I have been well funded for this task, to the tune of $12.6 million. For this, I am of course most grateful. It is a level of resourcing not available to past official historians. The flip side of deep government and War Memorial investment in the project is, however, an extremely tight timeline and reasonably rigid governance frameworks. We have six years to complete these dual series, including the authorship of one of the volumes. My authors will each have five years to finish their respective volumes. This is a great deal tighter than any Official History project to date. It is a tough ask. Yet funding allows for each author to be assigned a full-time research assistant. In terms of project management support, I have also employed a full-time project administrator/support officer. I am sure previous official historians are staggered by the staff and funds at my disposal, but I am sure they are equally staggered by the expectations of delivery. This is a different project from those that preceded it.

Perhaps another indication of the differences the project faces, labouring under considerable delivery expectations, are the administrative structures that surround it. The very first 'committee' established by me was the Official History Consultation Group. I raised this group for the sole purpose of providing expert external and scholarly advice on issues related to the Official History project, as they arose. The first task of this committee, when it met, was to examine the scope and volume structure of the official histories series as was approved in mid-2015 (largely unchanged from Professor Horner's earlier studies). The proposed volume structure was a single volume on East Timor, two volumes on Iraq and four on Afghanistan. The Consultation Group was unanimous in its conclusions that this was perhaps not the best spread of volumes and recommended changes. After all, as I mentioned earlier, this structure was a function of the long, complex process undertaken to get the Official History project approved. The question of the inclusion of East Timor in this series had been particularly vexed, and only agreed upon after approval was given to address both Iraq and Afghanistan. That is, a six-volume study of the Middle East was envisaged before the question of East Timor was decided. East Timor was subsequently 'added' to the project as a pseudo-independent volume. At no time was the original scope of the Official History project the product of considered analysis or calculations of all three conflicts in a seven-volume, 'dual' series.

In this light, the Consultation Group recommended not one but two volumes for East Timor, a single volume for Iraq (which might need to spit into two in the future) and three for Afghanistan. A chronological approach was to be maintained. No stand-alone thematic volumes concerning single-service activities, or activities at the political and strategic level, were considered appropriate. You might have noticed a mathematical mismatch here in that this totals six volumes, not the seven originally approved. The recommendation to reduce the series from seven to six volumes was made on scholarly and historical grounds. Yet I am not shy to admit that it also resulted in close to $1 million in salary savings that I knew, even then, would be required elsewhere. These recommendations were taken to the Memorial's senior management group, which approved them without question or complaint. The Memorial Council and the Department of Veterans' Affairs were informed of the outcome. The ease of passage of my recommendations in this regard gave me pause, and a sigh of relief. This was the type of support and the relationship between the project and its host institution that would allow us to succeed.

The second committee I raised is the Official History Records Access Steering Group. The purpose of this group is to act as an SES-level coordination body, above the 'operational' level of interaction between the project and select government departments, including Foreign Affairs and Trade, Prime Minister and Cabinet, Defence and the AFP. Other relevant agencies, particularly those with an intelligence and security bent, have requested direct and singular access to the project via the Official Historian and are not represented in this committee. More specifically, the steering committee will help identify the most appropriate methods by which necessary files and data can be made available, facilitate the flow of records into the project, and maintain protocols and pathways for project and external agency staff to work together. Last, it will act as a point of conflict resolution, to identify and resolve the difficulties that might arise with regard to the provision of appropriate and timely records to the Official History project.

Records

A further indicator that this Official History project cannot and will not be a mirror image of past experience is that the nature of records and proximity to the conflicts under examination. I anticipate, in general and philosophical terms, that research data behind the volumes will come in two types, requiring two distinct historical methodologies. The first will be oral sources. A significant benefit of conducting this project so close to the conclusions of the operations under scrutiny is the wholesale availability of veterans. Acknowledging the perpetual challenges of oral sources, the nuances, explanations and 'stories' behind events will not appear on a documentary record. The gap will be covered by a comprehensive interviewing program.

Not surprisingly, the second source of data for this project will come from written, visual and hardcopy documentary sources in a range of formats—from Cabinet papers to emails. These will be sources primarily from uniformed and civilian Defence (including organisations like the Defence Intelligence Organisation and the Australian Signals Directorate), but, given the nature of these conflicts, important contributions will be required from those other agencies represented on the Records Access Steering Committee—DFAT, PM&C and the AFP—as well as the Office of National Assessments, the United Nations, the International Committee of the Red Cross and so forth. Much Defence data exists on the 'Objective' records management system and is, more or less, searchable. In addition to Objective-accessioned material, other data, particularly from the earlier period (1999–2002), resides in more traditional repositories including the Army History Unit, Sea Power Centre – Australia, Office of Air Force History, various Defence headquarters, Defence Archives (Queanbeyan, Lidcombe and so on).

The procedure by which the project will access this type of information—across all relevant government agencies, including Defence—has been settled upon by the Records Access Steering Group. First, the project will develop 'requests for file lists' (or RFFs) by volume (which equates to by theatre and time period). That is an initial batch of six RFFs will be written by the project. These RFFs will indicate the types and nature of data sought by the project and, in the case of Defence, where the project thinks such information might have been generated or held. Next, the project will submit RFFs to relevant agencies through their representatives on the

Records Access Steering Group. On receipt of the project RFF, agencies will conduct internal record searches and prepare file lists, which will then be sent to the Official Historian for internal project distribution. For Defence, this will require collating file lists from multiple headquarters, commands and archives. Project authors will examine these lists, and determine a subset of files it wishes to view. This list will be returned to the relevant agency. On receipt of the returned file list, each agency will liaise directly with the project (through the Records Access Steering Group) to work out the details of access. In order to test the system described, an RFF based on the first East Timor (INTERFET) volume has recently been completed.

The final type of record relevant to the project is a large volume of data that has not been accessioned into Objective or Defence's legacy records management systems, nor catalogued into a physical collection within Defence, but rather data that sits unindexed and unaccessioned in a collection of hard drives returned from overseas, at Headquarters Joint Operations Command and other Defence repositories. This is a huge volume of data, appearing at upwards of 20 terabytes—literally millions of pages. These records are, at present, unsearchable and therefore of no use. However, Defence has initiated Project RORI; basically, a process to electronically 'ingest' these files, which stretch across the period from 1999 to the present, into Objective.

My philosophy

I think it appropriate to close with some comments on my personal outlook or philosophy as an Official Historian. I would begin by saying I suspect I differ very little from my predecessors in this regard. Official histories are, in many ways, a record of government actions and decisions based on government sources. They are a foundation and scaffold for future historians, and an accessible way for the public and the veteran community to gain insight into the operations and theatres under examination. This is particularly important today, given the serious disconnection between these 'wars' and the wider Australian public. I think it important too, given what I would describe as a significant mismatch between the public narrative of events in East Timor, Iraq and Afghanistan, and the true historical record. The perception of Australian activities and decision-making does not, in many ways, match wider understandings of those events. Here let me cast your minds back, for example, to the difficulties faced in gaining government approval for East Timor. There are reputations and legacies in play here that might not welcome a robust investigation and publication of the historical record. There are, possibly, institutional sensitivities at stake. There are also contemporary political and diplomatic considerations that might find a searching study of the recent past inconvenient. These are my challenges.

In response to problems of this type, let me offer a simple outlook that will certainly be captured in my brief to authors, and which represent a philosophical pillar of the project. We will not self-censor. We will include the good with the bad—frictions and mistakes are as valid a part of the historical record as triumphs. Successes in spite of institutional shortcomings enhance the legacy of those involved, not the reverse. We will write as we see it, and as the evidence trail indicates. If this outlook adds complications in future, then that will be dealt with then. The exception is, of course, security considerations. I have no problem with this at all. Others issues dressed up as security, however, might prove a different matter.

In terms of other aspects of Official History philosophy, one member of the author selection panel was inclined to ask potential candidates which of the past Official History series they would model their work most closely upon. It is a fair and interesting question. My answer would have been Gavin Long. The central reason here is that Long worked under the considerable weight of expectation set by Bean—so much so that his notebooks and correspondence abounds with efforts by actively serving officers to 'influence' him with an eye to how they might look in Bean 'mark two' series. Yet Long, particularly in *To Benghazi*, published in 1952, manages to my mind to weave in critiques and criticism where appropriate, without appearing cynical and within the context of what was expected of him. I have always appreciated this approach—a type of bravery in the context of his time. The only problem here is, perhaps, his over-subtlety. One needs to be aware of the problems to glean the full meaning of Long's tangential references. Most, I think, would have been lost on the wider public. To those within the tent, however, they would have stood out markedly. Given the framework, era and expectations he worked under, Long could never have been more explicit. I would hope to follow a similar line—with the caveat that with changing times and public expectations I need be much less discrete.

Yet Long had his faults—or, more accurately, he made his concessions and compromises. Again, to use the example of *To Benghazi*, in an otherwise comprehensive and excellent account, and admittedly with the multifaceted pressures incumbent upon him, Long perpetuated many of the misguided wartime interpretations of events in North Africa. Interestingly, somewhat akin to Bean, he later conceded that the 'one objective of the Australian war histories is frankly a nationalistic one—to contribute to the statement of a national tradition'.[3] Although far less interested than his predecessor in glorifying the ideal and achievement of the individual Australian soldier, Long nonetheless mirrored Bean's stressing of the primacy of Australian infantrymen on the battlefield. His conclusions are seriously undermined by a determination not to break the Anzac tradition of making Australian infantry, equipped with the individual and collective tools of inherited national character, the key determinant of victory. Long was unequivocal that the 'decisive work' in North Africa 'was done by ingenious and resolute foot soldiers'—making light of the all-important British logistics, gunners, machine-gunners and tank crews.[4] Well aware that at the time of writing there were still sufficient survivors left to challenge this rather ahistorical argument, Long chose to land the first blow, careful to make use of a colourful and obscuring analogy: 'To ascribe the success either to tanks as the overwhelming arm (as some writers have done), or to the artillery', says Long, 'is to present Hamlet without the Prince'—poetic nonsense, I am afraid.[5]

It is easy, however, to point fingers, and I admit freely and openly that the blow-torch has yet to be applied to me or my project. But at this early stage I chose not to follow this path. My aim is not a 'nationalistic' one—it is not celebratory or commemorative. It is historical, purely and simply. The day the project fails to engage with difficult and sensitive issues in a forthright manner is the day credibility is lost. There are simply

---

[3] Originally quoted by A.G. Austin in his review of D. Dexter, *The New Guinea Offensives*, Australian War Memorial, Canberra, 1961, in *Historical Studies*, vol. 10, no. 39, 1962, pp. 392–3. See also J. Ross, *The Myth of the Digger*, Hale & Iremonger, Sydney, 1985, p. 117; K.S. Inglis, 'The Anzac tradition', *Meanjin Quarterly*, vol. 24, no. 1, 1965, p. 32.
[4] G. Long, *Australia in the War of 1939–1945*, vol. 1: *To Benghazi*, Australian War Memorial, Canberra, 1952, p. 205; F. Berryman, 'The Battle of Bardia: The AIF's First Battle in World War II', Directorate of Military Training, AHQ, Papers of Lieutenant-General Sir Frank Berryman, AWM PR 84/370.
[5] Long, *To Benghazi*, p. 205.

too many veterans who know better—and that is not my style in any case. Yet I say this now, when philosophies are cheap and words simple to cast … ask me again in six years time.

All of which brings me back to the question at the heart of the conference that led to the production of this book. That is, does Bean loom large for me and the most recent Official History series, or is he withdrawing into the shadows? Like any good historian, let me give an annoyingly qualified answer. As I have alluded to throughout this talk, my project and Bean's epic undertaking share little common ground in terms of process, context and the mechanics of researching and writing. In this regard, Bean feels of little use to me. He has little to tell. Even in terms of audience, times have changed dramatically since Bean's volumes were published. I feel the educated public and veteran community is more cynical, for example—in positive and negative ways. They are perhaps more willing to accept and digest criticisms of Defence and government decisions and actions than the past. I am in this regard perhaps freer to tell the blunt truth than Bean (or Long) would have been. On the other hand, there will be a portion of our readership so enamoured of the Bean-inspired connection between military achievement and national identity as to reject some of our more difficult findings and conclusions out of hand. Where Bean does perch on my shoulder, however, is less connected to the conduct of my project than to the weight of expectation I believe I place on myself. Bean made the conception of what an Official History is in Australia, and what it represents. It is that legacy I feel above all.

20

Final reflections

John Blaxland

Niche Wars sets out to help provide some meaning to an otherwise hard to explain, let alone understand, series of choices made by successive Australian governments from 2001 to 2014. A string of decisions was made that saw Australian forces deploy carefully calibrated contributions to various places across the Middle East, particularly in Afghanistan and Iraq, but also in neighbouring countries. The book's authors have made contributions spanning Australia's commitment of troops to Afghanistan after the 9/11 attacks in the United States through the decision to support the US invasion of Iraq and then dealing with the consequences of that decision both in Iraq and back in Afghanistan.

Building on contributions made at the 'War in the Sandpit' conference on Australia's involvement in the wars in Afghanistan and Iraq, the book outlines a wide range of observations and potential lessons for Australia as it considers the utility of force and the pitfalls of short-term thinking in the pursuit of its national interests.

The book helps us to understand the choices made as well as the incomplete and, at times, incorrect information at hand that led to certain fateful decisions. While not addressing the Brereton Report of November 2020[1] in any detail as it was released on the eve of publication, this book helps to explain some of the context of the gravely flawed decisions that

---

1   Inspector-General of the Australian Defence Force, *Afghanistan Inquiry Report* ('the Brereton Report'), afghanistaninquiry.defence.gov.au/sites/default/files/2020-11/IGADF-Afghanistan-Inquiry-Public-Release-Version.pdf (retrieved 24 November 2020).

led to the atrocities reported upon by Brereton—ones that have brought shame on the ADF, the Australian Army and the special forces. It also is intended to help consider the implications arising from the recent past for contingencies that might arise in future. The benefit lies in the broad range of views, including those of politicians, senior commanders, government advisers, international counterparts, diplomatic and aid agency representatives, operational-level decision-makers, contingent commanders, and men and women of the Army, Navy and Air Force.

Niche Wars serves an important purpose: one that reflects on the mission of the Strategic & Defence Studies Centre (SDSC) at The Australian National University, to understand Australian military operations, Australian Defence policy and security affairs of the Asia Pacific, or Indo-Pacific, writ large. This is all within the context of the field of strategic studies that was defined, in Australia's case, by SDSC's founder, Professor Tom Millar and his successors as head of SDSC, Robert O'Neill, Desmond Ball, Paul Dibb, Hugh White, Brendan Taylor, myself and now Brendan Sargeant.

SDSC teaches three degree programs: a Bachelor of International Security Studies and a Master of Strategic Studies at the Acton campus, and the Military and Defence Studies Program, as part of the master's degree taught by SDSC, at the Australian Command and Staff College in the Canberra suburb of Weston. As noted in the introduction, a range of autobiographical and biographical accounts of certain aspects of the wars in Iraq and Afghanistan have already been written. Yet there remained a need for a book that would be useful for courses taught on these degree programs about Australia's experience—one written from the point of view of the practitioners, the crafters and implementers of Australian defence policy.

The inspiration for this book came from a discussion between myself and Colonel Marcus Fielding—the President of Military History and Heritage Victoria (MHHV)—himself the author of *Red Zone Baghdad*, a book written as a reflection on his experiences on deployment to Iraq in 2008 and 2009. As Fielding observed in the foreword to this book, we became fast friends working together in the lead-up to and conduct of the deployment of the International Force East Timor (INTERFET) sent in response to the crisis in East Timor following the vote over autonomy that led to East Timor's independence. Our first collaborative work after I joined academia was the 2014 conference held to mark the fifteenth

20. FINAL REFLECTIONS

anniversary of the intervention in East Timor. That resulted in *East Timor Intervention: A Retrospective on INTERFET*, published by Melbourne University Press in 2015.

I note that the collaboration between MHHV and SDSC goes back to the conference arranged by MHHV and SDSC that led to *Australia 1942: In the Shadow of War*, edited by Peter Dean and published by Cambridge University Press in 2012. Building on this experience, the 'War in the Sandpit' conference drew inspiration from this model and has delivered the array of speakers and authors now assembled in this book.

The key questions addressed in the chapters of this book are worth revisiting at this juncture: what happened? How well did Australians understand the nature of the fight in which they were becoming involved? Were there other viable approaches to the options taken along the way? Did Australia's contribution add value to the coalitions? And what lessons can be learned for the future? The aim of the conference and this book has been to distil some key observations and lessons for the Australian Defence Force and Australia more widely, as it ponders its future circumstances. So how well did we do in answering these questions?

In terms of what happened, this book did not set out to offer a comprehensive review of every force contribution over the duration. That is for the official historians to grapple with. Instead, selected contributions are made by those who were directly involved in decision-making or in the conduct of operations. Most of the contributors spoke directly at the conference, although we invited some to contribute afterwards. Part 1, on the selection on policy and strategy, covered the contributions from Robert Hill, Ric Smith and Chris Barrie. Part 2, concerning the experience on operations in and around Iraq and Afghanistan, concerned the contributions from Dan McDaniel, Chris Westwood, Anthony Rawlins, Peter Jones and Jim Molan. Part 3, on joint forces, enablers and partners, is covered by the chapters from Michael Crane, Mick Lehmann, Elizabeth Boulton, Alan Ryan, Col Speedie and Steve Mullins, David Savage and Karen Middleton. The fourth and final part covers the lessons and legacies, with chapters from William Maley, Dan Marston, Peter Leahy, Craig Stockings and John Blaxland. In fact, virtually every chapter has lessons identified.

At this juncture, it is worthwhile recapping the key lessons identified in the preceding chapters. The main points identified for parts 1 to 3 of the book are as outlined in the introduction, but the key lessons from Part 4 are worth covering in additional detail here.

Maley listed seven lessons for military deployments. First, military deployments always need to be linked to a political strategy. Second, it is not possible to stabilise a disrupted state such as Afghanistan on a province-by-province basis. Third, aid can act as a fuel for conflict rather than function as a flame retardant. Fourth, stability can prove remarkably tenuous. Fifth, in the long run, reliance on 'strongmen' tends to be at the expense of sustainable institutional development. Sixth, time is the ultimate security commodity, and it is often in short supply in undertakings of this kind. Seventh, treating assistance as a means to some other end runs the risk of devaluing the people affected.

Looking at the US and British experience in Iraq and Afghanistan from 2001 to 2004, Dan Marston observed the following lessons were identified, if not learned. First, there was a lack of clear and realistic strategic debates for use of force by both countries. Second, there were breakdowns in civilian–military relations in both countries. Third, there were breakdowns in trust between the two key allies, especially in Iraq. Fourth, there was a tactical-level reform on the battlefield by both the United States and United Kingdom; however, winning tactically on the battlefield does not equate to strategic victory. Fifth, there were problems created by ignoring the 'mosaic of the battlefield' and attempting to apply simplistic narratives and solutions to complex scenarios.

Peter Leahy draws a list of nine lessons and legacies from Australia's experience in Afghanistan and Iraq. First, the ADF should be ready for the most likely conflict. Second, have a strategy. Third, you cannot go to war quickly without introducing risk. Fourth, you cannot make a flexible and versatile force out of nothing. Fifth, equipping the force is difficult, expensive and time-consuming. Sixth, doctrine is important. Seventh, when designing the force, a clear mission is essential. Eighth, 'whole of government' should mean whole of government; and ninth, a combined arms approach is essential. In compiling his nine points, Leahy acknowledges the significance of the work of Dr Albert Palazzo, who wrote the redacted report on the Australian Army's experience in the Iraq War, made public through the revelations of Fairfax journalist David Wroe.[2]

He also suggests that there are no clear legacies from these conflicts, but there are three candidates. First, he calls for a parliamentary convention to debate and approve the commitment of ADF elements to conflict. Second, he argues that such commitments should not be based solely or even primarily on protecting the Australian–US alliance but on clearly articulated Australian national interests. Third, he calls for an obligation to look after the wounded and a dedication to making them the best reintegrated generation of soldiers in the nation's history. To Leahy, and many others, the obligation to learn from the effort and sacrifice of those soldiers involved in Afghanistan and Iraq is a sacred one that must be honoured.

In terms of how well understood was the nature of the fight in which we were becoming involved, this book indicates that Australia had a lot to learn. At each critical juncture, decisions were made that, even without the benefit of hindsight, could have been made slightly if not significantly differently. No one knows the future, and the decisions made at any point in time cannot easily be judged fairly looking back. But some observations can be made about the importance of thinking through the longer-term ramifications of decisions, thinking through the strategy; that is, the ways, the means and, importantly, the ends of a plan; to make sure it is as carefully considered as any decision can be, informed by the past and the present.

One of the striking features of the experience of Australia's wars in Afghanistan and Iraq, as outlined in these pages, is how each of the decision points along the way seems to have been reached and acted on, mindful of one underlying long-term concern—namely, maintenance and support of the US alliance. Yet this was undertaken principally with short-term priorities and concerns in mind. It was these short-term factors that drove the tangible contributions the government decided to offer at each juncture.

---

2 Palazzo, *The Australian Army and the War in Iraq 2002–2010*.

The rotation of naval forces in the Gulf, for instance, was contingent on US priorities and the contribution calibrated to what Australia could sustain without a significant increase in the size of the fleet. Essentially, Australia maintained a peacetime naval force structure, despite the rhetoric of an existential global so-called War on Terror. Similarly, the RAAF tailored contributions to fit in with routine training and operational priorities. Over time, of course, the cumulative effects of such decisions meant that Australia's contributions were hard to explain in other than quite woolly terms.

Moving to land forces, the Australian Government envisaged the contribution of the special forces in October 2001 as a one-off and short-term contribution. Subsequent land force contributions to the war in Iraq also were carefully contained to exclude post-conflict, or so-called Phase 4, operations to aid in the reconstruction of post-invasion Iraq. Then again, the return of special and conventional land forces to Afghanistan was with relatively short-term priorities in mind. As one quite senior officer cynically confided in 2006 when Australia was redeploying land forces to Afghanistan, the mission was accomplished: Australia had managed to get the Dutch into Uruzgan Province and Australia into NATO. This betrayed a remarkably superficial understanding of what it means to commit Australian young men and women into probable combat. It also reflects the ongoing lack of planning beyond the horizon, with the longer term ramifications in mind.

Little did planners seem to realise that a rotation of land forces, centred on an engineer regiment, the First Reconstruction Task Force (RTF1), would make ensuing demands on Australian forces that successive Australian governments simply were not prepared to meet. Indeed, the deployment of RTF1 came at a time when a crisis in East Timor stretched the ADF, and particularly its land forces, to the edge. As I pointed out in *The Australian Army from Whitlam to Howard*, the unprecedented operational tempo saw five of the six Regular Army commanding officers of the infantry battalions in the Royal Australian Regiment deployed on operations concurrently.[3] This was not sustainable without either capping Australia's involvement to carefully calibrated niche contributions or significantly expanding the force.

---

3   Blaxland, *The Australian Army from Whitlam to Howard*, p. 317.

A similar point again can be made about Australia's contribution to Iraq from 2005 onwards. As the authors of several chapters have pointed out, Australia's contribution to the Al Muthanna Task Group (AMTG) and the subsequent Overwatch Battle Group (West) (OBG(W)) was particularly constrained, to the point where British and US allies questioned the reliability, if not fidelity, of their Australian partners. Arguably, it might have been better to stay away than to make such a token force contribution in southern Iraq.

This pointed to the enduring peacetime mindset that saw no great urgency in expanding the land force in anything remotely akin to the expansion of forces during the Second World War (with its equivalent in terms of land forces of 14 divisions), let alone the period of Confrontation and the Vietnam War.

The Vietnam War parallel is particularly instructive, for it is here that the Australian Army, with its nine infantry battalions and associated arms and services that made up the brigade-sized 1st Australian Task Force, managed to maintain a rotation of forces through Phuoc Tuy Province in South Vietnam from 1965 to 1972. Eager to avoid the heightened domestic political controversy associated with the expanded force enabled by conscription in the 1960s, the Australian Government did not seriously consider a significant force expansion that might have enabled a more robust and holistic force contribution. That was understandable on one level, although arguably an expansion of the force could have been achieved without conscription simply by better and more targeted advertising and improved conditions of service. Instead, repeated rotations placed an unreasonable strain, particularly on the special forces, to the point where their practices led to controversy and even disrepute.

The Vietnam parallel is also instructive in terms of thinking through what matters most to Australia. Beyond seeking to be seen as supportive of the US alliance, Australia's Defence White Paper of 2016 lists three strategic priorities: a secure and resilient Australia, with secure northern approaches and proximate sea lines of communication; a secure nearer region, encompassing maritime South-East Asia and South Pacific; and a stable Indo-Pacific region and a rules-based global order.[4] Yet, ironically, Australia's carefully calibrated and constrained force contribution to operations in Afghanistan and Iraq reveals a certain dissonance here. The

---

4   Department of Defence, *2016 Defence White Paper*, Canberra, p. 33.

contrast with Australia's contribution to the East Timor intervention in 1999 is noteworthy. For that operation, Australia was prepared to be the lead nation, accept hundreds of casualties, if needs be, and assume the leadership role to ensure that the 22-nation coalition was successful in its mission. By 2020, Australian defence policy belatedly placed greater emphasis on security priorities closer to home in the Indo-Pacific region.[5]

In contrast, the approach taken in Afghanistan and Iraq stands in marked contrast. Despite having a significant stake in Uruzgan, Australia was deeply reluctant to offer to lead the provincial efforts on behalf of the coalition. Similarly, Australia was reluctant to stay for Phase 4, stabilisation operations, after the initial apparent victory in Iraq in 2003, or to expand the remit of its forces in southern Iraq when it did reluctantly redeploy there after repeated appeals from US and British allies from 2005 onwards.

In addition, there was little consideration of how to make a more profound and long-lasting contribution in a province like Uruzgan. This was in part because there was little if any appetite for taking responsibility for the province and driving the agenda there, with the long term in mind. In part this was driven by the lack of a coherent and sustained strategy for effective governance that dealt with the profound levels of corruption in Afghanistan. Absent this kind of strategic vision from the United States and other coalition partners, let alone signs of competent and effective governance emanating from the capital Kabul, there was little appetite for Australia to allow itself to be overexposed by its military contributions there. It bears repeating the point made by one senior officer commenting in mid-2006, the 'mission's accomplished' already. Australia had managed to 'get the Dutch into Uruzgan and us into NATO'.[6] But this cynical calculus simply was not enough to justify the blood and treasure spent in the dust of Uruzgan. Critics might say that this is unfair as many good people tried very hard, over successive rotations, to make a real difference in Uruzgan. That is true. The point, though, is not to lay blame at the feet of the practitioners who did their best in difficult circumstances. Instead, it is to question the lack of thought-through strategy for what the ADF would do there and what effect it would have on those who served there, let alone what long-term effects their actions would generate in country. For this, the senior-most military leadership and their political masters

---

5   Department of Defence, *2020 Defence Strategic Update*, Canberra, 2020.
6   Personal recollection of author.

must share responsibility: the military for not offering more frank, fearless and far-sighted advice, and politicians for not thinking beyond the prism of their own domestic political cycles.

As Craig Stockings has pointed out, the Official History of Australia's involvement in Iraq and Afghanistan is in train, but we might have to wait a while longer before those volumes are published. This work does not seek to cover this gap, but it does include an assembly of some important voices; some with unique vantage points as actual eyewitnesses, and others who have deep scholarly expertise and capacity to make judgements. This volume is not a formal history, so no attempt has been made to present the material chronologically. What this means is that the reader has been able to take a more eclectic route to understanding Australia's niche wars in Afghanistan and Iraq. After all, such thematic treatments are just as valid, and can be just as educative as formal histories.

There is merit for Defence to have external agencies undertake conferences of this type as part of the organisational learning process or as lead-in activity to the production of official histories. Indeed, many of the Official History authors attended the conference and expressed an appreciation of the information presented and the discussions that followed.

For Australia, the contributions made to the wars in Afghanistan and Iraq were deliberately constrained ones. Lessons were learned, experience was gained, capabilities were enhanced and alliance ties were burnished, but the experience was deliberately confined to the theatre of operations. Deployed forces put their heart and soul into their work. Yet there was a genuine reluctance in Canberra to embrace wholeheartedly the demands of the operational areas where Australian troops deployed. As a result, the mission often seemed opaque, the command authority constrained and the story allowed to be told through the media tightly managed. This too-clever-by-half strategy set the scene for some of the most shameful conduct of Australia's military history whereby unlawful killings came to be accepted in certain quarters as part of the norm. Looking back, in the hearts of veterans, there is a palpable sense of disappointment, even shame. Perhaps, as it considers future contingencies, where more than niche contributions might be required, Australia can learn from this experience—that it should commit troops when it has formulated clear-eyed strategic goals that we all can live with.

Appendix 1: Australian units and formations deployed to Afghanistan and the Middle East, 2001–14

NICHE WARS

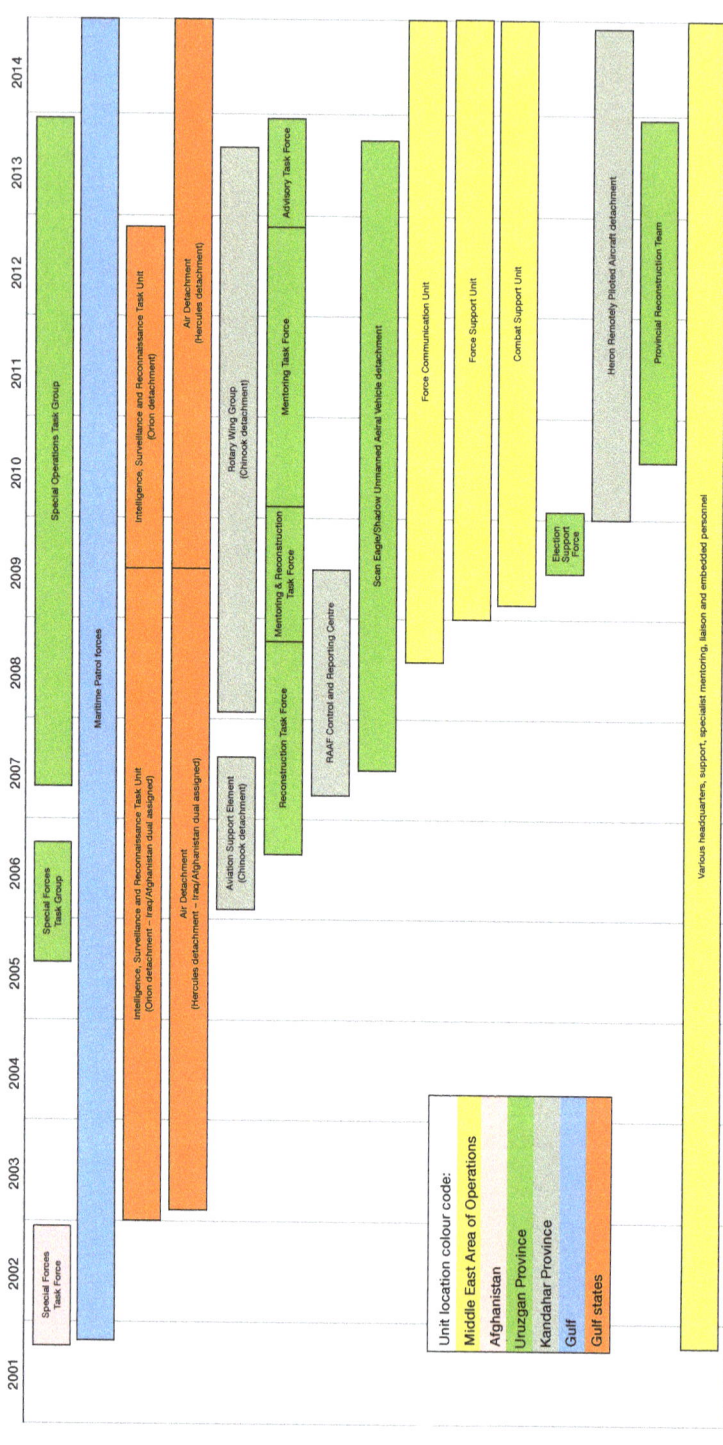

Appendix 2: Chronology: Australia's military involvement in Afghanistan, 2001–present

The following timeline has been adapted from the timeline produced by the Parliamentary Library.[1]

Milestones	Details
14 September 2001	Prime Minister John Howard announced that the government was invoking Article IV of the ANZUS Treaty in response to the terrorist attacks against the United States.
4 October 2001	The government directed the Chief of the Defence Force to have a range of military assets, including special forces, available to support the US under the ANZUS Treaty.
22 October 2001	The first contingent of the Special Forces Task Group was officially farewelled in Perth as it departed to assist the US-led International Coalition Against Terrorism.
25 October 2001	The government announced the deployment of Royal Australian Navy, Army and Air Force assets and personnel in support of coalition operations. The Army's 16th Air Defence Regiment (16AD Regt) was officially farewelled from Adelaide to support the Australian maritime element in the war against terrorism.

---

1 Australian Parliamentary Library, 'Australia's military involvement in Afghanistan since 2001: A chronology', www.aph.gov.au/About_Parliament/Parliamentary_Departments/Parliamentary_Library/pubs/BN/1011/MilitaryInvolvementAfghanistan (retrieved 21 January 2019).

9 November 2001	A contingent of four F/A-18 Hornets was officially farewelled from RAAF Base Williamtown as part of Australia's contribution to the fight against terrorism. Although it was not disclosed at that time, the detachment was based at Diego Garcia.
27 November 2001	The remaining soldiers from the Special Forces Task Group, making a total of 150 personnel, departed Perth to assist the coalition in Afghanistan.
3 December 2001	The Australian Defence Force (ADF) advance party arrived in Afghanistan and was operating under Australian command in theatre.
5 December 2001	Additional ADF personnel arrived in Afghanistan to assist the advance party.
15 January 2002	Minister for Defence Robert Hill confirmed that around 150 special forces personnel were in Afghanistan.
24 January 2002	The Australian Government announced that Brigadier Gary Bornholt would replace Brigadier Ken Gillespie (later Chief of Army) as Australian Force Commander of Australia's contribution to the coalition in March 2002.
February 2002	The second contingent of approximately 80 personnel, forming the Hornet detachment, was officially farewelled for operations in support of the coalition in mid-February.
17 February 2002	The first contingent of Hornet personnel was officially welcomed home to Williamtown following a three-and-a-half-month deployment.
1–17 March 2002	Australian Special Forces Task Group soldiers took part in Operation ANACONDA involving US, Afghan and coalition forces.
15 March 2002	The first contingent of B-707 Tanker Transport aircraft, aircrew and support personnel from RAAF 84 Wing prepared to depart for Manas Air Base, Kyrgyzstan. The aircraft would provide air-to-air refuelling support for operations in Afghanistan.
28 March 2002	The second contingent of the Special Forces Task Group was officially farewelled in Perth.

APPENDIX 2

March–April 2002	On 28 March, the first B-707 aircraft arrived at Manas, and was shortly followed by a second RAAF tanker. A small team of RAAF mechanics and technicians and a team of logistics experts were deployed as part of the detachment. After six months in theatre, the first contingent of the Special Forces Task Group in Afghanistan was replaced by the second contingent.
3 April 2002	The first contingent of the Special Forces Task Group was officially welcomed home from Afghanistan at Campbell Barracks, Swanbourne, WA, following its six-month deployment. One member was presented with the Distinguished Service Cross.
19 April 2002	Australia's continued military commitment to the war against terrorism was assured by the Minister for Defence, Robert Hill.
7 May 2002	It was announced that the Hornet detachment deployed to Diego Garcia had completed its mission and would return to Australia. This was the second air combat contingent under Operation SLIPPER, and it was not replaced.
16 June 2002	Minister for Defence Robert Hill announced: '[A] third rotation of Special Forces Task Group soldiers will deploy to Afghanistan in August as part of Australia's ongoing contribution to the international coalition against terrorism.' The authorised strength of special forces personnel operating in Afghanistan at that time was 150.
18 June 2002	A second B-707 contingent was officially farewelled from RAAF Base Richmond, NSW, to support air-to-air refuelling operations in Afghanistan from neighbouring Kyrgyzstan.
3 July 2002	The first contingent of B-707 aircrew and support personnel officially returned to Richmond following a three-and-a-half-month deployment in support of the coalition.
22 July 2002	ADF personnel deployed to Afghanistan, Kyrgyzstan and the Gulf in support of coalition operations had reached around 850 to 1,300.

30 August 2002	Six months after departing Australia, the second contingent of the Special Forces Task Group was officially welcomed home from Afghanistan at Campbell Barracks.
29 September 2002	Approximately 80 RAAF personnel returned to Richmond following a three-and-a-half-month deployment to Kyrgyzstan. This was the final deployment of the RAAF's B-707 aircraft to Kyrgyzstan as the fleet of B-707s were progressively retired from service. Responsibility for air-to-air refuelling operations was transferred to Australia's European coalition partners. The RAAF prepared to deploy two AP-3C Orion aircraft for maritime operations in the Gulf.
20 November 2002	As the focus of coalition operations in Afghanistan moved towards reconstruction efforts, the government announced: '[The] third rotation to Afghanistan will complete Australia's special forces contribution. The SASR Task Group will begin withdrawing from Afghanistan in late November …'. The minister noted that operational tasking for Australia's special forces elements in Afghanistan was insufficient to justify their continued deployment.
17 December 2002	The third contingent of the Special Forces Task Group officially returned to Perth. On their return, the Meritorious Unit Citation was awarded to the SAS Regiment.
21 February 2003	By February 2003, approximately 2,000 ADF personnel were reportedly involved in two operations in the Middle East: Operations SLIPPER and BASTILLE (the latter involved the forward deployment of ADF elements to the Middle East). Australia's military commitment in the Middle East at that time comprised an Australian command team 'in tactical control of the multinational interception force in the Persian Gulf' to support the enforcement of UN sanctions against Iraq. Australia maintained tactical control of six coalition vessels, including HMA Ships *Anzac*, *Darwin* and *Kanimbla*. In addition, a RAAF Orion detachment had been deployed to the Middle East in January 2003 and continued to conduct maritime patrols in the Gulf.

APPENDIX 2

18 April 2003	Following the withdrawal of special forces elements at the end of November 2002, it would appear that Australia's military contribution to Afghanistan had been reduced to an Army officer deployed to the United Nations Assistance Mission in Afghanistan under Operation PALATE.
November 2003	An Army engineering officer was deployed to Afghanistan to contribute to the coalition Mine Action Coordination Centre.
13 July 2005	The government announced Australia's renewed military commitment to Afghanistan with a deployment of 150 special forces personnel to conduct similar tasks undertaken during the 2001–02 deployment. The special forces deployment was approved for a 12-month period.
24 August 2005	The first contingent of the Special Forces Task Group was deployed to Afghanistan; the first since Australian forces withdrew in September 2002. The task group comprised approximately 190 personnel from the SAS Regiment, 4th Battalion Royal Australian Regiment, Incident Response Regiment and logistics support. The task group's mission was to conduct combat patrols in remote areas as well as reconnaissance and surveillance operations in collaboration with other contributing countries. The mission was scheduled to run until September 2006.
16 September 2005	The ADF flagged that a military provincial reconstruction team might be deployed to Afghanistan around mid-2006. It was also noted that Army mine clearance specialists had been deployed to Afghanistan since 2003 and continued to assist in the removal of unexploded ordnance under Operation SLIPPER. An Army officer role, deployed to the United Nations in Afghanistan under Operation PALATE, has also remained in place since 2003.

10 January 2006	The government announced that an Army CH-47 Chinook helicopter detachment would be deployed to Afghanistan in March 2006. The detachment was expected to remain in Afghanistan for the duration of the Special Forces Task Group deployment (until September 2006). However, should Australia deploy a reconstruction task force, the detachment's mission could be extended.
21 February 2006	The government announced that Australia would contribute a 200-strong reconstruction task force to Afghanistan for a period of two years.
25 February 2006	After returning to Australia from Afghanistan in January 2006, west coast–based Special Forces Task Group members were officially welcomed home. Two members of the SAS Regiment received the Medal for Gallantry. The second contingent of the Special Forces Task Group took over from the first contingent sometime in early 2006. The Special Forces Task Group mission was expected to remain in Afghanistan until September 2006.
4 March 2006	East coast–based Special Forces Task Group members were officially welcomed home from Afghanistan.
13 March 2006	Some 110 members of the 5th Aviation Regiment were deployed to Afghanistan with two Chinooks. The contingent was to provide heavy troop and medical evacuation airlift support to the 200-strong Special Forces Task Group already operating in Afghanistan.
8 May 2006	The first Australian reconstruction task force for Afghanistan, expected to comprise a 240-personnel deployment in July 2006, was announced. The Chinook helicopter mission was extended until April 2007 to support the insertion of the reconstruction force.
13 June 2006	The government announced that, from July 2006, the ADF would contribute a reconstruction task force to Uruzgan Province in Afghanistan. The first Reconstruction Task Force (RTF1) was expected to deploy in July 2006.

APPENDIX 2

25 July 2006	The first rotation of personnel from the Australian Army's Chinook detachment departed for Afghanistan. The Army helicopter commitment was scheduled to cease in July 2007.
9 August 2006	The government announced that an additional 150 personnel would deploy to reinforce RTF1 and provide increased protection. This would bring the total RTF commitment to 400 personnel.
23 August 2006	The RTF1 advance party departed for Afghanistan.
18 September 2006	Approximately 400 personnel forming RTF1 arrived in Afghanistan.
26 November 2006	East coast–based members of the 200-strong Special Forces Task Group were officially welcomed home in Sydney. Two members received gallantry awards (Star of Gallantry and the Medal for Gallantry), and a Unit Citation for Gallantry was awarded to combat elements of the task group. The task group as a whole received the Meritorious Unit Citation. The Special Forces Task Group was deployed for a period of 12 months and conducted three rotations (each approximately four months in duration).
2 December 2006	West coast–based members from the Special Forces Task Group were officially welcomed home. Four members received gallantry awards and a unit citation for gallantry was awarded to combat elements of the task group. As a whole, the task group received the Meritorious Unit Citation.
22 February 2007	Minister for Defence Brendan Nelson noted that the Special Forces Task Group had returned to Australia in September 2006. Nelson also noted that Australia's military commitment to Afghanistan in February 2007 was approximately 400 personnel, including trade, engineer and infantry personnel.
8 April 2007	Members from the 5th Aviation Regiment, comprising 110 Australian Army personnel and two Chinooks, returned to Australia following their deployment to Afghanistan.

10 April 2007	Prime Minister John Howard announced that another Special Operations Task Group of around 300 personnel were to deploy to Uruzgan, this time for a two-year mission. The role of the Reconstruction Task Force Protection Company Group, around 120 personnel, was extended until August 2008. Seventy-five RAAF personnel were to deploy to Kandahar airfield to provide an air surveillance radar capability and assume control of a portion of Afghan operational air space from mid-2007. The overall military commitment to Afghanistan was expected to reach 950 personnel by mid-2007, eventually peaking at around 1,000 personnel in mid-2008.
15 May 2007	Special Operations Task Force deployed to Afghanistan in support of the International Security Assistance Force (ISAF) operations in Uruzgan. The task force was made up of personnel from the SAS Regiment, 4th Battalion, Royal Australian Regiment (Commando), Incident Response Regiment and logistics support.
29 May 2007	The main RAAF contingent, including members from Darwin-based 114 Mobile Control and Reporting Unit and the RAAF's Combat Support Group, was farewelled from Darwin shortly after a small advance party from RAAF 41 Wing (Williamtown) had arrived in Afghanistan.
3 September 2007	The government announced the addition of a 10-member mortar section, to support RTF operations in Afghanistan. Personnel were to be drawn from the 2nd Battalion, Royal Australian Regiment.
4 October 2007	By October 2007, approximately 900 ADF personnel had been deployed to Afghanistan (predominantly in Uruzgan and Kandahar), and another 110 were expected to deploy in February 2008 with two Chinooks.
8 February 2008	Two of the 5th Aviation Regiment's recently upgraded Chinooks were deployed to Afghanistan.

APPENDIX 2

19 February 2008	Minister for Defence Joel Fitzgibbon announced that the government would maintain its current commitment in Afghanistan but would place a new emphasis on training Afghan National Army members. Fitzgibbon announced that an Operational Mentoring and Liaison Team (OMLT) would soon be embedded within an Afghan army battalion (known as a *kandak*).
20 February 2008	During the February 2008 Senate Additional Estimates hearing, the Chief of the Defence Force, Air Chief Marshal Angus Houston, noted that Australia's contribution to Operation SLIPPER included, at that time:

> In addition, Operation SLIPPER receives support from the RAAF AP-3C aircraft and the C-130 Hercules aircraft which are dual assigned to both Operation SLIPPER and Operation CATALYST. This month we also redeployed two CH-47 Chinook medium-lift helicopters with associated flight crew and support staff, which totals 93 personnel.
>
> … The government yesterday announced that further adjustment to the reconstruction task force is warranted to increase emphasis on the training of Afghani security forces. The provision of an operational mentoring and liaison team, or OMLT, will see us developing and mentoring an Afghan *kandak*, or infantry battalion. This adjustment will be achieved within our existing force capability; that is, an authorised establishment of 1,078.

13 March 2008	Fifteen soldiers from Darwin's 8/12 Medium Regiment, who spent six months in the United Kingdom as part of a bilateral program, were deployed in support of UK operations in Helmand Province.
April–May 2008	In April 2008, the third Reconstruction Task Force (RFT3) completed its six-month tour of Afghanistan and was replaced by RTF4, comprising 400 combat engineers, infantry, cavalry and support staff.

4 June 2008	Chief of Army Lieutenant General Peter Leahy announced that Army operational tours would be extended from six to eight months, beginning with the first Mentoring and Reconstruction Task Force (MRTF1), to be deployed to Afghanistan in October 2008.
29 June 2008	The Army's Chinook detachment was officially welcomed home after being replaced by elements from Townsville's 5th Aviation Regiment.
10 July 2008	RAAF personnel deployed to Afghanistan's Control and Reporting Centre in Kandahar for six months were officially welcomed home. The RAAF had provided personnel to this theatre of operations since April 2007. A third RAAF contingent had already deployed to Afghanistan, and a fourth contingent was commencing force preparation training.
15 July 2008	In his speech to the Brookings Institution, the Minister for Defence, Joel Fitzgibbon, summarised Australia's contribution and rationale for operations in Afghanistan:

> Australia's contribution in Afghanistan is a substantial one. It includes a Reconstruction Task Force of some 400 personnel, a Special Operations Task Group of around 300 special forces soldiers, an Air Force Control and Reporting Centre, a Rotary Wing Group, logistics support and a national Command Element. More than 1000 personnel in all. This makes us the ninth largest troop contributor and the largest non-NATO force in Afghanistan …

8 September 2008	Darwin-based troops from the Army's 1st Brigade (Light Armoured Brigade) deployed to Afghanistan as part of the MRTF1.
21 October 2008	The MRTF1 took over from RTF4 on 16 October 2008. In addition to reconstruction efforts in Uruzgan, the new rotation's role also included capacity-building and mentoring of the Afghan National Army. The RTF mission ran for more than two years with the first deployment commencing in August and September 2006. Four rotations took place during this time.

APPENDIX 2

23 October 2008	Members of the RTF4 were officially welcomed home following their six-month deployment in Afghanistan.
2 November 2008	Two Army Chinooks and 65 personnel were officially welcomed home following their eight-month deployment to Afghanistan. A third rotation was expected to deploy in February 2009 and begin flying operations in March.
16 January 2009	Trooper Mark Donaldson was awarded the Victoria Cross: 'For most conspicuous acts of gallantry in action in a circumstance of great peril in Afghanistan, as part of the Special Operations Task Group during Operation SLIPPER, Uruzgan, Afghanistan.'
23 January 2009	The first Force Support Unit (FSU-1) deployed to the Middle East Area of Operations (MEAO) to provide logistic support for all Australian military operations in the Middle East Area of Operations and MEAO Afghanistan.
29 April 2009	Prime Minister Kevin Rudd announced that Australia would increase its troop commitment in Afghanistan to 1,550 personnel. The increased troop level aimed to enhance the ADF's training mission so that the Afghan National Army could take responsibility for security in Uruzgan sooner. This announcement was the first statement made about Australia's future military drawdown. Some 120 additional personnel would be deployed as part of the Election Support Force.
5 May 2009	Australian Army officer Brigadier Damian Cantwell was appointed commander of the ISAF Election Task Force.
15 May 2009	Around 600 military personnel, predominantly from the 1st Battalion, Royal Australian Regiment, were deployed to Afghanistan as part of the second MRTF contingent.
9 July 2009	The RAAF's two-year mission commanding the Control and Reporting Centre at Kandahar Airfield was officially completed. The command role was transferred to the United States Air Force.
8 August 2009	Personnel from the MRTF1 were officially welcomed home to Australia after their eight-month deployment to Afghanistan.

12 August 2009	The contingent of 120 personnel, who had arrived in Afghanistan on 24 July 2009, commenced operations in support of Afghan national elections.
20 August 2009	Afghanistan's second presidential election was held, along with provincial council elections.
11 October 2009	Members of the RAAF's 41 Wing were officially welcomed home and acknowledged for completing the ADF's two-year commitment commanding the Control and Reporting Centre in Kandahar.
23 October 2009	The fourth Chinook detachment prepared to return home to Australia following their eight-month deployment to Afghanistan.
4 December 2009	The ADF's Force Communications Unit 3 (FCU3) was officially farewelled as part of Operation SLIPPER. FCU3 is a joint deployment with elements located in the MEAO and Afghanistan.
13 January 2010	Australia's first leased Heron Uninhabited Aerial Vehicle (UAV) commenced initial operations in Afghanistan. Five months previously, an Australian contingent of predominantly RAAF personnel had commenced working with the Canadian UAV detachment in Afghanistan to become familiar with the system.
20 January 2010	Members of the first Mentoring Task Force (MTF1) contingent, mostly made up from the Army's 7th Battalion, Royal Australian Regiment, deployed to Afghanistan at the same time as communication and logistic support elements were deployed to the MEAO. While the term 'reconstruction' has been removed from the title, MTF1 continues the same reconstruction activities that were previously conducted by MRTFs 1 and 2.
11 February 2010	Members of MRTF2 were officially welcomed home from Afghanistan following their eight-month deployment.
26 February 2010	Major General Ash Power was appointed the first Australian officer to serve as Senior Military Adviser to Afghanistan's Defence Minister, General Abdul Rahim Wardak.

APPENDIX 2

3 March 2010	MTF1 trains the Afghan National Army's 2nd and 4th Kandaks.
18 March 2010	The Minister for Defence, John Faulkner, announced that the personnel strength currently deployed to Afghanistan will remain at 1,550 for the year. The government announced that 10 personnel will be drawn from within Defence's embedded Afghanistan staff 'to develop a training concept for Afghanistan's Combat Arms Artillery School' located in Kandahar.
30 March 2010	The fifth helicopter detachment comprising two Chinooks commenced operations in Afghanistan and is expected to remain for eight months.
17 April 2010	The second contingent of the Second Force Support Unit returned to Australia from the MEAO and Afghanistan after being replaced by the Third Force Support Unit, which commenced operations on 11 April 2010.
31 May 2010	The ADF's mentoring role training elements of the Afghan military was expanded when MTF1 assumed responsibility for mentoring the Afghan National Army's 4th Brigade and a *kandak* previously mentored by the Netherlands. The Dutch are expected to transition further *kandak* elements to the ADF as they withdraw from Afghanistan by August 2010. A French-mentored *kandak* will also transition to Australian responsibility later in the year.
23 June 2010	Minister for Defence John Faulkner announced that with the Dutch withdrawing in August 2010, ISAF have agreed to new arrangements establishing a US-led multinational command structure in Uruzgan, which will comprise military and civilian elements. He also foreshadowed that Australia's military presence in Afghanistan might be drawn down within the next two to four years.
9 July 2010	A RAAF C-130 Hercules detachment was officially welcomed home following a deployment to the MEAO in support of Operations SLIPPER and KRUGER. Their replacements had already commenced flying operations in the Middle East.

3 October 2010	Prime Minister Julia Gillard's first official travel was to Afghanistan, where she thanked troops for their bravery and dedication.
4 October 2010	The Prime Minister noted that progress was being made in training and through the Provincial Reconstruction Teams, and estimated a transition process of two to four years.
12 October 2010	The Prime Minister announced the date for a formal parliamentary debate on Afghanistan. A commitment to hold this debate was contained in the Australian Labor Party–Greens Agreement signed following the August 2010 federal election.
19 October 2010	Opening the parliamentary debate on Afghanistan, Prime Minister Julia Gillard highlighted Australia's exit strategy for Afghanistan, stating: 'The international community and the Afghan Government are agreed on a clear pathway forward.'
23 March 2011	In a parliamentary update, the Defence Minister Stephen Smith focused on the transfer of security responsibility in Afghanistan, emphasising that 'transition will be a process rather than a single event' and that 'we believe the Uruzgan transition process can occur over the next three years, between 2012 and 2014'.
13 October 2011	The Defence Minister stated that Afghan forces were 'on track' to take over security in Uruzgan 'by 2014'. He also confirmed that there would continue to be an Australian presence in Afghanistan after 2014.
21 November 2011	Prime Minister Gillard updated parliament on the progress of Australia's whole-of-government effort in Afghanistan. She reported on the progress made by ISAF and provided a plan for the next three years, whereby Australia would transition into more of a training role, with possible special forces mandate.
24 November 2011	Defence Minister Smith updated parliament on a number of aspects of Australia's commitment to the conflict, including detainee management and transfers and an update of detainee allegations.

APPENDIX 2

28 November 2011	Following President Karzai's announcement of a second tranche of districts to be handed over to Afghan security responsibility, Prime Minister Gillard said that this 'underlines the progress made this year'.
3 February 2012	Defence Minister Smith indicated his belief that Afghan national security forces would play the lead security role in 'most if not all' of Afghanistan by mid-2013. Smith also noted there was a 'good prospect' that Uruzgan would be in the third tranche of territories to be handed over to Afghan security control.
9 February 2012	Defence Minister Smith emphasised that the international community needed to be making decisions about their post-2014 commitment to Afghanistan. Smith also outlined key issues that the government believed needed to be discussed at the upcoming NATO Summit in Chicago (20–21 May 2012).
18 March 2012	Defence Minister Smith again noted that Australia expected that Uruzgan would be part of the 'third tranche' of areas to be transferred to Afghan security control.
17 April 2012	Prime Minister Gillard foreshadowed the forthcoming NATO–ISAF meetings in Brussels and Chicago and emphasised the success so far of the counterinsurgency mission in Afghanistan. The PM also flagged forthcoming transition stages and the expectations for ongoing support in Afghanistan.
19 April 2012	In their statement to the NATO–ISAF Foreign Affairs and Defence Ministers' Meeting (16–19 April 2012), the Foreign and Defence ministers outlined that Australia would be open to providing training and a special forces contribution—'under the right mandate'—in addition to financial contributions to the ANSF.
10 May 2012	In this parliamentary update, the Defence Minister focused on 'detainee management'. Smith detailed the detainee management process, how it is monitored and how allegations of mistreatment are dealt with.

13 May 2012	The Afghan Government announced a third set of geographical areas to start the transition process, including Uruzgan.
16 May 2012	In the lead-up to the NATO Summit in Chicago, the Prime Minister and Minister for Defence announced that Australia would contribute $100 million annually for three years from 2015 'to help sustain and support Afghan National Security Forces beyond the transition process'.
20 May 2012	During the NATO Summit in Chicago, Prime Minister Gillard and Foreign Minister Bob Carr announced that Australian aid to Afghanistan would grow from $165 million per year—the 2011–12 budget figure—to $250 million per year by 2015–16. Also during the NATO Summit, Prime Minister Gillard and Afghan President Hamid Karzai signed the agreement to a comprehensive long-term partnership between Australia and the Islamic Republic of Afghanistan.
24 May 2012	Defence Minister Smith updated parliament on a number of aspects of Australia's commitment to the conflict, including outcomes from the NATO–ISAF Chicago Summit, ADF and civilian casualties, and detainee management issues.
31 May 2012	The government announced that Australia was taking on the leadership role of Combined Team – Uruzgan (CT-U). There would be no change in average troop numbers or 'authorised strength'. Australia would take command of CT-U in late 2012.
8 July 2012	Australia signed a memorandum of agreement with the Aghanistan Government to facilitate Australia's development assistance contribution between 2012 and 2017. This would focus on education, rural development and financial and electoral management.
17 July 2012	The Australian Government welcomed the formal start of the transition process in Uruzgan, noting that the transition 'is on track for completion over the next 12 to 18-month period'.

APPENDIX 2

16 August 2012	Defence Minister Smith again updated parliament on Australia's commitment to the conflict, including Australian and civilian casualties, high-profile attacks by the Taliban, green-on-blue incidents, detainee management and allegations of mistreatment made against Australian personnel.
29 August 2012	The Prime Minister made a public statement concerning the recent deaths of five soldiers in Afghanistan, owing to an insider attack and a separate helicopter crash.
9 October 2012	Defence Minister Smith's paid a fifth visit to Afghanistan, where he discussed the transition progress with ISAF commanders and local Afghan leaders.
14 October 2012	The Prime Minister addressed troops in Afghanistan, emphasising the importance of the mission in response to acts of terrorism, such as the 9/11 attacks and the Bali bombings of 2002.
31 October 2012	Prime Minister Gillard addressed parliament once more on Australia's commitment to the conflict, including the progress of transition arrangements, Australia's whole-of-government effort including AusAID and the AFP, and the need for resolve in supporting Afghanistan post-2014.
22 November 2012	Defence Minister Smith announced that all four infantry *kandak* of the Afghan National Army's 4th Brigade were now operating independently and had taken control of forward operating bases and patrol bases in Uruzgan.
7 February 2013	Defence Minister Smith addressed parliament on Australia's commitment to the conflict, including transition arrangements, the reconciliation process, Australia's post-2014 mission, and support for veterans, including mental health problems such as PTSD.
20 February 2013	Defence Minister Smith discussed the transition progress with senior Afghan officials (including President Karzai) and ISAF commanders. Also discussed was the reconciliation process and the post-2014 international commitment to Afghanistan.

26 March 2013	The Prime Minister and Minister for Defence welcomed the ISAF decision to close the Multi-National Base–Tarin Kowt at the end of 2013. Following this closure, the majority of Australian forces would return home from Afghanistan.
16 April 2013	Defence Minister Smith's speech covered a range of topics, including the current status of the ADF transition in Afghanistan, Australia's post-2014 mission, Australian relations with the United States and NATO, and support for veterans, particularly addressing mental health issues.
3 May 2013	Prime Minister Gillard provided a summary of the current ADF transition arrangements and indicated that Australia would be prepared to provide training (and possibly special forces) assistance post-2014.
16 May 2013	Defence Minister Smith once again updated the parliament on the status of Australia's commitment to the conflict, largely regarding detainee management and his responses to allegations of misconduct by Australian personnel while in Afghanistan.
19 June 2013	Defence Minister Smith addressed parliament again on Australia's commitment to the conflict, including current strategy and mission and transition arrangements, Australia's post-2014 role, the Afghan-led peace and reconciliation process, and awards from operations in Afghanistan.
28 July 2013	Prime Minister Kevin Rudd visited Afghanistan to thank the troops and noted the improvements made in education and infrastructure.
6 August 2013	The Prime Minister attended the opening of an Afghanistan exhibition at the Australian War Memorial and provided personal reflections on Australia's involvement in the conflict.
23 October 2013	Defence Minister David Johnston addressed the ISAF Defence Ministers' meeting in Brussels, and discussed Australia's ongoing training mission in Afghanistan during 2014 and probably beyond.

APPENDIX 2

28 October 2013	Prime Minister Tony Abbott visited Afghanistan for a ceremony to mark Australia's drawdown in the conflict, and the cessation of the PRT. He also reaffirmed that Australia would support Afghanistan beyond 2014.
12 November 2013	The Prime Minister addressed parliament to discuss his recent visit to Afghanistan with the Opposition Leader, Bill Shorten. In acknowledging the progress made so far, he also presented some artefacts given by the Uruzgan governor as gifts.
11 December 2013	Defence Minister David Johnston updated parliament on the conclusion of operations in Uruzgan, as well as Australia's commitment to Afghanistan post-2014.
15 December 2013	The last combat troops were withdrawn from Afghanistan.
January– December 2014	Four hundred ADF personnel remain on Operation SLIPPER in Kandahar and Kabul tasked with training, advising and assisting Afghan National Security Forces.
December 2014	The final Heron UAV detachment leaves Afghanistan.
31 December 2014	Operation SLIPPER concludes, and the remaining troops undertaking train, advise and assist tasks with the Afghan National Security Forces are placed under Operation HIGHROAD.

Appendix 3: Chronology: Australia's military involvement in Iraq, 2003–09

Milestones	Details
20 March 2003	US, UK and Australian forces invade Iraq.
9 April 2003	US troops capture Baghdad. Saddam Hussein disappears.
21 April 2003	General Jay Garner becomes the civilian leader of Iraq when his Office for Reconstruction and Humanitarian Assistance is established.
1 May 2003	US President George W. Bush, aboard USS *Abraham Lincoln*, declares an end to major combat operations.
12 May 2003	L. Paul Bremer (appointed US Presidential Envoy and Administrator) arrives in Iraq as the head of the newly formed Coalition Provisional Authority and replaces General Jay Garner as civilian leader of Iraq.
22 May 2003	UN Security Council Resolution 1483 passed. The resolution empowers the US- and UK-led coalition, making it the legitimate and legal governing and peacekeeping authority in Iraq and recognising the creation of a transitional governing council of Iraqis.
14 June 2003	Lieutenant General Ricardo Sanchez assumes command of Combined Joint Task Force 7.

13 July 2003	The Iraqi Governing Council (comprising 25 Iraqis chosen under the supervision of the Coalition Provisional Authority) holds its inaugural meeting in Baghdad.
14 August 2003	UN Security Council Resolution 1500 passed, establishing the UN Assistance Mission for Iraq.
19 August 2003	Suicide truck bomb wrecks UN headquarters in Baghdad, killing 22 people, including UN envoy Sergio Vieira de Mello.
13 December 2003	US troops capture Saddam Hussein near Tikrit. Paul Bremer breaks the news with the announcement: 'We got him.'
2 March 2004	Almost 200 killed in a series of bomb blasts in Baghdad and Karbala at the climax of the Shia festival of Ashura.
8 March 2004	Iraq Governing Council approves Iraq's interim constitution.
31 March 2004	Four US civilian contractors are murdered and mutilated in Fallujah.
4–30 April 2004	First battle of Fallujah.
April 2004	Abu Ghraib prisoner abuse scandal breaks.
15 May 2004	Headquarters Combined Joint Task Force 7 disbands, and Headquarters Multi-National Force – Iraq and Headquarters Multi-National Corps – Iraq are established.
28 May 2004	Iyad Allawi is chosen as Prime Minister of the Iraqi interim government.
1 June 2004	Iraqi Governing Council dissolved to make way for Iraqi Interim Government led by Ayad Allawi. Ghazi al-Yawar is named President.
8 June 2004	UN Security Council Resolution 1546, adopted unanimously by the UN Security Council, establishes the multinational force in Iraq. This provides a mandate for the coalition's occupational mission in Iraq.
June 2004	General George Casey assumes command of Multi-National Force – Iraq.
June 2004	Multi-National Security Transition Command – Iraq is established.

APPENDIX 3

23 June 2004	John D. Negroponte appointed US ambassador to Iraq.
28 June 2004	Coalition Provisional Authority transfers sovereignty to Iraqi Interim Government. Coalition Provisional Authority is dissolved. Bremer leaves Iraq.
November 2004	Second battle of Fallujah.
19 December 2004	A suicide car bomb blast in Najaf, 300 metres from the Imam Ali shrine and near crowds of people, kills 52 and wounds at least 140. On the same day a car bomb explodes in Karbala, killing 14 and injuring at least 52.
31 January 2005	Iraqis elect the Iraqi Transitional Government in order to draft a permanent constitution. Although some violence and a widespread Sunni boycott mar the event, most of the eligible Kurd and Shia populace participates. The Shia-led United Alliance dominates election for interim parliament. The government is headed by Prime Minister Ibrahim al-Jaafari.
16 March 2005	Iraqi National Assembly holds its first meeting.
21 June 2005	Zalmay Khalilzad replaces John Negroponte as US ambassador to Iraq.
15 October 2005	Referendum ratifies new Iraqi constitution by 78 per cent despite Sunni Arab opposition, which almost vetoes it.
19 October 2005	Saddam Hussein goes on trial charged with crimes against humanity for the killing of 148 Shia men and boys in Dujail after an assassination attempt in 1982. He pleads not guilty.
8 November 2005	UN Security Council Resolution 1637, brought forward by Denmark, Japan, Romania, the United Kingdom and the United States, is passed, allowing the extension of the Multi-National Force – Iraq mandate to 31 December 2006.
15 December 2005	Parliamentary elections. Sunnis vote in strength.
10 February 2006	Final results give Shia Alliance a near majority with 128 seats, Sunnis 58 and Kurds 53.

22 February 2006	Al-Qaeda destroys Shia al-Askari mosque in Samarra, which sparks widespread sectarian violence, provoking fears of civil war.
21 May 2006	New Prime Minister Nuri al-Maliki chairs his first cabinet meeting.
7 June 2006	US aircraft kill al-Qaeda leader in Iraq, Abu Musab al-Zarqawi.
September 2006	Sheik Abdul Sattar Buzaigh al-Rishawi forms the Anbar Awakening Council (also known as 'Anbar Awakening') to counter the influence of al-Qaeda. The Anbar Awakening Council is trained and equipped with assistance from coalition forces.
5 November 2006	A court in Baghdad finds Saddam Hussein guilty of crimes against humanity and sentences him to be hanged because of the Dujail killings.
18 November 2006	UN Security Council Resolution 1723, submitted by Denmark, Japan, Slovakia, the United Kingdom and the United States, extends the Multi-National Force – Iraq's mandate until 31 December 2007.
23 November 2006	Suspected Sunni Arab militants use suicide car bombs and mortar rounds on the capital's Shia Sadr City slum, killing at least 215 people and wounding 257.
6 December 2006	Iraq Study Group Report released. The bipartisan Iraq Study Group, led by former US Secretary of State James Baker and former Democratic Congressman Lee Hamilton, concludes that 'the situation in Iraq is grave and deteriorating' and that 'US forces seem to be caught in a mission that has no foreseeable end'.
30 December 2006	Saddam Hussein is executed.
23 January 2007	In the 2007 State of the Union address, George W. Bush announces that he has decided to deploy reinforcements of more than 20,000 soldiers and marines to Iraq.
10 February 2007	General David Petraeus replaces General George Casey as commander of Multi-National Force – Iraq.

APPENDIX 3

14 February 2007	Prime Minister Nouri al-Maliki launches a US-backed crackdown in Baghdad aimed at pulling Iraq back from the brink of civil war.
26 March 2007	Ryan Crocker replaces Zalmay Khalilzad as US ambassador to Iraq.
28 May 2007	Iranian and US ambassadors to Iraq meet in Baghdad to discuss ways to improve security in the country. The talks end a three-decade diplomatic freeze between the two nations.
15 June 2007	US military completes its troop build-up, or 'surge', to 160,000 soldiers.
Mid-2007	Following the success of the Anbar Awakening Council, the coalition begins a controversial program to recruit Iraqi Sunnis for the formation of 'Guardian' militias to secure various Sunni neighbourhoods, a form of armed neighbourhood watch of concerned local citizens. The militias are later named the 'Sons of Iraq'.
1 August 2007	Main Sunni Arab bloc pulls out of Prime Minister al-Maliki's cabinet, plunging the government into crisis.
14 August 2007	Numerous al-Qaeda bomb attacks against the minority Yazidi community in Qahtaniya kill 411 people. More than 100 homes and shops are destroyed in the blasts.
29 August 2007	Shia cleric Moqtada al-Sadr imposes ceasefire on Mahdi Army militia for six months after clashes with police.
17 September 2007	Iraqi government announces that it is revoking the licence of the US security firm Blackwater USA over the firm's involvement in the deaths of eight civilians, including a woman and an infant, in a firefight that followed a car-bomb explosion near a State Department motorcade.
18 December 2007	At the request of the Iraqi Government, the UN Security Council passes Resolution 1790, which extends the mandate of the Multi-National Force – Iraq until 31 December 2008.
12 January 2008	Parliament votes to allow members of Saddam's Baath Party to return to government jobs, winning US praise for achieving a benchmark step towards reconciling warring sects.

21 February 2008	Thousands of Turkish troops cross into northern Iraq to hunt for Kurdish PKK guerrillas. Eight days later, Turkish forces withdraw.
March 2008	The Green Zone in Baghdad comes under repeated rocket attack, killing two US government officials and injuring several others.
25 March 2008	Al-Maliki launches crackdown on militias in Basra, sparking pitched battles with Moqtada al-Sadr's Mahdi Army. Fighting rages for a week in southern Iraq and Baghdad. Hundreds are killed.
7 July 2008	For the first time, Al-Maliki raises the prospect of setting a timetable for the withdrawal of US troops as part of negotiations over a new security agreement with the United States.
July 2008	Sons of Iraq grow to number 103,000. A program to integrate them into the Iraqi Army or police forces or to find alternative employment is developed.
19 July 2008	In a political breakthrough, Iraq's main Sunni Arab bloc rejoins the government after parliament approves its candidates for several vacant ministerial posts.
1 September 2008	The US military hands over the province of Anbar to Iraqi security forces—the first Sunni Arab province to be returned to Iraqi control since 2003.
16 September 2008	General Raymond Odierno replaces General David Petraeus as commander of Multi-National Force – Iraq.
24 September 2008	Parliament approves a provincial elections law. The presidency approves it formally on 7 October, paving the way for the election to take place by 31 January 2009.
15 October 2008	US forces announce that they have killed the second-in-command of al-Qaeda in Iraq, a Moroccan named Abu Qaswarah, in a raid in Mosul on 5 October.
4 November 2008	Senator Barack Obama wins the US presidential election.

APPENDIX 3

17 November 2008	Iraq and the United States sign an Iraqi–US Security Agreement, requiring the United States to withdraw its forces by the end of 2011. The agreement gives the Iraqi Government authority over the US-led mission for the first time, replacing the UN Security Council Resolution.
27 November 2008	Iraqi parliament approves the Iraqi–US Security Agreement after protracted negotiations between rival factions, removing the last major hurdle to the agreement. The Presidency Council subsequently endorses the Iraqi–US Security Agreement on 4 December.
14 December 2008	During a joint press conference with Prime Minister Nuri al-Maliki in Baghdad, President Bush dodges two shoes thrown at him from the audience.
30 December 2008	Memorandum of understanding between Iraq and Australia signed.
31 December 2008	UN Security Council Resolution 1790 expires.
1 January 2009	Iraqi–US Security Agreement comes into effect. Memorandum of understanding between Iraq and Australia takes effect.
31 January 2009	Provincial elections held in 14 of Iraq's 18 provinces.
27 February 2009	President Obama gives his 'Responsibly Ending the War in Iraq' speech at Camp Lejeune in North Carolina.
March 2009	Ryan Crocker stands down as US ambassador to Iraq.
21 April 2009	Christopher Hill is confirmed as US ambassador to Iraq.
30 April 2009	The United Kingdom declares an end to its combat operations in Iraq.
30 June 2009	In accordance with the Iraqi–US Security Agreement, all US combat forces are withdrawn from cities. Other non-combat US military advisers and trainers remain.
28 July 2009	Last group of 11 Australian Defence Force members, serving as part of Operation CATALYST, depart Baghdad.

30 July 2009 Last group of 11 Australian Defence Force members, serving as part of Operation CATALYST, arrive in Australia.

31 July 2009 Memorandum of understanding between Iraq and Australia expires.

Bibliography

Abbott, Prime Minister the Hon. T., MP, Address at Recognition Ceremony, Tarin Kowt, Afghanistan, 28 October 2013

Ahmed, A., 'Powerful Afghan police chief is killed in targeted suicide attack', *New York Times*, 20 March 2015

Al-Ali, N. and N. Pratt, *What Kind of Liberation? Women and the Occupation of Iraq*, University of California Press, Berkeley, 2009, doi.org/10.1525/9780520942172

Anderson, M., 'Where are the women? The unfortunate omission in the Army's COIN doctrine', Modern War Institute, United States Military Academy, West Point, 2017

Appelbaum, V.J., J. Horchert and C. Stöcker, 'Catalog advertises NSA toolbox', *Der Spiegel*, 29 December 2013, www.spiegel.de/international/world/catalog-reveals-nsa-has-back-doors-for-numerous-devices-a-940994.html (retrieved 14 March 2020)

Asia Foundation, *Afghanistan in 2017: A Survey of the Afghan People*, Asia Foundation, Kabul, 2017

Auerswald, D.P. and S.M. Saideman, *NATO in Afghanistan: Fighting Together, Fighting Alone*, Princeton University Press, Princeton, 2014, doi.org/10.7202/1027571ar

Austin, A.G., Review of D. Dexter, *The New Guinea Offensives*, in *Historical Studies*, vol. 10, no. 39, 1962

Australia–United States Ministerial Consultations 1999 Joint Communiqué, 3 November 1999, dfat.gov.au/geo/united-states-of-america/ausmin/Pages/australia-united-states-ministerial-consultations-1999-joint-communiqu.aspx (retrieved 31 March 2020)

Australian Broadcasting Corporation, 'Killing Field', *Four Corners*, 16 March 2020, www.abc.net.au/4corners/killing-field/12060538 (retrieved 19 March 2020)

Australian Civil-Military Centre, *Afghanistan: Lessons from Australia's Whole of Government Mission*, Australia Civil-Military Centre, Queanbeyan, 2016, www.acmc.gov.au/resources/publications/afghanistan-lessons-australias-whole-of-government-mission (retrieved 3 April 2020)

—— *Same Space—Different Mandates: A Civil–Military–Police Guide to Stakeholders in International Disaster and Conflict Response*, Australia Civil-Military Centre, Queanbeyan, 2015

Australian Human Rights Commission, *Change the Course: National Report on Sexual Assault and Sexual Harassment at Australian Universities*, Australian Human Rights Commission, Canberra, 2017

Australian War Memorial, 'Historians: Official History of Australian operations in Iraq, Afghanistan and East Timor', www.awm.gov.au/learn/understanding-military-history/official-histories/iraq-afghanistan-timor/oh (retrieved 21 October 2020)

Azadzoi, N. and R. Nordland, 'Afghanistan says it controls key city, but ravaged streets show otherwise', *New York Times*, 12 August 2018

Barry, B., *Harsh Lessons: Iraq, Afghanistan and the Changing Character of War*, Routledge, Abingdon, 2017, doi.org/10.4324/9780429031557

BBC News, 'Suspect reveals 9/11 planning', 22 September 2003

—— 'UK general attacks US Iraq policy', 1 September 2007, news.bbc.co.uk/2/hi/6973618.stm (retrieved 3 April 2020)

Berry, B., 'Bitter war to stabilize southern Iraq—British Army report declassified', International Institute for Strategic Studies, London, 10 October 2016

—— *Harsh Lessons: Iraq, Afghanistan and the Changing Character of War*, International Institute for Strategic Studies, London, 2017

Berryman, F., 'The Battle of Bardia: The AIF's first battle in World War II', Directorate of Military Training, AHQ, Papers of Lieutenant-General Sir Frank Berryman, AWM PR84/370

Blaxland, J., *The Australian Army from Whitlam to Howard*, Cambridge University Press, Melbourne, 2014

—— (ed.), *East Timor Intervention: A retrospective on INTERFET*, Melbourne University Press, Melbourne, 2015

—— *Strategic Cousins: Australian and Canadian Expeditionary Forces and the British and American Empires*, McGill-Queens University Press, Montreal, 2006

Bolger, D.P., *Why We Lost: A General's Inside Account of the Iraq and Afghanistan Wars*, Houghton Mifflin Harcourt, New York, 2014

Bongiorno, P., interview with Foreign Minister the Hon. Alexander Downer MP by 'Meet the Press', 18 November 2001

Boulton, E., *Teaming: An Introduction to Gender Studies, Unshackling Human Talent and Optimising Military Capability for the Coming Era of Equality: 2020 to 2050*, Australian Army, Canberra, 2017

Cameron, E. and J. Kamminga, *Behind Closed Doors: The Risk of Denying Women a Voice in Determining Afghanistan's Future*, Oxfam International, Oxford, 2014

Cantwell, J. with G. Bearup, *Exit Wounds: One Australian's War on Terror*, Melbourne University Press, Melbourne, 2012

Carney, S.A., *Allied Participation in Operation Iraqi Freedom*, Center for Military History, Washington, DC, 2011

Central Statistics Organization, *Afghanistan Statistical Yearbook 2016–17*, Central Statistics Organization, Kabul, 2016–17

Chayes, S., *Thieves of State: Why Corruption Threatens Global Security*, W.W. Norton, New York, 2015, doi.org/10.5038/1944-0472.9.2.1531

Chilcot, J., *Report of the Iraq Inquiry*, 6 July 2016, webarchive.nationalarchives.gov.uk/20171123123237/http://www.iraqinquiry.org.uk (retrieved 3 April 2020)

—— 'Statement by Sir John Chilcot', in *Report of the Iraq Inquiry*, 6 July 2016, webarchive.nationalarchives.gov.uk/20171123123519/http://www.iraqinquiry.org.uk/media/247010/2016-09-06-sir-john-chilcots-public-statement.pdf (retrieved 3 April 2020)

Civil–Military Fusion Centre, *Corruption and Anti-Corruption Issues in Afghanistan*, Civil–Military Fusion Center, Norfolk, VA, 2012

Clancy, T., *Executive Orders*, G.P. Putnam's Sons, New York, 1996

CNN Wire Staff, 'Obama announces Afghanistan troop withdrawal plan', CNN Politics, 23 June 2011

Coburn, N., *Losing Afghanistan: An Obituary for the Intervention*, Stanford University Press, Stanford, 2016

Commonwealth of Australia, *2016 Progress Report on the Australian National Action Plan on Women, Peace and Security: 2012–2018*, Commonwealth of Australia, Canberra, 2016

Connolly, P., *Counterinsurgency in Uruzgan, 2009*, Land Warfare Studies Centre, Canberra, 2013

Cosgrove, P., *My Story*, HarperCollins, Sydney, 2007

Coughlin, C., 'A last salvo from General Sir David Richards', 17 July 2013, www.telegraph.co.uk/news/uknews/defence/10185613/A-last-salvo-from-General-Sir-David-Richards.html (retrieved 2 April 2020)

Crompvoets, S., *The Health and Wellbeing of Female Vietnam and Contemporary Veterans*, Department of Veterans' Affairs, Canberra, 2012

Defence Abuse Response Taskforce, *Report on Abuse in Defence*, Commonwealth of Australia, Canberra, 2014

Defence Committee, *Pathway to Change: Evolving Defence Culture—A Strategy for Cultural Change and Reinforcement*, Department of Defence, Canberra, 2012

Department of Defence, *2016 Defence White Paper*, Department of Defence, Canberra, 2016

—— *2020 Defence Strategic Update*, Canberra, 2020

—— *Annual Report 2004–05*, Department of Defence, Canberra, 2005, www.defence.gov.au/annualreports/04-05/downloads/0405_dar_10_full.pdf

—— *The Australian Approach to Warfare*, Department of Defence, Canberra, 2002

Department of Defense, *US Army Counterinsurgency Handbook*, Skyhorse Publishing, New York, 2007

Donaldson, M., *The Crossroad*, Macmillan Australia, Sydney, 2013

Dougherty, J., 'What happens to "civilian surge" as military surge ends', CNN, 22 June 2011

Downer, A., interview transcript, 'Meet the Press', 18 November 2001

Echavez, C.R., S. Mosawi and L.W.R. Pilongo, *The Other Side of Gender Inequality: Men and Masculinities in Afghanistan*, Afghanistan Research and Evaluation Unit, Kabul, 2016

Economist, 'Iraq's grim lessons', 6 July 2016, www.economist.com/britain/2016/07/06/iraqs-grim-lessons (retrieved 3 April 2020)

Ellery, D., 'Captain Miller has a firm grasp of the navy's tiller', *Sydney Morning Herald*, 14 October 2011, www.smh.com.au/politics/federal/captain-miller-has-a-firm-grasp-of-the-navys-tiller-20111014-1v6i8.html (retrieved 1 April 2020)

Elliott, C.L., *High Command: British Military Leadership in the Iraq and Afghanistan Wars*, Hurst, London, 2015

Farrell, T., *Unwinnable: Britain's War in Afghanistan, 2001–2014*, Vintage, London, 2018

Ferguson, N., *The Square and the Tower: Networks, Hierarchies and the Struggle for Global Power*, Allen Lane, London, 2017

Fielding, M., *Red Zone Baghdad: My War in Iraq*, Echo Books, Canberra, 2016

Flood, P., *Report of the Inquiry into Australian Intelligence Agencies*, Department of Prime Minister and Cabinet, Canberra, 2004

Flynn, M.T., M. Pottinger and P. Batchelor, 'Fixing intel: A blueprint for making intelligence relevant in Afghanistan', Center for a New American Security, Washington, DC, 2010

Foster, K., *Don't Mention The War—The Australian Defence Force, the Media and the Afghan Conflict*, Monash University Publishing, Clayton, Vic, 2013

Frame, T. and A. Palazzo (ed.), *On Ops: Lessons and Challenges for the Australian Army Since East Timor*, NewSouth, Sydney, 2016

Frerks, G., 'Who are they? Encountering international and local civilians in civil–military interaction', in *Effective Civil–Military Interaction in Peace Operations*, ed. G. Lucius and S. Rietjens, Springer, Berlin, 2016

Gall, C., *The Wrong Enemy: America in Afghanistan, 2001–2014*, Houghton Mifflin Harcourt, New York, 2014

Gillard, Prime Minister the Hon. J., MP, Speech to the House of Representatives, Ministerial Statements, *Commonwealth Parliamentary Debates*, 19 October 2010

Gyngell, A., *Fear of Abandonment: Australia and the World Since 1942*, La Trobe University Press, Melbourne, 2017

Hayden, M., *Playing to the Edge: American Intelligence in the Age of Terror*, Penguin Press, New York, 2017

Heller, C., and W. Stofft (eds), *America's First Battles, 1776–1965*, University of Kansas Press, Kansas, 1986

Hill, Senator the Hon. R., 'Australian Special Forces to return from Afghanistan', media release, MIN 664/02, 20 November 2002

Hoffman, J.T. (ed.), *Tip of the Spear: US Army Small-Unit Actions in Iraq, 2004–2007*, Center of Military History, Washington, DC, 2010

Horn, B., *No Lack of Courage: Operation Medusa, Afghanistan*, Dundurn Press, Toronto, 2010

Horn, B. and E. Spencer, *Canadian Forces in Afghanistan*, Dundurn Press, Toronto, 2016

Horner, D., 'The higher command structure for joint ADF operations', in *History as Policy: Framing the Debate on the Future of Australia's Defence Policy*, ed. R. Huisken and M. Thatcher, ANU E Press, Canberra, 2007, doi.org/10.22459/HP.12.2007.10

—— *The Official History of Australian Peacekeeping, Humanitarian and Post-Cold War Operations*, vol. 2: *Australia and the 'New World Order'*, Cambridge University Press, Melbourne, 2011

House of Representatives, Debates, 17 September 2001

Howard, J., *Lazarus Rising: A Personal and Political Autobiography*, HarperCollins, Sydney, 2010

—— Ministerial statement to Parliament on Iraq, 14 May 2003

Howard, Prime Minister the Hon. J., MP, 'Address to the Australian troops', Campbell Barracks, Perth, 24 August 2005

—— 'Australian troops to be deployed to Afghanistan', statement, 17 October 2001

—— 'Troop deployment to Afghanistan', press conference transcript, 13 July 2005

Ibrahimi, N., *The Hazaras and the Afghan State: Rebellion, Exclusion and the Struggle for Recognition*, Hurst & Co., London, 2017

Inglis, K., 'The Anzac tradition', *Meanjin Quarterly*, vol. 24, no. 1, 1965

Inspector-General of the Australian Defence Force, *Afghanistan Inquiry Report* ('the Brereton Report'), afghanistaninquiry.defence.gov.au/sites/default/files/2020-11/IGADF-Afghanistan-Inquiry-Public-Release-Version.pdf (retrieved 24 November 2020)

Jackson, A. and S. Haysom, *The Search for Common Ground: Civil–Military Relations in Afghanistan, 2002–13*, Humanitarian Policy Group, London, 2013

Jahner, K., 'Green Beret who beat up accused child rapist can stay in Army', *Army Times*, 28 April 2016

Jones, P., 'The maritime campaign in Iraq', in *Naval Power and Expeditionary Wars: Peripheral Campaigns and New Theatres of Naval Warfare*, ed. B.A. Elleman and S.C.M. Paine, Routledge, New York, 2011, doi.org/10.4324/9780203833216

Kamal, M., 'L'offensive de Koundouz: Le contexte militaro-stratégique', *Les Nouvelles d'Afghanistan*, vol. 151, 2015

Keating, T.J., 'This was a different war: Interview with Vice Admiral Timothy J. Keating', *US Naval Institute Proceedings*, vol. 129, no. 6, 2003

Keegan, J., *Intelligence in War*, Pimlico, London, 2004

Khalilzad, Z., 'Why Trump is right to get tough with Pakistan', *New York Times*, 23 August 2017

Kilcullen, D., *Blood Year: Islamic State and the Failures of the War on Terror*, Black Inc., Melbourne, 2016

Knowles, R., H. Szoke, G. Campbell, C. Ferguson, J. Flynn, J. Lay and J. Potter, 'Expert Advisory Group on discrimination, bullying and sexual harassment: Report to Royal Australasian College of Surgeons', Royal Australasian College of Surgeons, Melbourne, 2015, www.surgeons.org/-/media/Project/RACS/surgeons-org/files/operating-with-respectcomplaints/expert-advisory-group/background-briefing-16-june-15-final.pdf?rev=7b721c1d5a264a5983f715783a3ab18f&hash=DE07ACB50DC25A6D5C8400405C164B43 (retrieved 20 October 2020)

Ladwig, W.C., *The Forgotten Front: Patron–Client Relationships in Counterinsurgency*, Cambridge University Press, Cambridge, 2017

Land Warfare Doctrine 0.0, 'Command, Leadership and Management', Department of Defence, Canberra, 2003

Langford, I., 'Australian special forces in Afghanistan: Supporting Australia in the "long war"', *Australian Army Journal*, vol. 7, no. 1, 2010, pp. 21–32

Lawrence-Wood, E., L. Jones, S. Hodson, S. Crompvoets, A. McFarlane and S. Neuhaus, 'Mothers in the Middle East Area of Operations (MEAO): The health impacts of maternal deployment to an area of operations', Applied Research Program, Department of Veterans' Affairs, Canberra, 2014

Ledwidge, F., *Losing Small Wars: British Military Failure in the 9/11 Wars*, Yale University Press, New Haven, 2017

Logue, J., *Herding Cats: The Evolution of the ADF's Embedding Program in Operational Areas*, Working Paper 141, Land Warfare Studies Centre, Canberra, 2013

Long, G., *Australia in the War of 1939–1945*, vol. 1: *To Benghazi*, Australian War Memorial, Canberra, 1952

Lucius, G., and S. Rietjens (eds), *Effective Civil–Military Interactions in Peace Operations: Theory and Practice*, Springer, Berlin, 2016

Ludlam, S., Debate on the War Powers Bill, 7 July 2011, scott-ludlam.greensmps.org.au/articles/debate-war-powers-bill

MacAskill, E. and J. Ball, 'Portrait of the NSA', *Guardian*, 3 November 2013, www.theguardian.com/world/2013/nov/02/nsa-portrait-total-surveillance (retrieved 26 April 2020)

McGoldrick, C., 'The state of conflicts today: Can humanitarian action adapt?', *International Review of the Red Cross*, vol. 97, no. 900, 2015, doi.org/10.1017/s181638311600028x

Mackenzie, M., *Beyond the Band of Brothers: The US Military and the Myth that Women Can't Fight*, Cambridge University Press, Cambridge, 2015, doi.org/10.1017/cbo9781107279155

McLagan, M., and D. Sommers, *Lioness* (documentary), Public Broadcasting Service, USA, 2008

Maley, W., 'Afghanistan on a knife-edge', *Global Affairs*, vol. 2, no. 1, 2016

—— *The Afghanistan Wars*, Palgrave Macmillan, New York, 2016

—— 'Civil–military interaction in Afghanistan: The case of Germany', in *Reconstructing Afghanistan: Civil–Military Experiences in Comparative Perspective*, ed. W. Maley and S. Schmeidl, Routledge, London, 2015, doi.org/10.4324/9781315749389

—— 'PRT activity in Afghanistan: The Australian experience', in *Statebuilding in Afghanistan: Multi-national Contributions to Reconstruction*, ed. N. Hynek and P. Marton, Routledge, New York, 2011

—— 'Studying host-nationals in operational areas: The challenge of Afghanistan', in *Routledge Handbook of Research Methods in Military Studies*, ed. J. Soeters, P.M. Shields and S. Rietjens, Routledge, London, 2014, doi.org/10.4324/9780203093801.ch6

—— 'Talking to the Taliban', *World Today*, vol. 63, no. 11, 2007

—— *Transition in Afghanistan: Hope, Despair and the Limits of Statebuilding*, Routledge, New York, 2018

—— 'The war in Afghanistan: Australia's strategic narratives', in *Strategic Narratives, Public Opinion and War: Winning Domestic Support for the Afghan War*, ed. B. de Graaf, G. Dimitriu and J. Ringsmose, Routledge, New York, 2015, doi.org/10.4324/9781315770734

—— *What is a Refugee?*, Oxford University Press, New York, 2016

Maley, W., and S. Schmeidl (eds), *Reconstructing Afghanistan: Civil–Military Experiences in Comparative Perspective*, Routledge, London, 2015

Maloney, S., *Enduring the Freedom: A Rogue Historian in Afghanistan*, Potomac Books, Washington, DC, 2005

Mansfield, D., *A State Built on Sand: How Opium Undermined Afghanistan*, Hurst & Co., London, 2016, doi.org/10.1093/acprof:oso/9780190608316.003.0007

Marston, D., 'Operation TELIC VIII to XI: Difficulties of twenty-first-century command', *Journal of Strategic Studies*, 2019, doi.org/10.1080/01402390.2019.1672161

—— '"Smug and complacent?" Operation TELIC: The need for critical analysis', *British Army Review*, vol. 147, 2009, pp. 16–23

Martin, M., *An Intimate War: An Oral History of the Helmand Conflict*, Hurst & Co., London, 2014

Mashal, M., M.F. Abed and Z. Nader, 'Attack at university in Kabul shatters a sense of freedom', *New York Times*, 26 August 2016

Mashal, M., M.F. Abed and J. Sukhanyar, 'Deadly bombing is among worst of Afghan war', *New York Times*, 1 June 2017

Masters, C., *No Front Line: Australia's Special Forces at War in Afghanistan*, Allen & Unwin, Sydney, 2017

McChrystal, S., United States Government Integrated Civilian and Military Campaign for Support to Afghanistan, Commonwealth Institute, 2009, www.comw.org/qdr/fulltext/0908eikenberryandmcchrystal.pdf (retrieved 5 May 2020)

Middleton, K., 'Shadow of the Towers', Part II, *Dateline*, SBS, 11 September 2011, www.youtube.com/watch?v=VW12K3cFGcU&t=3s (retrieved 1 April 2020)

—— *An Unwinnable War: Australia in Afghanistan*, Melbourne University Press, Melbourne, 2011

Miles, D., 'Gates wraps up Afghanistan visit with new insights', 8 May 2009, United States Department of Defense, www.defense.gov/news/newsarticle.aspx?id=54252 (retrieved 3 May 2020)

Miller, L., 'A peace "surge" to end war in Afghanistan', *New York Times*, 23 July 2017

Mills, C., 'Parliamentary approval for military action', House of Commons Library, 13 May 2015, researchbriefings.parliament.uk/ResearchBriefing/Summary/CBP-7166

Mohammadi, H., *Tasir-e jahanishodan bar farhang dar Afghanistan*, Entesharat-e Farhang, Kabul, 2014

Molan, J., *Running the War in Iraq*, HarperCollins, Sydney, 2008

Motwani, N., 'Afghanistan and the regional security contagion', in *Afghanistan—Challenges and Prospects*, ed. S. Bose, N. Motwani and W. Maley, Routledge, London, 2018, doi.org/10.4324/9781315161938-14

Neumann, B., L. Mundey and J. Mikolashek, *Operations Enduring Freedom, March 2002–April 2005*, Center of Military History, Washington, DC, 2013

Noble, R., 'The essential thing: Mission command and its practical application', *Australian Army Journal*, vol. 3, no. 3, 2006

Noetic Solutions, 'Strategic Command and Control Lessons—Scoping Study', Noetic Solutions, Canberra, 2013, www.defence.gov.au/FOI/Docs/Disclosures/343_10_11_Document.pdf (retrieved 31 March 2020)

Oakes, D., 'General defends Afghan warlord ties', *Sydney Morning Herald*, 7 December 2010

O'Connell, A.B. (ed.), *Our Latest Longest War: Losing Hearts and Minds in Afghanistan*, University of Chicago Press, Chicago, 2017, doi.org/10.7208/chicago/9780226265797.001.0001

Office of the Special Adviser on Gender Issues, 'Landmark resolution on Women, Peace and Security', United Nations, New York, www.un.org/womenwatch/osagi/wps (retrieved 25 March 2020)

Olson, R.G., 'The art of a deal with the Taliban', *New York Times*, 29 March 2017

Palazzo, A., 'Assessing the war in Iraq', Address to the Royal United Services Institute of New South Wales, 31 July 2012, www.rusinsw.org.au/Papers/20120731.pdf

—— *The Australian Army and the War in Iraq: 2002–2010*, Directorate of Army Research and Analysis, Canberra, 2011

—— 'The making of strategy and the junior coalition partner: Australia and the 2003 Iraq war', *Infinity Journal*, art. 6, vol. 2, no. 4, 2012, pp. 27–30, quoted in Palazzo, 'We went to Iraq for ANZUS', *Interpreter*, 25 March 2013, www.lowy institute.org/the-interpreter/we-went-iraq-anzus (retrieved 31 March 2020)

Parliament, Senate, *Select Committee on a Certain Maritime Incident* (report), The Committee, Canberra, 2002

Powell, C., 'Remarks to the National Foreign Policy Conference for Leaders of Nongovernmental Organizations', Washington, DC, 26 October 2001, avalon.law.yale.edu/sept11/powell_brief31.asp (retrieved 1 April 2020)

Ramage, G. and I. McPhedran, *Afghanistan: Australia's War*, HarperCollins, Sydney, 2014

Ricks, T.E., *Fiasco: The American Military Adventure in Iraq*, Penguin, New York, 2006

Rico, J., *Blood Makes the Grass Grow Green*, Presidio Press, New York, 2007

Ross, J., *The Myth of the Digger*, Hale & Iremonger, Sydney, 1985

Rudd, Prime Minister the Hon. K., MP, press conference, Parliament House, Canberra, 29 April 2009

Rynning, S., *NATO in Afghanistan: The Liberal Disconnect*, Stanford University Press, Stanford, 2012

Schlosser, N.J., *The Surge, 2007–2008: US Army Campaigns in Iraq*, Center of Military History, Washington, DC, 2017

Schmeidl, S., *The Man Who Would be King: The Challenges to Strengthening Governance in Uruzgan*, Netherlands Institute of International Relations Clingendael, The Hague, 2010

Schroen, G.C., *First In: An Insider's Account of How the CIA Spearheaded the War on Terror in Afghanistan*, Presidio Press, New York, 2005

Sexton, R., 'Aid as a tool against insurgency: Evidence from contested and controlled territory in Afghanistan', *American Political Science Review*, vol. 110, no. 4, 2016, doi.org/10.1017/s0003055416000356

Shah, T. and M. Mashal, 'Taliban assassinate Afghan police chief ahead of elections', *New York Times*, 19 October 2018

Sharan, T., *Dawlat-e Shabakahi: Rabeteh-i Qodrat wa Sarwat dar Afghanistan Pas az Sal-e 2001*, Vazhah Publications, Kabul, 2017

Sharan, T. and S. Bose, 'Political networks and the 2014 Afghan presidential election: Power restructuring, ethnicity and state stability', *Conflict, Security and Development*, vol. 16, no. 6, 2016, doi.org/10.1080/14678802.2016.1248431

Snelson, D., 'Liberating Iraq—The UK's maritime contribution', *Naval Review*, vol. 91, no. 4, 2003

Stern, J., 'The UN Security Council's Arria-formula meeting on vulnerable groups in conflict: ISIL's targeting of LGBTI individuals', *NYU Journal of International Law and Politics*, vol. 48, 2015

Stewart, C., 'How they found the Diggers' killer Hekmatullah', *Weekend Australian*, 3 October 2013, www.theaustralian.com.au/national-affairs/defence/how-they-found-the-diggers-killer/news-story/6883aa8eee237dcac676c67f259073d2 (retrieved 14 March 2020)

Stewart, K., 'International Women's Day 2006—inspiring potential', *Newsletter*, Defence Community Organisation—South Australia, 8 March 2006

Steyn, J.G. and E. Lang, *The Unexpected War: Canada in Kandahar*, Penguin, Toronto, 2008

Stockings, C., 'A continuing tradition … but a whole new ballgame: The Official Historian of Australian Operations in Iraq and Afghanistan, and Australian Peacekeeping Operations in East Timor', in *Charles Bean: Man, Myth and Legacy*, ed. P. Stanley, UNSW Press, Sydney, 2017, pp. 215–28

Strachan, H., R. Iron and J. Bailey (eds), *British Generals in Blair's Wars*, Ashgate Publishing, Farnham, UK, 2013

Studdert, H. and S. Shteir, *Women, Peace and Security Reflections: From Australian Male Leaders*, Australian Civil-Military Centre, Canberra, 2015

Sunstein, C.R., *Laws of Fear: Beyond the Precautionary Principle*, Cambridge University Press, Cambridge, 2005

United Nations Assistance Mission in Afghanistan, *Human Rights and Protection of Civilians in Armed Conflict: Special Report on Kunduz Province*, UNAMA and United Nations Office of the High Commissioner for Human Rights, Kabul, 2015

United States Marine Corps, *Command and Control*, Doctrine Publication 6, Department of the Navy, Washington, DC, 1996

Walt, S., 'Top 10 lessons of the Iraq War', *Foreign Policy*, 20 March 2012, foreignpolicy.com/2012/03/20/top-10-lessons-of-the-iraq-war-2 (retrieved 2 May 2020)

Warner, N., 'ASIS at 60' (speech), 19 July 2012, www.asis.gov.au/about-us/speech.html

Williams, G., 'Why Australia must learn from our mistakes in the Iraq War', *Sydney Morning Herald*, 27 March 2017, newsroom.unsw.edu.au/news/business-law/why-australia-must-learn-our-mistakes-iraq-war (retrieved 24 April 2020)

Winterbotham, F.W., *The Ultra Secret*, Weidenfeld & Nicolson, London, 1974

Wroe, D., 'The secret Iraq dossier', *Sydney Morning Herald*, 25 February 2017

www.ingramcontent.com/pod-product-compliance
Lightning Source LLC
Chambersburg PA
CBHW041733300426
44115CB00027B/2972